DISCONTINUOUS SYNTAX
HYPERBATON IN GREEK

DISCONTINUOUS SYNTAX

Hyperbaton in Greek

A. M. DEVINE

LAURENCE D. STEPHENS

New York   Oxford

Oxford University Press

2000

Oxford University Press

Oxford   New York
Athens   Auckland   Bangkok   Bogotá   Buenos Aires   Calcutta
Cape Town   Chennai   Dar es Salaam   Delhi   Florence   Hong Kong   Istanbul
Karachi   Kuala Lumpur   Madrid   Melbourne   Mexico City   Mumbai
Nairobi   Paris   São Paulo   Singapore   Taipei   Tokyo   Toronto   Warsaw

and associated companies in
Berlin   Ibadan

Published by Oxford University Press, Inc.
198 Madison Avenue, New York, New York 10016

Oxford is a registered trademark of Oxford University Press

Library of Congress Cataloging-in-Publication Data
Devine, A. M. (Andrew M.)
Discontinuous syntax : hyperbaton in Greek / A. M. Devine, Laurence D. Stephens.
p.   cm.
Text in English with phrases and examples in Greek.
Includes bibliographical references and index.
ISBN 0-19-513270-X
1. Greek language—Word order.   2. Oral-formulaic analysis.
3. Greek language—Syntax.   4. Rhetoric, Ancient.   5. Homer—Language.
I. Stephens, Laurence D.   II. Title.
PA373.D48   1999
485—dc21   99-15285

1 3 5 7 9 8 6 4 2

Printed in the United States of America
on acid-free paper

PREFACE

People still have a tendency to associate grammar with the smallminded pedantry of Terence Rattigan's schoolmasters. Such a dismissive attitude is rather anachronistic: grammar is nowadays a more abstract and theoretical subject than it used to be. In any case, we still need grammar; everyday activities like language instruction and the elicitation of textual meaning can't be performed without it. So it is time to revise and expand the doctrines of traditional grammar in a more theoretical and explanatory framework. In the present book we try looking at a basic problem of Greek syntax, namely phrasal discontinuity, in this new perspective.

We argue that there are pragmatically determined positions in Greek phrase structure, which are crosscategorial; these positions can be seen as a direct syntactic encoding of logical structure. Discontinuity has nonconfigurational origins, which are not merely a matter of the mechanics of syntax but can involve a different way of structuring meaning. As the Greek language develops from Homer to the classical period, it undergoes a change in syntactic typology which is reflected in a corresponding change in the rules for discontinuity. Nouns and adjectives in Greek both seem to require a fairly elastic mechanism for mapping from prima facie syntactic categories to semantic types; empirical evidence for this includes argument ranking effects. In the context of these assumptions, discontinuity emerges as a more natural and comprehensible feature of Greek syntax.

We have included a glossary covering some technical terms not used in traditional grammar. In a second appendix, selected Greek examples are transliterated and translated word-for-word.

During the course of our project we received generous help from many colleagues and friends. They are not responsible for the use we have made of their advice. (In coauthored work on syntax, all errors are said to be each other's.) We should like to mention in particular Martin Bloomer, Joan Bresnan, Maria Devine, Henriette de Swart, Mark Edwards, John Etchemendy, Bruce Hedin, Michael Jameson, Paul Kiparsky, Daphne Kleps, Hilary Mackie, Joseph Manning, Marsh McCall, Julius Moravcsik, Ian Morris, Rachel Nordlinger, Orrin Robinson, Adam Serfass, Susan Stephens, Susan Treggiari, Thomas Wasow. Sonia Moss and John Rawlings of Stanford Library have again handled our many requests with their characteristic courtesy and professional expertise.

Christmas 1998   A.M.D., *Stanford*
                                                  L.D.S., *Dallas*

CONTENTS

ABBREVIATIONS

Ach	*Acharnians*	Eur	Euripides
Aesch	Aeschines	*Euthyd*	*Euthydemus*
Ag	*Agamemnon* (Aeschylus)	*Euthyph*	*Euthyphro*
Ag	*Agesilaus* (Xenophon)	*Evag*	*Evagoras*
Alc	*Alcestis* (Euripides)	*Ex*	*Exordia*
Alc	*Alcibiades* (Plato)	*Gorg*	*Gorgias*
Amat	*Amatores*	*Heaut*	*Heauton Timorumenos*
An	*Anabasis*	*Hec*	*Hecuba*
Andoc	Andocides	*Hel*	*Helen*
Andr	*Andromache*	*Hell*	*Hellenica*
Antiph	Antipho	*HF*	*Hercules Furens*
Apol	*Apology*	Her	Herodotus
app. crit.	apparatus criticus	*Heracl*	*Heraclidae*
Ar	Aristophanes	*Hipp*	*Hippolytus*
Are	*Areopagiticus*	*Hipp Mai*	*Hippias Maior*
Arist	Aristotle	*IA*	*Iphigenia in Aulis*
Bacch	*Bacchae*	IG	Inscriptiones Graecae
Bus	*Busiris*	*Il*	*Iliad*
Clit	*Clitopho*	Isae	Isaeus
Crat	*Cratylus*	Isoc	Isocrates
Criti	*Critias*	*IT*	*Iphigenia in Tauris*
Cycl	*Cyclops*	*LGS*	*Lyrica Graeca Selecta*
Cyn	*Cynegetica*	*Locr*	IG IX².1.718
Cyr	*Cyropaedia*	*LSAG*	Jeffery 1990
DAA	Raubitschek et al. 1949	Lyc	Lycurgus
De Comp	*De Compositione Ver-*	Lys	Lysias
Verb	*borum*	*Med*	*Medea*
Dem	Demosthenes	*Mem*	*Memorabilia*
Din	Dinarchus	*Menex*	*Menexenus*
Eccl	*Ecclesiazusae*	*Od*	*Odyssey*
El	*Electra*	*Oec*	*Oeconomicus*
Ep	*Epistulae*	*Orest*	*Orestes*
Epid	*Epidemics*	*OT*	*Oedipus Tyrannus*
Eum	*Eumenides*	*Pac*	*De Pace*

Panath	*Panathenaicus*	*Rhet*	*Rhetorica*
Paneg	*Panegyricus*	*Sept*	*Seven against Thebes*
Pers	*Persae*	*Soph*	*Sophista*
Phaedr	*Phaedrus*	*Suppl*	*Supplices*
Phil	*Philebus*	*Symp*	*Symposium*
Philoct	*Philoctetes*	Thuc	Thucydides
Phoen	*Phoenissae*	*Tim*	*Timaeus*
Pl	Plato	*Trach*	*Trachiniae*
Polit	*Politicus*	*Troad*	*Troades*
Prot	*Protagoras*	Xen	Xenophon
PV	*Prometheus Vinctus*	*Vect*	*De Vectigalibus*
Rab Perd	*Pro Rabirio Perduellionis Reo*	v.l.	manuscripts vary
		/	caesura
Rep	*Republic*	|	end of line
Rhes	*Rhesus*	:	inscriptional punctuation

DISCONTINUOUS SYNTAX

HYPERBATON IN GREEK

1 Y₁ Hyperbaton in Prose

Our first chapter gives a preliminary syntactic account of premodifier hyperbaton (left branch discontinuity) in Greek prose. This type of discontinuity may at first sight appear to be a particularly strong indication of flat unstructured serial word order, but a closer analysis of the data reveals consistent cross-categorial patterning for premodifiers in both discontinuous and continuous phrases, which clearly calls for a phrase structural account.

SUBEXTRACTION

An echo question is a question in which the speaker repeats or paraphrases the words of another interlocutor, querying one or more constituents in order to ascertain that the message has been accurately received (often to suggest that the message is so preposterous that it must have been misheard)

    A. He's invited Don Pedro to dinner.
    B. He's invited WHO to dinner?

In echo questions, the interrogative *wh*-word is substituted in situ for the queried constituent: *who* appears in the direct object slot in the above example. In ordinary questions, however, the interrogative word does not remain in situ but is placed at the beginning of the clause, presumably reflecting a logical structure of the type $?x[P(x)]$

    Who has he invited to dinner?

In this sort of discourse situation, the interlocutors typically both know that Don Giovanni *(he)* has invited someone to dinner (this is the presupposition), and B is asking A to identify the someone. So

    He has invited x to dinner

is the presupposition, and

    x = who?

is the query.

Now suppose that instead of asking a completely openended question, the speaker knows that the invitee was a friend. Consequently, he wishes to identify one member of the set of individuals who are friends; he therefore uses the interrogative determiner *which*

Which friend has he invited to dinner?

Here the presupposition is that he has invited some friend to dinner, and the query is which one

(For x = which) (x is a friend) (he has invited x to dinner).

One can think of the answer being the result of set intersection: the interlocutor is asked to give the result of intersecting the set of his friends with the set of those he has invited to dinner. The distribution of information in the interrogative phrase is not uniform. The fact that the invitee is a friend, although it serves to restrict the set of individuals over which x ranges, is part of the presupposition and not part of the query. So one might think that it could stay in its regular direct object position while the interrogative determiner was placed at the beginning of the clause

*Which has he invited friend to dinner?

But this structure violates a rule of English syntax known as Ross's Left Branch Condition, which has been variously reanalyzed over the years (Corver 1990), most recently as a chain uniformity violation (Radford 1997). This rule constrains the extraction of determiners, adjectives, possessors and degree words. Even though the noun is part of the presupposition, the syntax requires that the whole noun phrase, and not merely its left branch, be placed at the beginning of the clause or "extracted" as a single unit

Which friend has he invited to dinner?

When the whole noun phrase is extracted, the interrogative carries the noun along with it, or "piedpipes" the noun, whereas in the illicit structure the interrogative has been "subextracted," leaving the noun in situ. The result is a discontinuous structure. The traditional term for this and other types of discontinuous structure in Greek grammar is *hyperbaton*. As noted, the discontinuous structure seems to show a better fit between syntax and meaning: only what is questioned is extracted. For this reason, some people hypothesize that the piedpiped noun is lowered back into the nuclear clause for semantic interpretation. On the other hand, it could also be that the mechanics of interrogation (and of focus) likes to function in terms of complete argument and adjunct phrases rather than in terms of subconstituents embedded within them (Drubig 1994; Kiss 1995). For instance, the Somali focus particle *baa* is used with complete noun phrases but not with just an adnominal modifier (Saeed 1984).

The Left Branch Condition evidently does not apply to Greek, nor indeed to various Slavic languages, notably Polish, since in these languages sub-extraction is permitted. Alongside questions in which the whole noun phrase appears at the beginning of the clause, we find questions with only the interrogative (which in Greek is probably an adjective) at the beginning of the clause

(1)   τίνα δύναμιν ἔχει Pl *Laws* 643a
      τίνα ἔχει δύναμιν Pl *Rep* 358b

      τίνι τεκμηρίῳ χρῶμαι; Pl *Gorg* 487c
      τίνι χρώμενος τεκμηρίῳ; Dem 20.115

      τίνα γνώμην ἔχειν περὶ ὑμῶν Dem *Ep* 2.8
      τίνα δ᾽ ἔχων ἕκαστος ὑμῶν γνώμην Aesch 1.186.

When we consider the answers to such questions, we find the same sort of informational structure as in questions: the presupposition remains the same, but instead of the query we have the informational focus

> Which car did he buy last week?
> He bought the RED car last week.

The presupposition is that he bought some car from a contextually fixed set of cars last week, and the new information is that it was the red one. Even when it allows focus to be placed at the beginning of the clause, English does not permit the right branch of the noun phrase to remain in situ, as in the following sentence with contrastively focused topics

> *The RED he bought car last week, the BLUE he has had car for years.

To the extent that it is used at all, a sentence like

> Raw he used to eat oysters

can only mean 'he used to eat oysters raw,' not 'he used to eat raw oysters.' Greek, on the other hand, has no problem with the prima facie subextraction of focused modifiers, which pattern along the same lines as the subextracted interrogative adjectives just noted (not surprisingly since interrogatives and focus are treated similarly in various languages); this is probably implicit in the following question and elliptical answer sequences

(2)   τίν᾽ ἔχει λοιπὴν δωρειάν, Λεπτίνη; οὐδεμίαν δήπου (scil. ἔχει λοιπὴν
      δωρειάν) Dem 20.123.

---

(1) What power it has (Pl *Laws* 643a). What power it has (Pl *Rep* 358b). What evidence do I use? (Pl *Gorg* 487c). Using what evidence? (Dem 20.115). To have what opinion about you (Dem *Ep* 2.8). Having what opinion will each of you...? (Aesch 1.186).
(2) What reward has he left, Leptines? None evidently (Dem 20.123).

(3)   πόσον γὰρ ἐδημηγόρει χρόνον Τίμαρχος; πολύν (scil. ἐδημηγόρει χρόνον) Dem 19.286

Ελ. ποίοις ἐπιστὰς βαρβάροις πυλώμασιν;
Με. τοῖσδ' (scil. ἐπιστὰς βαρβάροις πυλώμασιν) *Hel* 789.

The parallel patterning of adjectives and interrogatives is evidenced in sub-extraction from various superordinate phrase types, as illustrated by the following complex of evidence

NOUN PHRASE

(4)   ποίας πολίτης πατρίδος Ἕλληνος *IT* 495
Φεραίας τῆσδε κωμῆται χθονός *Alc* 476.

ADJECTIVE PHRASE

(5)   ὅσων... αἴτιοι κακῶν Dem *Ex* 6.1
τοσούτων αἴτιοι κακῶν Dem 28.19

τίνος... ἐπιστήμων τέχνης Pl *Gorg* 448e
ῥητορικῆς... ἐπιστήμων τέχνης Pl *Gorg* 449c

PREPOSITIONAL PHRASE

(6)   τίνος ἕνεκα καιροῦ Dem 23.182
τηλικούτων ἕνεκα... τεκμηρίων Dem 57.64

VERB PHRASE

(7)   τίνα ἔχει δύναμιν Pl *Rep* 358b
οὐδεμίαν ἔχει δύναμιν Pl *Euthyd* 296c

τίνι χρώμενος τεκμηρίῳ; Dem 20.115
τῷ αὐτῷ... χρησόμεθα τεκμηρίῳ Pl *Symp* 195e

ἐπὶ τίνα... στρατευσόμεθα πόλιν; Her 3.137
ἐπ' ἀροτῆρας... στρατευόμεθα ἄνδρας Her 7.50.

The pattern established by the above evidence for interrogative extraction and focus also occurs, as might be predicted, with other *wh*-words, namely exclamations

(3) How long had Timarchus been a public speaker? A long time (Dem 19.286). Standing at which foreign gate? At this one (*Hel* 789).

(4) Citizen of which Greek state? (*IT* 495). Inhabitants of this land of Pherae (*Alc* 476).

(5) All the evils they are responsible for (Dem *Ex* 6.1). Responsible for such great evils (Dem 28.19). Knowledgeable about which art? (Pl *Gorg* 448e). Knowledgeable about the art of rhetoric (Pl *Gorg* 449c).

(6) For the sake of which advantage? (Dem 23.182). For the sake of such important evidence (Dem 57.64).

(7) What power does it have? (Pl *Rep* 358b). It has no force (Pl *Euthyd* 296c). Using what evidence? (Dem 20.115). We will use the same evidence (Pl *Symp* 195e). Which city will we wage war against? (Her 3.137). We are waging war against men who are farmers (Her 7.50).

(8) ἐν οἵοις κείμεθ' ἄθλιοι κακοῖς *Phoen* 1639
     ἐν τοιοῖσδε κειμένη κακοῖς *Hec* 969

and relative clauses

(9) ἃς μὲν ὤμοσε... συνθήκας Dem 23.171
     τῆς γὰρ ἐπιθυμήσῃ γυναικὸς Her 1.216
     ἀφ' ἧς ὠμόσαθ' ἡμέρας Dem 18.26
     ἐφ' αἷς ἐκλήθησαν διαθήκαις Isae 4.13
     καθ' οὓς ἐπολιτευόμην χρόνους Dem 18.69
     τῶν ἐγὼ οἶδα ἀνθρώπων Her 7.238.

That this distribution of hyperbaton is systematic and not coincidental is typologically confirmed. In Mohawk (Baker 1996) one can say

> *Which did you buy basket?*
> *This I found gun*
> *John lost which I bought basket.*

The following provisional conclusion may be drawn from the Greek data cited so far. Interrogatives and other *wh*-word modifiers can optionally be subextracted and placed in an operator position that is structurally higher than (c-commands) the whole clause. Operators, unlike ordinary predicates and referring expressions, involve some form of logico-semantic computation (quantification, negation, modality, tense, etc.); they are placed in a position to the left of the material they have scope over in standard logical representations, and sometimes in syntactic word order too. Since the focused modifiers of hyperbaton pattern with *wh*-words, they too appear to be subextracted and placed in an operator position. (We shall argue in chapter 6 that more is involved than the term "subextraction" by itself suggests.) It is not the case that the head of the superordinate phrase is introduced into the noun phrase to create hyperbaton: for instance, the verb is not inserted between the adjective and the noun. Nor is the noun extraposed out of the nuclear phrase, as some theories of hyperbaton assume. Rather, the focused modifier is taken from its normal position in the noun phrase and placed in a left peripheral operator position. However, the parallel between *wh*-words and modifiers in hyperbaton does not extend beyond this very general principle. In the first place, the modifiers in prose Yı hyperbaton have strong focus, not the weak (informational) focus that they would have if they were merely answers to implicit questions and the

---

(8) To what disasters are we wretchedly subjected? (*Phoen* 1639). Find myself in such an evil situation (*Hec* 969).

(9) The agreement he swore to (Dem 23.171). The woman he desires (Her 1.216). From the day on which you swore to the peace treaty (Dem 18.26). The will they were summoned to witness (Isae 4.13). During the periods of my political activity (Dem 18.69). Of all the men I know (Her 7.238).

declarative counterparts of the interrogative examples; this matter is investigated in detail in chapter 2. Secondly, the domain of *wh*-word extraction is typically the nuclear clause (the clause minus any fronted topicalized material), whereas hyperbaton, as we shall see, has various narrower phrasal domains. In the examples cited, the *wh*-words and the hyperbaton modifiers are both extracted from the same superordinate phrases and are both occupying operator positions, but (at least in a structural analysis, as opposed to one based on simple serial precedence) they are not the same operator positions; they just seem that way because of the coincidence of the beginning of higher and lower phrasal projections. In fact, we have to deal with a whole range of different positions, more like what we find with the quantifiers in the following French sentences (de Swart 1992)

> Max a vendu *beaucoup* de livres (NP)
> Max a *beaucoup* vendu de livres (VP)
> *Combien* Max a-t-il vendu de livres? (CP),

or with floating quantifiers in English

> (All) the students (all) will (all) have (all) been (all) given (all)
> a copy of Rutilius Namatianus.

To the extent that hyperbaton co-occurs with an interrogative, one would expect the *wh*-word to be outside the hyperbaton

(10)   τί μάλιστ᾽ ἐν ἅπασι διεσπούδασται τοῖς νόμοις; Dem 20.157
τίσι γὰρ τῶν πραγμάτων ἐγκρατὴς γέγονε Φίλιππος ἁπάντων
Dem 19.300 (Y₂ hyperbaton)

and similarly for relative clauses

(11)   οἷς πολλὰ καὶ καλὰ σύνισμεν ἔργα Aesch 3.241
ἐν οἷς οἱ περὶ τῆς εἰρήνης ἐγίγνοντο λόγοι Aesch 2.74.

However, where the modifier is a strong topic, the topic is outside the interrogative even in hyperbaton

(12)   οὗτοι δὲ τί ποιοῦσιν οἱ νόμοι; Dem. 21.30
ταυτὶ τίνος τὰ φορτί᾽ ἐστί; Ar *Ach* 910
τὸ σὸν τί ἐστι πρᾶγμα; Pl *Apol* 20c.

---

(10) What has been guarded against most in all the laws? (Dem 20.157). By what means Philip gained complete political control (Dem 19.300).

(11) Whose many noble deeds we acknowledge (Aesch 3.241). In which the debate about the peace took place (Aesch 2.74).

(12) What do these laws accomplish? (Dem 21.30). Whose goods are these? (Ar *Ach* 910). What are you up to? (Pl *Apol* 20c).

CROSSCATEGORIAL ANALYSIS

Consider a noun phrase like καλῆς γυναικός. Such a phrase can appear as the complement of a range of lexical heads: verbs, prepositions, adjectives and other nouns: μέμνημαι [καλῆς γυναικός], περὶ [καλῆς γυναικός], ἄξιος [καλῆς γυναικός], ἔρως [καλῆς γυναικός]. In the simplest form of hyperbaton, the modifier, instead of being placed in its regular position next to the noun, is placed at the beginning of the phrase. Pending a more adventurous analysis to be proposed in chapter 6, we shall simply assume that it is in a structurally external and superior position which has scope over and c-commands the rest of the phrase: καλῆς [μέμνημαι γυναικός].

The idea of a parallelism in the composition of phrases of different categories (NP, AP, PP, VP) is implicit in some functionally based terminology of traditional grammar. For instance, not only verbs but also prepositions are said to have objects (*milites interfecit, contra milites*); verbs have subjects and objects, and verbal nouns occur with subjective and objective genitives (*timor militum*). The further idea that heads of different categories project structurally parallel phrases became central to syntactic theory when, with the movement away from generative semantics, it was no longer possible to account for cross-categorial parallelisms via (often rather abstract) transformations (Jackendoff 1977). The complex of data presented in this section is designed to show that in Greek the parallelism of structure across the phrasal (X-bar) spectrum extends to the Y1 hyperbaton operator position, which, consequently, is a structurally defined position exploited for a pragmatic function, namely focus marking.

First, we need to introduce some shorthand that will enable us to refer to the various hyperbaton structures and their components without repetitive circumlocution. Take a simple hyperbaton like

   (13)   εἰ... πολλὰ κατέλιπε χρήματα Andoc 1.119.

We refer to the noun phrase πολλὰ χρήματα as YP, to its first (leftmost) element (namely πολλὰ) as Y1, and to its righthand element (χρήματα) as Y2. Y1 and Y2 are defined by linear order irrespective of grammatical category. The superordinate phrase combining YP and its governing head X (κατέλιπε) is called XP. When there is no hyperbaton, XP is either [X YP] (κατέλιπε πολλὰ χρήματα) or [YP X] (πολλὰ χρήματα κατέλιπε). When there is hyperbaton, the order is [Y1 X Y2]. If the modifier is Y1, we call the resulting structure Y1 hyperbaton (πολλὰ κατέλιπε χρήματα). If the modifier is Y2, we call the result Y2 hyperbaton (χρήματα κατέλιπε πολλὰ).

For each category, we provide a preliminary and schematic diagram illustrating the relationship between the structure with continuous YP and the structure with Y1 hyperbaton by collapsing the two positions into a single tree. In a

(13) If he had left a great deal of money (Andoc 1.119).

dynamic framework, with a copying theory of movement, these diagrams can also be understood as showing the positions of the modifier before and after movement from its position inside YP to the external Y_1 position. The labelling of the nodes is rather uncertain. Apart from the notorious prevailing disagreement about the appropriate labelling of adjectivally modified noun phrases (Delsing 1993), the status of the Y_1 focus node is not too clear: it could be a specifier, an adjoined node, or the specifier or head of a separate focus projection: two of these options are diagrammed in Figure 2.2 in the next chapter. Interrogative extraction, which is focus related, is usually associated with specifiers, whereas German-type scrambling, which has a more topical flavour, is neatly handled via an array of adjunction positions (Müller & Sternefeld 1993). For terminological convenience, we will often simply refer to the Y_1 hyperbaton position as a specifier. Note that this position is probably available c-commanding any structure ranging from the lowest X′ to the complete phrase including adjuncts to XP. The status of the terminal nodes in the Y_1 hyperbaton structure may be different from that in the continuous YP structure, as discussed in chapter 6; they are left unlabelled for the time being. As throughout this work, we shall use a very simple, surface-oriented syntax, in which nominal inflections do not project syntactically, there are no agreement projections, and if movement exists at all it is mainly pragmatically driven. The present chapter is principally concerned to establish the syntactic preliminaries. That might strike some as a strange thing to say, since an analysis of hyperbaton in strictly autonomous syntactic terms should qualify as a complete and adequate account. However, the main interest of the data lies in how syntactic structure interfaces with pragmatic meaning and compositional semantics. This latter perspective will be more prominent in subsequent chapters.

Noun phrase

Figure 1.1 represents the relationship between the posthead continuous order and the hyperbaton order in noun phrase Y_1 hyperbaton, as illustrated by the following pair of examples

(14)   ἐπὶ σωτηρίᾳ τῶν ξυμπάντων πραγμάτων Thuc 8.72.1 (X YP)
         ἑτέρων παρεμβολῇ πραγμάτων Aesch 3.205.

Here are some further examples of noun phrase hyperbaton

(15)   ἑτέρων χώραν πρέσβεων Aesch 2.105
         τοιούτων εἰσηγητὴς αὐτῷ καὶ διδάσκαλος ἔργων Aesch 1.172
         τὴν τῶν μεγάλων καὶ πρώτων γένεσιν ἔργων Pl *Laws* 889a.

(14) For the salvation of the whole situation (Thuc 8.72.1). By the introduction of extraneous matters (Aesch 3.205).
(15) The function of other ambassadors (Aesch 2.105). His teacher and instructor in that conduct (Aesch 1.172). The major primary creations (Pl *Laws* 889a).

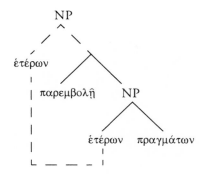

Figure 1.1
Noun phrase hyperbaton
ἑτέρων [παρεμβολῇ — πραγμάτων]

(16)   τὴν τοῦ ἀγαθοῦ εἰκόνα ἤθους Pl *Rep* 401b
       τὴν τῶν πολλῶν δόξαν ἀνθρώπων Pl *Prot* 353a.

Note that the focus c-commands the noun phrase, not the determiner phrase:
*τῶν πολλῶν τὴν δόξαν ἀνθρώπων. Compare the position of Y1 in the follow-
ing examples.

(17)   ἐν παγκάκων ἤθεσιν ἀνθρώπων Pl *Laws* 928e (PP)
       ὁ τούτου ἔρως τοῦ ἀνθρώπου Pl *Symp* 213c (DP).

Adjective phrase

(18)   μεστῇ πολλῶν ἀγαθῶν Xen *An* 3.5.1 (X YP)
       πολλῶν μεστὸν ἀγαθῶν Pl *Laws* 906a.

This is a simple adjective phrase hyperbaton, in which the head and its sister
noun phrase constituent exhaust the adjective phrase, as diagrammed in Figure
1.2. The genitive can be a complement genitive, a partitive genitive, or a genitive of comparison; the adjective can be a null head modifier

(19)   τῶν ἴσων αἴτιος... κακῶν Dem 19.29
       ὁ πάντων σχετλιώτατος ἀνθρώπων Andoc 1.124.

(16) The concept of good character (Pl *Rep* 401b). The opinion of the masses (Pl *Prot*
353a).
(17) When the character of men is completely evil (Pl *Laws* 928e). The love of this man
(Pl *Symp* 213c).
(18) Full of plentiful supplies (Xen *An* 3.5.1). Full of many good things (Pl *Laws* 906a).
(19) Responsible for the same disasters (Dem 19.29). The most wicked of all men
(Andoc 1.124).

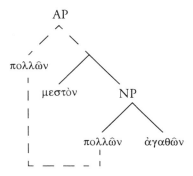

Figure 1.2
Adjective phrase hyperbaton
πολλῶν [μεστὸν — ἀγαθῶν]

(20)   πάσης μεῖζον᾽ εὐεργεσίας Dem 13.24
  τούτων... ἔνιοι τῶν ἀνδρῶν Dem 20.64.

Prepositional phrase

Hyperbaton in prepositional phrases will be analyzed in detail in chapter 5. For the time being, note that, in prose, hyperbaton is, apart from a few instances, illicit in prepositional phrases except for περὶ in its nonlocal meaning

(21)   περὶ τῶν ἄλλων τεχνῶν Pl *Clit* 410c
  τῶν ἄλλων περὶ νομέων Pl *Polit* 268b.

To the extent that it occurs, prepositional phrase hyperbaton is patterned like hyperbaton with other categories, as diagrammed in Figure 1.3. It also occurs with the socalled "improper preposition" ἕνεκα

(22)   ἕνεκα τῆς ἰδίας χρείας τοῦ σίτου Dem 50.6 (X YP)
  τῆς ἰδίας ῥᾳθυμίας ἕνεκα Dem 10.25 (YP X)
  τῆς ἰδίας ἕνεκα ῥᾳθυμίας Dem 8.49.

Verb phrase

The following pair illustrates simple verb phrase hyperbaton with a direct object YP

(20) Greater than every service rendered (Dem 13.24). Some of these men (Dem 20.64).
(21) Concerning the other skills (Pl *Clit* 410c). Concerning the other herdsmen (Pl *Polit* 268b).
(22) Because of their own need of food (Dem 50.6). For the sake of your own ease (Dem 10.25). For the sake of your own ease (Dem 8.49).

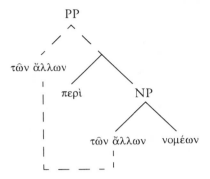

Figure 1.3
Prepositional phrase hyperbaton
τῶν ἄλλων [περὶ —νομέων]

(23)   ἠδικηκότα... πᾶσαν τὴν πόλιν Dem 24.8 (X YP)
πᾶσαν ἔβλαπτε τὴν πόλιν Dem 3.13.

This is diagrammed in Figure 1.4. Here are some further examples illustrating various other grammatical relations. If complements and adjuncts are attached at different bar levels in Greek, hyperbaton is not sensitive to the difference

(24)   πᾶσι βεβοηθήκατε τοῖς ἐν τοῖς ἔργοις ἐργαζομένοις Dem 42.31
εἰ πάσης ἄρξειε Θρᾴκης Dem 23.117, cp. Lyc 62
τούτοις ἐπαρθεὶς τοῖς ψηφίσμασι Dem 18.168
μιᾷ μόνον ἁλῶναι ψήφῳ Dem 21.75

Additional argument or adjunct

So far we have analyzed hyperbaton as if X plus YP always exhausted XP. If XP = X plus YP, then the only possible structure for hyperbaton is Y X Y. However, there are also cases in which, in addition to YP, there is a second complement or an adjunct (which we shall call ZP). Purely in terms of serial order, there are four possible locations for ZP, all of which are attested. ZP can be prehead or posthead, and in each case it can either precede or follow the Y element

ZP Y X Y
Y ZP X Y
Y X Y ZP
Y X ZP Y.

(23) That he had defrauded all the city (Dem 24.8). Injured all the city (Dem 3.13).
(24) You have aided all those working in the mines (Dem 42.31). If he should rule all Thrace (Dem 23.117). Having been encouraged by these decrees (Dem 18.168). That he was condemned by only one vote (Dem 21.75).

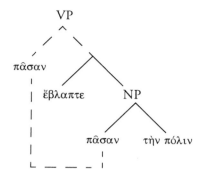

Figure 1.4
Simple verb phrase hyperbaton
πᾶσαν [ἔβλαπτε — τὴν πόλιν]

The distribution of ZP is not random but appears to correlate with informational content. Syntactic and phonological factors may also contribute to the outcome. So, as for word order in general, results are not entirely predictable without a complicated optimality calculus. When ZP is prehead, it tends to have some degree of focus, with first or second position depending inter alia on its salience relative to Y₁

(25)   πρὸς ὑμᾶς ἅπασαν ἐρῶ τὴν ἀλήθειαν Dem 23.187
        τὴν ἱερὰν ἀπὸ τῆς χώρας ᾤχετ᾽ ἔχων τριήρη Dem 4.34
        πολλοὺς καὶ θρασεῖς... τῇ πόλει ἐπαιρόμενος λόγους Dem 18.222
        πλεῖστον ἐκ τῆς πολιτείας εἰληφὼς ἀργύριον Aesch 3.173.

When ZP is located outside and after the YXY hyperbaton structure, its informational status varies

(26)   ἁπάντων μετασχὼν τῶν πόνων τῇ πόλει Aesch 3.191
        τοῖς μεγάλοις χρῆσθαι τεκμηρίοις περὶ τῶν μεγάλων Lys 7.33
        τὴν δὲ ἄλλην ἀνάγουσι ὁρτὴν τῷ Διονύσῳ οἱ Αἰγύπτιοι...
            κατὰ ταὐτά... Ἕλλησι Her 2.48.

In the Aeschines example, ZP is tail material, in the Lysias it is a second focus. The Herodotus example is more complex: here the hyperbaton is embedded

---

(25) I will tell you the whole truth (Dem 23.187). He made off from the land with the sacred trireme (Dem 4.34). Although he had uttered many insolent words against the city (Dem 18.222). Although he had made a vast amount of money from politics (Aesch 3.173).

(26) Sharing all its toils with the city (Aesch 3.191). To use significant evidence for significant issues (Lys 7.33). The Egyptians celebrate the rest of the festival to Dionysus in the same way as the Greeks (Her 2.48).

within a topicalization starting with the contrastive Y1 adjective ἄλλην and including the tail subject and indirect object; the focus is κατὰ ταὐτά. Between X and Y2, on the other hand, we find posthead tail pronouns

(27)   μεγίστων αἴτιον ἡμῖν ἀγαθῶν Pl *Phaedr* 266b
        τὴν αὐτὴν ἔχειν περὶ ἐμοῦ διάνοιαν Lys 24.21
        εἰ μείζων... γένοιτο παρ᾽ ὑμῶν βλάβη Dem 3.32.

It is interesting that in Polish (Siewierska 1984), a second argument can appear within the hyperbaton span, but it must precede rather than follow the verb unless it is pronominal.

The pragmatic differences elicited seem to correlate with discernible differences in scope and in the order in which arguments are composed with the head. Consider again

(28)   πρὸς ὑμᾶς ἅπασαν ἐρῶ τὴν ἀλήθειαν Dem 23.187

Here πρὸς ὑμᾶς is either a focus or a contrastive topic. Not only is this example quite different from a neutral (broad scope focus) sentence like

(29)   εἰρήκαμεν δ᾽ ὑμῖν πᾶσαν τὴν ἀλήθειαν Thuc 6.87.1,

it is also arguably different from

        ἅπασαν ἐρῶ πρὸς ὑμᾶς τὴν ἀλήθειαν.

The information is structured in such a way that in the one what is entire is the truth that will be told, in the other what is entire is the truth that you will be told. This has interesting implications for the syntactic analysis of hyperbaton. When posthead ZP is inside the hyperbaton in the surface order, the structure is Y1[[X ZP]Y2]

        μεγίστων [[αἴτιον ἡμῖν] ἀγαθῶν].

But when it is outside the hyperbaton, the structure is [Y1[XY2]]ZP

        [τοῖς μεγάλοις [χρῆσθαι τεκμηρίοις]] περὶ τῶν μεγάλων.

If the Y1 focus node were taken to c-command the maximal verb phrase in both structures, the difference would be lost

        *τοῖς μεγάλοις [[χρῆσθαι τεκμηρίοις] περὶ τῶν μεγάλων].

Beyond XP

In the data analyzed so far, we have seen what normally would be a branching noun phrase YP made discontinuous in such a way that a Y1, bearing narrow focus, is placed in an operator position at the left edge of the immediately

---

(27) Source of the greatest benefits for us (Pl *Phaedr* 266b). To maintain the same opinion of me (Lys 24.21). If I should incur greater harm from you (Dem 3.32).

(28) I will tell you the whole truth (Dem 23.187).

(29) We have told you the whole truth (Thuc 6.87.1).

superordinate phrase XP. Instead of continuous [X[Y₁Y₂]] (type ἐπάρξασα πάσης τῆς Ἀσίας), we find discontinuous [Y₁[XY₂]] in hyperbaton (type πάσης ἐπάρξασα τῆς Ἀσίας Lyc 62). Even when another argument appears between Y₁ and the head (πᾶσαν ὑφ᾽ αὐτῷ λαβὼν τὴν ἀρχὴν Dem 23.180), Y₁ is still attached to the superordinate phrase XP.

However, this schema does not cover all the possible landing sites for Y₁. Although hyperbaton has the appearance of a simple phrasal wrapping, it is also possible for Y₁ to skip over more than one node in such a way that it climbs beyond the specifier position of the superordinate phrase to be adjoined to, or land in the specifier position of, a not immediately dominating phrasal projection. Once again, this phenomenon is crosscategorial. The serial order of the elements following Y₁ varies reflecting the word order of the corresponding clause without hyperbaton. In noun and adjective phrase hyperbaton we find

$$Y_1[XV-Y_2]$$
$$Y_1[VX-Y_2]$$
$$Y_1[V-Y_2X].$$

The dash (–) marks the position that Y₁ would occupy in the absence of hyperbaton. In the first two structures, the Y-elements demarcate the domain of hyperbaton; that is, the domain of hyperbaton starts with the Y₁ constituent and ends with the Y₂ constituent, and both heads (X and V) are contained inside the hyperbaton. But in the third structure, $Y_1[V-Y_2X]$, Y₁ stands at the left edge of the domain of hyperbaton, but Y₂ is not the last constituent in the domain because X (the head of XP) follows rather than precedes Y₂. We could say that Y₁VY₂X was the domain of hyperbaton and Y₁VY₂ the span of hyperbaton. Usually, the domain and the span are coterminous: this is one situation in which they are not.

We will start with a noun phrase hyperbaton

(30)   μὴ μικροψύχου ποιεῖν ἔργον ἀνθρώπου Dem 18.269.

In this example, the adjective μικροψύχου appears neither in its neutral position next to ἀνθρώπου nor in the specifier position of the superordinate noun phrase (μικροψύχου ἔργον ἀνθρώπου), but in the specifier position of the infinitive verb phrase, resulting in the serial order Y₁VXY₂; the light verb ποιεῖν may facilitate this structure, since light verbs tend to be adjacent to their associated nonreferential nouns (Dover 1968). In the order Y₁VY₂X the head of the superordinate noun phrase is external to the span of hyperbaton, as in the following verse example

(31)   Εὐξένου δ᾽ ἀφικόμην | πόντου πρὸς ἀκτάς Rhes 428.

In adjective phrases too, the immediately superordinate head may be internal or external to the span of the hyperbaton

(30)   Not to behave like a meanspirited person (Dem 18.269).
(31)   I arrived at the shores of the Black Sea (Rhes 428).

(32)   ἁπάντων αἴτιος εἶναι τῶν συμβεβηκότων Dem 55.25
        πολλῆς μεστὸν ὄντα ὁρμῆς Pl *Ep* 325e
        τὸ πάθος... ὃ πάντων ἔφαμεν εἶναι τῶν θαυμαστῶν αἴτιον
        Pl *Polit* 270b.

The common verse practice of wrapping a noun phrase around its prepositional head

(33)   χλωραῖς ὑπ᾽ ἐλάταις *Bacch* 38,

is, as already noted, mostly illicit in prose. However, the preposition plus Y1 can appear to the left of a superordinate head, giving the order PN1VN2

(34)   ἐν τοῖς φονικοῖς γέγραπται νόμοις Dem 9.44
        ἐν τοῖς δημοσίοις ἀναγέγραπται γράμμασιν Aesch 2.58
        ἔς τε δὴ ὧν τὰς ἄλλας ἔπεμπε συμμαχίας Her 1.82
        ὑπὸ ταύτης ἀγόμενοι τῆς ἐλπίδος Pl *Phaedo* 68a
        μοι κατὰ ταύτην προσῆκε κρίνεσθαι τὴν γραφήν Isae 11.35.

A pronominal, or even rarely a nominal, argument may appear along with the verb within the hyperbaton span

(35)   εἰς τοσοῦτόν με κατέστησεν ἀγῶνα Lys 7.42
        ἐν πολλῇ ἂν ἔχεσθαι ὑμᾶς ἀπορίᾳ δοκῶ Antiph 5.65
        ἀπὸ τῶν ὑμετέρων ὑμῖν πολεμεῖ συμμάχων Dem 4.34
        ἐκ τούτου τὴν μορίαν ἀφανίζειν ἐπεχείρησα τοῦ χωρίου Lys 7.28.

Since NPN is illicit, it follows that NVPN should not occur either.

Next we turn to the question of exactly where in the tree the Y1 node is located. Consider an example like the following

(36)   καὶ περὶ τούτου Δημοσθένης μὲν καὶ Κτησιφῶν πολὺν ποιήσονται
        λόγον Aesch 3.28;

first comes a topic, then the conjoined subjects, and finally the verb phrase with its hyperbaton. A potential indeterminacy is introduced by the fact that the subjects are contrastive with the subject of the following clause (ὁ δέ γε

---

(32) That I was responsible for everything that had happened (Dem 55.25). Being full of great desire (Pl *Ep* 325e). The event which we said was the cause of all the portents (Pl *Polit* 270b).

(33) Beneath green pine trees (*Bacch* 38).

(34) It is written in the homicide laws (Dem 9.44). They are registered in the public archives (Aesch 2.58). He sent messengers to the other allies (Her 1.82). Inspired by the hope of... (Pl *Phaedo* 68a). It would be right for me to be prosecuted on this charge (Isae 11.35).

(35) He took me to court on so serious a charge (Lys 7.42). I think you would be in great difficulty (Antiph 5.65). He makes war on you at the expense of your allies (Dem 4.34). I tried to remove the sacred olive from this plot of land (Lys 7.28).

(36) And on this point Demosthenes and Ctesiphon will speak at length (Aesch 3.28).

νόμος), but this is still a fairly unambiguous example of verb phrase hyperbaton. Compare also

(37) οἱ κορυβαντιῶντες ἐκείνου μόνου αἰσθάνονται τοῦ μέλους ὀξέως
      Pl *Ion* 536c
      πονηρὰ φύσις... δημοσίας ἀπεργάζεται συμφοράς Aesch 3.147.

On the other hand, in

(38) ἑτέραν γάρ ἐγὼ γέγραφα μαρτυρίαν Aesch 1.47
      περὶ ὧν... μεγάλας... οἱ νόμοι διδόασι τιμωρίας Dem 18.12
      οὐδεμίαν ἐκείνου περὶ τούτων ποιησαμένου διαθήκην Isae 8.40

Y₁ is evidently in a position c-commanding the rest of the clause. But what about sentences in which the left edge of the verb phrase is simultaneously the left edge of the clause and of any other projections intermediate between the clause and the verb phrase? Strictly speaking, in a verb phrase hyperbaton where VP exhausts the clause or the hyperbaton begins the clause

(39) μεγάλας ἐπέθηκαν τιμωρίας (scil. οἱ νόμοι) Dem 47.2
      ἔπειθ᾽ ἕτερον ἐπήγετο ψήφισμα Aesch 2.110
      ἐνταῦθ᾽ ἕτερον νικᾷ ψήφισμα Δημοσθένης Aesch 3.68 (v.l.)
      πρὸ ἐμοῦ τοῦτ᾽ εἶχε τὸ φρόνημ᾽ ἡ πόλις Dem 18.206,

it is not possible to claim categorically that the verb phrase is the domain of hyperbaton without making the additional assumption that for hyperbaton, as opposed to interrogative extraction, the lowest operator position made available by the word order is the one used in interpreting the sentence. Given the choice between a phrasal and a clausal focus slot for hyperbaton, we have assumed the former. There is also an example with the subject between the verb and the Y₂ noun

(40) πολλὴν γάρ πάνυ κατέλιπεν ὁ πατὴρ αὐτῷ οὐσίαν Aesch 1.42;

contrast with focused subject and presupposed modifier

(41) οὐχ ὁ πατὴρ αὐτῷ τὴν πολλὴν οὐσίαν κατέλιπεν Isae 5.37.

Although it may be mechanically possible in the hyperbaton examples with postverbal subjects to treat all the material to the left of the subject as fronted,

(37) The Corybantians hear only that song clearly (Pl *Ion* 536c). An evil nature produces public disasters (Aesch 3.147).
(38) I have written another affidavit (Aesch 1.47). For which the laws prescribed great punishments (Dem 18.12). Although he had made no will concerning these matters (Isae 8.40).
(39) They imposed great punishments (Dem 47.2). Then he introduced another proposal (Aesch 2.110). Then Demosthenes carries another resolution (Aesch 3.68). Also before my time the city had this proud spirit (Dem 18.206).
(40) For his father left him a very great deal of property (Aesch 1.42).
(41) His father did not bequeath him his extensive property (Isae 5.37).

it is simpler to assume that the subjects have not been raised out of the verb phrase to subject position. This is because the sentences are not really designed to predicate information of the grammatical subject, but rather to quantify or identify the object. Such an assumption is rather natural for the pronominal subject of an unaccusative

(42)   πᾶσιν ἤρεσκε ταῦτα τοῖς ἄλλοις πρέσβεσιν Dem 19.157.

This then raises the question whether some examples with preverbal subject, like Dem 18.12 and Aesch 1.47 cited above, could not be verb phrase hyperbaton too, with the subjects in SpecVP and with Y1 adjoined to VP. We shall suggest in chapter 2 that hyperbata with verb phrase internal subjects are a direct encoding of pragmatic structure according to the predicational theory of focus; the grammatical subject is not a separate subject of predication in such structures.

When the focused modifier is additionally a topic, it can occur to the left of a regular focus

(43)   ταῦτα ἐς τοὺς πάντας Ἕλληνας ἀπέρριψε ὁ Κῦρος τὰ ἔπεα
        Her 1.153;

here Y1 is a focused topic, the primary focus is on the quantifier in the prepositional phrase, and the subject is again predictable tail material along with Y2: 'these words Cyrus addressed to ALL the Greeks.' In addition to these informational considerations, the distance from Y1 to Y2 may also be a factor entering into the calculus and lowering the frequency of higher domain hyperbaton. In movement theories, longer movements are said to be less economical and so less favoured. Presumably the further away Y2 is from Y1, the more difficult the sentence is to decode and consequently the less frequently distant landing sites are used. Y1 has to be held in limbo until the utterance reaches Y2 for the sentence to be construed with more than contextual guesswork

> Which chapter did you discuss Lucretius in?
> Which chapter did you discuss the remarkably challenging textual and interpretational problems associated with Lucretius' didactic verse in?

This factor is apparently involved in a syntactic joke in Aristophanes

(44)   οὐ πολὺν οὐδ᾽ ὁ πίθηκος οὗτος ὁ νῦν ἐνοχλῶν, | Κλειγένης ὁ μικρός, | ὁ πονηρότατος βαλανεὺς ὁπόσοι κρατοῦσι κυκησίτεφροι | ψευδο-λίτρου κονίας | καὶ Κιμωλίας γῆς, | χρόνον ἐνδιατρίψει Frogs 708.

(42)   These things were pleasing to all the other ambassadors (Dem 19.157).

(43)   These words Cyrus directed at the whole Greek people (Her 1.153).

(44)   Not for much longer either will this ape who is now bugging us, Cligenes the midget, the most good-for-nothing bathkeeper of all those who, mixing the ash, have domain over soap adulterated with lime and Cimolian clay, spend time among us (Frogs 708).

FOCUS IN CONTINUOUS NOUN PHRASES

For there to be hyperbaton as analyzed so far, two conditions must be met: there must be narrow focus on the modifier of a noun phrase and there must be an available superordinate head. Given these conditions, hyperbaton can create a pragmatically determined node, or exploit a pre-existing node for pragmatic purposes, such that it c-commands structures ranging all the way from the X′ dominating X and Y2 up to the full clause. Since hyperbaton is optional, the question arises: can focus be syntactically encoded within the continuous noun phrase, that is without exploiting the option afforded by hyperbaton of displacement to the edge of the superordinate phrase?

In order to find out whether focus can be encoded by marked word order in continuous noun phrases, obviously we first need to establish what is the unmarked word order for continuous noun phrases. Unfortunately, the analysis of simple branching noun phrases consisting of noun plus adjective (in either order) is a complex and major undertaking well beyond the scope of this work (Bergson 1960; Brunel 1964; Duhoux 1973; Dik 1997). The following is just a sketch of our underlying assumptions.

To establish the neutral or unmarked word order for restrictive adjectives, we need to look at noun phrases in which there is no internal pragmatic differentiation, for instance contexts in which the whole noun phrase is in focus, or it is part of a broad scope focus extending over a number of constituents, or it is part or all of the tail material. In such broad scope contexts, the neutral position for restrictive adjectives is postnominal. This is particularly so for intersective adjectives; these are prototypically simple properties denoting an extensional class determined for the most part independently of the noun they modify; for instance, adjectives of colour (*red*), shape (*square*), sex (*female*), material (*wooden*), nationality (*Athenian*), and so on

(45)   ἵπποι ἄγριοι Her 4.52
       νεφέλη λευκή Xen *An* 1.8.8.
       στολὴν Μηδικὴν Xen *Cyr* 8.5.18
       λάρνακας κυπαρισσίνας Thuc 2.34.3.

First the nominal class is established and then a restriction is applied to it. Scalar adjectives are a separate category: they tend to be further from the head in English ((*)*square large tables*) and to be prenominal in both Greek and Latin, also when used restrictively. Such adjectives include those of size (*large*), quantity (*numerous*), manner (*fast*) and value judgement (*good, pretty*). Although these adjectives can be interpreted absolutely, they are often interpreted relative to a comparison set, which depends on the noun and the context (*big flea, big elephant*).

(45) Wild horses (Her 4.52). A white cloud (Xen *An* 1.88). Median robe (Xen *Cyr* 8.5.18). Cypress coffins (Thuc 2.34.2).

In traditional Greek and Latin grammar, adjectives are broadly classified into two classes, determining adjectives (mostly intersective) and qualifying adjectives (mostly scalar adjectives and quantifiers). There has been a tendency to underestimate the multivariate nature of the problem of adjective-noun order. Specifically, it is not very likely that the variability of order preferences can be reduced to the direct effect of a single parameter, whether it be semantic category, syntactic structure or pragmatic salience. Table 1.1 gives the percentages of adjective-noun (AN) and noun-adjective (NA) orders for the attributive occurrences (both definite and indefinite) of eight adjectives of the determining class (*det*) and ten of the qualifying class (*qual*) in Herodotus (Dik 1997). Although it is true that the NA percentage is higher than the AN percentage for both classes of adjective, it is also clear, as the odds ratio $\omega = 3.34$ shows, that the correlation of AN order and determining class is quite strong. The odds *det N : N det* (1 : 1.66) are three and a third times greater than the odds *qual N : N qual* (1 : 5.54). As the value $\chi^2 = 39.35$ shows, the correlation is highly significant: there is less than one chance in ten thousand that it could arise at random in a sample of this size. Consequently adjective class is an independent variable (assuming it is not redundantly correlated with some other variable). These data establish adjective class as an irreducibly independent factor determining AN/NA order.

Furthermore, the correlation established in Table 1.1 interacts with the linguistic dimension of dialect. Its direction is reversed in Attic relative to Ionic. Table 1.2 gives the corresponding percentages for Thucydides (Bergson 1960). In Thucydides, as the odds ratio $\omega = 0.495$ shows, the odds *det N : N det* are just half of the odds *qual N : N qual*. The reversal in direction of the correlation results from a pronounced increase of the *qual N : N qual* odds relative to Ionic, while the *det N : N det* odds remain unchanged (1 : 2.44 in Thucydides and 1 : 2.44 in Herodotus according to Bergson's percentages). This can be seen most clearly from the order rates for the single adjective πολύς as given in Table 1.3 (Bergson's figures). As the odds ratio $\omega = 1.915$ shows, the πολύς *N :*

TABLE 1.1
Correlation of adjective class
and order preference in Herodotus

	AN %	NA %	Total
Determining	37.62	62.38	210
Qualifying	15.29	84.71	425

$$\omega = 3.34$$
$$\chi^2 = 39.35$$
$$p = 0.0001$$

TABLE 1.2
Reversal of adjective class correlation
in Thucydides

	AN %	NA %	Total
Determining	29.00	71.00	—
Qualifying	51.00	49.00	—
	$\omega = 0.495$		

N πολὺς odds have doubled in Thucydides as compared to Herodotus. This reversal of correlation is intractable for a single parameter theory based directly on semantics or pragmatics, since neither of these should vary for the same adjective in the same genre. It follows that the AN/NA order rates depend in part on a properly syntactic factor which can vary with dialect.

Table 1.4 gives some idea of the variability of order tendencies across dialect, genre, time, definiteness and adjective type (data from Bergson, Brunel, and Palm [excluding Hippocrates *Epid*], except for the righthand column which is based on our own count). A comparison of columns 1 and 2 illustrates the strong effect of definiteness. Prenominal position is far more common for adjectives in definite noun phrases than in indefinite noun phrases. The effect is so strong that it is unlikely to be entirely a reflex of any independent differences associated with definiteness, such as a higher incidence of descriptive adjectives. If a postnominal articulated adjective is a null head modifier noun phrase, and a postnominal indefinite adjective is simply a modifying adjective phrase, then the more cumbersome syntactic structure of the postnominal definites would explain their relative infrequency, as well as formalizing Aristotle's intuition that they have ὄγκος (*Rhet* 3.6). The more articulated syntax of the definites could also carry with it a more articulated (less integrated) semantics of adjective restriction, which would further limit the use of the definite postnominal type.

Comparison of columns 1 and 4 shows the strong tendency of plural παντές to prenominal position. Since only indefinite noun phrases are considered, the

TABLE 1.3
Change in order rates of πολὺς
from Ionic to Attic

	AN %	NA %	Total
Thucydides	54.00	46.00	—
Herodotus	38.00	62.00	—
	$\omega = 1.915$		

TABLE 1.4
Variation of AN rate
over dialect, genre, time, definiteness, adjective type

Definite	AN − %	DAN + %.	DemDN + %	παντές N − %	πολύς N − %	τὸν ἐμὸν N + %
Hippocrates			81.47			
Herodotus	29.90	73.91	58.69	68.43	38.00	21.95
Thucydides			44.88		54.00	100.00
Xenophon-H	21.18		80.00		60.00	99.75
Xenophon-Ph	59.29		52.00		86.00	90.90
Plato (*Rep*)	69.79	92.11	73.77	92.86	80.00	
Lysias			87.50		88.00	59.57
Demosthenes	47.79	97.22	68.86	91.30	76.00	52.29
Isocrates	72.46		16.00-67.00			45.28

effect of definiteness is controlled. The preference for prenominal position is so strong, even in Herodotus, that it is probably not entirely a reflex of the pragmatic salience of the universal quantifier but at least in part the syntactic reflex of the semantic property of quantifier scope. The effects of scopal requirements may also be relevant in the following set of examples involving *other*

(46)   ἀποδεξάμενοι ἔργα μεγάλα Her 7.139
    ἄλλα τε μεγάλα ἔργα ἀπέδεξαντο Her 8.17 (v.l.)
    ἄλλα ἀποδεξάμενος μεγάλα ἔργα Her 1.59 (YXY).

The last two examples contain ἄλλα, which has to take scope over the whole modified phrase ('other great deeds') and not just over the noun ('other deeds, which were great'). The latter reading is found with postnominal μέγας in the following noun phrase

(47)   ἄλλος βωμὸς μέγας Her 1.183

('another altar, which was large'). The prenominal position of the adjective in μεγάλα ἔργα, both in the continuous (Her 8.17) and in the hyperbaton (Her 1.59) versions, apparently results in a more hierarchical structure perhaps facilitating the desired scopal relation.

Column 6 gives the percentages of the prenominal order τὸν ἐμὸν N in our samples of different cases in the singular and plural. (The two Xenophon samples are *Anabasis* and *Cyropaedia* for the historical genre and *Memorabilia*, *Symposium* and *Oeconomicus* for the philosophical genre.) Instances involving

(46) Having performed great exploits (Her 7.139). Performed other great deeds (Her 8.17). Having performed other great deeds (Her 1.59).

(47) Another, large altar (Her 1.183).

hyperbaton, coordinate head nouns, and other modifiers coordinated or stacked with τὸν ἐμὸν have been excluded. At first sight, τὸν ἐμὸν N in Herodotus and the Attic orators seems to resist the prenominal ordering effect observed with other definite noun phrases in column 2. This resistance however is not a simple and uniform property of τὸν ἐμὸν, but depends on the semantic relation of the adjective to its head noun. Postnominal position (N τὸν ἐμὸν) is very strongly associated with kin terms

(48)   θυγατρὶ τῇ ἐμῇ Her 1.118
        παῖδα τὸν ἐμὸν Her 1.214
        τὸν κηδεστὴν τὸν ἐμὸν Dem 50.24
        ὁ πάππος οὑμὸς Dem 57.20
        τῆς μητρυιᾶς τῆς ἐμῆς Lys 32.17.

This correlation is illustrated for Herodotus, Lysias and Demosthenes in Table 1.5, where the order of presentation is altered to NA–AN for ease in stating the odds and odds ratios. The values of the odds ratios show that the kin term effect is quite strong in all three authors; the *NA : AN* odds for τὸν ἐμὸν with kin terms range up to six and a third times those for non-kin terms.

The resistance of kin terms to AN order is not the whole story. There exists a significant gradient in the rate of AN order for τὸν ἐμὸν which reflects a finer grained scale of semantic relations between the head noun and the adjective. Kin terms, of course, are prototypically relational nouns, which are two-place predicates (Löbner 1985). Their meaning inherently implies a relation to another entity of the sort expressible by complementation: *my brother* is 'he who is brother to me.' Other nouns are, or can be, relational too

(49)   δέσποιναν τὴν ἐμὴν Her 1.8
        δεσπότεα τὸν ἐμὸν Her 1.11
        τῶν ἡλικιωτῶν τῶν ἐμῶν Isoc *Are* 66.

TABLE 1.5
Preference for NA order of τὸν ἐμὸν
with kin terms

	Herodotus		Lysias		Demosthenes	
	NA %	AN %	NA %	AN %	NA %	AN %
Kin term	93.21	7.69	68.75	31.25	57.33	42.67
Non-kin term	71.43	28.57	28.13	71.87	26.47	73.53
	ω = 4.80		ω = 6.33		ω = 3.73	

(48) My daughter (Her 1.118). My son (Her 1.214). My father-in-law (Dem 50.24). My grandfather (Dem 57.20). My stepmother (Lys 32.17).
(49) My mistress (Her 1.8). My master (Her 1.11). My contemporaries (Isoc *Are* 66).

With nonrelational nouns such as simple concrete nouns, which are one-place predicates, τὸν ἐμὸν expresses simple possession: *my pencil* is not 'that which is a pencil to me' (unless used functionally) but 'the pencil which I own'

(50)   ἐπὶ τῆς ἐμῆς νέως Lys 21.7, 21.8
       τῶν ἐμῶν χρημάτων Dem 34.9
       τὸ ἐμὸν χρυσίον Dem 34.18.

With abstract nouns τὸν ἐμὸν often expresses a grammatical relation, for instance transitive subject (*my destruction of the Persians*), complement (*my destruction by the Persians*), unergative subject (*my assertion*), unaccusative subject (*my downfall*). *My assertion* is neither 'that which is an assertion to me' (relational) nor 'the assertion which I own' (possessive) but 'that which I asserted'

(51)   τῇ ἐμῇ προφάσει Lys 6.19
       τῆς ἐμῆς ἱππικῆς Lys 24.10
       ἡ... ἐμὴ γνώμη περὶ ὧν βουλεύεσθ' Dem *Ex* 56.3.

If we posit a scale (1) kin term > (2) relational non-kin > (3) concrete > (4) abstract, then we find that the farther to the left on this scale a noun falls, the more likely it is to take postposed τὸν ἐμὸν, and conversely the farther to the right the noun falls, the more likely it is to take preposed τὸν ἐμὸν. The percentages of the preposed type τὸν ἐμὸν N in the combined samples of Lysias and Demosthenes are presented in Table 1.6. The correlation of preposing with scale position is exceptionless. The values of $\bar{\chi}^2$, c_1, and c_2, calculated according to Bartholomew's test for ordered proportions (Fleiss 1973), mean

TABLE 1.6
Gradient of preposed τὸν ἐμὸν

Scale position of head noun	Prenominal %	Total
(1)	40.66	91
(2)	53.33	15
(3)	66.67	12
(4)	78.12	32

$$\bar{\chi}^2 = 12.5671$$
$$c_1 = 0.6177$$
$$c_2 = 0.6356$$
$$p < 0.005$$

(50) On my ship (Lys 21.7). My money (Dem 34.9). My money (Dem 34.18).
(51) My accusation (Lys 6.19). My riding of horses (Lys 24.10). My opinion on what you are deliberating about (Dem *Ex* 56.3).

that the gradient is highly significant: the probability is less than five in a thousand that this ordered gradience could have arisen at random in the absence of a genuine relationship to the posited semantic scale. It is clear that the different arguments and modifiers of a noun are projected to different positions of the noun phrase in the syntax (Giorgi & Longobardi 1991), and these different positions are the main cause of the observed gradience with τὸν ἐμὸν. With relational nouns τὸν ἐμὸν tends to be complement-like and occupy a posthead position in the noun phrase. Possessors and particularly subject arguments are more specifier-like and tend to occupy a prehead position in the noun phrase.

If we consider the evidence of the various tables taken together, two major correlations are evident. Tables 1.2, 1.3 and column 5 of Table 1.4 show that when genre and chronology are kept comparable, the rate of AN order increases from the Ionic to the Attic dialect. Columns 1, 3 and 5 of Table 1.4 show that when dialect is held constant there is a tendency for AN order to increase from historical narrative to oratory to philosophical or technical prose. Note the much higher DemDN rate for the selected texts of the Hippocratic Corpus as compared to Herodotus (column 3). Note also the consistently higher rate of AN in Xenophon's philosophical works as compared to his historical works (columns 1, 3, 5 and 6). The complete explanation of these trends awaits a deeper analysis of the data, and all we can do here is to make a few preliminary theoretical observations.

First we will consider how these trends could be driven by variation in the direct effects of a single parameter. If all that is involved is syntax, then there is a simple syntactic trend away from postmodification and towards premodification for some or all adjectives. If all that is involved is semantics, then scalar and intersective adjectives are occurring at different rates in the different texts. While this is unlikely for different dialects in the same genre, it is a very plausible component of the genre distinction. Philosophical-technical genres may have more abstract nouns and be more concerned with evaluating and measuring their nouns, while historical genres may be more prone to deal with intersective modifiers of concrete nouns. If all that is involved is pragmatics, then the pragmatic categories are occurring at different rates in the different texts. Again this is unlikely for the dialects, but a plausible component of the genre difference. Detached historical narrative has less need of strongly marked focus than empathetic oratory.

It is fairly clear that a single parameter account is not adequate. A purely syntactic explanation leaves no room at all for differential frequency of various categories of adjective and noun in different genres. A purely semantic account is by definition inapplicable to trends involving specific adjectives, as in columns 4 and 5 of Table 1.4. A purely pragmatic account might make unwelcome predictions for stylistic differences among authors in the same genre, and is in principle unsuitable for dialectal and diachronic trends. Furthermore, both the semantic and the pragmatic factors can also be interpreted as driving the trends by an indirect effect. For instance the relative frequency of scalar adjectives in two texts might be the same, but one text might have a stronger syntactic propensity to treat scalars as premodifiers. Or the relative frequency of focus in two texts might be the same, but one text might have a stronger syntactic propensity to front focused adjectives. Our tentative conclusion is that, while texts are no doubt liable to differ along any or all of the parameters discussed, there is an overall trend towards a more hierarchically structured noun phrase, in keeping with the long term diachronic trends of Greek syntax described in chapter 4.

Another important distinction in any analysis of modification is that between descriptively and restrictively used modifiers. As their name implies, restrictively used modifiers restrict reference, but descriptively used modifiers do not; they simply express an additional property of an independently established referent. *Red shirt* and *tall building* are usually restrictive, while *green grass* and *frightful monster* are usually descriptive. In a sentence like

> She married Jack's younger brother,

if Jack has one brother the adjective is used descriptively ('Jack's brother, who is younger than he is'), but if he has two brothers it is used restrictively ('the younger of Jack's two brothers'). Adjectives of speaker attitude and evaluation (*damned guerillas*) are normally used descriptively. In languages that allow both prenominal and postnominal adjectives, French, Italian and Modern Greek for instance (Siegel 1976; Longobardi 1994; Stavrou 1996), there is a clear tendency for descriptive adjectives to be prenominal. For instance in Italian

> un' iniziativa importante/un' importante iniziativa
> 'an important initiative'

the postnominal type normally has a restrictive reading and the prenominal type a descriptive reading (unless it is contrastively focused). This tendency is subject to various conditioning factors; a descriptive reading is more likely in definite than in indefinite noun phrases. In the following French example, the same adjective is first restrictive when the referent is introduced into the discourse and subsequently descriptive when the referent is a topic (Waugh 1976)

> J'ai vu un éléphant énorme... Cet énorme éléphant buvait de l'eau
> 'I saw an enormous elephant... this enormous elephant was drinking some water.'

In Greek, descriptive adjectives tend to prenominal position

(52)   τὴν παλαιὰν παροιμίαν Pl *Rep* 329a
        οἱ μὲν κατάπτυστοι Θετταλοὶ Dem 18.43
        ἡ μιαρὰ καὶ ἀναιδὴς αὕτη κεφαλὴ Dem 21.117.

(52) The old proverb (Pl *Rep* 329a). The damned Thessalians (Dem 18.43). This disgraceful and shameless person (Dem 21.117).

When descriptive adjectives cooccur with a demonstrative, they are prenominal not only when they are emphatic and precede the demonstrative

(53) τὰς πολυτελεῖς ταυτασ(ὶ) πομπάς Pl *Alc* 2.149c, 150a
      τὰ ἐλεινὰ ταῦτα δράματα Pl *Apol* 35b
      οἱ αὐθαίρετοι οὗτοι στρατηγοὶ Xen *An* 5.7.29,

but also in the neutral unemphatic word order where they follow the demonstrative

(54) ταῦτα τὰ καλὰ ὀνόματα Pl *Crat* 411a
      τοῦτο τὸ καλὸν ἀνάθημα Pl *Gorg* 472b.

In languages like French and Italian, intensionality is also a factor governing adjective position (Bolinger 1967; Siegel 1976; Higginbotham 1985). Consider modified noun phrases like

a beautiful dancer
an eloquent pianist.

The adjectives can be interpreted intensionally ('a dancer who dances beautifully,' 'a pianist who plays eloquently') or extensionally ('someone who is a dancer and is beautiful in her appearance,' 'someone who is a pianist and is eloquent in his speech'). Intensional uses in French and Italian tend to be in prenominal position and extensional ones in postnominal position

un gros buveur 'a heavy drinker'
un buveur gros 'a heavily-built drinker.'

More examples are cited in chapter 4. This factor is probably also relevant in Greek (Bergson 1960:56), although it is difficult to separate focus or descriptive use from intensionality in the Greek examples collected by Bergson: γυναικεῖος 'woman-like,' δούλειος 'servile,' ψυχρός 'useless,' Κορινθία κόρη 'hetaera,' Καδμεία νίκη 'Pyrrhic victory.' The intensional reading is not available in French and Italian when the adjective is used predicatively

Le buveur est gros 'The drinker is heavily-built.'

So the postnominal interpretation agrees with the predicative interpretation rather than with the prenominal interpretation. This again points to the postnominal type being less integrated. Further evidence comes from agreement in French and Spanish (Radford 1993)

de vieilles (fem. pl.) gens 'some old people'
des gens plus vieux (masc. pl.) que moi 'some people older than me'

(53) These expensive processions (Pl *Alc* 2.149c). These pitiable dramas (Pl *Apol* 35b). Those selfchosen generals (Xen *An* 5.7.29).
(54) These noble words (Pl *Crat* 411a). That wellknown beautiful offering (Pl *Gorg* 472b).

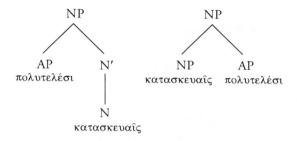

Figure 1.5
Continuous pre- and postmodifiers
πολυτελέσι κατασκευαῖς Thuc 2.65.2
κατασκευαῖς πολυτελέσι Thuc 1.10.2

> simpaticas (fem. pl.) mujeres y hombres/hombres y mujeres simpaticos (masc. pl.) 'nice [men and women]'

and from liaison in colloquial French, which applies between prenominal adjectives and nouns but not between nouns and postnominal adjectives. Various ways have been suggested for formalizing the distinction. For instance, some theories treat English postnominal adjective phrases

> an aunt fond of her nephews

as reduced relative clauses or small clauses. However, the idea that prenominal adjectives too are derived from reduced relative clauses (Chomsky 1957; Kayne 1994) cannot be extended to intensional adjectives of the type *former, alleged*. The high degree of integration between prenominal adjective and noun, and the constraint (in English, but not modern Greek) against complements between the adjective and the noun (*a fond of her nephews aunt*) have led to the suggestion that the adjective is a head or cohead of the noun phrase, or head-to-head adjoined to the noun (Sadler & Arnold 1994). More conservatively, the prenominal adjective is a sister of N or of N′, while the postnominal adjective is adjoined to NP, as illustrated in Figure 1.5. This is supported by the evidence of determiner spreading (p. 238): with definites, prenominal modifiers in Greek are a function from N to N, while postnominal modifiers are a function from DP to DP (as in Figure 6.6).

Focused restrictive adjectives

There is a further class of prenominal adjectives that we have only briefly alluded to so far. When a restrictive adjective carries narrow focus, the class–restrictor order is often not maintained; rather, the adjective appears to the left of the noun. This can easily be observed by comparing pragmatically neutral cases of restrictive adjectives with cases having unequivocal contrastive focus

(55)   ἵππους λευκούς Her 7.113
 αἱ μὲν οὖν πυρραὶ ἔχουσαι ἔστωσαν λευκὴν τρίχα Xen *Cyn* 4.8

 τις ἀνὴρ Ῥόδιος Xen *An* 3.5.8
 Ἕλλην τις ἀνήρ, καὶ ἄλλος δέ τις Μῆδος Xen *Cyr* 6.3.11
 Μακεδὼν ἀνὴρ Ἀθηναίους καταπολεμῶν Dem 4.10, cp. 11.17

 ἄνδρα τυφλὸν Her 2.137
 τυφλοῖς ὀφθαλμοῖς ὄψιν ἐντιθέντες Pl *Rep* 518c

 ἐνδεδύκασι δὲ κιθῶνας λινέους Her 2.81
 μετέβαλον ὧν ἐς τὸν λίνεον κιθῶνα Her 5.87.

In the second (and third) lines in each set of examples, the adjective is implicitly or explicitly contrastively focused and placed to the left of the noun. In a serial order account, the adjective and the noun would simply exchange places, but in a structural account the noun stays put and the adjective moves across the noun to a left peripheral focus position, as diagrammed in Figure 1.6. According to this account, the focus position is not the same position as that occupied by ordinary unfocused prenominal adjectives but external to it. This makes sense: premodifiers are more integrated than postmodifiers, but everything we know about focus points to it being less rather than more integrated than its unfocused counterpart. Examples with the definite article, like τὸν λίνεον κιθῶνα just cited, show the limitations of a simple mechanical conception of movement, since, in purely synchronic terms, they require some form of adjustment to take care of the determiner: τὸν κιθῶνα τὸν λίνεον → *τὸν

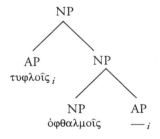

Figure 1.6
Focused adjective in continuous NP
τυφλοῖς ὀφθαλμοῖς

(55) White horses (Her 7.113). The tawny hounds should have some white hair (Xen *Cyn* 4.8). A man from Rhodes (Xen *An* 3.5.8). A Greek man and someone else from Media (Xen *Cyr* 6.3.11). A Macedonian defeating Athenians in war (Dem 4.10). A blind man (Her 2.137). Installing sight in blind eyes (Pl *Rep* 518c). They wear linen tunics (Her 2.81). They changed it to the linen tunic (Her 5.87).

λίνεον τὸν κιθῶνα. If the determiner is not repeated in the base structure, the adjective is not under the scope of the initial determiner and is interpreted as predicative. The problem is a technical one, and can be solved in various ways, which range from positing insignificant housekeeping rules to abstaining entirely from use of movement or of the movement metaphor in order to escape from this type of "movement paradox." A diachronic perspective is very enlightening. The article probably originally belonged to the adjective, and it is quite possible that what was originally fronted both in continuous nominals and in hyperbaton was a paratactic null head modifier. Inscriptional punctuation

(56)   τοις Ναυπακτιοις : νομιοις χρεσται *Locr* 19

suggests that the noun could form a constituent with a following verb to the exclusion of the fronted adjective, even when adjective and noun were adjacent. These ideas are explored in detail in chapters 4 and 6.

Y₁ hyperbaton

If we combine our analysis of focused restrictive adjectives in continuous noun phrases with our earlier crosscategorial analysis of Y₁ hyperbaton (which applies inter alia to focused restrictive adjectives), it becomes obvious that we are not dealing with two separate phenomena but with a single syntactic process. The noun phrase focus position is simply the lowest of a series of hierarchically ordered specifier-type positions in which the focused modifier can land. Consider the following examples

(57)   μάρτυρας ψευδεῖς παρεχόμενον Dem 29.5 (N A X)
        ψευδεῖς μαρτυρίας παρασχόμενος Dem 47.17, cp. 47.48 (A N X)
        ψευδεῖς ἀναγνόντα μαρτυρίας Dem 45.48 (A X N).

In the first example, the restrictive adjective ψευδεῖς is in its unmarked postnominal position. In the second example, it is in the noun phrase focus position (assuming it is focused and not merely prenominal). In the third, it is in the verb phrase focus position with Y₁ in hyperbaton. In a movement theory, ψευδεῖς starts out as Y₂ in a postverbal YP, then climbs cyclically through Y₁ in a postverbal YP to preverbal Y₁ in hyperbaton (stranding the noun in postverbal position). This is represented in Figure 1.7. (In the first two examples, the whole noun phrase is fronted to preverbal position.) If this movement theory is interpreted literally, in addition to the problem with the article already alluded to, there is a complication with prepositional examples like

(58)   ἐν τοῖς φονικοῖς γέγραπται νόμοις Dem 9.44

(56) To be subject to the Naupactian laws (*Locr* 19).
(57) Producing false witnesses (Dem 29.5). Having produced false evidence (Dem 47.17). Having read false depositions (Dem 45.48).
(58) It is written in the homicide laws (Dem 9.44).

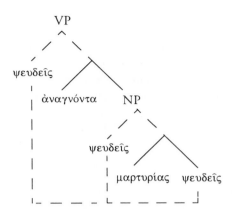

Figure 1.7
Narrow focus with restrictive adjective
ἀναγνόντα ψευδεῖς [μαρτυρίας —], ψευδεῖς [ἀναγνόντα μαρτυρίας —]

where, on the face of it, the preposition has to be picked up en route. The choice between the various syntactically available noun phrase structures is not random but depends on pragmatic factors that we will analyze in chapter 2, and on associated syntactic properties to be discussed in chapter 6.

Although YP and XP phrase structures are clearly recognizable in Greek, hyperbaton (perhaps more than any other aspect of "free word order") gives the beginning student of Greek the impression that the syntactic phrase in Greek is optional, that the disiecta membra of phrases can be arranged in a flat linear order which is entirely pragmatically determined. Our analysis has come to just the opposite conclusion. Hyperbaton is quintessentially structural. Focus Y_1 consistently seeks out a structurally identical position irrespective of the category or complexity of the projection. Some languages have a single clausal focus position, often adjacent to the verb, in which (continuous) focused noun phrases are regularly placed. What is so interesting about hyperbaton is that it extends this feature crosscategorially down to the lowest phrasal projection: not only clauses, but verb phrases, adjective phrases, some prepositional phrases, complex noun phrases and simple noun phrases too make structurally parallel positions available for focused modifiers.

2 The Meaning of Y₁ Hyperbaton in Prose

We start with a test designed to corroborate the idea that Y₁ hyperbaton encodes focus in prose. The next sections are devoted to an analysis of the contribution of Y₁ hyperbaton to the meaning of a clause. In the final section we discuss the relationship of form to function, asking how fragmenting noun phrases into discontinuous subconstituents could turn out to be a natural way to encode modifier focus.

Modifier class test

In chapter 1 we proceeded on the assumption that Y₁ hyperbaton is a focus construction in prose. In some examples this is selfevident from the context; on the basis of these the focus interpretation was generalized to pragmatically less transparent instances. A more objective source of evidence for this central assumption is afforded by the distribution of different types of modifiers in hyperbaton relative to their distribution in continuous noun phrases. Quantifiers (words such as *all, some, any, each,* numerals)

(1) πολλὰς εἶχε ἐλπίδας Her 5.36
     πάντας πεῖσαι τοὺς παριόντας Lys 7.18

and negative quantifiers

(2) οὐδεμίαν ὑμᾶς ποθεῖν ἀκοῦσαι πρόφασιν Lys 14.1
     οὐδεμίαν ἐκείνου περὶ τούτων ποιησαμένου διαθήκην Isae 8.40

are the most common category of modifier in hyperbaton, followed by demonstratives and other socalled pronominal adjectives, and adjectives of size and dimension

(3) τοὺς ταύτῃ χρωμένους τῇ ἐργασίᾳ Aesch 1.119

(1) He had considerable hope (Her 5.36). To persuade all those passing by (Lys 7.18).
(2) That you desire to hear no excuse (Lys 14.1). Although he made no will concerning these things (Isae 8.40).
(3) Those that follow this profession (Aesch 1.2).

(4) ἐξ ἄλλης ἐλθόντα κώμης Her 1.196

      μεγάλα τούτων οἶμαι σημεῖα δείξειν Aesch 3.177

and then restrictive adjectives, comparatives and superlatives. Nonrestrictively used modifiers and expressions of speaker evaluation which do not limit the reference of the noun, like descriptive instances of καλός, πονηρός, φαῦλος, χρηστός, are rare or nonoccurring. In general, it seems that the more a modifier is intrinsically restrictive, that is the more it fixes the identity or specifies the range of a class of referents by pointing to a specific individual or individuals or a complete subset of the set denoted by the noun, the more that modifier is associated with Y1 hyperbaton. Conversely, the more a modifier provides a secondary and nonrestrictive comment about its head noun, the less likely it is to appear in Y1 hyperbaton in prose. However, the reality of the preference for the class of quantifiers (including ordinals), demonstratives and pronominals (QDP) as compared with other adjectives, both restrictive and descriptive, was not adequately demonstrated in earlier work (de Vries 1938), for the simple reason that the QDP class is comparatively common in continuous phrases as well as in hyperbaton.

The genuineness and strength of the preference for the QDP class in Y1 hyperbaton is directly established by the following test. A sample was taken of over one hundred continuous noun phrases with adjectival modifiers in (D)AN order only from Aeschines and Andocides, for instance

(5) τοῖς δημοσίοις ἀγῶσιν Aesch 1.2

      τὴν ἄνισον πολιτείαν Aesch 1.5.

The sample was analyzed to determine the percentage of modifiers that belonged to the QDP class. Then the Y1 hyperbata in the same speeches were similarly analyzed. There results are presented in Table 2.1. Whereas nearly

TABLE 2.1
Semantic class of modifier

	QDP %	Other %	N
Y1 Hyperbaton	88.99	11.01	109
Continuous (D)AN	67.15	32.85	137

Odds ratio = 3.9538

$\chi^2 = 16.2613$, d.f. = 1

$p \ll 0.001$

(4) Coming from another village (Her 1.196). I think that I will present substantial proof of these things (Aesch 3.177).

(5) Public law suits (Aesch 1.2). Discriminating government (Aesch 1.5).

90% of the modifiers in Yı hyperbaton were quantifiers, demonstratives or pronominals, only slightly more than two-thirds of the modifiers in continuous noun phrases belonged to this class. So, as the odds ratio shows, the odds for the QDP class are nearly four times as great in Yı hyperbaton as in continuous structures. The chi-square shows that the difference is statistically significant, with a probability considerably less than one in one thousand of having arisen by chance. In a phonetic study of fundamental frequency in English, it was found that quantifiers and adjectives are more likely to receive a focus accent in English than ordinary nouns and verbs; interrogative pronouns were also prosodically prominent (O'Shaughnessy & Allen 1983). This correlates with the general structure of Yı hyperbaton (adjective in focus position). The test results do not support the weaker hypothesis that Yı hyperbaton simply encodes the semantic property of restrictiveness: if that were all there was to it, one would expect ordinary restrictive adjectives and QDP to occur at the same relative frequency as they do in continuous noun phrases. There must be some additional property, presumably focus (rather than simply phrase structural distinctions), that accounts for the higher relative frequency of QDP in Yı hyperbaton as compared with regular YP noun phrases.

Focus is not a unitary category, but comprises a family of related but different meanings. We distinguish focus in general from old or predictable information; we refer to the latter as tail information. Within the category of focus, we distinguish weak focus, which is purely informational, from strong focus. Within the category of strong focus, we sometimes distinguish simple strong focus, which is implicitly exclusive, from contrastive focus. These distinctions will be clarified and illustrated as the discussion proceeds.

It is not possible to prove that strong focus is involved in each and every Yı hyperbaton in prose; some degree of subjective contextual judgement is involved. It is fair to say that focus is possible in all or almost all instances. A more cautious account might define the Yı position in Yı hyperbaton as open not only to focus but also to certain logical operators, particularly quantifiers, even when they are used without strong focus. The association of Yı hyperbaton with focus is typologically supported: it is noted in descriptions of some Algonquian languages such as Fox and some Australian languages such as Kalkatungu. Dutch has a Left Branch Condition just like English, but in Dutch child language hyperbaton sometimes occurs alongside continuous structures (Hoekstra & Jordens 1994; van Kampen 1997), both with interrogatives and with demonstratives

> Welke wil jij liedje zingen?
> 'Which want you song to sing?'

> Die heb ik niet sok aan
> 'That have I not sock on'

> Ik wil die niet boek lezen!
> 'I want that not book to read.'

The Y1 elements in these examples gave the impression of being contrastively stressed, again pointing to a focus-based analysis of this type of hyperbaton.

FOCUS

Weak focus

Let us start with interrogative focus, just as we did in chapter 1. Using the popular metaphor of file change semantics, we can say that a *wh*-question word requests information to fill a blank (or empty field) in a file in the speaker's knowledge store. The part of the sentence not in interrogative focus, typically the presupposition, represents the material already in the file, or material that is "accommodated" to the pre-existing file. A question like

> Quis subegit Gallias?
> 'For *x* = who, *x* conquered Gaul?'

presupposes that there is someone such that he conquered Gaul and asks who it was. The existential presupposition can qualified or suspended

> Who, if anyone, conquered Gaul?

If the actual world is one in which someone conquered Gaul, tell me who it was; if not, don't bother. There may be other foci in addition to the *wh*-word

> Who conquered TRANSALPINE Gaul?

In fact there are some examples of ordinary Y1 hyperbaton in *wh*-questions.

Informational focus is the type of focus used in answer to interrogative focus, and in general for the straightforward communication of new information

> CAESAR conquered Gaul.

This type of focus simply fills the blank field in the interlocutor's knowledge file and updates the information state: Caesar belongs to the set of those who on the occasion in question conquered Gaul, and possible circumstances in which he does not belong to that set do not correspond to the real world and should be eliminated from the body of knowledge shared by the interlocutors. Counterassertive focus, on the other hand, requires deleting existing erroneous information and substituting new correct information in the file field.

Information crucially involves choosing from alternative possibilities. Questions define a range of alternative candidate answers, and assertions (answers to explicit or implicit questions) choose from that same range of alternatives. The available alternatives can be thought of as part of the presuppositional knowledge of the interlocutors. Focus structure is particularly important in text, where questions are implicit: it is a way of encoding which of the various possible implicit questions in the context the speaker is addressing (Roberts 1996; Calcagno 1996). Sometimes the presupposition is not directly and explicitly available in the previous discourse, but has to be reconstructed from the context

    A. Some Greek authors are very difficult

    B. I use the LOEB for authors like Pindar.

B's contribution to the conversation takes the form of an answer to an implicit question about which editions he uses for difficult authors.

One of the principles of cooperative communication is the maxim of quantity, according to which speakers make their contributions to the conversation as informative as, but not more informative than, is required by the context of the exchange. Typically, the questioner expects a complete answer and the interlocutor provides one. In answer to the question

    Who passed the Latin test?

if the class consists of four students, the answer

    JACK did

will probably be interpreted as not only true but also exhaustive, unless the interlocutor has reason to believe that the answer is based on incomplete information. The implicature of exhaustiveness can be cancelled, as in

    JACK did, for one

which is an explicitly partial answer, a subset of those who passed. But if the class has forty students, there would be less expectation of an exhaustive answer; the set of passing students would include Jack rather than being equal to Jack. Picking a salient or representative member from a set is obviously not the same thing as listing all members of the set. In fact, the interrogative focus in the original question is correspondingly more likely to be interpreted as nonexhaustive ('tell me some' rather than 'tell me all') if the class is large. Interestingly for interrogative hyperbaton

    Which ones passed the test?

is a more strongly exhaustive question than 'Who passed the test?', perhaps because it is less open ended and involves a set of discrete individuals and consequently a limited list of alternatives (Comorovski 1996; Szabolcsi & Zwarts 1993). German can add *alles* to a question to force an exhaustive reading. In English, intonation can be used to encode the exhaustive reading for both question and answer.

When the focus has an exhaustive meaning, the assertion holds for the set listed and is interpreted as negated for the complement of that set. For instance, in the above example

    JACK passed the Latin test

conveys that the remaining three students failed the Latin test, if the focus is interpreted as exhaustive: the sentence then means that Jack passed the Latin test and no other student passed the Latin test. In terms of updating the state of information in the discourse, the exhaustive interpretation involves not only adding Jack to the set of those who passed the test but also excluding all other students who took the exam from the set of those who passed. The nonexhaustive interpretation tells us for Jack whether he can truthfully be substituted for x in the file entry 'x passed the test.' The exhaustive interpretation tells us this for every student.

Strong focus

The narrow focus on *Jack* separates the new information from the presupposed or accommodated information (namely that someone passed the Latin test). As we saw in the preceding section, weak narrow focus makes no claim that the new information is complete, exhaustive and exclusive: it leaves open the possibility that the assertion is a partial answer to the (explicit or implicit) question. Strong narrow focus does make the claim to exclusivity. Strong focus differs from weak focus in not being purely informational; it has the additional property of much more directly evoking a set of alternatives to the focused item and excluding those alternatives from the scope of the assertion. Consequently, a sentence with a strong focus implicates its dual (combined internal and external negation). The implicature of

> JACK passed the Latin test

with strong focus on *Jack* is [[not Jack] not passed the Latin test], i.e. the complement to Jack relative to the students who took the test failed the test. This applies not only to situations in which naming a participant intrinsically suggests the exclusion of alternatives

> PAUL ate the last cherry

but also to situations compatible with a potentially larger focus set

> PAUL ate some cherries.

Strictly speaking, we need to distinguish two different sets: the overall set of alternates including the focus, and the complement of focus within that set (the alternatives to the focus). We use the term *alternates* to refer to the former and the term *alternatives* to refer to the latter. It is important to understand that it is not the existence of a set of alternates that is specific to strong focus. Suppose that the extensional denotation of *who?* is the set of persons (Hamblin 1973), more precisely the set of contextually relevant persons including any furry or feathered friends promoted to personhood. Then the denotation of *who?* in 'Who ate the last cherry?' is just the contextually relevant set of alternate persons. Any new information can be said to be chosen from a set of alternates, and any assertion made that contributes to the information store is chosen relative to a set of possible alternate assertions. What is specific to strong focus is that the set of alternatives is evoked and negated. Weak focus presupposes a set of alternatives, strong focus not only presupposes but also evokes and negates a set of alternatives. Counterassertion is the strongest form of strong focus; it arises when the speaker suspects that the interlocutor may have mistaken information, or wishes to be absolutely sure that he does not, or knows that he does.

In English strong focus, and particularly counterassertive strong focus, tends to be encoded by greater prosodic prominence than weak focus. Strong focus seems to stand between weak focus and the cleft in the strength of its connotation of exhaustiveness

> BRUTUS stabbed Caesar. CASSIUS did too (weak focus)
> (*)BRUTUS stabbed Caesar. CASSIUS did too (strong focus)
> *It was BRUTUS that stabbed Caesar. It was CASSIUS that did so too.

Perhaps exhaustiveness is asserted in strong focus sentences and presupposed in clefts; according to another view (van Leusen & Kálmán 1993) it is presupposed in strong focus too. The same hierarchy seems to hold for existential presupposition in negative sentences, which is more difficult to abandon in clefts than in strong focus sentences

> BRUTUS didn't stab Mark Anthony. In fact noone did
> It wasn't BRUTUS that stabbed Mark Anthony. In fact noone did.

Many of the problems with the above understanding of strong focus relate not so much to the claim that it negates the set of alternatives as to the definition of that set. The set of alternatives which are implicitly negated by the strong focus in

> Prof. Jones works on HOMER

is not necessarily accessible. One is not necessarily expected to be able to answer the question 'Who does Prof. Jones not work on?' for the focus to be computed. One can distinguish 'x, maybe also y' (weak focus), 'x, not not x' (open ended strong focus), 'x, not y' (closed set strong focus). Even if it were theoretically possible to list the negated set, it might be vague in the discourse: for instance, all other authors, or all other Classical authors, or all other Greek authors. On the other hand, the set of alternates may also have been explicitly established in the previous context. In a conversation about Greek authors, Plato would be included in the negated set of alternatives, but in a conversation about Greek poets he would not. Crucially, the set of alternatives has to be contextually relevant and salient. Strong focus on HOMER is not intended to exclude the fact that Prof. Jones also works on Dorothy Sayers or on his garden. In episodic sentences, the set of alternates is bound by the situation

> Prof. Jones gave the lecture on HOMER

negates the set of lectures on different topics relevant for the particular occasion described, not for some other conference on an entirely different subject five years earlier.

Contrastive focus

These problems largely disappear with explicitly contrastive focus, in the narrow sense that the alternative set is explicitly listed

> JACK passed the Latin test, but PEGGY and ARTHUR did not.

Here Jack was not necessarily the only student to pass the test, but he was the only student to do so out of the set of three students under consideration. As we understand it, there are two types of strong focus: simple strong focus and contrastive focus. In sentences with contrastive topics, something different is often asserted about each topic, resulting in the familiar symmetrical argument pairing sentences like

> BILL likes CATS, but HIS WIFE prefers DOGS.

This is parallel to simple strong focus in that what is asserted for the focus is negated for the complement set of alternatives, as made explicit in the second clause. Single contrastive focus merely excludes the contrasted alternatives from the scope of the assertion in each clause

> BILL likes cats, and HIS WIFE does too.

A suspended contrast

> BILL likes cats

implies that his wife does not like cats or at least that absolutely no claim is being made about her preferences. A suspended contrast is intonationally quite different from a string identical sentence with simple strong focus; the latter would mean that Bill exhausted the discourse relevant set of cat-lovers. Entities in contrastive focus need not be completely mutually exclusive, in that they be members of the same powerset

> Sometimes he writes about HOMER, sometimes about HOMER and
> APOLLONIUS (sometimes H & not A, sometimes H & A).

Adjectives

In our overview of the basics of focus, to keep the examples simple we consistently used nouns as the carriers of focus. But for Y₁ hyperbaton, we need to consider narrow focus on adjectives. This raises some additional questions involving the interaction of focus with modifiers. Modifiers often supply more specific information than their modifiees. In Haruai (Comrie 1993) this property seems to be grammaticalized in a rule that assigns stress in the minor phrase consistently to the adjective rather than to the noun, irrespective of word order. In English as already noted, modifiers have a greater tendency than nouns to attract focus (O'Shaughnessy & Allen 1983). There is an evident affinity between the property that focus has of excluding the set of alternatives and the property that restrictive adjectives have of specifying a subset.

Usually, there is little point in asserting something of a subset, if it is also true of the entire set

> Black cats bring bad luck
> (*)Black cats have tails.

The difference is that with strong narrow focus on the modifier, *cats* becomes presuppositional and there is a much stronger implicature that other types of cats do not bring bad luck and do not have tails, respectively

> BLACK cats bring bad luck
> (*)BLACK cats have tails.

As we saw with nouns, this is not necessarily the case when the focus is contrastive rather than simple strong focus.

In the clearest instances, those involving highly intersective adjectives, the restriction can in principle be analyzed in extensional terms (which is why such adjectives are sometimes called extensional adjectives). To interpret *red shirt*, we intersect the set that is the extension of the adjective (things that are red) with the set that is the extension of the noun (things that are shirts), giving the set of things that are both red and shirts, that is *red shirts*. Red shirts are a subset of all shirts. The set of shirts has been restricted to only those that are red. Restrictive modification is a function that takes a set as its input (*shirts*) and produces a subset as its output (*red shirts*). When the adjective has strong narrow scope focus (*RED shirts*), the effect of the focus is to evoke and exclude the complement, that is those shirts that are left over from the contextually relevant set of shirts when the red ones are removed. The set of alternatives is also a subset of all shirts, whereas for strong narrow focus on unmodified nouns, the set of alternatives is just a set of other entities. The selection can be from alternates actually available in the real world

> The LONG book is the better one,

or from alternates potentially available in other possible worlds

> Prof. Jones has written a LONG book.

In the first example, there are two books physically available, a long one and a short one. In the second example, Prof. Jones wrote a long book although he could have written a short one. Both contrast with emphatic *lo-o-ong*, which means 'very long.'

It is at this point that we encounter a difference between adjectives and nouns in the way the set of alternates is computed. To keep things simple in the following example, let us assume that just as all students are either male or female, so they are binarily classified as either smart or dumb. Take a sentence with strong focus on the adjective, like

> The SMART students passed.

The implicature is that the dumb students failed: the relationship between the set of students that are dumb and the set of students that failed is brought under active consideration in the discourse. Without the strong narrow focus, any such implicature would depend on assumptions about how informative the speaker was trying to be or able to be, and there would be no presupposition that a set of students sharing some property passed the test. As before, the implicature represents the dual (internal plus external negation) of the original assertion: the complement of the set of smart persons relative to the domain of students did not pass: [[NOT smart] NOT pass]. Note that the internal negation [NOT smart] is lexicalized as *dumb*; similarly, but with a prefix, *intelligent – unintelligent*. Now assume that in the class in question the students were a doctor, two lawyers, an electrical engineer and an expert in Celtiberic epigraphy. If we say

>   The LAWYERS passed,

the implicature again is that the complement to the set of lawyers did not pass, but there is no lexicalization for the set {doctor, electrical engineer, Celtiberic epigrapher}: this set is a nonce creation of the situation, not an established and recurring distribution in our everyday experience.

In other words, the relative contribution of the pragmatic context seems to be greater with nouns than with adjectives. The complement of *false* entities is regularly and consistently *true* entities, irrespective of the discourse context, whereas the set of alternatives for *dog* is less consistently *cat*, and the set of alternatives for *flower* varies considerably according to the context. One could say that for adjectives the set of alternatives was more lexically predictable. This observation relates to a posited difference in the way nouns and adjectives are organized in the lexicon, or, to put it in psycholinguistic terms, in semantic memory (Gross et al. 1989). Nouns often evidence a hierarchical (hyponymous) relationship, for instance *animal – bird – duck – mallard*. Sometimes they are associated pairwise, as in *pencil and paper, bow and arrow*. For adjectives, the basic relationship seems to be antonymy, the contrast between opposite poles of a gradable property (Bierwisch 1967). (We understand antonymy broadly to include complementarity.) Interest in this topic goes back to Greek philosophy, for instance the Pythagorean συστοιχία and Aristotle's ἀντικείμενα (Raible 1981). Many of the antonymous pairs of adjectives with the highest text frequency involve positive and negative values along some form of measurable scale: *tall – short, wide – narrow, deep – shallow, old – new, fast – slow, heavy – light, hot – cold, loud – soft, light – dark*. Others are less overtly physically quantifiable: *rough – smooth, drunk – sober, clean – dirty*. Derivational negation is most common with evaluative (not purely dimensional) adjectives (Bierwisch 1989): *legal – illegal, honest – dishonest, plausible – implausible*. The unmarked member of an antonymous pair, which is the default choice for degree questions, is normally the perceptually salient end of the scale (Givon 1995)

How tall is he?
How wide is it?
How loud was it?
How fast does it go?

The antonymous relationship involves a specific pair of lexical items, not just any two contradictory or contrary properties: *alive – dead*, and *old – new* are antonymous pairs, while *alive – lifeless* and *old – recent* are not. The relationship is not always biunique: *bad – good, evil – good; happy – sad, happy – unhappy*. Bipolarity is the most usual, but tripolarity or multipolarity are also possible. For the man in the street, *liquid – solid* is a binary contrast, for the physicist there is a ternary contrast: *liquid – gaseous – solid*. The colours are the best established instance of a multiple contrast of equipollent items: *red – yellow – green – blue*. So while the principles governing the lexical organization of nouns either exclude formation of a set of alternates

> *It's not a duck, it's a mallard

or are more or less context dependent in this regard

> It's not a cat, it's a dog
> It's not a pencil, it's paper (pragmatically unlikely),

the principles governing the lexical organization of adjectives determine the set of alternates to a significant degree. Consequently, it is often easier to interpret strong narrow scope focus on an adjective (as in Yı hyperbaton in Greek) than on a noun when the sentence is presented out of context

> Jack ate a BIG apple (not a small one)
> Jack ate a big APPLE (not some other conceivable edible entity).

That is not to say that context does not also contribute to the set of alternates for adjectives. The normal alternative for red wine is white wine, but in a winery that does not make white it has to be rosé. A sufficiently rich context can create a nonce set of alternatives from incompatible adjectives that is just as random as one involving nouns (van Leusen & Kálmán 1993), for instance

> not the red apple, the ripe one
> not the Amerindian lexicographer, the blonde one.

The excluded alternative can also depend on the noun (just as adjective interpretation itself often does in one way or another)

> It's just LUKEWARM coffee that puts me in a bad mood
> It's just LUKEWARM champagne that puts me in a bad mood.

In addition to polar opposites, gradable properties commonly have various intermediate stages or closely related properties that seem to cluster with the polar opposites (Gross et al. 1989): *wet* is asssociated with *damp, moist, soggy, waterlogged* for instance. Focus on *wet* excludes *dry*, but it is less clear what is the status of the associated terms. If the focus is metalinguistic, that is if it is a question of choosing precisely the term *wet*, then all other terms are definitionally excluded.

In another group of adjectives that are common in hyperbaton, the restriction is more "logical" in character. This is the case with comparatives, superlatives, ordinals, and identity adjectives (*same, other, similar, unlike*). For instance, comparatives in *-er* and superlatives in *-est* require some form of logical computation that excludes lower points on a scale in a contextually relevant set of entities: *third line, taller centurion(s), tallest centurion(s)* exclude the first and second line and shorter centurions in the context of the battle under discussion.

Weak and strong focus on modifiers

The mechanisms for the exclusion of alternatives can become quite confusing until one realizes that different types of focus exclude alternatives in different ways. In many contexts, simply by using one adjective, related incompatible adjectives are automatically excluded. In a broad scope weak focus sentence like

He was wearing a red shirt,

shirts of other colours are automatically excluded, if we make the pragmatically natural assumption that he was wearing one monochrome shirt. This is achieved in the absence of any specific mechanism for the exclusion of alternatives such as is associated with strong focus. For scalar modifiers and quantifiers, the weak focus situation is a little more complex, since it involves some additional pragmatic reasoning. In a sentence like

Caesar killed many Gauls,

the listener knows that, provided the speaker is not exaggerating, *many* does not truthfully represent a situation in which no more than *a few* Gauls were killed. The listener also knows that although *many* does truthfully describe a situation in which all the Gauls were killed (since *all* entails *many*), the speaker would not have chosen the quantifier *many* because it is less than maximally informative (Horn 1981; Koenig 1991). Once again, weak focus does not involve exclusion of the alternatives in the way strong focus does. The difference is clearly illustrated when the step of pragmatic reasoning is omitted, as in the following example involving the slightly different class of numerals (Hirschberg 1985)

> The month of February has twenty-eight days, and so do all
>   the other months (weak focus)
> *The month of February has twenty-EIGHT days, and so do all
>   the other months (strong focus).

The precision associated with the strong focus reading arises from the implicit exclusion of the other numerals in the set of alternates (21-27, 29). Strong focus evokes and excludes the set of alternatives; weak focus does not, and so permits upward compatibility ('28 or more') in the joke context. Returning to our *many* example, in a situation in which Caesar in fact killed all the Gauls, it would be quite possible for weak and strong focus to elicit 'yes' and 'no' responses to otherwise comparable questions

> A. Did Caesar kill many Gauls?
> B. Yes. In fact, he killed all of them.
> A. Was it MANY Gauls that Caesar killed? (cleft)
> B. No. It was ALL of them.

Contrastive focus also behaves differently from simple strong focus. The latter is particularly associated with negation of polar opposites, as just described. A sentence like

> Cinderella is the PRETTY sister

negates the polar opposite of *pretty* (*ugly*) for Cinderella and implicitly assigns it to the other two sisters. But when two adjectives are in explicit contrastive focus, the negated complement is the other adjective, which need not be the polar opposite

> No. The older sisters are the PRETTY ones, but Cinderella is the
> BEAUTIFUL one;

here the set of alternates is simply the contrasted adjectives under consideration, which in this instance both come from the upper end of the scale of physical attractiveness. When a nonpolar opposite is used in counterassertion, as in our example, the result often has a metalinguistic flavour.

Υ₁ HYPERBATON

The Υ₁ adjective

Now that we have reviewed some basic information about what focus is and how it works with modifiers, we are in a position to embark on our analysis of Υ₁ hyperbaton in Greek prose. Let us see how the principle of antonymous negation works in the various classes of adjectives used in Υ₁ hyperbaton.

For restrictive adjectives, we find examples like the following

> (6)   ἀληθεῖς κατ' ἀλλήλων ἔχοντες δόξας Aesch 3.213 (true, not false)
>   ψευδῆ συντάξας καθ' ἡμῶν κατηγορίαν Aesch 2.183 (false, not true)

(6) Having true opinions concerning each other (Aesch 3.213). Having put together a false charge against us (Aesch 2.183).

(7)   θηλείας μετασχόντα φύσεως Pl *Laws* 872e (female, not male)
δημοσίας ἀπεργάζεται συμφοράς Aesch 3.147 (public, not personal)
ἰδίους δ᾽ εὑρίσκειν πολέμους Dem 2.28 (personal, not public).

Although demonstratives are adjectives, they have an evident determiner-like function

(8)   ἐπ᾽ ἐκεῖνον τρέψεται τὸν λόγον Isae 5.3 (that other, not this)
περὶ ἐκείνου εἴπω τοῦ νόμου Dem 24.144 (that other, not this)
τούτοις ἐπαρθεὶς τοῖς ψηφίσμασι Dem 18.168 (these, not others).
ἐγὼ μὲν δὴ τοιαύτη συμβεβίωκα τύχῃ Dem 18.258 (of this sort, not
of another sort); cp. τοιαύτῃσι περιέπιπτον τύχῃσι Her 6.17
τηλικαύτην δ᾽ ἀνελόντας μαρτυρίαν Dem 28.5 (of such significance,
not of less).

The article does not appear as the sole Y₁ element in hyperbaton

(9)   *τοῖς ἐπαρθεὶς ψηφίσμασιν.

When focus is on uniqueness, one finds μόνος, and when focus is on referentiality, one finds the demonstrative. When the "article" does in occur in hyperbaton, in verse, it is in fact the older demonstrative

(10)   τῆς γὰρ πέφυκα μητρός *OT* 1082.

There is also probably a syntactic reason for the absence of the article in hyperbaton. Unlike demonstratives, possessive pronouns and interrogative adjectives, which were adjectives in Greek, the article probably had true determiner status. It could not appear productively without an accompanying adjective in null head modifier phrases apart from certain well defined usages, and its appearance in Y₁ position in hyperbaton would presumably constitute a true Left Branch Condition violation even in Greek.

Other pronominal adjectives include adjectives of identity, which like demonstratives serve to specify referents, although less directly

(11)   ἑτέρων παρεμβολῇ πραγμάτων Aesch 3.205 (other, not the same)
τὴν γὰρ αὐτὴν τούτῳ ποιησάμενος τῶν γεγραμμένων τάξιν
    Dem 18.56 (same, not different)
ἐξ ἄλλης ἐλθόντα κώμης Her 1.196 (another, not this).

---

(7) Sharing in female nature (Pl *Laws* 872e). Produces public disasters (Aesch 3.147). Find their own personal wars (Dem 2.28).

(8) He will have recourse to that argument (Isae 5.3). I may speak about that law (Dem 24.144). Encouraged by these decrees (Dem 18.168). I have lived with such success (Dem 18.258). Having destroyed so important an item of evidence (Dem 28.5).

(9) Encouraged by the decrees.

(10) I was born of that mother (*OT* 1082).

(11) By the introduction of extraneous matters (Aesch 3.205). Adopting the same order of accusations as this man (Dem 18.56). Coming from another village (Her 1.196).

Adjectives of size and measure exclude their polar opposites

(12) βραχύς μοι λείπεται λόγος Aesch 3.175 (short, not long)
       μικρὸν διαλιπὼν χρόνον Aesch 3.89 (small, not large)
       μεγάλας ἐπέθηκαν τιμωρίας Dem 47.2 (large, not small),

as do quantifiers

(13) πολλὴν προσήκει πρόνοιαν ὑπὲρ εὐσεβείας ἔχειν Aesch 2.114
          (much, not a little) ·
       πολλῶν ἦρξε τριήρων Lys 14.36 (many, not a few)
       ὀλίγας ἄρξας ἀρχὰς Lys 20.5 (few, not many)
       πάσας ἐξελύσατε τὰς παρασκευὰς τὰς τοῦ πολέμου Dem 18.26
          (all, not some).

We also find negative quantifiers

(14) μηδεμίαν παραλείπειν ἡμέραν Aesch 3.220 (not > zero)
       οὐδεμίαν πώποτε φανήσεται πρεσβείαν εἰς προεδρίαν καλέσας
          Aesch 3.76 (not > zero)

and cardinal numerals

(15) μιᾷ μόνον ἁλῶναι ψήφῳ Dem 21.75 (one, not >1)
       τρία καὶ εἴκοσιν ἐπιβιόντα ἔτη Isae 2.45 (23, not < 23).

Ordinal numerals, comparatives, and superlatives—both true superlatives (-est)
and intensifier superlatives (very)—specify referents by excluding lower points
on the scale of comparison

(16) πρώτην δ᾽ ἐξελθὼν στρατείαν Aesch 2.168 (not > first)
       οὐδὲν ἐλάττονος ἄξιον σπουδῆς Dem 18.5 (not < the same amount)
       πλείστας μὲν στρατηγήσαντες στρατηγίας Andoc 1.147
          (not < very many)
       μεγίστοις περιπέπτωκα κινδύνοις Andoc 4.2 (not < very great)
       ἐπ᾽ αἰσχίσταις στερηθεὶς αἰτίαις Lys 7.41 (not < very disgraceful)
       τῆς δικαιοτάτης ἂν τύχοι τιμωρίας Antiph 1.27 (not < the most just).

(12) Little remains for me to say (Aesch 3.175). With only a short delay (Aesch 3.89).
They imposed great penalties (Dem 47.2).
(13) Ought to have much consideration for piety (Aesch 2.114). He commanded many
triremes (Lys 14.36). Having held few offices (Lys 20.5). You halted all the preparations
for war (Dem 18.26).
(14) To leave not a single day (Aesch 3.220). He will be found not to have ever invited
a single embassy to the seat of honour (Aesch 3.76).
(15) That he was condemned by only a single vote (Dem 21.75). That he lived another
23 years (Isae 2.45).
(16) Going out on my first military expedition (Aesch 2.168). Worthy of no less serious
attention (Dem 18.5). Having held very many military commands (Andoc 1.147). I have
fallen into the greatest danger (Andoc 4.2). Having been deprived on the most disgraceful
charges of... (Lys 7.41). She would get the most just punishment (Antiph 1.27).

Contrastive focus excludes what it is explicitly contrasted with

(17)   ἄλλα τε καταστρέψασθαι ἔθνεα... καὶ δὴ καὶ Σκύθας Her 2.110
       (others – Scythians)
       εἴπας ἐς σὲ μάταια ἔπεα χρηστῆς εἴνεκα συμβουλίης Her 7.15
       (worthless – valuable)
       μικρὸν ἀναλώσαντες χρόνον πολλῷ... ἔσεσθ᾽ ἐμπειρότεροι
       Dem 18.173 (little – by much)
       ὀλίγα μὲν γὰρ ἦλθον ἔχοντες χρήματα, πολλῶν δὲ προσεδεήθησαν
       Lys 19.21 (few – many)
       πολλὰς αὖ ηὑρήκαμεν ἀρετὰς μίαν ζητοῦντες Pl *Meno* 74a
       (many – one)
       πλεῖστα πάντων γεγραφὼς ψηφίσματα οὐδεμίαν πώποτε γραφὴν
       πέφευγε παρανόμων Aesch 3.194 (very many – none).

The exclusion of alternatives in Y1 hyperbaton in prose is not merely a side
effect of the restrictive or specificational properties of this type of adjective with
weak or broad scope focus. On the other hand, the effect of focus in hyperbaton is usually much weaker than it would be in counterassertion. Most of the
time, the speaker is not conveying his belief that the audience is misinformed
and that they need to correct their file entry accordingly. Rather he is just
deliberately making the point that it is the Y1 modifier rather than its polar
opposite (or any of its other potential alternatives) that applies, and ensuring
that the audience is aware that the alternatives are positively excluded.

Descriptive adjectives

There are situations in which focus on an adjective is inappropriate, because
the context does not permit the construction of a set of alternates. If you are in
Grace Brothers department store and declare

       I like the BLACK shirts,

your remark will be accepted as perfectly felicitous: perhaps they have better
stitching than the other shirts, or perhaps your washing machine has broken
down. But if you are in a store which is known to sell only black shirts, say the
Camiceria Benito, the same remark will leave people puzzled, since they do not
carry shirts in alternative colours, least of all the red ones favoured by semanticists. Your remark is the contextual equivalent of

(17) That he had subdued other tribes... and also the Scythians (Her 2.110). Having
spoken to you foolish words in response to good advice (Her 7.14). Having spent a little
time... you will be much more experienced (Dem 18.173). They came having little
money but they needed a lot (Lys 19.21). We have again found many virtues while looking for one (Pl *Men* 74a). Having proposed the most motions of all men was never
accused for proposing a single illegal one (Aesch 3.194).

I like the BLACK coal.

What strong focus on *black* does is to evoke and negate the set of alternatives, that is the complement of the set of things that are black relative to the extension of the noun (shirts). In contexts in which a particular situation, or simply the way the world is, precludes the existence of a complement, focus just does not compute. In the phrase *black coal*, the adjective is much more likely to be used descriptively than restrictively. Descriptive adjectives convey additional information without restricting reference: *black coal* draws your attention to the fact that the coal is black, but does not restrict reference to a submass of the coal in question. Restrictive *black* in *black shirts* involves an intersection resulting in a subset of shirts in the store (those that are black): only part of the shirts is included in the set of black things. Descriptive *black* is just one of the family of sets to which all the shirts in the store belong: the entire set of shirts is included in the set of black things. Although the descriptive–restrictive distinction is particularly associated with adjectives, a similar distinction is found with nouns in sentences like

The bastard took my golf balls.

Here there is a prosodically encoded distinction between an anaphoric, attributive reading and a referentially restrictive reading.

As already noted in chapter 1, in Greek descriptive adjectives tend to be prenominal in pragmatically neutral word order (while restrictive adjectives tend to be postnominal)

(18)   τῇ νεογάμῳ γυναικί Her 1.37
         ἡ δεινὴ ἀγγελία Xen *Cyr* 7.5.52.

No distinction is being drawn in these particular contexts between a newly wed and a previous wife, nor between two different messages. Descriptive adjectives are not vacuous, just because they do not contribute to the identification of the referent. They can serve to emphasize a predictable or previously established property, contrast it with some other property in the context, indicate the speaker's attitude, or simply assert a nonrestrictive property that the interlocutor may be unaware of

You need to fix your worn brakes, sir!

Adjectives with plural proper names can often be interpreted as either restrictive or descriptive

the fierce Parthians.

With singular proper names, the restrictive interpretation is more difficult, because it presupposes more than one referent with the same name in the discourse context

(18) The newly wedded wife (Her 1.37). The terrible news (Xen *Cyr* 7.5.52).

> clever Peter
> pretty Polly
> the divine Callas.

As with common nouns, the descriptive adjective with proper names may recall and emphasize a known property

> The notorious Al Capone

or indicate the speaker's attitude

> (19)   τοῦ καταράτου Κυρηβίωνος Dem 19.287
> οἱ μὲν κατάπτυστοι Θετταλοὶ Dem 18.43.

However, in a phrase like

> The notorious Mrs Jones

the descriptive adjective may predicate notoriety of Prof. Jones' wife as new information to the listener.

Descriptive adjectives can be used emphatically, and the linguistic encoding of such emphasis may be quite similar, though not identical, to that of focus on restrictive adjectives. In English, both are encoded by prosodic prominence, but often with different durational and intonational properties. A sentence like

> This is our BEAUTIFUL new papyrologist, Miss Smith

would in most contexts have an emphasized descriptive adjective. When spoken with the prosody used for a focused restrictive adjective, it would be appropriate, if potentially embarrassing, in a context where there were two new papyrologists only one of whom was beautiful. Although descriptive emphasis does not restrict reference, it can be used as a sort of intensifier superlative, in which case it excludes other grades of the same property; or it may simply highlight the salience of the modifier relative to the rest of the message. The latter is the case for contrastive descriptive adjectives

> The BLACK earth yielded its GOLDEN crop.

Conversely, a regular restrictive adjective with focus can be made more salient by emphasis.

In Greek prose, emphasized descriptive adjectives can appear before a demonstrative within the noun phrase (p. 28); here are some further examples

> (20)   τὴν καλὴν ταύτην νίκην νενικηκὼς Aesch 1.64
> τὰς καλὰς ταύτας κόμας ἀποκερεῖ Pl *Phaedo* 89b
> ψυχαγωγηθέντες τοῖς... κακοήθεσι τούτοις ἀντιθέτοις Aesch 2.4.

---

(19) That bastard Cyrebio (Dem 19.287). The damned Thessalians (Dem 18.43).
(20) Having won this glorious victory (Aesch 1.64). You will have that beatiful hair cut (Pl *Phaed* 89b). Deceived by those malicious antitheses of his (Aesch 2.4).

So can contrastively focused adjectives, although not necessarily in the same prenominal slot

(21)   τοῦ κοινοῦ τούτου βίου Pl *Phil* 22d (cp. τρεῖς βίοι ibid. 22a)
πρῶτον μὲν τοίνυν οἱ περὶ τῆς βλάβης οὗτοι νόμοι πάντες...
ἔπειθ᾽ οἱ φονικοὶ Dem 21.43.

But, unlike focused adjectives, descriptive adjectives are rare or nonoccurring in Υı hyperbaton in prose. Not only is there a hierarchy DQP > restrictive > descriptive, but the descriptive type is scarcely attested in hyperbaton

*τὴν καλὴν ταύτην νενικηκὼς νίκην
*τὰς καλὰς ταύτας ἀποκερεῖ κόμας
*τοῖς... κακοήθεσι τούτοις ψυχαγωγηθέντες ἀντιθέτοις.

When adjectives that are commonly used descriptively appear in hyperbaton in Greek prose, they tend to be restrictive

(22)   καλὸν μὲν γὰρ ἡγεῖτο... ἐπιτήδευμα τὴν εὐθημοσύνην Xen *Cyr* 8.5.7
καλὴν γ᾽... ἀπειλήφασιν... χάριν Dem 9.65
καλλίστην οὖν εἶναι πρόφασιν Lys 12.6.

One prima facie exception to this rule

τὸν χρηστὸν λέγεις Θεόδωρον Pl *Phaedr* 266e

probably has a name in apposition to a null head modifier ('Do you mean that first rate man, Theodorus?'), in view of examples like

(23)   τὸν ἰατρὸν Ἐρυξίμαχον Pl *Symp* 185d
τὸν δὲ κάλλιστον Πάριον Εὐηνὸν Pl *Phaedr* 267a.

One might think that the relative absence of Υı hyperbaton with descriptive adjectives in prose was a question of style or subject matter, a simple statistical consequence of there being less occasion for emphatic (or unemphatic) descriptive adjectives in many styles of prose than in verse with its passages of highly coloured narration or expansive lyricism. One problem with this null hypothesis is that the absence of descriptive adjectives in prose is a predictable consequence of the semantics of prose hyperbaton. If we take an example like

(24)   διασῴζοντες τὴν παλαιὰν παροιμίαν Pl *Rep* 329a

and create a participial phrase hyperbaton by fronting the descriptive adjective

(21) Of this combined type of life (Pl *Phil* 22d). First then all these laws about damage... then the homicide laws (Dem 21.43).

(22) He thought that orderliness was a good habit (Xen *Cyr* 8.5.7). They have received a fine reward (Dem 9.65). They had an excellent excuse (Lys 12.6).

(23) Erixymachus the doctor (Pl *Symp* 185d). The illustrious Parian Evenus (Pl *Phaedr* 267a).

(24) Maintaining the old proverb (Pl *Rep* 329a).

τὴν παλαιὰν διασῴζοντες παροιμίαν

we get a structure like

(25)   ὁ παλαιὸς κελεύει νόμος Dem 20.99.

But in the Demosthenes passage, the adjective is restrictive and contrastive and the noun correspondingly backgrounded: the OLD law versus the NEW law (unlike νόμος παλαιὸς at Aristophanes *Birds* 1353). Obviously, this would be inappropriate in the Plato passage, where there is no question of distinguishing between old and new proverbs. Emphasis by itself is insufficient to license hyperbaton in prose. For hyperbaton to be felicitous in prose, there must be a set of alternates. Hyperbaton encodes the logical operation of ranging over the set of alternates, identifying the correct alternate(s), and excluding those that remain. Consider a situation in which Jack has one car (which is very bright red) and six shirts (one of which is red). Last Saturday

> Jack washed his re-e-e-d car (emphasis)
> Jack washed his RED shirt (strong narrow focus).

As fas as garments are concerned, the shirt that got washed was the red one and no others. As far as automobiles are concerned, there is no way in which *red* can serve to restrict the carwashing in this way: it relates only to the noun *car*. What got washed was the car, which incidentally was very red. This difference is directly reflected in the Greek syntactic rule we are examining. In the case of the shirts, *red* can be separated from the noun it modifies and can appear in Y_1 hyperbaton under strong narrow focus. In the case of the car, *red* is forced to remain in the same noun phrase as the noun it modifies.

The Y_2 noun

In many sentences having a single strong narrow focus, information is organized into a simple binary structure consisting of the focus and the cofocus. The cofocus in this simple type is tail material, although of course various other more complex structures also occur. The cofocus is often just called the presupposition. There is an ongoing theoretical discussion about the technical definition of the term presupposition; we shall use it in an informal and intuitive sense as referring to the common ground information about the world that the interlocutors bring with them, augmented by the information established up to the current state of the discourse. Not all cofoci are presuppositions; sometimes the cofocus is new information "accommodated" to the common ground which is introduced as though it were presupposed, whereas in fact the common ground has to be adjusted to accept it. For instance, a cleft like

> It was Clara Petrella who was singing at the opera last night

(25)   The old law prescribes (Dem 20.99).

can be felicitous even in a situation in which the listener is unaware, and the speaker knows that the listener is unaware, that there was an opera performance last night. The listener first incorporates the information to be accommodated into the common ground and then treats it like a presupposition in processing the focus structure. Focus driven accommodation is neatly illustrated by situations in which the listener has been inattentive. For instance, say Jack has momentarily dozed off during Prof. Jones' Roman history lecture; the first sentence he hears when he wakes up is

> Then the Gauls attacked the RIGHT wing of the Roman army;

on the basis of the contrastive focus, he can reconstruct what he has missed; his best guess would be that the Gauls had previously attacked the left wing of the Roman army. Conversely, not all presuppositions are cofoci. Firstly, the cofocus is usually not just any old presupposition, but one that relates to a question under active consideration in the discourse. Secondly, presuppositions can be foci as well as cofoci

> It wasn't flunking the Tertullian course that Jack regretted so much as failing the Prose Comp. test;

here the contrastive foci of the cleft are presuppositions introduced by the factive verb *regret*. Presuppositions can also be focused when they are reactivated in the discourse. However, in sentences having a strong narrow focus, the presupposition typically appears as tail material.

Let us now consider the informational status of Y2 nouns in hyperbaton in light of the above characterization of the cofocus. Most Y2 nouns are open to interpretation as tail material, although it would often be difficult unequivocally to exclude weak focus as a possible alternative. In some cases, the noun is more or less explicitly established in the antecedent discourse

(26)   ἀφ᾽ ὧν ἂν πλείστην δόξαν ἔχοι... πλείστην δ᾽ ἂν ἔχοι δόξαν
       Pl *Amat* 135b
       πολλὰς ἀρχὰς ἦρξεν... ὀλίγας ἄρξας ἀρχὰς Lys 20.5
       ἀνεγνωκέναι τοὺς Σόλωνος νόμους... τοὺς Σόλωνος ἀνεγνωκέναι
       νόμους Dem 20.103
       ἀντὶ τῶν ἀπολιπόντων μὲν ναυτῶν ἑτέρους ἐμισθωσάμην ναύτας
       Dem 50.12
       ἢν δὲ οἱ ἐπελθόντες μάντιες ἀπολύσωσι, ἄλλοι πάρεισι μάντιες
       Her 4.68

(26) From which he can get the most recognition... and he would get the most recognition (Pl *Amat* 135b). He held many magistracies... having held few magistracies (Lys 20.5). To have read the laws of Solon... to have read the laws of Solon (Dem 20.103). In place of the sailors who deserted I hired other sailors (Dem 50.12). If the later diviners acquit him, other diviners appear (Her 4.68).

(27)   κλίμακας προσθέντες... πολλὰς προσθέντες κλίμακας Thuc 3.23.1
       ἔπειθ᾽ ἕτερον ἐπήγετο ψήφισμα Aesch 2.110 (fourth ψήφισμα
       mentioned in this section of the speech).

It is common enough for strong quantifiers to quantify over a domain already
established in the discourse or the discourse context, and for restrictive adjectives and demonstratives to pick members from a discourse established set as in
the ἕτερος examples just cited. More generally, the prediction is that normally
a nonbranching or continuous branching YP is the first of two occurrences of a
noun, and hyperbaton the second, and that the reverse order should be much
less common. It is also possible that there may be a stronger association of Y1
hyperbaton with repeated nouns than of nonbranching or branching continuous YP.

In other cases, the noun has impoverished descriptive content relative to the
verb. Either it is an internal accusative or easily predicted from the selectional
restrictions of the verb along with the context, as in *dance a dance* or *mail a letter* respectively

(28)   πλείους τραπόμενος τροπὰς τοῦ Εὐρίπου Aesch 3.90
       τοιαῦτα ἁμαρτάνει ἁμαρτήματα Lys 31.23
       ἅπαντες γὰρ ἀπαγορεύουσιν οἱ νόμοι Aesch 3.50.

Sometimes the Y2 noun is just semantically light, like *person, matter* etc.

(29)   ταῦτα πλεῖν ἢ διακοσίων ἰδόντων ἀνθρώπων Lys 3.27
       τί γὰρ ἄν τις τοιούτῳ πιστεύσειεν ἀνθρώπῳ Aesch 2.130
       τὰ δ᾽ ἐν Φωκεῦσι διεφθάρη πράγματα Aesch 2.131
       τοῖς λοιποῖς ἐπιχειροίη πράγμασιν Dem 18.27.

In other instances the noun is accessible or inferable from the context

(30)   ὁρᾶτε τοῖς ὀφθαλμοῖς... ἴστε... αὐτοί, καὶ οὐδὲν ἑτέρων δεῖσθε
       μαρτύρων Aesch 3.119
       τὸ πορνικὸν τέλος... τοὺς ταύτῃ χρωμένους τῇ ἐργασίᾳ Aesch 1.119;

in the first example third person testimony is evoked as contrastive with eyewitness observation, in the second mention of a category member evokes the
category. Finally, the noun may arguably be backgrounded relative to the main

(27) Placing ladders... placing many ladders (Thuc 3.23.1). Then he proposed another
motion (Aesch 2.110).
(28) Turning more turns than the Euripus (Aesch 3.90). Offends with such offences
(Lys 31.23). All the laws forbid (Aesch 3.50).
(29) Although more than two hundred people saw this (Lys 3.27). Why would anyone
trust such a man? (Aesch 2.130). The Phocian situation was ruined (Aesch 2.131). He
could proceed with his remaining business (Dem 18.27).
(30) You see with your own eyes... you know by yourselves and you need no other witnesses (Aesch 3.119). The tax on prostitution... those practising this profession (Aesch
1.119).

information conveyed by the modifier, as illustrated by the English paraphrases given with the following examples

> πολλὴν προσήκει πρόνοιαν ὑπὲρ εὐσεβείας ἔχειν Aesch 2.114:
> 'great is the forethought that he should have concerning piety'
> τὴν αὐτὴν ἀπόδοτέ μοι χάριν... ἥνπερ ἐγὼ ὑμῖν Aesch 2.143
> 'the same as I did for you is the favour you should do for me.'

Because of the rather subjective nature of the judgements we can make about backgrounding, it is hard to say to what extent, if at all, the Y2 noun in hyperbaton could be weak (purely informational) focus rather than tail material. Consider the following

> (31)   εἰς τὴν ἐσχάτην ἐμπέσοιεν ἀθυμίαν Aesch 3.65.

The noun is certainly prima facie new information: despondency fills the field 'what would they fall into?'. So the sentence could involve the superimposition of a strong focus (the superlative) on a simple (broad scope) weak focus verb phrase. However, the verb phrase material seems to be backgrounded relative to the superlative. Superlatives are often used to pick that member of a previously established set that has the extreme value of some property. We can continue to call the unfocused material in such sentences the presuppositional frame, rather than reverting to a more neutral term like cofocus, if we assume that by backgrounding material that is new or not easily predictable the speaker forces the listener to accommodate such material and accept it as though it were presupposed.

Informational structure

Our analysis will involve the following informational categories: weak focus, strong focus, strong topic, tail. Since it is theoretically possible for each one of these to be distributed either with broad scope over the prototypical YP or with narrow scope over its adjective (Y1) or noun (Y2) subconstituents, it is evident that, even for a single noun phrase, there is a considerable range of pragmatic differences that languages may encode either in the syntax or phonologically or both.

The range of informational contrasts is particularly clear in Hungarian, which has separate syntactic slots for topic, focus and neutral constituents. If the noun phrase is distributed into more than one slot, a separate inflection is required for each slot. Here are some examples (Szabolcsi 1983)

> Mari látott két zöld biciklit
> Mary saw two green bikes
> 'Mary saw two green bikes'

(31) They should fall into the worst despondency (Aesch 3.65).

[Zöld biciklit]$_{FOC}$ látott Mari kettőt
'What Mary saw two of was green bikes'

[Biciklit]$_{TOP}$ [kettőt]$_{FOC}$ látott Mari zöldet
'As for bikes, Mary saw exactly two which were green.'

The last example has topic, focus and tail cooccurring in a single clause with hyperbaton. There is also a version with amplificatory Y2 adjective and prosodic dislocation. Topic Y1 is additionally reported for Serbocroatian (Progovac 1996)

Marijanina se udala   ćerka
Marianna's self married daughter
'As for Marianna, her daughter got married.'

The following examples illustrate the difference between broad and narrow scope focus as it applies to YP

It was the CUCUMBER SANDWICHES that the butler forgot
   (broad scope focus on YP: not the cake)
It was the CUCUMBER sandwiches that the butler forgot
   (narrow scope focus on Y1: not the ham sandwiches)
It was the cucumber SANDWICHES that the butler forgot
   (narrow scope focus on Y2: not the cucumber canapes)
It was the [CUCUMBER] [SANDWICHES] that the butler forgot
   (double narrow scope focus: not the ham canapes).

Now let us review some of the main informational structures relevant for an analysis of Y1 hyperbaton. (Those specific to Y2 hyperbaton are omitted here; they will by given in chapter 3). 'YP' is used to indicate broad scope application to YP, 'Y1' and 'Y2' to indicate narrow scope application to the subconstituent in question; square brackets delimit the scope of the pragmatic category.

YP Weak focus (I saw a [black cat] in the park yesterday)

(32)   [χλανίδιον λευκὸν] περιβαλλόμενος Her 1.195

YP Strong (contrastive) focus (It was a [BLACK CAT] that I saw in the park yesterday, not a dog)

(33)   χωρὶς τῆς ἄλλης αἰσχύνης καὶ ἀδοξίας... καὶ [μεγάλοι κίνδυνοι] περιεστᾶσιν ἐκ τούτων τὴν πόλιν Dem 19.83

YP Strong topic (As for [BLACK CATS], unlike dogs they bring bad luck)

(34)   [σώματα δὲ ἀγαθὰ καὶ καλὰ] πότερον ἐκ Βοιωτῶν οἴει πλείω ἂν ἐκλεχθῆναι ἢ ἐξ Ἀθηναίων; Xen Mem 3.5.2

(32) Putting on a white mantle (Her 1.195).
(33) Apart from the other shame and disgrace... also great dangers threaten the city as a result of this (Dem 19.83).
(34) As for fine, strong bodies, do you think more could be selected from the Boeotians or from the Athenians? (Xen Mem 3.5.2).

YP Tail (Talking about black cats, flea shampoo is a must for [black cats])

    (35)   ὡς οὖν καινοτομοῦντός σου περὶ τὰ θεῖα γέγραπται
           [ταύτην τὴν γραφήν] Pl *Euthyph* 3b (the γραφή is old information)

Y1 Strong focus, Y2 Tail/backgrounded (It was a [BLACK] [cat] that I saw, not a white one)

    (36)   [κούφων ἁμαρτημάτων] αἴτιον Pl *Laws* 863c (continuous)
           [μεγάλας] ἐπέθηκαν [τιμωρίας] Dem 47.2 (hyperbaton)

Y1 Strong focus, Y2 Strong focus (It was a [BLACK] [CAT] that I saw, not a white dog)

    (37)   τῷ [καλλίστῳ ὀνόματι] χρώμενος δεινοτάτων ἔργων διδάσκαλος
           καταστάς Lys 12.78

Y1 Strong topic, Y2 Tail/backgrounded (Talking about cats, as for [BLACK] [cats], they bring you bad luck)

    (38)   δυώδεκα ὦν μηνῶν ἐόντων ἐς τὸν ἐνιαυτὸν τοὺς [τέσσερας] [μῆνας]
           τρέφει μιν ἡ Βαβυλωνίη χώρη, τοὺς δὲ ὀκτὼ τῶν μηνῶν ἡ λοιπὴ
           πᾶσα Ἀσίη Her 1.192 (continuous)
           [ταύτην] μὲν οὖν εἰς τὸν μέλλοντα χρόνον ἀνέγραψαν
           [τὴν πολιτείαν] Arist *Ath Pol* 31.1 (hyperbaton).

In this analysis, Y1 hyperbaton occurs in the categories strong focus plus tail and strong topic plus tail, which fits with the conclusion of the preceding separate analyses of the pragmatic status of the adjective and of the noun in Y1 hyperbaton. Other categories are less likely or outright impossible. The combination strong focus plus weak focus is intrinsically more difficult, since narrow scope strong focus on the modifier is typically correlated with a noun that is part of the presupposition or at least backgrounded:

        I saw a [BLACK] [cat] in the park yesterday

is inappropriate as an out-of-the-blue utterance or at the beginning of a conversation, unless cats can be established as predictable by the physical discourse context or the shared experience of the interlocutors. This particular pragmatic combination appears felicitously as

        I saw a [cat] in the park yesterday, which was [BLACK],

    (35) So he has made this accusation against you on the grounds that you are a religious radical (Pl *Euthyph* 3b).

    (36) Responsible for MINOR offences (Pl *Laws* 863c). They imposed HEAVY penalties (Dem 47.2).

    (37) Using the most excellent phraseology he became the instigator of the most terrible deeds (Lys 12.78).

    (38) Of the twelve months in the year the Babylonian land supports him for four months and for the other eight the entire rest of Asia (Her 1.192). This constitution they drew up for the future (Arist *Ath Pol* 31.1).

which in Greek is not a Y₁ hyperbaton at all, but one type of Y₂ hyperbaton. Broad scope weak focus and weak focus plus tail are both theoretically conceivable assignments for Y₁ hyperbaton: in fact, they are common enough in verse but rare or nonoccurring in prose. Strong focus plus strong focus, as in double contrast, is also rare or nonoccurring. In an example like

(39)   πολλοὺς μὲν ἔχων φίλους Ἰφικράτης, πολλὰ δὲ χρήματα κεκτημένος
       Dem 21.62

the nouns are not strongly contrastive, as they are in the following example with contrastive topics and Y₂ hyperbaton

(40)   ἄνθρωποι... ἀπέθανον... πολλοί, καὶ χρήματα πολλὰ... ἑάλω
       Thuc 7.24.2.

A generalization emerging from this analysis is important for the question of how the syntax interfaces with the pragmatics. It is that in prose Y₁ hyperbaton does not normally occur in broad scope structures. Hyperbaton in prose exists to distribute pragmatically nonuniform subconstituents of the noun phrase into their appropriate pragmatically determined syntactic positions, namely Y₁ and Y₂. Broad scope structures, being pragmatically uniform, do not naturally trigger hyperbaton in prose: in terms of the tripartite structure (p. 78), if both Y elements are in the nuclear scope or if both are in the restriction, there will be no Y₁ hyperbaton. The converse prediction, from the syntax back to the pragmatics, fails because hyperbaton is not obligatory. Nonuniform structures can alternatively piedpipe one subconstituent into the position that would have appropriately been assigned to the other; this was illustrated in the examples marked "continuous" in the data.

When the above analysis is applied to a body of text, two features soon become apparent: firstly, the judgements involved in assigning individual instances to a particular category can be rather subjective; and secondly, some categories are far more common than others. While this could be a practical obstacle, for instance in a statistical study, it is also theoretically instructive to understand why things are just this way. Restriction is a prototypical function of adnominal adjectives, and often what is restricted is a class already established in the discourse or else a relatively vacuous class like *person* or *thing*. These tendencies are quite observable in written language and become overwhelming in spontaneous natural conversation (Thompson 1988). Y₁ hyperbaton exhibits not so much a different set of properties from simple modification as the same sort of properties in an exaggerated form. Whereas an adjective with weak narrow focus is restrictive, an adjective with strong narrow focus is not only restrictive but also, in one sense or another, exclusive. If it stands in hyperbaton, the Y₂ noun is not merely preferentially but obligatorily

(39) Iphicrates, possessing many friends and having acquired a lot of money (Dem 21.62).
(40) Many men died and much property was captured (Thuc 7.24.2).

predictable, presupposed or accommodated material. After a weak focus adjective, a nontail noun is relatively uncommon, particularly in spoken language, but still grammatical; after a strong focus adjective in Y1 hyperbaton, it is marginal or ungrammatical.

Three conclusions emerge from the above analysis. First, the distribution of pragmatic categories in Y1 hyperbaton is skewed relative to continuous YP structures; this proves that Y1 hyperbaton is not a pragmatically meaningless syntactic variant of the continuous YP structure. Second, the specific pragmatic categories that actually occur in Y1 hyperbaton are fairly consistently narrow focus on the adjective and tail status for the noun. Third, Y1 hyperbaton is optional. Optionality manifests itself along two parameters. Y1 hyperbaton may fail to occur either because a strong focus plus tail is not syntactically actuated by hyperbaton but, for instance, by piedpiping. Or Y1 hyperbaton may be absent because a text avoids strong foci in general. In other words, in one condition the pragmatics is there but the syntax fails to encode it, in the other the pragmatics is itself absent so that the syntax gets no chance to encode it. Both Y1 and Y2 hyperbaton are attested even in the earliest prose texts

(41)   τὸν μὲν δεξιὸν ὑποδεῖται πόδα, τὸν δὲ ἀριστερὸν ἐπιλήθεται
        Pherecydes of Athens 105 Jacoby
        ἰσχὺν ἔχοντα μεγίστην Acusilaus of Argos 22 Jacoby.

The first example is a canonical contrastive focus Y1 hyperbaton, the second a canonical topic Y2 hyperbaton. However, there are significant differences in the frequency of hyperbaton from one author to another, particularly between the orators and the historians. In this regard, Xenophon and Aeschines seem to be writing in different languages. While this is perplexing from the perspective of the rather stable word order of English (the closest analogy would be variability in the use of clefts), it is not unexpected in light of the situation in a language like Russian. Descriptions of word order in Russian classify sentences as emotive or nonemotive. The two types have different word order and different prosody. Nonemotive sentences are typical in scientific writing but can also occur in speech, emotive sentences are associated with colloquial speech and with literature that reflects colloquial speech (King 1993). So it is natural to associate the high frequency of hyperbaton in the orators with a more emotive style that makes greater use of pragmatically marked word order, and the lower frequency in the historians with a preference for a more detached and analytical style.

Complex structures

One variation on the basic pragmatic structure of Y1 hyperbaton is for there to be an additional strong focus on the verb

(41) He put a shoe on his right foot but forgot his left one (Phercydes 105). Having the greatest strength (Acusilaus 22).

(42)   πολλοὶ μὲν δὴ συγκατακαίονται τοῖσι μάντισι βόες, πολλοὶ δὲ
περικεκαυμένοι ἀποφεύγουσι Her 4.69;

here the number of events in which the oxen are burned to death is contrasted
with the number of events in which they escape singed.

A different type of complexity arises when there are two modifiers, for
instance a demonstrative and an adjective, a quantifier and an adjective, or a
demonstrative and a quantifier. There can be narrow focus on either or focus
on both

these RED shirts (not these black ones)
THESE red shirts (not those red shirts)
THESE RED shirts (not those black ones).

When both modifiers are focused, either each modifier contributes to the identification of the referent (*these* does not exhaust the set of red shirts and *red*
does not exhaust the set of shirts), or *red* is an amplification designed to support the deixis (*these* does exhaust the set of red shirts). In fact, so long as the
focus appears in the outer operator slot, even a descriptive adjective can occur
preverbally in Y₁ hyperbaton

(43)   πάντα ταῦτα τὰ καλὰ λέγουσι ποιήματα Pl *Ion* 533e.

Both adnominal quantifiers and restrictive adjectives are interpreted in
terms of a relation between the set denoted by the noun and another set.
Modification represents a function from set to subset, adnominal quantification can be seen as a function from set to set of sets. A noun phrase with an
adjective specifies both intersected sets but gives no details about their quantificational relationship. A noun phrase with a quantifier specifies only one of the
intersected sets but explicitly states the quantificational relationship characterizing the intersection. So *some red shirts* is the set of sets containing some entities that are in the denotation of both *red* and *shirt*, and *all the red shirts* is the
set of sets containing all the entities that are both red and shirts. In a simple
sentence like

Some red shirts were sold

the common noun serves to pick out shirts as a subset from the universe of all
entities, in symbols $\lambda x[P(x)]$. The restrictive adjective takes the set of shirts and
intersects it with the set of red things to produce a subset, namely the set of red
shirts: $\lambda x[P(x) \land Q(x)]$. Finally, the quantifier defines the numerical relationship between the set of red shirts and the set of things sold as greater than zero;
the intersection between the two sets involved in the main predication is not

(42)   Many oxen are burned to death along with the diviners, but many escape scorched
(Her 4.69).
(43)   They compose all those beautiful poems (Pl *Ion* 533e).

null, in symbols $A \cap B \neq \emptyset$. Focus involves a further complication, since the exclusivity or exhaustiveness of strong narrow focus

The RED shirts were sold

endows the focus with something like the quantificational properties of *only*. The non-red shirts are evoked and assigned to the set of things that were not sold. The red shirts are then a superset of the shirts sold ($A \supseteq B$), and the non-red shirts are a subset of the unsold shirts ($\neg A \subseteq \neg B$).

The analysis just given is indicated for the sort of integrated reading of the noun phrase that corresponds to its usual syntactic structure in English, where, for instance in terms of categorial grammar, adjectives represent a function from noun to noun and determiners a function from noun to noun phrase. In languages having flatter, less configurational phrases, it might break down both for the adjective and for the quantifier. If the adjective is completely unintegrated

Some shirts were sold, ⟨and they were⟩ red
Some shirts were sold, red ⟨ones⟩,

the settheoretical relationship is between shirts and things that get sold, not red shirts and things that get sold, so long as the unintegrated syntax is reflected in the semantics. We will discuss this distinction in more detail as it relates to integrated and unintegrated interpretations of Y₂ hyperbaton in chapter 4. Conversely, the adjective could be integrated but the quantifier could be adverbial rather than adnominal

Red shirts were sold in some number.

The same sort of issue is directly raised by the syntax of the quantifier πολλοί. When πολλοί quantifies over a noun that is also modified by an adjective of measure or evaluation, as a rule the quantifier and the adjective are coordinated, and more often than not both are prenominal

(44)   πολλοὺς καὶ μεγάλους οἴκους Isoc *De Pace* 4
        μετὰ πολλῶν καὶ ἀγαθῶν ξυμμάχων Thuc 5.60.5
        πολλοί τε καὶ ἀξιόλογοι ἄνθρωποι Thuc 6.60.2
        πολλοὶ μὲν καὶ φιλάνθρωποι λόγοι Dem 45.4
        πολλοὺς λόγους καὶ ταπεινοὺς Dem 21.186
        πόλεις πολλαὶ καὶ μεγάλαι Xen *An* 2.4.21.

Many and *few* express the size of a set, and properties like measure and evaluation are presumably semantically compatible with size, at least in that they all belong to the class of scalar adjectives. Exceptions with contiguous quantifier and adjective are rare in prose and may tend to involve nonscalar adjectives

(44) Many great houses (Isoc *De Pac* 4). With the support of many good allies (Thuc 5.60.5). Many important men (Thuc 6.60.2). Many kindly words (Dem 45.4). Many humble words (Dem 21.186). Many large cities (Xen *An* 2.4.21).

(45) πολλοὺς ἁδροὺς χοίρους Xen *Oec* 17.10
ῥάβδοισι ἰτεΐνῃσι πολλῇσι Her 4.67.

For the general sensitivity of coordination to adjective class (Risselada 1984), compare

> tall and handsome actors
> *tall and notorious actors.

The difference in syntactic structure between the uncoordinated and the coordinated type is presumably as illustrated in Figure 2.1.

Quantifiers like *many* arguably have two readings, a proportional reading and a cardinal reading (Partee 1988). The proportional reading is similar to a partitive (it has been called a covert partitive), so that *many hoplites* is like *many of the hoplites*, whereas on the cardinal reading it just means a relatively large number of hoplites. While the proportional reading implicitly quantifies over a contextually identifiable set, the cardinal reading can introduce individuals into the domain of discourse without presupposing their existence: 'there were hoplites in large numbers who...'. Both readings make reference to some standard of comparison, which is defined partly on the basis of linguistic structure and partly on the basis of what is to be expected given the context. Caesar spills more blood when he kills many Gallic warriors than when he kills many Gallic chieftains. Since we are concerned with how focus works in quantifier plus adjective combinations, we should perhaps mention an interesting focus effect found with *many* and *few* (but not with strong quantifiers like *all or most*)

> Many Theban soldiers were killed in the battle, and the remainder
> fled

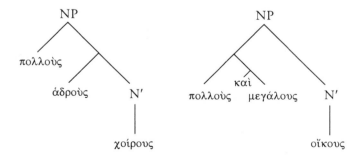

Figure 2.1
Hierarchical and parallel structure
of quantifier plus adjective

(45) Many fine pigs (Xen *Oec* 17.10). With many willow wands (Her 4.67).

Many Theban soldiers were killed in the battle, although the overall casualties both of the Thebans and of their allies were light.

The first example has a proportional use of *many*, which quantifies over Theban soldiers. If the second example is proportional, it quantifies over soldiers killed in the battle, and if it is cardinal it establishes the latter as the standard of comparison, giving interpretations such as 'Considering what normally happens in battles of this sort, although the proportion of the Theban army that got killed was small, the proportion of overall casualties suffered by the Thebans was high / there was a high number of Theban casualties relative to the casualties of the other allies.' This reading is particularly associated with strong narrow focus on the adjective only (many THEBAN soldiers); it may involve a modification of the tripartite structure (Herburger 1997; de Hoop & Solà 1996).

With all this in mind, consider an example like the following, which theoretically admits a number of different readings

(46)   παραλαβὼν Σικελίας πολλὰς καὶ μεγάλας πόλεις Pl *Ep* 7.331e.

An English expression like *many great cities of Sicily* lends itself to a proportional (strong) interpretation: 'many of the great cities of Sicily.' As noted, a proportional interpretation is close to a partitive: πολλὰς τῶν μεγάλων πόλεων. But it is quite likely that, when coordinated with an adjective, πολλοί is not quantificational sensu stricto but has an adjectival, and therefore cardinal (weak) interpretation, just as it does when preceded by the article

(47)   τὰ πολλὰ καὶ μεγάλ᾽ ἀγαθά Dem 19.35.

However, this still leaves us with the question whether the coordinated adjective contributes to the standard of comparison. In principle, we could get the following three possible readings (Gil 1982): (1) cities which are great and are many judged by the standard of the total number of cities in Sicily or the total number of cities that rulers take over in general; (2) cities which are great and are many judged by the standard of the total number of great cities in Sicily; (3) a batch of great cities in Sicily and a separate batch of many cities in Sicily. The third reading is presumably excluded for the combination of quantifier and adjective (as it is for English *many great cities*), although it is available for coordinated adjectives (*yellow and red roses*) both in continuous noun phrases and in hyperbaton

(48)   χρυσέων καὶ ἀργυρέων μετάλλων Her 3.57 (YP)
        ἐν τῷ χρύσεά τε καὶ ἀργύρεα ἔνι μέταλλα Her 7.112 (YXY).

---

(46) Taking over many great cities of Sicily (Pl *Ep* 7.331e).
(47) The numerous great benefits (Dem 19.35).
(48) Gold and silver mines (Her 3.57). In which there are gold and silver mines (Her 7.112).

Whereas English admits both the other two readings for quantifier plus adjective, the Greek coordinating syntax maps more directly onto the first reading. There are obvious consequences, since there are more cities than great cities in Sicily.

Now we can see what happens when either the quantifier or the adjective or both are focused. Here is an example of Yı hyperbaton with focus on the quantifier only

(49)   πολλὰς ἔχοντι σάρκας ἀλλοτρίας Pl *Rep* 556d.

The following (continuous) examples have contrastive focus on the adjective

(50)   πολλὰς μὲν κουριδίας γυναῖκας... πλεῦνας παλλακὰς Her 1.135
πολλὰ μὲν χρύσεα ποτήρια... πολλὰ δὲ ἀργύρεα Her 7.190.

Note the absence of coordination in both types and the fact that the adjectives do not belong to the quantifier-compatible scalar class. The coordinated type, which is common in null head modifier phrases

(51)   πολλοὺς καὶ ἀγαθοὺς Lys 13.28
πολλὰ καὶ ἀνόσια Pl *Rep* 416e
μεγάλων καὶ πολλῶν Dem 36.22,

is found in hyperbaton with both adjectives in the Yı position

(52)   πολλὰ καὶ καλὰ σύνισμεν ἔργα Aesch 3.241
πολλοὺς καὶ θρασεῖς... ἐπαιρόμενος λόγους Dem 18.222
τοὺς μὲν πολλὰ καὶ μεγάλα ποιήσαντας ὑμᾶς ἀγαθὰ Dem 26.7
τοὺς μὲν πάνυ πολλὰ καὶ παντοῖα κεκτημένους ἔπιπλα Xen *Oec* 3.2.

So both the hierarchical and the parallel type can occur in hyperbaton, and the difference has at least the potential of carrying over into the semantic interpretation. The hierarchical example from *Republic* 556d says that the extra pounds carried around by the rich man were numerous (whatever his weight would otherwise have been), while the parallel example from *De Corona* 18.222 says that the threats of Philip had been both numerous and insolent (whatever the ratio of insolent to polite ones). *Many, red shirts* entails *many shirts*, but *many [red shirts]* does not entail *many shirts*. Similarly, πολλοὺς καὶ θρασεῖς λόγους entails πολλοὺς λόγους but πολλὰς [σάρκας ἀλλοτρίας] does not entail πολλὰς σάρκας: think of a twiggy-like character with a beer belly.

(49) Carrying around a lot of extra pounds (Pl *Rep* 556d).
(50) Many legally wedded wives... even more concubines (Her 1.135). Many gold cups... and many silver ones (Her 7.190).
(51) Many good men (Lys 13.28). Many unholy deeds (Pl *Rep* 416e). Many important facts (Dem 36.22).
(52) We are well aware of their many noble deeds (Aesch 3.241). Although he had uttered many insolent words (Dem 18.222). Those who have done you many good deeds (Dem 26.7). That some people have acquired many items of equipment of all sorts (Xen *Oec* 3.2).

Noun phrases having both a noncoordinating quantifier (like πᾶς) and a restrictive adjective show various outcomes in Y1 hyperbaton. In one type, the quantifier is focused and the adjective is backgrounded or tail material

(53)   πᾶσιν ἤρεσκε ταῦτα τοῖς ἄλλοις πρέσβεσιν Dem 19.157
πᾶσιν ἐναντίον εἰσενήνοχε τοῖς οὖσι νόμοις Dem 24.32
πάντων ἐπικρατεῖν τῶν ἀνθρωπίνων λογισμῶν Aesch 1.84
ἅπαντας... μεγάλους εἶναι τοὺς δημοσίους ἀγῶνας Lyc 7.

In a second type, the adjective is a strong topic or focus and the quantifier is in Y2 position, rather like a floated quantifier

(54)   ταῦτ᾽ οὖν ἐψηφίσασθε ἐξαλεῖψαι πάντα τὰ ψηφίσματα Andoc 1.76
τούτων ἄρχειν πασῶν τῶν τεχνῶν Pl *Gorg* 517e.

In a third type, both the quantifier and the adjective seem to be focused

(55)   πάντων... μεγίστων αἴτιος κακῶν Dem 18.143.

So whether the adjective or quantifier appears in Y1 or in Y2 position depends mainly on its pragmatic status. The same sort of variation occurs in Fox with quantifiers and demonstratives in hyperbaton (Dahlstrom 1987), where the sentence 'These four songs are used' is recorded with both the following orders (the first being the more usual)

These are used four songs
Four these are used songs.

ASSOCIATION WITH FOCUS

The focal scope distinctions analyzed in the preceding section can be recognized with particular clarity in the situation known as association with focus, where adverbials like *only, even*, modals like *ought, must*, adverbial quantifiers like *always, often*, particles like γε, δή, μέν, and negation are narrowly interpreted with one subconstituent of YP. For instance, consider how *only* associates with different focus constituents in the following sentences

He only wears RED shirts (Y1 focus: no black shirts)
ONLY (he wears P shirts) (P = red)
He only wears red SHIRTS (Y2 focus: no red sweaters)
ONLY (he wears red *x*) (*x* = shirts)

(53) These things were pleasing to all the other ambassadors (Dem 19.157). He has introduced a law inconsistent with all the existing laws (Dem 24.32). That it prevails over all human reasoning (Aesch 1.84). One ought to think that all public trials are important (Lyc 7).
(54) You decreed that all these decrees should be cancelled (Andoc 1.76). To be master of all these arts (Pl *Gorg* 517e).
(55) Responsible for all the greatest evils (Dem 18.143).

He only wears RED SHIRTS (YP focus: no sweaters)
　　ONLY (he wears x) (x = red shirts)
He only wears RED SHIRTS (double focus: no black sweaters)
　　ONLY (he wears Px) (P = red, x = shirts)
He only WEARS red shirts (V focus: he doesn't sell them)
　　ONLY (he V red shirts) (V = wear)
He only WEARS RED SHIRTS (VP focus: that is all he does)
　　ONLY (he does VP) (VP = wear red shirts).

Association with focus can affect truth conditions, most obviously via quantification:

She only does verse composition in LATIN

means that Latin compositions are a superset of her verse compositions, so she does not do Greek verse composition;

She only does VERSE composition in Latin

means that verse compositions are a superset of her Latin compositions, so she does not do Latin prose composition. If in fact she does Greek verse composition, the first sentence is false but the second one is not necessarily false. If in fact she does Latin prose composition, then the second sentence is false but the first one is not necessarily false.

If it is correct that Y1 hyperbaton encodes focus, then we expect association of particles and adverbials to be with Y1 when a narrowly focused adjective stands in hyperbaton. We will test this prediction in the rest of this section. It is a reasonable prediction to make, since it is just what we find in Fox (Dahlstrom 1995): here is an example with an emphatic particle

kotaka=¢i·h=meko　nekeh·kahama·ko·pi oškinawe·h...
other=EXCLAM=EMPH designate-AFFIXES young man...
'ANOTHER young man had been designated (for me to marry)';

and here is an example with *only*

še·ški· mani ki·h=awato·pena ¢i·ma·ni
only this FUT=take-AFFIXES　canoe
'Let's take only THIS canoe.'

Only

Both adverbial μόνον and adjectival μόνος, whether meaning 'exclusively' or 'merely' (scalar interpretation), can associate with subconstituents of YP when YP is continuous

(56) εἰ μίαν μόνον συλλαβὴν παραλλάξειαν Aesch 3.192
      ἐν μόνῳ τούτῳ τῷ δικαστηρίῳ Dem 23.66
      τρεῖς δὲ μόναι ψῆφοι Dem 23.167.

Association with focus can also occur when YP is discontinuous. In Yı hyperbaton, association is, as predicted, with the modifier. μόνον can occur immediately following a focused Yı with which it associates, like English *only* when it is a noun-phrase modifier: 'they drank only TEA'

(57) τοῖσι πατρίοισι μοῦνον χρᾶσθαι θεοῖσι Her 1.172
      μιᾷ μόνον ἁλῶναι ψήφῳ Dem 21.75
      μιᾶς δὲ μόνον μνησθήσομαι πράξεως Isoc *Panath* 127.

Alternatively, it can be postposited to the verb, while associating with Yı across the verb, like English *only* when it is a verb-phrase modifier: 'they only drank TEA'

(58) τὴν Ἑλλάδα πᾶσαν, οὐχὶ τὰς ἰδίας ἀδικοῦσι μόνον πατρίδας
      Dem 19.11.

Adjectival μόνος can appear directly preceding or following a Yı (or Y₂) modifier with which it associates

(59) ἔτι τοίνυν ταύτην μόνην ἀνάγνωθί μοι τὴν ἐπιστολήν, τὰς δ᾽ ἄλλας ἔα
      Dem 23.162
      ταύτας δὲ μόνας ἀναγκασθεὶς τὰς λητουργίας λειτουργῆσαι Isae 5.36
      ἐκείνου μόνου αἰσθάνονται τοῦ μέλους ὀξέως Pl *Ion* 536c
      μόναις ταύταις ἀπαγορεύουσιν οἱ νόμοι ταῖς γυναιξὶ Dem 59.86
      μόνος οὗτος ἠρεμεῖ ὁ λόγος Pl *Gorg* 527b.

A matrix verb may intervene between μόνος and Yı

(60) μόνην δ᾽ ἂν μοι δοκοῦμεν ταύτην τοῖς ἐνθάδε κειμένοις ἀποδοῦναι
      χάριν Lys 2.75.

In all the instances cited, μόν- associates with the narrow scope focus on the modifier in hyperbaton, not with the noun nor with the verb nor with the

(56) If they altered only a single syllable (Aesch 3.192). In this court alone (Dem 23.66). Only three votes (Dem 23.167).

(57) To worship only the ancestral gods (Her 1.172). To be convicted by only a single vote (Dem 21.75). I shall mention only a single action (Isoc *Pan* 127).

(58) They are injuring the whole of Greece, not only their own countries (Dem 19.11).

(59) So read for me just this one more letter, and foget about the rest (Dem 23.162). Having been forced to undertake only these public services (Isae 5.36). They hear only that song clearly (Pl *Ion* 536c). The law forbids only these women... (Dem 59.86). Only this argument remained intact (Pl *Gorg* 527b).

(60) This seems to me to be the only thanks we can give to those who lie here (Lys 2.75).

whole verb phrase. It explicitly excludes those members of the set of alternates denoted by the noun (plus the rest of the restriction) that are not in the subset denoted by the Y1 modifier.

The difference between putting μόν- in the position preceding and in the position following the modifier may involve the relative importance of identification ('THESE alone') and exclusion ('ONLY these'). In the former case, the modifier is likely to be new information and the focus operator *only* adds explicit exclusivity. In the latter case, the modifier could be old information; then the new information is just the fact of exclusivity and the whole rest of the assertion is already presupposed. This pragmatic distinction may not correlate systematically with the syntax. However, it is interesting that in Demosthenes 59.86 just cited, which has the order μόναις ταύταις, the demonstrative, while contrastive, refers to a previously introduced category of women; the emphasis is on the exclusivity; the fact that these women are forbidden to attend the sacrifices has already been established a few lines above; the point is that all other women are permitted to do so. In Demosthenes 23.162, also just cited, which has the order ταύτην μόνην, ταύτην presents a new letter and μόνην actually gets reinforced by τὰς δ᾽ ἄλλας ἔα.

Particles

Here are a couple of examples of the contrastive particle μέν narrowly associating with a Y1 modifier in hyperbaton

(61)   τοῦτο μὲν οὖν παράνομον ἦν τὸ ψήφισμα... ἐκείνοις δὲ τοῖς προτέροις ψηφίσμασι... Dem 7.25
ἅπαντας μὲν οὖν χρὴ νομίζειν μεγάλους εἶναι τοὺς δημοσίους ἀγῶνας... μάλιστα δὲ τοῦτον Lyc 7.

Here are some examples with καί 'also, too, even' and γέ 'at least':

(62)   πρὸς γὰρ τοῖς ἄλλοις κακοῖς καὶ τοῦθ᾽ εὕρηνται σόφισμα Dem 55.31
εἰ δὲ καὶ ταύτης κύριος τῆς χώρας γενήσεται Dem 3.16
ἐὰν μή τι καὶ τῶν τοιούτων φθέγξηται ῥημάτων Aesch 1.38
ταύτης γε μετέχειν τῆς ἀρετῆς Pl *Prot* 323a.

Note that while *only* explicitly excludes the alternatives, *also* includes them and *even* includes them with the connotation that the proposition applies to them more predictably than it does to the focus. This association of the Y1 modifier in hyperbaton with focus particles is one of the clearest indications that the Y1

(61) This decree was unconstitutional... but to those earlier decrees... (Dem 7.25). One ought to think that all public trials are important... but particularly this one (Lyc 7).

(62) In addition to their other evil deeds, they have dreamed up this scheme too (Dem 55.31). If he becomes master of this land too (Dem 3.16). Without also using some of this type of disgraceful language (Aesch 1.38). To share in this excellence (Pl *Prot* 323a).

position is not simply assigned to weak focus quantifiers and restrictive modifiers but is indeed a strong focus position.

Negation

It is not clear exactly how negation is applied to sentences with strong narrow focus. Take a sentence like

> Jack didn't read AESCHYLUS last night.

On one approach, we have a simple propositional negation of the corresponding positive sentence, and the semantics of focus is carried over from the positive sentence

> NOT (Jack read AESCHYLUS last night).

Another approach treats negation as a two-place operator with a presuppositional restrictive clause and association with focus, like *only*

> NOT (Jack read x last night) (x = Aeschylus).

Negative declarations are rather uninformative creatures. They do not usually give a complete list of the entities for which the negative declaration holds, but just cite an example. In a conversation about Greek tragedians, the above example does not mean that Aeschylus was the only author that Jack did not read last night; perhaps he also did not read Sophocles. Strong focus associating with a negative is not like a simple strong focus but more like a contrastive focus. The set of alternatives is evoked and contrasted with the focus, but it is not necessarily asserted, except in a situation in which there are two alternates one of which is presupposed to be true. If the above sentence is uttered with the intonation appropriate to ordinary exclusive focus, the negative does not associate with the focus and the sentence means 'Aeschylus is the author that Jack failed to read last night.'

Negative focus also agrees with contrastive focus in triggering the same sort of implicatures. Our example will normally be interpreted to mean that Jack did read an author other than Aeschylus (more precisely that he did read some or all of the complement of Aeschylus within the domain of relevant authors). However, this implicature can easily be cancelled

> Jack didn't read AESCHYLUS last night; in fact he didn't read any author at all, but went out drinking with his friends.

With the qualification that the restrictor clause is more like an implicature than a presupposition, we will adopt a framework in which negation associates with strong narrow focus, resulting in structures parallel to those already given for association with *only*

> He doesn't wear RED shirts (Yı focus: some other colour)
> NOT (he wears P shirts) (P = red)

He doesn't wear red SHIRTS (Y2 focus: some other red garment)
NOT (he wears red x) (x = shirts)
He doesn't wear RED SHIRTS (YP focus: some other garment)
NOT (he wears x) (x = red shirts).

The negative may also associate with the verb (he doesn't wear them, he sells them) or more broadly with the verb phrase (he doesn't wear red shirts, but he does vote communist).

In hyperbaton, as predicted, the negative normally associates narrowly with the Y₁ modifier

(63)   οὐκ ἂν ἑτέρων ἔδει σοι μαρτύρων Lys 7.22, cp. Aesch 3.119
μὴ μικροψύχου ποιεῖν ἔργον ἀνθρώπου Dem 18.269
ἔστιν ἡσυχία δικαία... ἀλλ᾽ οὐ ταύτην οὗτος ἄγει τὴν ἡσυχίαν
        Dem 18.308
οὐδὲν ἐλάττονος ἄξιον σπουδῆς Dem 18.5
τὴν Ἑλλάδα πᾶσαν, οὐχὶ τὰς ἰδίας ἀδικοῦσι μόνον πατρίδας
        Dem 19.11
οὐ μικρὰς ἔχομεν αἰτίας Isae 10.20
οὔτι πάντας ἄγων τοὺς Μινύας, ἀλλ᾽ ὀλίγους τινάς Her 4.148.

A couple of points call for further comment. In most of these examples, there is verb phrase or sentential negation and the negative associates with the focused Y₁ adjective. The result is that the antonym or polar opposite is implicated: for instance, in Lysias 7.22 ¬ἑτέρων = τῶν αὐτῶν. However, in Isaeus 10.20 we seem to have rather simple lexical negation with regular focus on the resulting positive adjective: *no small* = *large*. Secondly, association of a negative with different foci usually has pragmatic rather than semantic consequences, as noted in the next section: 'he doesn't wear RED shirts' versus 'he doesn't wear red SHIRTS.' However, semantic distinctions can arise with some quantifiers, as illustrated by the last example (Herodotus 4.148). The text in this example means that the number of Minyans that Theras took with him was not equal to the entire number of Minyans; if, on the other hand, the negative had not associated narrowly with the quantifier but with the verb (so that the quantifier was outside the scope of the negative), it would have meant that the number of Minyans that Theras took with him was zero (οὐκ ἄγων = 'leaving behind').

---

(63) You would not need other witnesses (Lys 7.22). Not to behave like a meansiprited person (Dem 18.269). There is a type of disengagement which is just... but that is not the sort of disengagement that this man practises (Dem 18.308). Meriting equally serious attention from me (Dem 18.5). They are injuring the whole of Greece, not only their own countries (Dem 19.11). We have no small reasons (Isae 10.20). Taking not all the Minyans, but just a few (Her 4.148).

MEANING AND SYNTAX

Some linguistic facts—for instance, that the word *table* has a *t* in it—are idiosyncratic, arbitrary and not motivated by any general linguistic principle or mechanism. Other facts recur in a variety of unrelated languages and reflect discernible general properties of language. The prosodic mechanisms that typically signal focus in English, pitch obtrusion and increase in duration and intensity, have an immediately recognizable iconic origin: items that are informationally more significant are made substantively higher (or lower) toned, longer lasting and louder. However, it remains a prima facie mystery why launching phrases into discontinuous fragments should be related to focus in any way. As a first step to answering this question, we shall briefly review some logical representations that have been suggested for focus.

There is no particular reason why logical analysis should be restricted to semantic meaning; it is a very useful tool for the elucidation of pragmatic meaning too. Focus can contribute to both types of meaning. Weak focus typically relates to pragmatic meaning:

$$[\text{BRUTUS}]_{\text{WK FOC}} \text{ stabbed Caesar}$$

is true in the same situations as

$$\text{Brutus stabbed } [\text{CAESAR}]_{\text{WK FOC}}.$$

The two assertions are just designed to fit different gaps in the information store of the listener. In the former case, the speaker takes it that the listener knows that Caesar got stabbed, but does not know who did it; in the latter case, that he knows that Brutus stabbed at least one person but not who got stabbed. In both cases weak focus is noncommittal about the distinction between a complete and a partial answer to the implicit question raised by the discourse context. The situation with strong focus is rather different. We have conservatively referred to the exhaustive and exclusive component in the meaning of strong focus as an implicature. But it is quite a strong implicature, and to the extent that it is not easily defeasible, it contributes to semantic meaning.

$$[\text{BRUTUS}]_{\text{STR FOC}} \text{ stabbed Caesar}$$

is a false answer to the question 'Who stabbed Caesar?', unless the other conspirators are pragmatically discounted and subsumed under the name of Brutus. Contrastive anaphors and, as already noted, adverbials associated with focus can also involve semantic meaning

Jack punched Bill and then he kicked him / ...HE kicked HIM
She always has COFFEE for breakfast / ...coffee for BREAKFAST.

Five main theories of focus have been proposed over the last thirty years. Two of these are one-dimensional: the predicational or cleft theory and the movement or operator-variable theory. The other three are two-dimensional:

the in situ interpretation theory (known as alternative semantics), the structured meaning theory, and the higher order unification theory. We shall review them in that order (as best we can, since some of this literature gets rather technical).

Predicational theory

Take a simple broad scope focus sentence like

Hector killed Patroclus.

Let K stand for *killed*, *h* for *Hector* and *p* for *Patroclus*. Then in simple predicate logic, abstracting away from tense, our sentence can be represented as follows: $K(h,p)$. This can be taken to mean that Hector and Patroclus stand in the killing relation such that Hector is the killer and Patroclus gets killed. In a compositional, Montague style semantics, the representation would be a bit more structured: $(K(p))(h)$, equivalent to $\lambda x[(K(p))(x)](h)$, meaning that Hector has the property of killing Patroclus or is a member of the set of those killing Patroclus. This captures the subject-predicate structure using lambda abstraction. (Lambda is a type of set-generating operator.) Now take a cleft sentence like

It was Hector that killed Patroclus,

the cleft being a quintessential strong focus construction. One early proposal (Gazdar 1979) simply represented the cleft by lambda abstracting on the focused item, in this particular sentence yielding a representation no different from the one just given. This suggests that something is missing, since the pragmatic meaning of the cleft is not the same as that of broad scope focus. The cleft makes the presupposition that someone killed Patroclus, while the simple broad scope focus does not. Furthermore, the cleft typically conveys exhaustiveness. Finally in this particular cleft the subject-predicate relation seems to have been reversed. In the simple sentence *killed Patroclus* is predicated of Hector, whereas in the cleft version the focus material seems to be predicated of the rest of the sentence, that is of the presupposition. To remedy these problems, a more complex representation was proposed for clefts (Atlas & Levinson 1981): adapting for a singular subject, $\lambda x(x = h)\ (\iota x K(x,p))$, 'the individual that has the property of killing Patroclus has the property of being identical to Hector.' The subject-predicate reversal is achieved by independently justifiable type shifting operations, which reverse the referential and predicative roles of the simple sentence. The lambda operator maps an entity onto the property of being that entity; so it maps Hector onto the property of being Hector, which allows a predicative reading for a referential expression like Hector. The iota operator is used to achieve the inverse result, namely to map a property onto the unique entity having that property; so it maps the property of killing Patroclus onto the entity having that property, Patroclus' killer. One can think of these type shifting operations as analogous to morphological operations forming verbal nouns like infinitives and gerunds from verbs.

Finally, we come to the simple strong focus version of our sentence:

> HECTOR killed Patroclus.

According to the predicational theory of focus (Löbner 1990:168), this has just the representation accorded the cleft in the preceding paragraph. This is tantamount to saying that clefts are simply syntactic spellouts of the logical representation of strong focus. The rather radical school of generative semantics, which used complex and abstract transformational derivations as a syntax-semantics interface, even produced the suggestion that in English simple focus was syntactically derived from an underlying cleft. Although there are serious problems with this idea for English (Jackendoff 1972), it was pointed out that such a derivation was plausible as a diachronic development in some languages (Takizala 1973). Relative clauses, which are a typical ingredient of cleft constructions (Schachter 1973), are a classical example of a syntactic operator (the relative pronoun) fulfilling a function comparable to that of a semantic operator. Our example 'HECTOR killed Patroclus' is interpreted as 'The one who killed Patroclus is HECTOR,' i.e. the unique individual in the denotation of the relative clause is Hector. The relative clause ranges over a contextually given set of Trojan warriors and picks out the one who killed Patroclus; the latter is then equated with Hector.

At all events, the essential insight of the predicational theory of focus is that, whatever the grammatical structure of the sentence, in its informational structure the focus is the predicate. The focus structure imposes a superpredication on the sentence, and the main grammatical predication is reduced to a subpredication. So in a hyperbaton sentence like

> The RED shirts were sold

the adjective is the informational predicate, even though grammatically it is embedded in the subject noun phrase. In its strong focus version, this is not a "thetic" sentence with a nontopical predicate internal subject ('The next thing that happened was that the red shirts got sold.') but an inverted predicational sentence ('The shirts that got sold were the red ones.'). A subordinate predicate (*red*) has become the primary predicate, and the primary predicate (*sold*) has been subordinated.

Movement theory

The movement theory identifies the focus and separates it from the presupposition by overt or covert syntactic movement. A syntactic operator-variable relationship results between the moved focus and its trace, similar to that obtaining between a scoped quantifier and its trace. The syntactic variable is thought of as a counterpart to the variable in predicate logic, and the operator as a counterpart of the quantifier that specifies the quantification applied to the variable. In a simple sentence such as

Prof. Jones likes Jack

Jack is interpreted as directly referring, but in a sentence such as

Prof. Jones likes everyone

everyone cannot be interpreted as being directly referential like *Jack*; so the sentence is interpreted as

'For all x, where x is human, Prof. Jones likes x,'

x being a variable that ranges over all the humans that Prof. Jones knows or all those that are relevant to the current discourse. In a sentence like

Every student spent Christmas in his home town

we need to range over students and their respective home towns. Similarly, a sentence with focus such as

Prof. Jones likes JACK

is interpreted as

'For x = Jack, Prof. Jones likes x,'

and a sentence with double focus like

PROF. JONES likes JACK

is interpreted as

'For x = Prof. Jones, y = Jack, x likes y.'

In this respect variables are rather like the pronoun *it* in a sentence such as

Every time Prof. Jones writes a book, *it* gets good reviews,

in which *it* ranges over the various books written by Prof. Jones. Interrogatives are focus-related: for instance, in Yoruba interrogative words and focused phrases are both extracted and placed sentence initially followed by the focus particle *ni* (Carstens 1985). Like focus, interrogatives can also be thought of as involving some form of quantifying operation or variable binding: interrogatives are sometimes called "quasi-quantificational."

Who does Prof. Jones like?

is interpreted as

'For x = who, Prof. Jones likes x?'.

The idea is that all one needs to do to interpret *Jack* is to retrieve the corresponding entity, but interpreting *everyone* or a focused or interrogative item requires some form of computation ranging over various entities, in which the entities are separate from the slot in the sentence into which they are inserted; and that this operator-variable articulation is needed not only for an artificial truth-conditionally oriented language like predicate logic, but also at some interpretive level of natural language to account for observable syntactic regularities associated with focus that, either overtly or covertly, mimic the posited quantifying process. In the first place, many languages, including English, move interrogative words to a peripheral operator position; Hungarian can move quantifiers to their proper peripheral scopal positions in the surface syntax. Similarly, a number of languages have a fixed slot into which focused words, often including interrogatives, are moved from their canonical positions in the clause. Why would all sorts of unrelated languages take focused words and interrogatives out of their regular positions and put them into a dedicated slot if not to serve some interpretive purpose? Secondly, some languages have rules of pronominal reference in which quantifiers and focused words, which remain in situ, behave like interrogatives, which are extracted. Here are some typical examples; the subscript i indicates coreference:

> His$_i$ mother LOVES Jack$_i$ (both arguments tail)
> *His$_i$ mother loves JACK$_i$ (focus on Jack)
> *His$_i$ mother loves everyone$_i$ (quantifier)
> *Who$_i$ does his$_i$ mother love? (interrogative)
> ?Which man$_i$ does his$_i$ mother love? (specific interrogative).

The phenomenon is called weak crossover because, in a language like English, the extracted object was thought to pass over the possessive pronoun on its way to the operator position. Coreference is impossible both with interrogatives and with quantifiers and focused objects, which suggests that the latter are interpretively moved just as the former are overtly moved. Such movement was supposed to take place at an abstract syntactic level of representation called logical form, at which the overt syntax is massaged to prepare it for semantic interpretation, particularly with respect to scopal relations. Whatever factor or combination of factors is invoked to explain the much-discussed phenomenon of weak crossover (argument ranking, phrase structure, linear precedence), the question remains why strong focus behaves in a number of examples like a syntactic operator.

A third, less familiar item of evidence involves the availability of collective interpretations with numerals and quantifiers like *many*. Consider a sentence such as

> Seven students carried the piano upstairs.

This naturally gets a collective interpretation: the piano was carried upstairs by a group of seven students. However, when the quantifier is focused (not in metalinguistic counterassertion), it tends to get a distributive interpretation even in a contextually improbable example like ours: the number of students who individually performed acts of carrying the piano upstairs was seven. Perhaps the focus restructures the sentence by moving the quantifier to a position from which it naturally gets a distributive reading. Note again the association of focus with quantification in the narrow sense of ranging over a set of individuals.

The movement theory is a theory of covert (and for some languages like Greek, overt) syntax: it needs to be taken in conjunction with some assumptions about semantic interpretation. When it was originally suggested (Chomsky 1976), it was endowed with an equational semantics similar to that of the predicational theory ('The *x* such that Prof. Jones likes *x* is Jack.'). So movement theory could be understood as setting the structural stage for predicational interpretation.

The main empirically based criticism of the movement theory has involved the phenomenon of syntactic islands. The problem, which is interesting both in its own right and because hyperbaton itself is a prima facie island violation, is too complex to discuss here in more than its briefest outline. Movement in logical form is supposed to mimic overt syntactic movement (that was one of the main arguments for the existence of a separate level of logical form). Even with interrogatives, this principle creates some difficulties. Take a sentence like

Inspector Parker interviewed the reporter who met the diplomat.

Complex noun phrases, such as noun phrases containing relative clauses, tend to be strong islands. (Exceptions like Hindi topicalization [Dwivedi 1994] are supposed not to involve movement.) So we cannot extract a question word out of the relative clause and put it in the main clause interrogative slot

*Who did Inspector Parker interview the reporter who met?

According to the principle in question, languages that allow interrogatives to remain in situ should not permit this type of question either. However, in Japanese regular questions like

You read books that who wrote?

are fine. With focus, the principle breaks down massively

Inspector Parker only interviewed the reporter who met the eyewitness who had seen the DIPLOMAT.

If relative clauses are islands, the focus *diplomat* cannot be moved to a position adjacent to the focus operator *only*. Yet, while the sentence is a bit difficult to compute, it is certainly not ungrammatical (although apparently some speakers differentiate bare focus and association with focus in this regard [Culicover 1993]). The response to these problems has been very similar for interrogatives and for focus. On one approach, the idea that movement in logical form is sensitive to island constraints is rejected outright ("no subjacency at LF"). Another approach distinguishes the focus from the focus phrase, typically the complete argument or adjunct phrase in which the focus is embedded (Nishigauchi 1990; Fiengo et al. 1988; Drubig 1994; Kiss 1995; Krifka 1996). It is the whole focus phrase rather than just the focus that moves. So piedpiping would not be merely a property of overt syntax, but would extend to logical form. According to a third proposal, the nested focus analysis (Rooth 1996), the focus sensitive domain is expanded cyclically from the most embedded phrase to the complete noun phrase, a solution that is reminiscent both of the cyclical movement of interrogatives through complementizer slots, and also of the focus phrase theory just noted, in that the focus operator associates with the focus via the intermediary of a larger structure that does not violate island constraints. These proposals help to resolve the apparent difference in locality constraint between association with focus and focus in ellipsis construal, as in the following gapping example

> The Classics Department only appointed the guy who studies TIBERIUS and the History Department NAPOLEON.

Two-dimensional theories

These theories originated from the perceived need to identify and interpret focus in the semantics without any preparatory syntactic movement of the focused constituent in logical form, given the problem of insensitivity to islands just mentioned. We call these theories two-dimensional, since they posit a second layer of representation in addition to the regular one. The best known of these theories is the socalled alternative semantics (Rooth 1985, 1992), which was developed for sentences where *only* associates with focus and then generalized to other types of focus

> Mary only introduced BILL to Sue.

The focused phrase is said to have two semantic values, its ordinary semantic value and its focus semantic value, the latter reflecting the set of alternates. Focus is perceived to involve an additional component of meaning (besides the simple propositional content of the sentence), which relates the sentence to the set of pragmatically related sentences. The syntactic domain of *only*, the verb phrase in the above example, is assigned as the domain of the focus semantic value. The set of alternates {Jack, Peter, Charles, Bill} is not accessed directly but via the set of verb phrase alternates {introduce Jack to Sue, introduce Peter to Sue, etc.}. Focus quantifies over the properties expressed by the verb phrase and its alternatives; it encodes a relation between the real verb phrase and the set of alternatives to the verb phrase, such that if Mary has a contextually relevant property of the form 'introducing y to Sue,' extensionally $\lambda x[\text{introduce } (x,y,s)]$, then it is the property 'introducing Bill to Sue', $\lambda x[\text{introduce } (x,b,s)]$. The theory is evidently designed to explain focus in situ, which is just what prose hyperbaton is not. However, the concept of the verb phrase as a domain of quantification for *only* or as a possible domain for narrow bare focus is very suggestive, particularly the idea of introducing a syntactically covert phrase level focus operator at (for English) the level of logical form (Rooth 1992)

> Mary [[introduced BILL to Sue]$_{VP}$ FOC]$_{VP}$.

The next two-dimensional theory is the structured meaning theory. This theory accesses the focused entity more directly than is possible in alternative semantics. Focus is thought to induce an additional partition of the meaning of the clause into two parts, a background part (presuppositional frame) and a focus part. When the former is applied to the latter, the ordinary semantic representation results. The partitioned structure is seen as an argument of the focus operator, whereas in alternative semantics the two arguments were the phrase in the focus domain and the set of alternates. Sticking with the familiar "introduction" example, we get the following type of structured meaning representation: ONLY ($\langle \lambda x$[introduce (m,x,s)], $b \rangle$) 'Mary only introduced BILL to Sue.' One interesting feature of this theory is the suggestion (Jacobs 1991) that bare focus involves a silent focus operator, referred to as ASSERT, that associates with or binds the focus in its domain, just as *only* does: ASSERT ($\langle \lambda x$[introduce (m,x,s)], $b \rangle$) 'Mary introduced BILL to Sue.' It is a natural step to link such a semantic representation with the syntactic operator representation of the movement theory. Positing an ASSERT or FOCUS operator also allows bare focus to be thought of in terms of the familiar tripartite operator structure (Partee 1995; Roberts 1995; von Fintel 1994)

FOC (Mary introduced x to Sue) (x = Bill).

The restrictor of the operator is the presuppositional frame and the nuclear scope is the assertion (here, strong focus represented equationally). The suitability of this structure for representing strong focus is not coincidental. The operation of ranging through alternates and/or exhaustively excluding those not corresponding to the focus is akin to quantification. The relationship between focus and interrogatives can be included if focus operators are thought of as quantifying over possible answers to an implicit question. For reasons that will become apparent in the next section, it helps to think of the tripartite structure in the order FOCUS – nuclear scope – restrictor, rather than in the more usual order with the restrictor preceding the nuclear scope (which we shall continue to use for quantifiers in deference to the syntactic continuity of adnominal quantification).

The third theory is the higher order unification theory (Pulman 1997). This theory builds on the parallel between focus and ellipsis. Unlike alternative semantics, it can access the focused item directly, and unlike structured meanings, it is not so bound by ordinary constituency, although in many respects the theories seem quite similar. Consider a bare argument ellipsis like the second clause in the following example

Caesar slaughtered the Gauls; and the Germans too.

Resolution of ellipsis can be thought of as a procedure rather like using a macro (user defined key or variable) in word processing: information that has already been used is reinstantiated and combined with new information. Simple syntactic approaches to ellipsis resolution (not involving movement at logical form) require the string *Caesar slaughtered* to be copied over from the antecedent clause to the elliptical clause (or deleted from the latter), and ordinary semantic approaches to ellipsis require the semantic translation of the same string to be copied over. These approaches are not quite straightforward because *Caesar slaughtered* is, according to our usual phrase-structural notions, not a syntactic or semantic constituent, just a string of words (Reinhart 1991). Higher order unification is a logical tool that allows information to be combined without any particular dependency on the semantic translation of syntactic constituents. The antecedent clause is decomposed in such a way that a predicate is abstracted and applied to an element parallel to the remnant material in the ellipsed clause. In our example, the antecedent is decomposed into λx[slaughtered (Caesar, x)] (the Gauls), and then the lambda abstract is applied to *the Germans*, thereby resolving the ellipsis (Dalrymple et al. 1991). Now, in the elliptical clause, the ellipsed material is repeated and consequently presupposed background material (even if it was focused in the antecedent clause), whereas the material that appears overtly includes the new or contrastive information, that is the focus (in our example, *the Germans*). So if the theory is one possible way of handling sentences in which the presupposition is ellipsed, perhaps it could also be used for sentences in which the presupposition is overt. The evoked alternate sentences correspond to the antecedent of the ellipsis, and the focus structure controls the decomposition directly rather than indirectly through an ellipsis. The particular relationship between Yı hyperbaton and ellipsis is explored in chapter 6.

To recapitulate: In the movement theory, the focus is separated from the presupposition at logical form. In the structured meaning and unification theories, the abstracted presupposition is predicated of the focus. In the predicational theory, the focus is predicated of the presupposition, which reflects the pragmatic structure more faithfully.

Hyperbaton

We have just conducted a brief and nontechnical survey of a range of abstract and hypothetical logical machinery proposed by various formal semanticists, most of whom are probably not particularly familiar with the phenomenon of hyperbaton. In fact, one of the island violation arguments adduced against the movement theory of focus was just that hyperbaton is impossible (scil. in English). What is so interesting is that, confronted with the problem of focus in English, these analysts came up with formulations in terms of just those properties that are overt and empirically discernible syntactic characteristics of hyperbaton in Greek — the separation of the focus from the presuppositional frame and a phrasal domain for the focus operator, the latter most conspicuously in alternative semantics, the former, in one guise or another, in the other theories.

The combination of these two principles leads directly to a theory of hyperbaton. Suppose that the phrasal domain for the focus operator associating with a focused modifier Y_1 in Greek is just a projection of X, so that we get cross-categorial focus domains of the type

> only wore a RED shirt
> only in the BLUE car
> only proud of his ELDER daughter
> only a composer of MINOR symphonies

(64)   FOC μετασχόντα [θηλείας] φύσεως cp. Pl *Laws* 872e

　　　FOC μετασχὼν [ἁπάντων] τῶν πόνων τῇ πόλει cp. Aesch 3.191

　　　FOC περὶ [τῶν ἄλλων] νομέων cp. Pl *Polit* 268b

　　　FOC μεστὸν [πολλῶν] ἀγαθῶν cp. Pl *Laws* 906a

　　　FOC παρεμβολῇ [ἑτέρων] πραγμάτων cp. Aesch 3.205.

The phrasal domain of the focus operator endows it with a minimal functional complex within which it is interpreted, by including the head X in its domain. Now suppose, again following alternative semantics, that the operator FOC is assigned a syntactic node that c-commands its domain. The syntactic property of c-command actuates in the syntax the domain of the logical operator. This idea can be executed in a couple of different ways. The first, which we will use because it is simplest, is to make the operator node the specifier position in XP. A more abstract and articulated approach is to make it the head of a functional projection 'Focus Phrase.' Either way, at this stage we have a mismatch between the posited syntax and the pragmatic structure. The syntax has a bipartite structure

　　　FOC [X YP (Z)].

Any linear order or hierarchical structure inside the focus domain is grammatically determined. (In this formulation, we have made XP head initial and ignored the relative order of elements inside YP.) But the focus structure is not bipartite but tripartite; in other words, FOC is a two-place rather than a one-place operator. It requires a distinction inside XP between focus and presupposition:

　　　FOC (nuclear scope) (restriction)

if, for focus, we use the order with restriction last, as already suggested. In a language which allows the syntax to satisfy the structure of pragmatic meaning, the focused constituent will be taken out of the core XP and placed in a separate position corresponding to the nuclear scope (or to the operator), in syntactic terms a specifier c-commanding the core XP. Since the syntax permits

---

(64) Sharing in female nature (Pl *Laws* 872e). Sharing all its toils with the city (Aesch 3.191). Concerning the other herdsmen (Pl *Polit* 268b). Full of many good things (Pl *Laws* 906a). By the introduction of extraneous matters (Aesch 3.205).

piedpiping, one possible result of this is simply the location of the whole of YP in the specifier node, giving the type

> θηλείας φύσεως μετασχόντα
> πολλῶν ἀγάθων μεστὸν
> ἑτέρων πραγμάτων παρεμβολῇ.

It remains possible that the modifier was string vacuously fronted within the noun phrase (Speas 1991). But since Greek syntax also allows discontinuity, another syntactically licit option is to place just the Υı focus in the specifier node, giving a more faithful syntactic implementation of the pragmatic structure

> θηλείας μετασχόντα φύσεως Pl *Laws* 872e
> ἁπάντων μετασχὼν τῶν πόνων τῇ πόλει Aesch 3.191
> τῶν ἄλλων πέρι νομέων Pl *Polit* 268b
> πολλῶν μεστὸν ἀγαθῶν Pl *Laws* 906a
> ἑτέρων παρεμβολῇ πραγμάτων Aesch 3.205.

This, of course, is Υı hyperbaton. Trees to illustrate the derivation, with and without a separate Focus Phrase, are given in Figure 2.2. Note that in the structure with a separate Focus Phrase, the head position (FOC) is just that which is occupied by overt illocutionary verbs in the account of complement clause hyperbaton in chapter 3.

According to the idea just proposed, the syntax constructs surface expressions that correspond to structured units of pragmatic meaning. The question of what licenses Greek syntax to ignore the semantic structure of modification in favour of the pragmatic structure of focus is the subject of chapters 4 and 6. According to the theory of hyperbaton developed in those chapters, Υı is

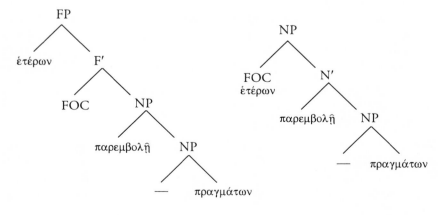

Figure 2.2
Υı hyperbaton with and without a focus phrase
ἑτέρων παρεμβολῇ πραγμάτων

mostly interpreted as a null head modifier and Y1 foci mainly range over entities, corresponding to (null head) syntactic noun phrases. It may be that one of the effects of strong focus on modifiers is to turn them into null head noun phrases. As the theory provisionally stands at this point, Y1 focus will have to range over modifiers and quantifiers (corresponding syntactically to adjectives in Greek), which will require a more complex and less uniform semantics for focus in noun phrases. For instance, there will be tripartite structures like 'FOC P, P = red, he was wearing a shirt that had the property P.' This is also the case for socalled "categorial" analyses of questions, which abstract over the queried category (Hausser & Zaefferer 1979), and so can capture the relationship between queried and focused constituents.

There is a further complication involving the relation of the hyperbaton tripartite structure to the canonical tripartite structure based on the relational approach to generalized quantifiers. In a broad scope (sentential) focus reading of a sentence

> All the hoplites attacked

the tripartite structure is ALL (x is a hoplite) (x attacked). So the quantifier is the operator, the noun is the restrictor and the predicate is the nuclear scope, and the sentence expresses the quantificational relationship between those who are hoplites and those who attacked. From the pragmatic perspective, in this sentence the quantifier and the nuclear scope are new information and the subject noun is presupposed or topical. Single narrow scope focus can modify these assignments. The quantifier can end up as part of the presupposition or it can itself be the focus

> All the HOPLITES attacked
> ALL the hoplites attacked
> Only all the HOPLITES attacked (association with focus).

In such cases, the discourse seems to superimpose the pragmatic structure on the basic quantificational structure. It can also superimpose a new focus structure on a previously established one

> A. He only taught GRADUATE students on Mondays
> B. Actually, he only taught graduate students on FRIDAYS.

Phrasal domain of hyperbaton

It has been said of Hungarian that it is a language that wears its logical form on its sleeve (Szabolcsi 1997). In the matter of focus-presupposition structure, we have identified a similar propensity in Greek. In fact, a sentence in which a Y1 (or a simple focused constituent) has sentential scope and the subject is postverbal

(65)   πολλὴν γὰρ πάνυ κατέλιπεν ὁ πατὴρ αὐτῷ οὐσίαν Aesch 1.42

(65) For his father left him a very great deal of property (Aesch 1.42).

directly encodes in its surface syntax the structure posited by the predicational theory, according to which the subject of the predication is not ὁ πατὴρ but the whole presupposition of which ὁ πατὴρ is just one component. What is particularly interesting about Greek is that this propensity does not merely involve a single clausal division between focus and presupposition, but extends down to the level of the phrase. Each [X YP]$_{XP}$ phrase is treated as a minipredication with its own subsidiary focus-presupposition structure. It is a reasonable speculation that this less integrated, more textured focus structure may be a residue of the less integrated and more paratactic syntax of prehistoric Greek. In this less configurational type of syntax, smaller focus constituents are placed at the edge of smaller focus domains. This is because all modifiers (not merely focused ones) are more independent than they are in languages like English, and because instead of a single integrated clause this stage of the language tends to operate with smaller paratactic phrases, which in turn produce smaller domains for focus and other word order rules. We can illustrate this with the following Homeric pastiche

(66)   [τόν δ᾽ ἴφθιμος βάλεν Αἴας]
         [τείχει ὕπο Τρώων] [Ἑλένης πόσιν ἠϋκόμοιο]
         [δεξιτερὸν κατὰ μαζὸν].

Each hemistich is a separate syntactic and prosodic phrase, and within each of these phrases the modifier and its noun are arranged in such a way that they are separated by the superordinate head. The availability of a phrasal focus position in classical prose is a residue of this type of syntax. We present this theory of hyperbaton in detail in chapter 4.

Islands for hyperbaton

Since we are interpreting Yı hyperbaton in prose in terms of (real or metaphorical) focus movement, we need to return briefly to the question of islands. By definition, noun phrases are not islands for hyperbaton, but it does not follow that hyperbaton should be insensitive to islands in general. In other words, just because in Greek modifiers can escape out of their noun phrases, that does not mean that they can also escape out of their clauses. Consider the following English sentences

> I saw the man whose accomplice stabbed Caesar.
> You saw the man whose accomplice stabbed who?
> *Who did you see the man whose accomplice stabbed?

> Prof. Jones went to lunch after he had finished his paper on Tibullus
> Prof. Jones went to lunch after he had finished what?
> *What did Prof. Jones go to lunch after he had finished?

(66) The strong Ajax hit him with a missile, beneath the wall of the Trojans, husband of Helen with the lovely hair, on the right breast.

In the first set of examples, an interrogative is wrongly extracted out of a relative clause, in the second set out of an adjunct temporal clause; consequently, such clauses are islands for interrogative extraction. At least with certain matrix verbs, finite indirect statements, being complement clauses, are less constrained than adjunct clauses like temporal and causal clauses

> What did you believe that Prof. Jones said?
> *What did you leave when Prof. Jones said?

Although statistical proof may not be feasible, there are a number of subordinate clauses having finite verbs that, unlike infinitival complement clauses discussed in chapter 3, are probably islands for hyperbaton. The claim is that even though hyperbaton is more common in main clauses than in subordinate clauses for purely pragmatic reasons, there is a further properly syntactic constraint against the extraction of a Y element out of these clauses. We will refer to hyperbaton that crosses the clause boundary as long hyperbaton.

The claim that hyperbaton is essentially clause bound does not refer to the fronting of a topical Y element ahead of the complementizer slot (probably adjunction to CP)

> (67)   μάρτυρες δ᾽ εἰ μὲν πολλοὶ παρεγένοντο Antiph 2.9 (Y2 quantifier)

nor to the embedding of an entire subordinate clause within a main clause in such a way that it is straddled by YP

> (68)   μάρτυρας, ὡς ἀφῆκα αὐτὸν τῶν ἐγκλημάτων, παρέσχετο ψευδεῖς
>   Dem 45.5 (Y2 hyperbaton).

Further, it does not rest simply on the distance between Y1 and Y2, nor on instances where minimality problems might, at least temporarily, make it unclear which noun phrase was governed by which verb, as in the following example (in which we have modified a passage with hyperbaton entirely within a subordinate clause to create an island violation)

> (69)   (*)ταύτην τότε εἰσβάλλουσιν εἰς τὸ πλοῖον τὸ γραμματείδιον ἵνα
>   ἔχοιεν ἐμοὶ τὴν αἰτίαν ἐπιφέρειν (cp. Antiph 5.55 ἵνα ταύτην
>   ἔχοιεν ἐμοὶ τὴν αἰτίαν): purpose clause;

taking ταύτην as a null head modifier results in a garden path effect.

The following examples, modified as above, illustrate the sort of island constraints that seem to apply to hyperbaton

(67) If there had been many witnesses (Antiph 2.9).
(68) He produced false witnesses to the effect that I had released him from the charges (Dem 45.5).
(69) Then they dropped the note into the boat, so that they could have this charge to bring against me (Antiph 5.55).

(70)   (*)τὴν δὲ προτέραν συνέβαινε ὅτε ἐπρεσβεύομεν πρεσβείαν
       ἐμοὶ... ἀπιέναι (cp. Aesch 2.82 ὅτε τὴν προτέραν ἐπρεσβεύομεν
       πρεσβείαν): temporal clause

       (*)ἐν αὐτῷ οὐδὲν ἴσασι πρίν γ' ἤδη ὦσι τῷ κακῷ (cp. Antiph 1.29
       πρίν γ' ἤδη ἐν αὐτῷ ὦσι τῷ κακῷ): temporal clause

       (*)πάντα τὰ τοιαῦτ' ἄξιός εἰμι ἐπαίνου τυχεῖν ὅτι προηρούμην
       πολιτεύματα (cp. Dem 18.108 ὅτι πάντα τὰ τοιαῦτα
       προηρούμην πολιτεύματα): causal clause

       (*)δυοῖν γὰρ πάντες ὄντοιν... ὦν ἕνεκα τίθενται οἱ νόμοι (cp. Dem
       25.17 ὦν ἕνεκα πάντες τίθενται οἱ νόμοι): relative clause

       (*)ἐξ ἑτέρας ἐρωτήσατ' αὐτὸν... πότερον ᾤχετο πρεσβεύων πόλεως ἢ
       ταύτης αὐτῆς (cp. Dem 19.147 πότερον ἐξ ἑτέρας ᾤχετο
       πρεσβεύων πόλεως): indirect question.

The last example is less obviously illicit than the others, because indirect questions, like indirect statements, are complement rather than adjunct clauses, and so less resistant to extraction, particularly those with *whether*. This distinction is well supported crosslinguistically, although there is some parametric variation, and different types of movement obey different constraints (Müller & Sternefeld 1993). For instance, interrogative extraction from complement clauses in German is easier than from subject clauses and much easier than from adjunct clauses (Webelhuth 1990). In Tzotzil (Mexico: Aissen 1992), focus cannot be extracted out of a relative clause or an indirect question. Russian allows scrambling of a constituent out of a finite indirect statement

> Ja slyšal čto novuju mašinu Marija skazala čto Andrej kupil
> 'I heard that Maria said that Andrew bought a new car,'

but German does not

> *Ich hörte dass ein neues Auto Maria sagte dass Andreas
> gekauft hat (Grewendorf & Sabel 1994).

Hungarian, which has a sentential focus slot preceding the main verb, allows extraction of both a focus and an interrogative from a complement clause with a "bridge" verb, particularly in the spoken language (Marácz 1989)

> Kit   gondolsz   hogy János látott?
> who you think-INDEF that John saw
> 'Who do you think that John saw?'

(70) It happened that when we were were on the first embassy, I left... (Aesch 2.82). They know nothing until they are caught up in the actual crime (Antiph 1.29). I deserve praise because I chose all those policies (Dem 18.108). There are two reasoons why all laws are made (Dem 25.17). Ask him whether he was on an embassy from another city or from this very one (Dem 19.147).

Marit   gondolod   hogy láttam
Mary you think-DEF that I saw
'You think that I saw Mary.'

In Greek, there are some verse examples in which the matrix verb, as superordinate head, separates the predicate of the finite complement from its argument or adjunct, suggesting some type of clause union

(71)   σοὶ δ᾽ ὡς ἀνάγκη τούσδε βούλομαι φράσαι | σῴζειν *Heracl* 205
       χὤπως μὲν ἐκ τῶνδ᾽ οὐκέτ᾽ οἶδ᾽ ἀπόλλυται *OT* 1251
       εἰ δ᾽ ἐστὶν ὅσιος αὐτὸς οἶδεν εἰς ἐμέ *Heracl* 719.

When weak or strong topics are extracted from finite complement clauses, they
are often syntactically integrated into the main clause, appearing as objects of
the matrix verb in a construction known as prolepsis

(72)   τοὺς νόμους ἐσκόπουν ὅπως ἀκριβῶς καὶ καλῶς ἕξουσιν Isoc *Paneg* 78
       βούλομαι δὴ ταύτην ὡς ἔστιν ἀληθὴς ἐπιδεῖξαι σαφῶς πᾶσιν ὑμῖν
       Dem 29.10.

When the extracted noun phrase could be the object either of the matrix verb
or of the complement clause verb, the result is indeterminate between simple
extraction and prolepsis with null or trace object

(73)   οὐ ταῦτα λέγεις ὅτι διδάσκων διαφθείρω; Pl *Apol* 26b
       τούτους δὴ τοὺς δεσμοὺς ἔλεγον ὅτι χαλεπὸν οὐδὲν συνδεῖν
       Pl *Polit* 310e.

Prolepsis can also apply in hyperbaton to a Y1 adjective (consequently a null
head modifier) or to a Y1 noun

(74)   ὁρᾷς τὸν εὐτράπεζον ὡς ἡδὺς βίος Eur Frag 1052.3 Nauck
       (Y1 modifier)
       ἤκουσα τοὺς ναύτας ὅτι | σοὶ πάντες εἶεν συννεναυστοληκότες
       Philoct 549 (Y1 noun).

Object YPs again show indeterminacy

(71) I want to say to you that it is necessary for you to save these ⟨children⟩ (*Heracl*
205). And I do not know how she perished after this (*OT* 1251). But he himself knows if
he has behaved in a holy way towards me (*Heracl* 719).
(72) They made sure that the laws would be precise and good (Isoc *Pan* 78). I want to
demonstrate clearly to all of you that this one is true (Dem 29.10).
(73) Isn't it by teaching these things that you say I corrupt them? (Pl *Apol* 26b). These
were the bonds that I said it was not at all difficult to create (Pl *Polit* 310e).
(74) You see how sweet is a life of luxury (Eur Frag 670.2). I heard that all the sailors
were shipmates of yours (*Philoct* 549).

(75) τοιοῦτον μέντοι καὶ ἐγὼ οἶδα ὅτι πάθος πάθοιμι ἂν Pl *Gorg* 522b
       τουτονὶ δεῖ μαθεῖν ὑμᾶς... τὸν νόμον τί ποτ᾽ ἐβούλεθ᾽ ὁ θείς
       Dem 23.37
       φυλακὰς ἅπαντες ἴσασιν ὅτι βέλτιόν ἐστι καθιστάναι καὶ ἡμερινὰς
       καὶ νυκτερινὰς Xen *Oec* 20.8 (Y1 noun).

Although it may have originated as an adjunct clause construction in paratactic syntax, in the classical language prolepsis functions as a restructuring device that provides an alternative to straight long extraction out of complement clauses, both for continuous constituents and for Y elements in hyperbaton.

Consider once more our example of a focus deeply embedded in a syntactic island; we will edit it by introducing a modifier with strong narrow scope focus

> Inspector Parker only interviewed the reporter who met the eyewitness who had seen the TALL diplomat.

Extrapolating from the hypothesis about hyperbaton islands just presented, we could say that if the focused modifier is thought of as undergoing overt syntactic movement, such movement is strictly local. Y1 is neither required to remain in situ nor to move to a sentential focus slot. We do not get 'only the TALL interviewed...' but 'who had the TALL seen...'. Y1 does move, but only within the bounds of its own clause. It is (definitionally) insensitive to left branch type noun phrase islands, but respects higher level clausal islands. In fact, as we shall argue in chapter 6, it is far more constrained than the extraction of interrogatives, since it is probably subject to the same sort of argument ranking restrictions in simple sentences that are commonly associated with interrogatives in complex sentences.

---

(75) I know that I too would suffer the same fate (Pl *Gorg* 522b). You must learn what the man who enacted this law intended (Dem 23.37). Everyone knows that it is better to post sentries both by day and by night (Xen *Oec* 2.8).

3 Hyperbata Varia

In this chapter we survey a whole range of other types of phrasal discontinuity: Y₂ hyperbaton, genitive hyperbaton, conjunct hyperbaton, clitic hyperbaton, specifier hyperbaton, nonhead X hyperbaton, double hyperbaton, attribute YP hyperbaton, and hyperbaton in nonfinite clauses. We also discuss the important difference between Y₁ hyperbaton in verse and Y₁ hyperbaton in prose. Anyone who tends to develop allergic reactions from sustained exposure to even fairly coarse-grained philological classification and analysis can perhaps read lightly in this chapter; but not too lightly, since much of theoretical significance emerges even at this preliminary stage in the argument.

Y₂ HYPERBATON

In the type of hyperbaton analyzed in chapters 1 and 2, the modifier preceded the superordinate head. The canonical hyperbaton structure Y_1XY_2 was actuated with the adjective in Y_1 position and the noun in Y_2 position: AXN. In this section, we are concerned with a type of hyperbaton that is, prima facie, the mirror image of Y_1 hyperbaton. We call this type Y_2 hyperbaton. Compare the following examples

   (1)   ἐπ᾽ ἀροτῆρας... στρατευόμεθα ἄνδρας Her 7.50 (Y₁ hyperbaton)
           ἐπ᾽ ἄνδρας στρατευόμεθα ἀγαθούς Her 7.53 (Y₂ hyperbaton).

Our nomenclature classifies hyperbaton on the basis of grammatical category: in Y_1 hyperbaton the modifier precedes X, in Y_2 hyperbaton it follows X. In practice, this categorial difference correlates with a pragmatic one. In Y_1 hyperbaton, the Y_1 adjective typically has strong focus and the Y_2 noun is tail material, whereas in one type of Y_2 hyperbaton, for instance, the Y_1 noun can be a topic and the Y_2 adjective a weak focus. However, it is not difficult to devise

---

(1) We are making war against men who are farmers (Her 7.50). We are making war against valiant men (Her 7.53).

unusual sentences in which this correlation between grammatical category and pragmatic value is reversed

> It was a shirt that he was wearing that was coloured red
> As for red ones, he was wearing a shirt.

Such a reversal is typical in the chiastic structures in which hyperbaton often occurs in colloquial Polish

A. Podobno   mają   piękny dom
   Apparently they have a beautiful house

B. Nieprawda! Dom mają   kiepski, ale piękny mają   ogród
   Nonsense! House they have lousy, but beautiful they have garden.

B's reply consists of two Y₂ hyperbata: *dom* is a repeated topic noun and *piękny* a contrastive topic modifier: 'what they have beautiful is their garden.' According to the analysis presented in chapters 1 and 2, Y₁ hyperbaton in prose does not involve extraposition of the noun to the right of the superordinate head, but, for restrictive adjectives, movement (or its nonderivational equivalent) of the adjective cyclically through the YP focus position across the superordinate head to the XP focus position. So Y₁ hyperbaton is associated with (surface) prenominal adjectives. Y₂ hyperbaton, by contrast, is associated with (surface) postnominal adjectives. In chapter 4, we present an analysis of Y₂ hyperbaton, according to which Y₂ hyperbaton does not involve extraposition of the adjective to the right of the superordinate head X but movement of the noun to a weak focus position preceding X: XNA → NXA

(2)   παρεχόμενοι νέας ὀγδώκοντα... Her 8.44 (X YP)
       νέας παρεχόμενοι ὀγδώκοντα Her 6.8

       σφάζοντες ἵππους λευκούς Her 7.113 (X YP)
       ἵππον ἔχων λευκόν Xen *An* 7.3.26
       ἀπ' ἵππου τε μαχόμενος λευκοῦ Her 9.63.

When Y₂ hyperbaton is not used, the whole YP commonly occurs in the weak focus preverbal position

(3)   ἄνδρας ἀγαθοὺς τιμᾶν Her 7.135 (YP X)
       ἐπ' ἄνδρας στρατευόμεθα ἀγαθούς Her 7.53

       ὀδμὴν δὲ βαρέαν παρέχεται Her 2.94 (YP X)
       ὀδμὴν παρεχόμενον βαρέαν Her 6.119

---

(2) Supplying eighty ships (Her 8.44). Supplying eighty ships (Her 6.8). Killing white horses (Her 7.113). Having a white horse (Xen *An* 7.3.26). Fighting from a white horse (Her 9.63).

(3) To honour valiant men (Her 7.135). We are making war against valiant men (Her 7.53). It gives off a strong smell (Her 2.94). Giving off a strong smell (Her 6.119).

(4)   χρόνου βραχέος διελθόντος Dem 5.5 (YP X)
        ἐπειδὰν δὲ χρόνος διέλθῃ βραχύς Dem 20.86

        ἡ πόλις ἐν κακοῖς τοῖς μεγίστοις ἐγίγνετο Andoc 1.58 (P YP X)
        τὴν δὲ πόλιν ἐν κακοῖς οὖσαν τοῖς μεγίστοις Andoc 1.51.

The Y₁ noun in hyperbaton may additionally be modified or quantified by prenominal adjectives

(5)   πάντες οἱ πόλεμοι γεγόνασι οἱ Ἑλληνικοί Dem 9.22
        τοῖς μὲν τοίνυν ἄλλοις ἅπασιν ἀνθρώποις ὁρῶ τοῖς κρινομένοις
        Dem 21.136.

An additional argument or adjunct (Z) may be placed either internal or external to the YXY structure, as was the case for Y₁ hyperbaton

(6)   κακὰ δ'ἐργαζόμενον τὰ μέγιστα τὴν πόλιν Dem 5.6 (YXYZ)
        ἔπαινον εἶχε οὐκ ὀλίγον πρὸς τῶν πολιητέων Her 1.96 (YXYZ)
        λόγους προὔπεμπον ἐς τὸ Ἄργος ξυμβατηρίους Thuc 5.76.1 (YXZY)
        οἰκίαν ᾠκοδόμηκεν Ἐλευσῖνι τοσαύτην Dem 21.158 (YXZY)
        δωρειὰς καὶ προδόσεις δοὺς ἑκάστῳ αὐτῶν μεγάλας Dem 50.7
        (YXZY).

Like Y₁ hyperbaton, Y₂ hyperbaton is crosscategorial

(7)   γῆς περίοδος πάσης Ar *Clouds* 206
        ὑπ' ἀνδρὸς χλαῖναν εὐγενοῦς Eur Frag 603.4
        αἰσχύνης πέρι κακῆς Pl *Laws* 647b
        τῶν ὀρεινῶν Θρᾳκῶν πολλοὺς τῶν αὐτονόμων καὶ μαχαιροφόρων
        Thuc 2.96.2.

Y₂ hyperbaton is used for quite a range of different pragmatic values. So the
question arises, how a single serial order YXY interfaces with multiple pragmatic values in a type of syntax that tends to be discourse configurational. The
most concrete approach would go as follows. If there is one serial order, then
there is just one syntactic structure; consequently, the syntax neutralizes the
pragmatic distinctions. At the other extreme is a discourse structural approach,

(4) A short time having elapsed (Dem 5.5). After a short time has elapsed (Dem 20.86).
The city was getting to a terrible situation (Andoc 1.58). That the city is in a terrible situation (Andoc 1.51).
(5) All the Greek wars have taken place (Dem 9.22). I see that for all other men who are
being prosecuted (Dem 21.136).
(6) Doing the greatest injury to the city (Dem 5.6). He won no small praise from his
fellow-citizens (Her 1.96). They sent to Argos proposals for peace (Thuc 5.76.1). He has
built such a large house at Eleusis (Dem 21.158). Giving each of them large bonuses and
advance payments (Dem 50.7).
(7) A map of the whole earth (Ar *Clouds* 206). In the bed of a noble man (Eur Frag
603.4). About disgraceful dishonour (Pl *Laws* 647b). Many of the mountain-dwelling
Thracians who are independent and carry sabres (Thuc 2.96.2).

according to which for each pragmatic value there is a separate syntactic structure. While the concrete approach is probably superficial, syntactic structures posited purely on the basis of distinctions in pragmatic (or, for that matter, semantic) meaning are in principle suspect. However, prosody, which is quintessentially (although not exclusively) structural and hierarchical, often provides evidence that more structure exists than is discernible in purely syntactic terms. For instance, in Finnish "there is a close connection between word order and intonation" (Karttunen 1989), and, in Bulgarian, prosody makes a critical contribution to the disambiguation of free word order structures (Rudin 1986). In the following sections, we will review the most important classes of Y_2 hyperbaton.

Weak focus Y_2 hyperbaton

In the simplest type of Y_2 hyperbaton, [Y_1X] is an ordinary weak focus and the Y_2 adjective specifies an additional restriction on the noun, and so represents a second weak focus. Some of the clearest instances involve split subject phrases

(8) ταὶ θυγατερες ἀνελοσθο ταὶ γνεσιαι IG V.ii.159 (Tegea)
μετὰ ταῦτα ναυμαχία γίγνεται ἐπ' Αἰγίνῃ μεγάλη Thuc 1.105.2
κρίσις γίνεται μεγάλη τῶν γυναικῶν Her 5.5
λύγξ τε τοῖς πλείοσιν ἐνέπεσε κενὴ Thuc 2.49.4
διακωλύοντες τὰ ἱερὰ μὴ γίγνεσθαι τὰ νομιζόμενα Antiph 5.82
οἱ πόλεμοι γεγόνασιν οἱ Ἑλληνικοί Dem 9.22
ἀνὴρ ἐν τοῖσι Μήδοισι ἐγένετο σοφὸς Her 1.96
ἱππομαχία τις ἐγένετο βραχεῖα Thuc 2.22.2.

For instance, in the two Thucydides examples, first of all an event is reported ('a sea battle took place,' 'a cough affected most people') and then comes the Y_2 restriction. This structure is quite different from the strong focus plus tail structure of Y_1 hyperbaton. The adjective does not have exclusive meaning and the event is not presupposed. Thucydides is not trying to make the point that it was a dry cough rather than some other type of cough that afflicted most patients, nor Antipho to imply that irregular religious rites were performed without hindrance. This difference between Y_1 and Y_2 hyperbaton is illustrated by the following examples

(9) ὁ παλαιὸς κελεύει νόμος Dem 20.99
νόμος δ' εἴη πάτριος Andoc 1.110;

---

(8) Let his legitimate daughters take it (IG V.ii.159). After that a great sea battle took place at Aegina (Thuc 1.105.2). A great dispute arises among his wives (Her 5.5). A dry cough affected the majority (Thuc 2.49.4). Preventing the regular religious rites from being performed successfully (Antiph 5.82). There once was a wise man among the Medians (Her 1.96). A short cavalry battle took place (Thuc 2.22.2).
(9) The old law prescribes (Dem 20.99). That there is an old law (Andoc 1.110).

Demosthenes is contrasting the old law with a new one, Andocides is establishing that a law exists and saying that it belongs to the class of νόμοι πατρίοι. The additional specification of the Y2 adjective can be contrastive

(10)   τὸν ὀφθαλμὸν παράβαλλ᾽ ἐς Καρίαν | τὸν δεξιόν, τὸν δ᾽ ἕτερον
        ἐς Καρχηδόνα Ar *Knights* 173
        ἀνδρῶν ἐρῶ πρεσβυτέρων... ὀνόματα καὶ μειρακίων Aesch 1.155
        (NVA καὶ N),

but not normally in combination with a tail presupposition. For instance, if the Aeschines example were read as a Y1 hyperbaton, it would involve a cancellation of the implicature of exclusivity: 'it is of OLDER men that I shall cite the names, and of YOUNG men.' In verse, Y2 can be a descriptive adjective: here are a couple examples from Homer

(11)   θεοὺς νεμεσίζετο αἰὲν ἐόντας *Od* 1.263
        πλοκάμους ἔπλεξε φαεινοὺς *Il* 14.176.

According to the analysis presented in chapter 4, the Y1 noun forms a phrase with the verb X, and the Y2 modifier is adjoined to this phrase, as illustrated for object YP in Figure 3.1 (derivationally in Figure 4.5). The subject Y1 nouns are also probably verb phrase internal. If one looks back over the examples cited, two generalizations suggest themselves: first, the verbs are all intransitive, and second, apart from the inscriptional ἀνελοσθο which is predictable information, they are all simple verbs of occurrence or existence. (The possible unaccusative ἐδούλευσεν at Xen *Ath Pol* 3.11.3 is textually uncertain [Gigante 1951].) Existential-presentational verbs are a familiar class in English, licensing both expletive *there* and extraposition of a relative clause or prepositional phrase from a subject phrase (the latter with indefinites only)

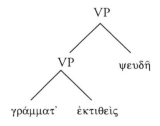

Figure 3.1
Simple Y2 hyperbaton
γράμματ᾽ ἐκτιθεὶς ψευδῆ Dem 25.50

(10)   Now turn your right eye towards Caria, the the other one towards Carthage (Ar *Knights* 173). I will cite the names of the older men and of the young men (Aesch 1.155).
   (11)   He was in awe of the immortal gods (*Od* 1.263). She plaited her glossy hair (*Il* 14.176).

UNACCUSATIVE (APPEARANCE)
A student who was tall/with a red shirt arrived
There arrived a student who was tall/with a red shirt
A student arrived who was tall/with a red shirt

UNERGATIVE
A student who was tall/with a red shirt laughed
*There laughed a student who was tall/with a red shirt
*A student laughed who was tall/with a red shirt

TRANSITIVE
A student who was tall/with a red shirt destroyed the dictionary
*There destroyed the dictionary a student who was tall/with a red shirt
*A student destroyed the dictionary who was tall/with a red shirt.

Many of our subject Y_2 hyperbaton examples could be paraphrased with an expletive *there* or an extraposed relative clause: 'There took place a sea battle...,' 'A sea battle took place which was quite large.' Although the subject is pre-verbal (not γίγνεται ναυμαχία), the sentences have a clearly eventive character. If there is a predicational relationship, it is with an implicit time-place topic. The same structure is found with presentational sentences

(12)   ἔπεστι κολοσσὸς λίθινος Her 2.149 (YP)
        κρηπὶς δ' ὑπῆν λιθίνη Xen *An* 3.4.7.

Similar restrictions on subjects in Y_1 hyperbaton are discussed in chapter 6. We may conclude that this type of Y_2 hyperbaton was easier than other types for subject YPs. Any such constraint is weaker or absent in the more paratactic syntax of Homer

(13)   Ἄρης ἐνάριζε μιαιφόνος *Il* 5.844

and in the onomastic structure of inscriptional signatures

(14)   Εὐθυκαρτιδης : μ'ἀ:νεθεκε : hο Ναhσιος *LSAG* Pl. 55.3
        Ἀριστοδαμος ἐποιϝεσε hἀργειος *LSAG²* Pl. 74.6
        Ηιπποθεριδες : ἀνεθεκεν : Ἀχαρνευς *DAA* 246.

Similar subject phrase Y_2 hyperbata are licensed by proper names also in Attic prose

(15)   Σόλωνος εἰπόντος Ἀθηναίου τὴν γνώμην Aesch 3.108.

---

(12) On top there is a stone colossus (Her 2.149). Underneath was a stone foundation (Xen *An* 3.4.7).
(13) Murderous Ares was stripping his armour (*Il* 5.844).
(14) Euthycartides the Naxian dedicated me (*LSAG* Pl. 55.3). Aristodemus the Argive made this (*LSAG²* Pl. 74.6). Hippotherides the Acharnian dedicated this (*DAA* 246).
(15) After Solon the Athenian had expressed his opinion (Aesch 3.108).

Nonlexical Y$_2$ hyperbaton

In nonlexical Y$_2$ hyperbaton, the adjective is a demonstrative or a possessive personal pronoun. Let us start with demonstratives. The neutral word order for demonstratives is before the noun, but they are often postnominal too. After proper names, demonstratives are particularly frequently postposed

(16) Πρόδικος ὅδε Pl *Prot* 340c, d, e
     Προδίκου τουτουΐ Pl *Prot* 341a,

presumably because with proper names they regularly have a deictic rather than their usual restrictive function. When they actually do restrict the reference of a proper name, they are focused and preposed

(17) οὗτος Σωκράτης Pl *Phaedo* 115c
     ὑπὸ τουτουΐ τοῦ Μαρσύου Pl *Symp* 215e.

In the following instances from Andocides

(18) κατὰ (μὲν) τὸ ψήφισμα τουτὶ Andoc 1.80, 1.85
     ὁ νόμος ὅδε Andoc 1.99

the postnominal demonstrative refers to documents that have already been cited in the speech, whereas in the following instances

(19) τουτουσὶ τοὺς νόμους Andoc 1.86
     οὑτοσὶ ὁ νόμος Andoc 1.87

the prenominal demonstratives refer to laws that are about to be introduced in contrast to previously cited ones. When the demonstrative is explicitly contrastive, it is normally prenominal

(20) οὔτ’ ἐν ταύτῃ τῇ μάχῃ οὔτ’ ἐν ταῖς ἄλλαις Thuc 6.69.1
     τουτὶ τὸ ῥῆμα ἀλλὰ μὴ τουτί Dem 18.232,

unless the noun is treated as topical

(21) πόλεσι γὰρ ταύταις μόναις Thuc 7.55.2.

Here is a set of examples from Herodotus further illustrating this pragmatic distribution

(22) ταύτην τὴν μάχην... κρίνω ἰσχυροτάτην γενέσθαι Her 1.214
     (strong focus in topic phrase)

(16) Prodicus here (Pl *Prot* 340c). Of Prodicus here (Pl *Prot* 341a).
(17) This Socrates who... (Pl *Phaedo* 115c). By this Marsyas (Pl *Symp* 215e).
(18) According to this decree (Andoc 1.80). This law (Andoc 1.99).
(19) These laws (Andoc 1.86). This law (Andoc 1.87).
(20) Neither in this battle nor in the others (Thuc 6.69.1). This word but not that one (Dem 18.232).
(21) These cities alone (Thuc 7.55.2).
(22) I consider this battle to have been the hardest fought (Her 1.214).

(23)   ἐκ ταύτης τῆς πόλιος Her 2.41 (simple topic phrase)
περὶ τῆς χώρης ταύτης Her 2.13 (no focus)
τὰς ἐν τῇ πόλι ταύτῃ γυναῖκας Her 2.60 (no focus; "donkey" reference).

In a number of examples, postposed demonstratives occur in Y₂ hyperbaton

(24)   τὰς ἀνάγκας ἀκούσητε ταύτας Dem 2.29
τοῦ ἀγῶνος ἕνεκα τουτουί Dem 48.55
ἐπὶ τῆς αἰτίας ὄντα ταύτης Aesch 2.4
τὰς μαρτυρίας μοι λέγε πρῶτον ταυτασί Dem 19.200
ὁ χρόνος διελήλυθεν οὗτος Dem 2.25
μεγίστου γὰρ πολέμου συστάντος ἐκείνου Isoc *Pac* 71.

The weak informational status of such demonstratives is particularly clear in an example like the following with explicitly contrastive nouns

(25)   οὐ μόνον... διὰ τὴν πρᾶξιν ὀργίζεσθαι ταύτην ἀλλὰ καὶ διὰ τὸν λόγον τοῦτον Lyc 58.

It is possible that some postnominal possessive pronouns have a similar weak informational status both in continuous YPs

(26)   ταῦτα δὲ λέγοντος τοῦ πατρὸς τοῦ ἐμοῦ Andoc 1.22

and in Y₂ hyperbaton

(27)   τὸν πατέρα ἔφη τὸν ἐμὸν παρεῖναι Andoc 1.17
ὑπὸ τῶν ἐχθρῶν πεισθεὶς τῶν ἐμῶν Lys 7.39
τὴν μητέρα γήμαντος τὴν ἐμὴν Dem 45.3.

The evidence just cited indicates that these nonlexicals in Y₂ hyperbaton tend to differ from regular Y₂ hyperbaton adjectives in being very light and often predictable, and semantically in often involving not an independent restrictive modification but some form of secondary deictic reference. Turning to the syntax, they differ categorially by definition, since they are nonlexical (closed class) adjectives, and they give the impression of being potentially syntactically

(23) From this city (Her 2.41). Concerning this country (Her 2.13). The women in that particular town (Her 2.60).

(24) You listen to these handicaps of theirs (Dem 2.29). Because of this law suit (Dem 48.55). While he was on the subject of this charge (Aesch 2.4). First read these depositions for me (Dem 19.200). This time has passed (Dem 2.25). When that very great war broke out (Isoc *Pan* 71).

(25) To be angry not only because of what he has done but also because of what he has said (Lyc 58).

(26) When my father said these things (Andoc 1.22).

(27) He said that my father was present (Andoc 1.17). Persuaded by my enemies (Lys 7.39). Having married my mother (Dem 45.3).

postpositive to the informationally salient element of the noun phrase. So beside broad scope postposition

(28)   οἱ χρηστοὶ πρέσβεις οὗτοι Dem 18.30

we find postadjectival examples, including contrastive ones like the following

(29)   τρεῖς μὲν βίοι... τοῦ κοινοῦ τούτου βίου... Pl *Phil* 22a-d
        ἐν τοῖς τριάκοντ᾽ ἐκείνοις ἐτέσι... ἐν τοῖς ἑβδομήκοντα Dem 9.25.

There is also evidence to suggest that ὅδε could be prosodically appositive, metrical evidence from bridges

(30)   ὅτ᾽ ἦν παῖς ἥδε μοι Eur *Suppl* 1098 (Porson's bridge)
        τόνδε λέβητα *Cyclops* 343 MS (split anapaest)

and inscriptional evidence from phrase punctuation

(31)   : αι δε τιρ τα γραφεα : ταϊ καδαλεοιτο : *LSAG* Pl. 42.6
        hος δ᾽ αν τοδε πιεσι : ποτεριο : Nestor's cup.

Elided ὅδε can be prosodically prepositive (*OT* 219, *Hippolytus* 1151, *Andromache* 875); however in one example

(32)   ὅς γ᾽ ἡλίου τόδ᾽ εἰσορᾶν ἐμοὶ φάος | μόνος δέδωκας *Philoct* 663

if τόδ᾽ coheres syntactically with anything, it is with the preceding ἡλίου and not with the following VY2 structure, since it is precaesural.

Taken together, this evidence suggests a syntactic, and at least for ὅδε, also a prosodic difference between nonlexical and lexical adjectives. On a straight nonderivational approach, perhaps the nonlexical was simply adjoined to a preceding head. A derivational structure is illustrated in Figure 3.2: the determiner phrase does not land in the focus position of the demonstrative phrase (as in the continuous type) but in that of the superordinate verb phrase. Some form of movement analysis seems appropriate for a case like the following

(33)   ἵν᾽ εἰδῆθ᾽ ἡλίκα πράγμαθ᾽ ἡ μιαρὰ κεφαλὴ ταράξασ᾽ αὕτη δίκην
        οὐκ ἔδωκε Dem 18.153;

here an emphatic subject noun phrase appears between a participle and its extracted object, stranding the demonstrative. Although it is convenient to refer to this type of Y2 hyperbaton as nonlexical hyperbaton, it should perhaps

(28) These excellent ambassadors (Dem 18.30).
(29) Three different types of life... of this combined type of life (Pl *Phil* 22d). In those thirty years... in the seventy (Dem 9.25).
(30) When I had this daughter alive (Eur *Suppl* 1098). This cauldron (*Cyclops* 343).
(31) If anyone damages this writing (*LSAG* Pl. 42.6). Whoever drinks from this cup (Nestor's cup).
(32) Who alone have been responsible for my seeing this light of the sun (*Philoct* 663).
(33) So that you may know how much trouble this bastard stirred up without being punished (Dem 18.153).

be defined in informational terms as Y₂ tail hyperbaton. In that case, the classification would be entirely discourse conditioned. Then if a nonlexical adjective has focus, it will be classified as a case of regular Y₂ hyperbaton

(34)   θεοὺς δὲ σέβονται μούνους τούσδε Her 5.7.

Conversely, if a lexical adjective in Y₂ hyperbaton is tail material, it would presumably be classified with the nonlexical type

(35)   παῖδα ἀνόητον χαίροντα ἤδη εἶδες;... ἄνδρα δὲ οὔπω εἶδες ἀνόητον
        χαίροντα; Pl *Gorg* 497e.

Topic Y₂ hyperbaton

Although some Y₂ hyperbata with complement phrases involve weak focus

(36)   ἔπαινον εἶχε οὐκ ὀλίγον Her 1.96
        οἰκίαν ᾠκοδόμηκεν... τοσαύτην Dem 21.158
        γράμματ᾽ ἐκτιθεὶς ψευδῆ Dem 25.50
        νέας αὐτοῖσι ἀνδράσι εἶλον Ἑλληνίδας πέντε Her 8.17,

in many others the [Y₁X] structure is established or predictable information

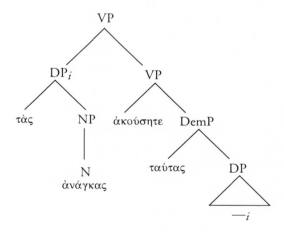

Figure 3.2
Nonlexical Y₂ hyperbaton
τὰς ἀνάγκας ἀκούσητε ταύτας Dem 2.29

(34) The only gods they worship are these (Her 5.7).
(35) Did you ever see a foolish child rejoicing?... did you ever see a foolish man rejoicing? (Pl *Gorg* 497e).
(36) He won no small praise (Her 1.96). He has built such a large house (Dem 21.158). Publishing false letters (Dem 25.50). They captured five Greek ships with their crews (Her 8.17).

(37)   ἐπ᾽ ἄνδρας στρατευόμεθα ἀγαθούς Her 7.53
      ἐπὶ γὰρ πόλεις... μέλλομεν ἰέναι μεγάλας Thuc 6.20.2
      ὅτε ἵππευεν,... ἵππους ἐκτήσατο λαμπροὺς Lys 19.63
      στρατιὰν ἔχων οὐ πολλὴν Thuc 8.61.1, cp. 1.95.6.

A related type establishes a new or contrastive topic

(38)   ἐσθῆτι δὲ χρεωμένους Μηδικῇ Her 5.9
      ἐσθῆτα δὲ φορέουσι οἱ ἱρέες λινέην μούνην Her 2.37
      ἀγαθὸν μὲν πεποιηκὼς μηδέν Aesch 3.226.

We can illustrate with an example used by Bolinger half a century ago (Bolinger 1952); it has an indefinite object and an intensional verb

> I'm looking for a VACANT HOUSE (broad scope YP focus or double focus)
> I'm looking for a VACANT house (cp. Y_1 hyperbaton)
> I'm looking for a house that's VACANT (cp. topic Y_2 hyperbaton).

Note that the last sentence can be the answer to the question 'What sort of a house are you looking for?' or to the question 'What are you doing?'. In the former situation, *I'm looking for a house* (= [Y_1X]) is presupposed material and the new information (the weak focus) is the adjective *vacant* (= Y_2). This corresponds to topic Y_2 hyperbaton. In the latter situation, both are weak foci: this corresponds to focus Y_2 hyperbaton. Now sentences with double foci are complex; in effect they answer two questions simultaneously. Our example, for instance, could be decomposed into the following dialogue

> A. What are you doing?   B. I'm looking for a house.
> A. What sort of a house are you looking for?   B. One that's vacant.

In this little dialogue, *I'm looking for a house* serves first as a focus and subsequently as a presupposition. This suggests that, in the single sentence version, it could have both functions simultaneously via a process akin to accommodation. First it is asserted, then there is a subsidiary update in the information state allowing it to serve as a presupposition for the second (and primary) focus on the adjective. (As we shall see in chapter 4, this type of minor update should be carefully distinguished from a regular clausal update.) This idea would elucidate the relationship between focus Y_2 hyperbaton and topic Y_2 hyperbaton (and account for the fact that some examples, with contextually unsurprising [Y_1X] material, seem indeterminate between the two types). So, as far as the Y_2 adjective is concerned, the [Y_1X] structure has a topical function in both types.

---

(37) We are making war against valiant men (Her 7.53). We intend to march against large cities (Thuc 6.20.2). When he served in the cavalry... he procured fine horses (Lys 19.63). With a small force (Thuc 8.61.1).

(38) Wearing Median clothes (Her 5.9). The priests wear only linen clothing (Her 2.37). Having done nothing good (Aesch 3.226).

The difference between the two types relates to the status of [Y₁X] in the common ground of knowledge at that point in the discourse when it is uttered, not at the point when the Y₂ adjective is interpreted.

As in the subject focus type, topic [Y₁X] structures tend to be informationally lean. The noun is mostly indefinite and often nonreferential. The closest thing in English seems to be the literary construction 'Answer gave he none' with a quantifier. Since 'shirt wore he red' is out of the question, we could fall back on paraphrases like 'The clothes they wear are in the Median style,' 'As for the clothes they wear, they are in the Median style,' 'They clothes-wear Median ones.' The first paraphrase treats [Y₁X] as the notional subject and the Y₂ adjective as the focus and notional predicate. The second paraphrase emphasizes the status of [Y₁X] as contrastive topical material. The third reflects the nonindividuated status of the noun, which we shall argue in chapter 6 is a particularly important ingredient of Y₁ hyperbaton in prose. All three paraphrases take the verb to be part of the topical structure: $[Y_1X]_{TOP}Y$, not $[Y_1]_{TOP}XY$, therefore 'Clothes-wear, they do Median ones' rather than 'Clothes, they wear Median ones.' However, the interrogative evidence we shall cite in the next paragraph indicates that in principle both structures were available. The same is true for German split topicalization (van Geenhoven 1998)

> Katzen had jedes Kind welche gesehen
> Katzen gesehen had jedes Kind welche
> 'Each child saw some cats.'

In the following example, the intervening subject indicates that only the Y₁ noun has been topicalized

(39) τούτοις οὐσίαν ὁ πατὴρ κατέλιπε πολλήν Isae 7.5

We know for certain that the informational distinction between focus and topic can be structurally encoded in Greek syntax, because we can observe it unequivocally in sentences with interrogative pronouns (Thomson 1939). The material to the left of a "postponed" interrogative is that part of the presupposition of a question that has been topicalized—an argument phrase, an adjunct phrase or some larger fragment of the clause

(40) τὰς δ᾽ ἐμὰς τύχας | τίς ἄρ᾽ Ἀχαιῶν... ἔχει; *Troad* 292 (object)
      ἀτὰρ θυγατρὸς τῆς Ἐρεχθέως τί μοι | μέλει; *Ion* 433 (oblique complement)
      ἁ δὲ τάλαιν᾽ ἄλοχος τίνι μοι, τέκνον, ὤλετο μοίρᾳ; *Phoen* 1566 (subject)

___

(39) Their father left them a great deal of property (Isae 7.5).

(40) But who of the Achaeans has control of my destiny? (*Troad* 292). But what do I care about the daughter of Erechtheus? (*Ion* 433). But by what fate, my child, did my wretched wife perish? (*Phoen* 1566).

(41) καὶ σκῦλα γράψεις πῶς ἐπ' Ἰνάχου ῥοαῖς; *Phoen* 574 (VP fragment)
      σοί τε γὰρ παίδων τί δεῖ; *Med* 565 (both arguments).

The topicalized material is strongly contrastive in context in all these examples. The position of enclitic μοι after the interrogative indicates that the interrogative is initial within the nuclear clause and not simply in situ: consequently the topical material is adjoined to CP. Here is an example with two preinterrogative arguments from Bulgarian (Rudin 1986)

> Ivan knigite   dale   da donese?
> Ivan books-the whether to bring-3SING
> 'Should Ivan bring the books?'.

For verb phrase topicalization, compare English sentences like

> They told him to inscribe the spoils, and [inscribe the spoils]TOP
> he did by the streams of Inachus.

Topicalization in interrogative sentences also occurs in prose

(42) τὰ δίκαια δὲ πότερον ὁ ἑκὼν ψευδόμενος... οἶδεν ἢ ὁ ἄκων;
      Xen *Mem* 4.2.20
      τρέφεται δὲ... ψυχὴ τίνι; Pl *Prot* 313c
      σοὶ δὲ πῶς φαίνεται...; Pl *Crat* 403b.

Interrogative sentences which have both topicalization and Y2 hyperbaton fall into two classes. In the first, the Y2 modifier is itself the interrogative

(43) εἰσφορὰς λογίζῃ πόσας; Isae Frag 2 Forster (see app. crit.)
      φίλοι γάρ εἰσιν ἀνδρὶ δυστυχεῖ τίνες; *HF* 559
      ἔχει δ' ὄνησιν τοῖσι θύουσιν τίνα; *Bacch* 473
      μορφὴν ἔχον τίν'; *Ion* 1420.

In the second class, the Y1 noun is in the topic position, either by itself or together with other material, and the Y2 modifier is stranded in the nuclear clause after the interrogative

(44) φιλίαν δὲ παρὰ τίνων ἄν ποτε λάβοις τοσαύτην...; Xen *Cyr* 3.1.28
      παῖδας δὲ δὴ τί τούσδ' ἀποκτεῖναι θέλεις; *HF* 206 (verb outside YP)

---

(41) How will you inscribe the spoils at the streams of Inachus? (*Phoen* 574). What need have you of children? (*Med* 565).

(42) Does the intentional deceiver or the unintentional know what is just? (Xen *Mem* 4.2.20). What is a soul nourished by? (Pl *Prot* 313c). What is your opinion (Pl *Crat* 403b).

(43) How much do you calculate for taxes? (Isae Frag 2). What friends does an unfortunate man have? (*HF* 559). What advantage do they bring to the celebrants? (*Bacch* 473). What does it look like? (*Ion* 1420).

(44) From whom would you ever get so great friendship? (Xen *Cyr* 3.1.28). Why do you ask to kill these boys? (*HF* 206).

(45)   ὄγκον γὰρ ἄλλως ὀνόματος τί δεῖ τρέφειν | μητρῷον...;   *Trach* 817.

Both classes are illustrated in Figure 3.3. The topicalized material that precedes an interrogative tends to be either strongly relevant to the discourse context and presupposed by the discourse, as in *HF* 206 just cited, or actually repeated from preceding discourse, as in the *Cyropaedia* passage, where φιλίαν picks up an earlier φιλία τῇ ἐμῇ, or a contrastive topic, often in a μὲν... δὲ structure. There is a type of in situ interrogative in English (Ginzburg 1992) which is licensed by the repetition of topiclike material from the preceding discourse

    A. We're reading tragedy this quarter
    B. And you're reading which play exactly?

This type is not quite the same as an echo question; it asks for additional information rather than confirmation of information already provided.

If the conditions licensing topicalization in interrogatives are applied to Y2 hyperbaton, it is clear that not all prima facie instances would qualify. For instance, the interrogative proves topicalization in

(46)   χρόνον δ᾽ ἐμείνατ᾽ ἄλλον ἐν Τροίᾳ πόσον;   *Hel* 113

which meets the criterion of repeated material, since it picks up on

(47)   πόσον χρόνον γὰρ διαπεπόρθηται πόλις;   *Hel* 111

two lines before. However the status of superficially comparable examples like

(48)   ἐγὼ δ᾽ ἐπειδὴ χρόνον ἔμειν᾽ ὅσον με χρῆν   *Hel* 612

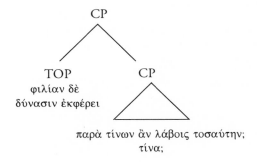

Figure 3.3
Topic Y2 hyperbaton in questions
φιλίαν δὲ παρὰ τίνων ἂν λάβοις τοσαύτην; Xen *Cyr* 3.1.28
δύνασιν ἐκφέρει τίνα; *Ion* 1012

(45) Why should someone vainly enjoy the name of mother (*Trach* 817).
(46) How much time other than that did you stay in Troy? (*Hel* 113).
(47) How long is it since the city was destroyed? (*Hel* 111).
(48) I, when I had remained as long a time as I was required to (*Hel* 612).

(49)   χρόνον μὲν οὐκ ἂν ἦμεν ἐν Θρᾴκῃ πολύν Ar *Ach* 136

is not so unequivocal, and most of the examples cited in this section do not look as though they involved adjunction of Y_1 or V' to CP. So one solution would be simply to assign the same structural position to focus and to topic Y_2 hyperbaton. Here we will consider an alternative approach. Presumably, topical V'-structures can also be adjoined to lower projections, just as in Y_1 hyperbaton the adjective can appear in a range of positions lower than that used by the interrogative. For instance, the following example in which *power* is weakly topical and contrasted with *reputation*, involves conjoined verb phrases

(50)   ὁ γὰρ ἀνὴρ καὶ δύναμιν ἔχει μεγάλην καὶ ὀνομαστός ἐστιν
       Xen *Hell* 6.1.4.

If one accepts this line of reasoning, it leads to a fairly abstract structure. Although the topic type Y_2 hyperbaton looks identical to the focus type, it is actually derived by an additional "movement." Just as in the interrogative type (illustrated in Figure 3.3) the V' δύνασιν ἐκφέρει in this example moves as a constituent out of the nuclear verb phrase to be adjoined to CP, so the V' στρατιὰν ἔχων in Thucydides 8.61.1 cited above moves as a constituent out of the nuclear verb phrase (where it would remain in the focus type) to be adjoined to it

$$_{VP}[στρατιὰν ἔχων] \ _{VP}[[—] οὐ πολλὴν].$$

It is reasonable to assume that this more complex structure is reflected in the intonation.

Comparative texts

Here are some examples of comparative texts with Y_1 and Y_2 hyperbaton. The English paraphrases are intended to capture some of the difference in informational structure between the two constructions.

> πολλὰ κατέλιπε χρήματα Andoc 1.119 '[if] he had left a GREAT
>   amount of property'
> χρήματα λαβὼν πολλὰ Her 6.17 'capturing property in large
>   quantities'
>
> πολλὴν γὰρ πάνυ κατέλιπεν ὁ πατὴρ αὐτῷ οὐσίαν Aesch 1.42
>   'for GREAT indeed was the property that his father left him'
> τούτοις οὐσίαν ὁ πατὴρ κατέλιπε πολλήν Isae 7.5 'to the afore-
>   mentioned, as for property, their father left them a great deal'
>
> πολλὰ καὶ καλὰ ἔδωκε δῶρα τῷ Ὑστάσπᾳ Xen *Cyr* 8.4.26
>   'he gave MANY FINE gifts to Hystaspas'

---

(49)   We wouldn't have stayed long in Thrace (Ar *Ach* 136).
(50)   The man both has great power and is famous (Xen *Hell* 6.1.4).

καὶ ἄλλα δῶρα ἔδωκεν αὐτῷ πολλὰ καὶ καλά Xen *Cyr* 8.5.17
    'he also gave him other gifts, which were many and beautiful.'

ψευδεῖς παρασκευάζονται λόγους Isae 1.17 'they are preparing FALSE
    arguments'

γράμματ' ἐκτιθεὶς ψευδῆ Dem 25.50 'publishing letters that are
    forged'

μικρὸν διαλιπὼν χρόνον Aesch 3.89 'with hardly ANY delay'

ἐπειδὰν δὲ χρόνος διέλθῃ βραχύς Dem 20.86 'after an interval of
    short duration'

ἐκεῖνον ἐπέδειξα τρία καὶ εἴκοσιν ἐπιβιοῦντα ἔτη Isae 2.45 'I showed
    that it was TWENTY-THREE years that he continued to live'

ἔτη γὰρ ἤδη βεβίωκεν ἐνενήκοντα καὶ τέτταρα Aesch 2.147 (cp. Lys
    19.55) 'for the years that he has lived now amount to ninety-four.'

GENITIVE HYPERBATON

Genitive positions in continuous YPs

To develop a clear account of genitive hyperbaton, we need first to analyze the positions available to genitives that are not discontinuous from the noun phrases with which they are associated. These positions are most evident when both the genitive and the head noun are articulated. Genitive positions can then be classified according as they are internal or external to the determiner phrase with which they are associated, and according as they are in Y_1 or in Y_2 position in the resulting complex structure. (The internal type probably originates as demonstrative pronoun plus external genitive.) Let us start with possessives. We can illustrate with a simple lexical genitive like the ethnic τῶν Ἀθηναίων, which is obviously common enough in Thucydides

(51)   τὰς ναῦς τῶν Ἀθηναίων Thuc 7.74.2 (external Y_2)
        τῶν Ἀθηναίων τῷ περὶ τὰς ναῦς ἐρύματι Thuc 8.55.3 (external Y_1)
        τὰς τῶν Ἀθηναίων ναῦς Thuc 7.23.3, 7.36.3 (internal Y_1)
        ὅλον τὸ στράτευμα τὸ τῶν Ἀθηναίων Thuc 8.50.5 (internal Y_2).

The main distinction for possessives is between Y_1 internal and Y_2 external. Although it is not always possible to make an unequivocal classification of the pragmatic status of the genitive, in transparent passages clear trends emerge. External Y_2 tends to be a simple modifier position, apparently just a sister to the head determiner phrase. Internal Y_1 can clearly be a functionally (pragmat-

(51) The ships of the Athenians (Thuc 7.74.2). The fortification of the Athenians around the ships (Thuc 8.55.3). The ships of the Athenians (Thuc 7.23.3). The entire army of the Athenians (Thuc 8.50.5).

ically) defined position used for contrastive or exclusive focus (whereas internal Y₂ is likewise restrictive but typically without strong focus)

(52)   τὸ στρατόπεδον τῶν Ἀθηναίων Thuc 4.94.2 (external)
τὸ τῶν Ἀθηναίων στρατόπεδον Thuc 2.25.2, 3.5.2, 7.73.3 (internal).

The external instance occurs in a paragraph of which the topic is the Athenian army and in a sentence of which the subject is the Athenian general: unlike in the internal examples, Ἀθηναίων does not serve to contrast opposing armies nor even to identify the army in question out of the set of all possible armies, but merely provides tail material helping the audience to keep track of a discourse active referent. Both positions are further illustrated in the following passages

(53)   οἱ μὲν ὁπλῖται τῶν Χαλκιδέων... νικῶνται ὑπὸ τῶν Ἀθηναίων...
οἱ δὲ ἱππῆς τῶν Χαλκιδέων... νικῶσι τοὺς τῶν Ἀθηναίων ἱππέας
Thuc 2.79.3;

first the Chalcidian hoplites are contrasted with the Chalcidian cavalry, then the latter are contrasted with the Athenian cavalry (first $xP : yP$, then $yP : Qy$); consequently Q is internal. In the account of the siege of Syracuse, when mention is made of the Athenian wall and the Syracusan counterwalls, the genitive is normally in the posthead position

(54)   τὰ τείχη τῶν Ἀθηναίων Thuc 7.3.4, 7.46.1, 7.51.2
τὸ παρατείχισμα τῶν Συρακοσίων Thuc 7.42.4
τὸ τείχισμα τῶν Ἀθηναίων Thuc 7.2.4.

But in two passages in which an (explicit or implicit) contrast is drawn between the Athenian and the Syracusan walls

(55)   ὅσον οὐ παρεληλύθει τὴν τῶν Ἀθηναίων τοῦ τείχους τελευτὴν
ἡ ἐκείνων τείχισις Thuc 7.6.1
παροικοδομήσαντες καὶ παρελθόντες τὴν τῶν Ἀθηναίων οἰκοδομίαν
Thuc 7.6.4

the genitive is internal. The pragmatic principles controlling the distribution and the positions used are, mutatis mutandis, clearly comparable to what was established for restrictive adjectives in chapter 1, and a derivational account

(52) The army of the Athenians (Thuc 4.94.2). The army of the Athenians (Thuc 2.25.2).
(53) The hoplites of the Chalcidians are conquered by the Athenians, but the cavalry of the Chalcidians conquers the cavalry of the Athenians (Thuc 2.79.3).
(54) The wall of the Athenians (Thuc 7.3.4). The crosswall of the Syracusans (Thuc 7.42.4). The wall of the Athenians (Thuc 7.2.4).
(55) Their wall had practically passed the end of the wall of the Athenians (Thuc 7.6.1). Building across and passing the construction of the Athenians (Thuc 7.6.4).

would reflect the same sort of movement posited for focused adjectives and illustrated in Figure 1.6.

An internal position is available to argument genitives as well as possessive genitives

(56) μετὰ δὲ τὴν τῶν Ἀργείων ἀπόστασιν ἐκ τῆς ξυμμαχίας Thuc 5.81.1
μετὰ τὴν τῶν ἀνδρῶν ἐς τὴν νῆσον διακομιδὴν Thuc 3.76.1.

The external Υι position is well attested for possessives in Herodotus

(57) τῶν Συρίων τοὺς κλήρους Her 1.76
τῶν βασιλέων τοὺς παῖδας Her 3.15
τῶν Ἰώνων τοὺς στρατηγούς Her 5.109, contrast τοὺς τῶν Ἀθηναίων στρατηγοὺς Thuc 4.66.3,

but in our Thucydides sample it seems to be restricted to special cases where for instance the possessive is topical in some phrasal domain (cp. τοῦ δὲ Μαρσύου τὸ εὖρος Xen *An* 1.2.8) or has the flavour of a source complement and is followed by a heavy branching or conjoined noun phrase

(58) ἵνα... Ἀθηναίων τήν τε οὖσαν καὶ τὴν μέλλουσαν δύναμιν καθέλητε
Thuc 6.92.5
δείσαντες τῶν Ἀθηναίων τὸ τολμηρὸν καὶ τὴν νεωτεροποιίαν
Thuc 1.102.3.

Partitives and arguments occur commonly in an external position

(59) τῶν ὁπλιτῶν τὸ στῖφος Thuc 8.92.5.
μετὰ δὲ τῆς Ποτιδαίας τὴν ἀποτείχισιν Thuc 1.65.3
περὶ τοῦ μισθοῦ τῆς ἀποδόσεως Thuc 8.85.3.

An almost grammaticalized version of the distinction between internal and external genitives is found with nonlexicals. For instance, the reflexive possessive αὑτοῦ is contrastive and normally internal, while the simple anaphoric possessive αὐτοῦ is usually syntactically postpositive to the head noun, to a modifier or more rarely to a superordinate head

(60) τὴν χώραν αὐτοῦ Dem 17.6
τὰς ἑαυτοῦ χώρας Dem 7.28

(56) After the defection of the Argives from the alliance (Thuc 5.81.1). After the transfer of the men to the island (Thuc 3.76.1).

(57) The farms of the Syrians (Her 1.76). The sons of the kings (Her 3.15). The generals of the Ionians (Her 5.109). The generals of the Athenians (Thuc 4.66.3).

(58) So that you may destroy both the present and the future power of the Athenians (Thuc 6.92.5). Fearing the audacity and the revolutionary spirit of the Athenians (Thuc 1.102.3).

(59) The mass of the hoplites (Thuc 8.92.5). After the investment of Potidaea (Thuc 1.65.3). Concerning the payment of the wages (Thuc 8.85.3).

(60) His country (Dem 17.6). His own lands (Dem 7.28).

(61) τὴν γυναῖκ᾽ αὐτοῦ Dem 18.204, 41.12
τὴν ἑαυτοῦ γυναῖκ᾽ Dem 59.110, 46.13

τὸν πατέρ᾽ αὐτοῦ Dem 23.111, 24.126
τὸν μὲν ἑαυτοῦ πατέρα Dem 22.56.

(62) τῶν ἰδίων αὐτοῦ πονηρευμάτων Dem 25.60
προσέβαλλον αὐτῶν τῷ τείχει Thuc 3.52.2.

Genitive positions in hyperbaton

With this analysis in hand, we are in a position to give an account of genitive
hyperbaton. Both external positions can be used in genitive hyperbaton, typically Y₁ for topic or focus, Y₂ for tail genitives

(63) τῆς οἰκίας ταύτης ἔστηκε τὰ οἰκόπεδα Aesch 1.182
τῶν συνθηκῶν ἀνάγνωθι τὰ ἀντίγραφα Aesch 1.115
χωρὶς μὲν γὰρ τῶν Περσέων ἐκέετο τὰ ὀστέα Her 3.12

ἡ στρατία ἥξει τῶν Ἀθηναίων Thuc 4.42.3
καὶ τοὺς προτέρους στρατιώτας νοσῆσαι τῶν Ἀθηναίων Thuc 2.58.2
τὴν πρᾶσιν ἐποιήσατο τοῦ ἀγῶνος Aesch 1.115.

Both internal positions also occur with hyperbaton. The following examples of
Y₁ internal genitives have contrastive focus

(64) τὸ Δημοσθένους ἐπιγράφειν ὄνομα Aesch 3.159
τοὺς Ἀθηναίων κάλει πρέσβεις Aesch 2.59
τὴν τῶν δικαστῶν... θεασώμεθα δύναμιν Pl *Polit* 305b
τὴν τῆς αὐτοῦ ποίμνης ἄριστα μεταχειριζόμενος μουσικήν
Pl *Polit* 268b
τὴν τῆς πόλεως ὁρῶν ῥώμην Pl *Alc* 1.135e.

On the other hand, in the following examples of Y₂ internal genitive hyperbaton, the genitive is in one way or another predictable in context

(61) His wife (Dem 18.204). His own wife (Dem 59.110). His father (Dem 23.111).
His own father (Dem 22.56).
(62) His private crimes (Dem 25.60). An attack was being made on their wall (Thuc
3.52.2).
(63) The foundations of that house still stand (Aesch 1.182). Read the copy of the
agreement (Aesch 1.115). The bones of the Persians lay separately (Her 3.12). That the
army of the Athenians would come (Thuc 4.42.3). Also the original troops of the Athenians fell ill (Thuc 2.58.2). He effected the sale of the case (Aesch 1.115).
(64) To write the name of Demosthenes (Aesch 3.159). Call the ambassadors of the
Athenians (Aesch 2.59). Let us consider the function of judges (Pl *Polit* 305b). Performing best the music of his own herd (Pl *Polit* 268b). Seeing the strength of the city (Pl *Alc*
1.135e).

(65)   τῆς ἀρχῆς ἀπόδειξιν ἔχει τῆς τῶν Ἀθηναίων Thuc 1.97.2
       τὴν αὔξην μοι δοκεῖ ἀπεικάζειν τὴν τῶν νέων Pl *Crat* 414a
       τοὺς νόμους ἧκεν ἔχων τοὺς τῶν ἐπικλήρων Dem 37.45
          (cp. Dem 47.71)
       τὰς δ᾽ ἐπιστολὰς ὑμῖν ἀναγνώσομαι τὰς τοῦ Φιλίππου Dem 19.187
       τὰς δὲ συμβουλίας πιστοτέρας ὑπολαμβάνετ᾽ εἶναι τὰς τῶν πρέσβεων
          Dem 19.5.

To sum up, both the external and the internal Y2 positions are used for established information. In Demosthenes 19.187 (just cited), an example of internal
Y2, it is not a question of whether to read Philip's letters or someone else's. The
same holds for the external Y2 position. In Thucydides 2.58.2 (repeated here)

καὶ τοὺς προτέρους στρατιώτας νοσῆσαι τῶν Ἀθηναίων

there is no need to distinguish between an earlier force of Athenians and an
earlier force of some other city. Our examples for external Y1 position are split
by dialect. It is not the case in Aeschines 1.115 (likewise repeated here)

τῶν συνθηκῶν ἀνάγνωθι τὰ ἀντίγραφα

that it is useful in the discourse context to distinguish between a copy of the
agreement in question and a copy of some other document. However, in
Herodotus 3.12, the Persians are contrastive and the bones are tail, but, as
already noted, Herodotus has less constraint on external Y1 possessives in continuous YPs too. On the other hand, internal Y1 position is consistently associated with some form of contrast.

Y₁ HYPERBATON IN VERSE

Genre differences between prose and verse in the frequency and use of hyperbaton are not in themselves unexpected. For instance, both in Finnish (Leino
1986) and in modern Georgian (Boeder 1989) hyperbaton is less constrained
in verse than in ordinary speech. In Greek, not only is hyperbaton far less
restricted in verse in terms of absolute frequency, it is also less constrained in
terms of the pragmatic values it can assume. In prose Y1 hyperbaton is consistently associated with strong focus, but in verse this constraint does not apply.
This complicates our story in two ways. Since Y1 hyperbaton in verse encodes
not only strong focus on the modifier but also simple weak focus, we get firstly
a difference in pragmatic meaning without a prima facie difference in syntactic
structure

(65) They also contain an exposition of the domination of the Athenians (Thuc
1.97.2). It seems to depict the growth of the young (Pl *Crat* 414a). He came having with
him the laws concerning heiresses (Dem 37.45). I will read you the letters of Philip (Dem
19.187). You consider the advice of the ambassadors more reliable (Dem 19.5).

(66)   σὸν μὲν ἐχθαίρων λέχος | καινῆς δὲ νύμφης ἱμέρῳ πεπληγμένος
      Med 555 (YXY; strong Y₁ focus)
      ἢ σὸν ἐχθαίρων λέχος; *Med* 697 (YXY; weak Y₁ focus)

and secondly a difference in syntactic structure without a prima facie difference in pragmatic meaning from neutral unmarked word order

(67)   σὸν δέμας θηρώμενος *Phoen* 699 (YP X)
      καὶ σὸν ἐκσῶσαι δέμας *Hel* 1092, cp. *Orest* 405, *Med* 531 (YXY).

In this section, we will document this difference between verse and prose. We will also briefly note differences in the admissibility of Y₁ hyperbaton involving prepositional phrases. Our objectives in this section are limited to a preliminary presentation of the pertinent evidence; analysis and explanation will come in later chapters.

Nonlexical Y₁ hyperbaton

We distinguish nonlexical hyperbaton from clitic hyperbaton (discussed later in this chapter). Nonlexical hyperbaton involves a demonstrative or a pronominal possessive adjective as the Y₁ modifier. Like ordinary lexical hyperbaton, nonlexical hyperbaton is crosscategorial

NOUN PHRASE

(68)   τύραννον τῆσδε γῆς *Hel* 1058, cp. *Rhes* 388, *Heracl* 111 [X YP]
      τῆσδε φάρμακον νόσου *Hipp* 479

      ἄναξ τῆσδε χθονός *HF* 8 [X YP]
      τῆσδε κοίρανος χθονὸς *Med* 71, *Alc* 507

ADJECTIVE PHRASE

(69)   ὃς κακῶν τῶνδ᾽ αἴτιος *IA* 895 (NAX)
      τῶνδ᾽ ὃς αἴτιος κακῶν *Med* 332 (AXN)

PREPOSITIONAL PHRASE

(70)   ἐν τῇδ᾽ ἡμέρᾳ *Hipp* 22, *Andr* 803 [X YP]
      τῇδ᾽ ἐν ἡμέρᾳ *Hipp* 726, *Med* 1231

      ἔν γ᾽ ἐμοῖς δόμοις *Andr* 934 [X YP]
      σοῖσιν ἐν δόμοις *Troad* 943, *Hel* 1651

(66) Hating your bed and struck with love for a new bride (*Med* 555). Or hating your bed (*Med* 697).

(67) Looking for your person (*Phoen* 699). And to save your life (*Hel* 1092).

(68) The king of this land (*Hel* 1058). A cure for this disease (*Hipp* 479). King of this land (*HF* 8). Ruler of this land (*Med* 71).

(69) Who is responsible for these evils (*IA* 895). Who is responsible for these evils (*Med* 332).

(70) On this day (*Hipp* 22). On this day (*Hipp* 726). In my house (*Andr* 934). In your house (*Troad* 943).

VERB PHRASE

(71)   λιποῦσα τούσδε... δόμους *Hel* 1526 [X YP]
        τούσδ᾽ ἂν ἐκλίποι δόμους *Hipp* 796.

In prose, when demonstratives and possessives are used in Y1 hyperbaton, it is regularly with strong narrow focus, either simple focus or focused topic

(72)   ταύτην ἀνθ᾽ ἁπάντων ἀπαιτοῦμεν ὑμᾶς τὴν χάριν Lys 18.23
        ἵνα ταύτην ἔχοιεν ἐμοὶ τὴν αἰτίαν ἐπιφέρειν Antiph 5.55
        ὑπὸ ταύτης ἀγόμενοι τῆς ἐλπίδος Pl *Phaedo* 68a
        ἀπὸ τῶν ὑμετέρων ὑμῖν πολεμεῖ συμμάχων Dem 4.34
        τίν᾽ οὖν ῥᾳστώνην... ὁ σός, ὦ Λεπτίνη, ποιεῖ νόμος Dem 20.28.

This type can also occur in verse

(73)   τούσδε γε στέρξεις νόμους *Hipp* 461
        οὗτος ἦν τεθῇ νόμος Eur *Suppl* 541
        τὸ μὲν σὸν σπεύδων ἀγαθὸν *Hec* 120;

an example of association with focus depends on Nauck's οὐ at Euripides Frag 795.3; but the vast majority of verse examples do not have strong narrow focus

(74)   τοῖσδ᾽ ἐπιστένεις τέκνοις *Med* 929
        τούσδ᾽ ἂν ἐκλίποι δόμους *Hipp* 796
        σοῖς ἁμιλλῶμαι λόγοις *Hipp* 971.

There is no question in these examples as to which children to grieve over, which house to depart from, or whose words to contest, respectively. This type is practically absent in prose; there are a few examples in which, while the Y2 noun is tail material, the status of the nonlexical is less clear

(75)   τοῦθ᾽ ὑμῖν ἀναγνώσεται τὸ ἐπίγραμμα Dem 20.112
        τούτους τε εἰσήγαγον τοὺς κωπέας Andoc 2.11
        οὐκ ἂν ἡ ἡμετέρα κατέστη μήτηρ Isae 3.5.

The two demonstratives may be noncontrastive topics; the possessive in the Isaeus example could apparently be a contrastive focus. Additional evidence for this difference is provided by negation. Negation is focus sensitive, and can

(71) Leaving this house (*Hel* 1526). He would leave this house (*Hipp* 796).

(72) This is the thanks that we ask of you in return for everything (Lys 18.23). So as to have this accusation to bring against me (Antiph 5.55). Induced by this hope (Pl *Phaedo* 68a). He makes war on you at the expense of your own allies (Dem 4.34). What relief does your law give, Leptines...? (Dem 20.28).

(73) You are going to be satisfied with these rules (*Hipp* 461). If this law is instituted (Eur *Suppl* 541). Furthering your interests (*Hec* 120).

(74) You lament over these children (*Med* 929). He would leave this house (*Hipp* 796). I contest your words (*Hipp* 971).

(75) He will read you this inscription (Dem 20.112). I supplied the oar spars (Andoc 2.11). Our mother would not have become ⟨heiress⟩ (Isae 3.5).

associate with a narrow focus. In prose a demonstrative in hyperbaton is a narrow focus, and if there is no other focus in the clause, the negative is likely to associate with the hyperbaton modifier, as discussed in chapter 2

(76)   οὐ ταύτην οὗτος ἄγει τὴν ἡσυχίαν Dem 18.308.

This can also happen in verse; in the following example (and also at *Andr* 935) the Y1 possessive is probably one of the foci associated with the negative

(77)   οὐ γὰρ σ᾽ ἔγωγε τῇδ᾽ ἐμῇ θάψω χερί *Alc* 665.

What is interesting is that there are some verse examples in which the negative does not associate with the hyperbaton modifier but with some other constituent not in hyperbaton at all

(78)   οὔτ᾽ ἦλθες ἐς τόνδ᾽ ἐξ ἐμοῦ κληθεὶς τάφον *Alc* 629
        οὐ σῆς προυνοησάμην φρενός *Hipp* 685.

In the *Alcestis* passage, the negative associates with the narrow focus ἐξ ἐμοῦ: 'The invitation which resulted in your coming to this funeral was not from ME'); while in the *Hippolytus* example the negation has clausal scope. In both examples, the negative does not associate with the nonlexical hyperbaton modifier because the modifier is not a narrow focus.

In nonlexical hyperbaton, Y1 is very commonly placed immediately preceding the head, irrespective of the category of X

(79)   τῶνδε διάλυσις κακῶν *Phoen* 435
        τὰς τῶνδ᾽ ἴστορας βουλευμάτων *IT* 1431
        τῶνδ᾽ ἀπότροποι κακῶν *Phoen* 586
        τῶνδε διάδοχος δόμων *Alc* 655
        τήνδ᾽ ἐς πυράν Eur *Suppl* 1065
        τόνδ᾽ ἐς οἶκον *Hel* 46

(80)   τήνδε πορσύνων χάριν Eur *Suppl* 132
        τήνδε διασῶσαι πόλιν *Phoen* 783
        σὸν οἰκήσειν δόμον *Hipp* 1010
        σὴν καθαιμάξαι δέρην *Orest* 1527.

An additional constituent can stand between the nonlexical and the head or between the head and the Y2 noun

(76) That is not the sort of disengagement that his man practises (Dem 18.308).

(77) I shall not bury you with this hand of mine (*Alc* 665).

(78) You did not come to this funeral invited by me (*Alc* 629). Didn't I foresee your intentions (*Hipp* 685).

(79) The termination of these evils (*Phoen* 435). Those having knowledge of this plot (*IT* 1431). Averters of these evils (*Phoen* 586). Heir to this house (*Alc* 655). Onto this pyre (Eur *Suppl* 1065). To this house (*Hel* 46).

(80) Doing this favour (Eur *Suppl* 132). To save this city (*Phoen* 783). To dwell in your house (*Hipp* 1010). To cut your throat (*Orest* 1527).

(81)   ποῦ τόνδε Θανάτῳ φῄς ἀγῶνα συμβαλεῖν; *Alc* 1141
        τὸν σὸν Ἑλλὰς ἀποτείσει φόνον *IT* 338

        τοῖσδ᾽ ἀνέστεμμαι κάρα | πλεκτοῖσι φύλλοις *Hipp* 806
        οἳ τήνδ᾽ ἐπεστράτευσαν Ἕλληνες πόλιν *Troad* 22.

Finally, another modifier can precede the Y1 nonlexical

(82)   Σκαμανδρίους γὰρ τάσδε διαπερῶν ῥοὰς *Troad* 1151
        Φεραίας τῆσδε κωμῆται χθονός *Alc* 476
        ἐπεὶ πετραίαν τήνδ᾽ ἐσήλθομεν †χθόνα *Cycl* 382
        τὴν ἑπτάπυργον τήνδε δεσπόζων πόλιν *HF* 28
        βίᾳ δ᾽ ὁ καινός μ᾽ οὗτος ἁρπάσας πόσις *Troad* 959
        τὴν ἐν οἴκοις σὴν καταστήσει κόρην *Andr* 635.

As noted in chapter 2, this pattern hardly occurs with descriptive adjectives in prose, but it is found with strong focus on the external modifier

(83)   οἱ διερωτῶντες ὑμᾶς οὗτοι πεφήνασι ῥήτορες... Dem 3.22.

Hyperbaton with prepositional phrases

Whereas hyperbaton with prepositional X is practically restricted to περί in prose, it occurs freely with other prepositions in verse

(84)   ἐν τῇδ᾽ ἡμέρᾳ *Hipp* 22, *Andr* 803 (X YP)
        τῇδ᾽ ἐν ἡμέρᾳ *Hipp* 726, *Med* 1231

        ἔν γ᾽ ἐμοῖς δόμοις *Andr* 934 (X YP)
        σοῖσιν ἐν δόμοις *Troad* 943, *Hel* 1659

        μυρίων ὑπ᾽ ἀγγέλων *Andr* 562
        κρεμαστοῖς ἐν βρόχοις *Hipp* 779
        αἰσχροῖς ἐπ᾽ ἔργοις *Hipp* 721
        χλωρὰν δ᾽ ἂν᾽ ὕλην *Hipp* 17.

Prepositional phrase hyperbaton is analyzed in more detail in chapter 5. In verse, as in prose, a verb may stand between PrepY1 and Y2, expanding a continuous prepositional phrase

(81) Where do you say that you fought this battle with death (*Alc* 1141). Greece will atone for your murder (*IT* 338). I am crowned on my head with these plaited leaves (*Hipp* 806). The Greeks who marched against this city (*Troad* 22).

(82) Passing over these streams of the Scamander (*Troad* 1151). Inhabitants of this land of Pherae (*Alc* 476). When we came into this rocky land (*Cycl* 382). Ruling this seven-gated city (*HF* 28). This new husband having taken me by force (*Troad* 959). He will make your daughter in the house ⟨regret⟩ (*Andr* 635).

(83) These orators who keep putting questions to you have shown up (Dem 3.22).

(84) Today (*Hipp* 22). Today (*Hipp* 726). In my house (*Andr* 934). In your house (*Troad* 943). By thousands of messengers (*Andr* 562). In a hanging noose (*Hipp* 779). Having behaved disgracefully (*Hipp* 721). In the green forest (*Hipp* 17).

(85)   ἐς τηλουρὸν ἥκομεν πέδον *PV* 1
     ἐν τοιοῖσδε κειμένη κακοῖς *Hec* 969
     ἐπ' ἀκταῖς νιν κυρῶ θαλασσίαις *Hec* 698.

Given that prose does not allow ordinary prepositional phrase hyperbaton, it follows that there is also a constraint against $Y_1VPrepY_2$. This constraint applies in Polish too (Siewierska 1984)

     O tej   mówiliśmy dziewczynie
     about this we spoke   girl
     *Tej mówiliśmy o dziewczynie
     this we spoke about girl
     'We spoke about this girl.'

Verse, which allows prepositional phrase hyperbaton, predictably also does allow $Y_1VPrepY_2$, although it is less common the $PrepY_1VY_2$

(86)   σὴν μολόντ' ἐφ' ἑστίαν *Hec* 1216
     Ὁμολωΐσιν δὲ τάξιν εἶχε πρὸς πύλαις *Phoen* 1119
     μελαίνη κειμένους ἐπὶ χθονί Archilochus 130.2 West
     ἀργενναῖς ἐτράφης Ἰδαίαις παρὰ μόσχοις *IA* 574 (AVAPrepN).

We note in passing that this structure also occurs in Y_2 hyperbaton with both adjective and genitive modifiers

(87)   λιμένας ἦλθες εἰς εὐηνέμους *Andr* 749
     εὐνὰς ἤλυθον πρὸς Ἕκτορος *Rhes* 660
     βρέτη πεσούσας πρὸς πολισσούχων θεῶν *Sept* 185.

At first sight, the genitive examples seem hopelessly scrambled, but the *Rhesus* structure is probably just a verse counterpart of prose examples like

(88)   ἐπὶ σκηνὴν ἰόντες τὴν Ξενοφῶντος Xen *An* 6.4.19,

the equivalent of σκηνὴν ἰόντες ἐπὶ Ξενοφῶντος. A similar interpretation is available for the adjective type in the *Andromache* example (p. 242).

Lexical Y_1

In prose, there are strict constraints on adjectives in Y_1 hyperbaton, as analyzed in chapter 2. Basically, an adjective can only be used in Y_1 hyperbaton if it has narrow strong focus. Consequently descriptive adjectives, emphatic or other-

(85) We have come to a distant land (*PV* 1). Being in such trouble (*Hec* 969). I found him on the seashore (*Hec* 698).

(86) Coming to your hearth (*Hec* 1216). He had his post at the Homoloid gate (*Phoen* 1119). Lying on the black earth (Archilochus 130.2). You were brought up as a cowherd beside the white heifers of Mt Ida (*IA* 574).

(87) You came to a sheltered harbour (*Andr* 749). I came to Hector's couch (*Rhes* 660). Falling before the images of the gods that protect the city (*Sept* 185).

(88) Coming to Xenophon's tent (Xen *An* 6.4.19).

wise, and restrictive adjectives not in strong focus never, or hardly ever, occur in Y₁ hyperbaton in prose. In verse, this constraint is simply absent. Descriptively used adjectives are well attested in Y₁ hyperbaton in tragedy, particularly in contexts favouring their occurrence, such as the ornamental style of lyric or the highly coloured narrative of messenger speeches

(89)   λευκὸν ἐδίδοσαν γάλα *Bacch* 700
λευκὸν ἐσχέας γάλα *Cycl* 389
λευκὴν τ᾽ ἀπέστρεψ᾽ ἔμπαλιν παρηίδα *Med* 1148
λευκὴν ἔδαπτον σάρκα *Med* 1189 (v.l.)

(90)   στικτῶν τ᾽ ἐνδυτὰ νεβρίδων *Bacch* 111
πολιῷ τεμεῖν σιδάρῳ *Heracl* 758
φόνιον δ᾽ ἀπόπαυσον Ἅιδαν *Alc* 225
τὸ κλεινὸν ἤλθομεν Φοίβου πέδον *Andr* 1085
τόν τ᾽ ὠκυρόαν διαβὰς Ἀξιὸν *Bacch* 569.

There is no question here of white milk being chosen rather than other qualities of contextually available milk (*Bacch* 700, *Cycl* 389), nor of Jason's bride's other cheek being a different colour (*Med* 148); and so on.

Perhaps the most familiar category of descriptive adjective in verse is the Homeric ornamental epithet (Parry 1971; Untermann 1984). Some Homeric epithets draw attention to permanent properties of a unique definite referent, so that a restrictive interpretation is theoretically impossible

(91)   εὐρεῖα χθῶν
ἀπείρονα πόντον
λευκοῖο γάλακτος *Od* 9.246.

Others involve a contextually unique definite referent in one way or another

(92)   μέγα τόξον *Il* 4.124
πικρὸν ὀϊστόν *Il* 4.118
πλοκάμους... φαεινοὺς *Il* 14.176.

In the *Iliad* 4 examples, both the bow and the particular arrow in question have already been established in the context, so that the adjectives do not restrict reference but express additional properties of an established referent. In the *Iliad* 14 example, there is no variation in the luminosity of Hera's hair; it could have been dull or it could have been glossy; in the actual world, it was

(89) Gave their white milk (*Bacch* 700). Pouring in white milk (*Cycl* 389). She turned her white cheek to the opposite side (*Med* 1148). They were eating into the white flesh (*Med* 1189).

(90) Garments of dappled fawnskin (*Bacch* 111). To cut with the grey iron (*Heracl* 758). Stop murderous Hades (*Alc* 225). We came to Phoebus' famous land (*Andr* 1085). Crossing the swift-flowing Axius (*Bacch* 569).

(91) The wide earth. The endless sea. Of white milk (*Od* 9.246).

(92) Great bow (*Il* 4.124). Bitter arrow (*Il* 4.118). Glossy hair (*Il* 14.176).

glossy, and all of it was glossy. When a descriptive adjective in a definite description picks up a previous restrictive adjective ('the aforementioned small elephant'), it gets interpreted relative to the class of Y2, whereas ornamental descriptive adjectives ('the large elephant') are interpreted relative to a superordinate class, in this case animals. In a third group, the epithet occurs in an indefinite phrase; particularly when it is prenominal, a restrictive interpretation is natural

(93)   εἴλετο δ' ὀξὺν ἄκοντα *Od* 14.531
        ἔπορον δέ μοι ἀγλαὰ δῶρα *Od* 16.230
        αἰτήσασα θεοὺς περικαλλέ' ἄεθλα *Od* 24.85.

The only qualification here is that in Homer's heroic world low quality products were not much in evidence, so the function of restriction is almost reduced to confirming the predictable. Descriptive adjectives occur freely in Y1 hyperbaton in Homer

(94)   λευκοὺς δ' ἐπέρησεν ὀδόντας *Il* 5.291
        ξανθὴν ἀπεκείρατο χαίτην *Il* 23.141
        ἐΰτριχας ὡπλίσαθ' ἵππους *Il* 23.351

(and also in Y2 hyperbaton: *Iliad* 3.329, 369 etc.). It was suggested in chapter 2 that this difference between prose and verse in the acceptability of descriptive adjectives in Y1 hyperbaton was probably not merely a reflex of their far higher incidence in verse texts.

Some verse instances of restrictive adjectives in Y1 hyperbaton involve narrow strong focus, just as in prose

(95)   πλείστων ἁψάμενος λόγων *Alc* 964
        ἐκ δισσαῖν θνῄσκετ' ἀνάγκαιν *Andr* 516
        καὶ γὰρ ἀπ' ἐχθρῶν ἥκετε πύργων *Andr* 515
        πεισθεὶς ἀφανῆ;... φανερὰν δ' ἔσχεθες ἄτην *Hipp* 1289
        παλαιὰ καινῶν λείπεται κηδευμάτων *Med* 76
        οὐ χρὴ 'πὶ μικροῖς μεγάλα πορσύνειν κακὰ *Andr* 352.

There is no reason to assume that the syntactic and pragmatic principles licensing

---

(93)   He took a sharp javelin (*Od* 14.531). They gave me beautiful gifts (*Od* 16.230). Having asked the gods for very beautiful prizes (*Od* 24.85).

(94)   It pierced his white teeth (*Il* 5.291). He cut off a lock of golden hair (*Il* 23.141). He prepared his fair-maned horses (*Il* 23.351).

(95)   Having touched on very many questions (*Alc* 964). You are condemned to die by two separate sentences (*Andr* 516). You come from an enemy city (*Andr* 515). Persuaded about unseen things, you got a clearly seen ruin (*Hipp* 1289). Old marriage ties are left behind by new ones (*Med* 76). You should not inflict major wrongs in return for minor ones (*Andr* 352).

(96) μεγίστων αἴτιος κακῶν *Med* 1080

are any different from those licensing

(97) μεγίστων αἴτιος κακῶν Dem 18.143, cp. Aesch 3.188.

However, it is probable that in verse restrictive adjectives in Y₁ hyperbaton need not have an exclusive or contrastive meaning. Ordinary weak focus is apparently sufficient to license Y₁ hyperbaton in verse for lexical (as well as nonlexical) adjectives

(98) χρυσέαις ἐζευγμέναι | πόρπαισιν Eur *El* 317
      διὰ δ' αἰθερίας στείχοντε πλακὸς Eur *El* 1349
      χρυσέην ἐπέθηκε κορώνην *Il* 4.111
      πατρώϊον ἵκετο δῶμα *Il* 21.44
      ὀξὺν ἔχων πέλεκυν *Il* 17.520.

In chapter 4, we will offer an explanation for how a language could come to have the pragmatically less restricted Y₁ hyperbaton found in verse, and how it could subsequently develop the sort of constraints obtaining in prose. We will also suggest that the two types of Y₁ hyperbaton are actually associated with different structural positions. At this preliminary stage, our aim is merely to substantiate the difference between the two genres. In case anyone is still sceptical and inclined to dismiss the difference between prose and verse as a reflex of different subject matter and (nonsyntactic) stylistic convention, we cite the parallel of Polish, where a quite similar situation obtains, mutatis mutandis (Siewierska 1984). In colloquial Polish speech, hyperbaton is associated with strong focus, optimally with symmetrical contrast. However, in literary prose hyperbaton can also occur with weak focus and with unfocused nonlexicals. When presented with examples of the exclusively literary type of hyperbaton out of their literary context, native speakers of Polish either rejected them saying that they did not understand why the Y₁ modifiers were in hyperbaton, or corrected them into colloquially acceptable hyperbata by stressing the Y₁ modifier so as to induce a strong narrow focus.

HYPERBATA MINORA

Conjunct hyperbaton

Consider the following Polish examples (Giejgo 1981)

Słynnego przywitaliśmy językoznawçe
famous   we greeted   linguist

(96) Responsible for the greatest evils (*Med* 1080).
(97) Responsible for the greatest evils (Dem 18.143).
(98) Wearing golden brooches (Eur *El* 317). Going across the heavenly region (Eur *El* 1349). He put on a golden tip (*Il* 4.111). He came to his father's house (*Il* 21.44). Having a sharp axe (*Il* 17.250).

> Językoznawçe przywitaliśmy słynnego
>   linguist   we greeted   famous
> 'We greeted a famous linguist'
>
> Szynkę kupił i chleb
>   ham bought and bread
> 'We bought ham and bread.'

The first example is a Y_1 modifier hyperbaton, the second a Y_2 modifier hyperbaton. In the third, the verb is straddled not by a noun and its modifier but by a pair of conjuncts. We call this conjunct hyperbaton, and it is well attested in Greek too

(99)   Οἰνόην αἱρέουσι καὶ Ὑσιάς Her 5.74
        τὰς νέας ἐνέπρησαν καὶ τὸ τεῖχος ἅπαν Her 9.106
        πάντα ἄνθρωπον φεύγουσι καὶ παντὸς ὁμιλίην Her 4.174
        τούς τε Σκύθας κατεστρέψατο καὶ τοὺς Θρήικας Her 2.103
        πολλὴν δυσκολίαν ἔχοντα καὶ ταραχὴν Dem 5.1
        σκέλεα δὲ ἀποτάμνουσι καὶ τὴν ὀσφὺν ἄκρην καὶ τοὺς ὤμους τε
          καὶ τὸν τράχηλον Her 2.40
        ἵν᾽ ἀθανάτοισι φόως φέροι ἠδὲ βροτοῖσι Il 11.2.

These examples illustrate direct and indirect object conjunct hyperbaton and various expansions thereof.

In subject conjunct hyperbaton, agreement is normally with the associated conjunct, sometimes suggesting bare argument ellipsis or right node raising, and sometimes having the flavour of a comitative construction

(100)   σύ τε γὰρ Ἕλλην εἶ καὶ ἡμεῖς... Xen An 2.1.16
        ἐγὼ μὲν λέγω, ἔφη, καὶ Σεύθης τὰ αὐτά Xen An 7.7.16
        Εὐρύλοχος ἔσχατον εἶχε τὸ εὐώνυμον καὶ οἱ μετ᾽ αὐτοῦ
          Thuc 3.107.4.

The Y_2 conjunct can be a possessive

(101)   τῶν Πανοπέων τὴν πόλιν ἐνέπρησαν καὶ Δαυλίων καὶ Λιλαιέων
          Her 8.35
        Γοργοῦς ὄμματ᾽ ἔχων ἠδὲ βροτολοιγοῦ Ἄρηος Il 8.349

---

(99) They capture Oenoe and Hysiae (Her 5.74). They burned the ships and all of the wall (Her 9.106). They avoid all people and association with everyone (Her 4.174). He subdued the Scythians and the Thracians (Her 2.103). That they involve much difficulty and confusion (Dem 5.1). They cut off the legs, the loin end, the shoulders and the neck (Her 2.40). To bring light to the immortals and to mortals (Il 11.2).

(100) You are a Greek and so are we (Xen An 2.1.16). "Seuthes and I," he replied, "have the same to say" (Xen An 7.7.16). Eurylochus and those with him held the far left wing (Thuc 3.107.4).

(101) They burned the cities of Panopeus, Daulis and Lilaea (Her 8.35). Having the eyes of the Gorgon and of men-destroying Ares (Il 8.349).

(102)   εἰ μὴ Νὺξ δμήτειρα θεων ἐσάωσε καὶ ἀνδρῶν *Il* 14.259.

Prepositional complements and adjuncts can omit the preposition from the second conjunct under certain conditions

(103)   ἀπὸ κτηνέων ζώουσι καὶ ἰχθύων Her 1.216
        μιν σὺν παιδὶ περισχόμεθ᾽ ἠδὲ γυναικι *Od* 9.199
        παρὰ νηὸς ἀνήϊον ἠδὲ θαλάσσης *Od* 10.274;

contrast with repeated preposition

        ἐν Ἐλεφαντίνῃ Πέρσαι φρουρέουσι καὶ ἐν Δάφνῃσι Her 2.30.

In these examples, the single preposition is used for a single overall situation, the repeated preposition when reference is to two locally separate situations.

Conjunct hyperbaton is a purely structural phenomenon: it is completely crosscategorial. In addition to being a verb, as in the examples cited so far, the superordinate head X can be a preposition (in prose περί)

(104)   παίδων τε πέρι καὶ γυναικῶν Pl *Rep* 450c
        λύπης τε πέρι καὶ ἡδονῆς Pl *Rep* 464b
        νεῶν ἄπο καὶ κλισιάων *Il* 16.45

or an adjective

(105)   ἐλευθερίας ἡ πόλις μεστὴ καὶ παρρησίας γίγνεται Pl *Rep* 557b
        τῶν νόσων αἰτίους εἶναι καὶ τῆς ἀποβολῆς τῶν ἀρχαίων σαρκῶν
            Pl *Gorg* 518d
        ἠνορέῃ πίσυνοι καὶ κάρτεϊ χειρῶν *Il* 11.9
        πτωχῷ λευγαλέῳ ἐναλίγκιον ἠδὲ γέροντι *Od* 16.273.

The superordinate X can also be a noun, with various types of conjunct Y modifiers—quantifiers or genitives or adjectives

(106)   πέντε ναῦς καὶ πεντήκοντα Thuc 8.29.2
        πολλοὺς λόγους καὶ ταπεινοὺς Dem 21.186
        ἵππων τε πόδες πολλοὶ καὶ ἀνθρώπων Thuc 5.10.2
        καλὸν δὲ ἔργον καὶ ἐπιφανὲς Pl *Laws* 829c

(102) If Night, tamer of gods and men, had not saved me (*Il* 14.259).
(103) They live off livestock and fish (Her 1.216). We protected him with his child and wife (*Od* 9.199). I made my way up from the ship and the sea (*Od* 10.274). The Persians have guards at Elephantine and at Daphnae (Her 2.30).
(104) In the matter of women and children (Pl *Rep* 450c). As regards pain and pleasure (Pl *Rep* 464b). From the ships and the huts (*Il* 16.45).
(105) The city becomes full of freedom and free speech (Pl *Rep* 557b). That they are responsible for their diseases and for their loss of weight (Pl *Gorg* 518d). Trusting in their valour and the strength of their hands (*Il* 11.9). Resembling a wretched old beggar (*Od* 16.273).
(106) Fifty-five ships (Thuc 8.29.2). Many humble words (Dem 21.186). Many feet of horses and men (Thuc 5.10.2). A noble and distinguished deed (Pl *Laws* 829c).

(107)   κακῶν δὲ ἀνθρώπων καὶ ἀδίκων Pl *Laws* 899d
         μεγάλοις λίθοις καὶ ὀλισθηροῖς Xen *An* 4.3.6.

Finally, X itself may be coordinate

(108)   πολλὰ καὶ παθόντες κακὰ καὶ ποιήσαντες Aesch 2.172.

It is likely that branching and heavier conjuncts more strongly induce conjunct hyperbaton. A partly similar sort of heavy conjunct shift is found in English

> Jack and Arthur came
> Jack came and the emeritus professor who has spent thirty years
>   studying the grammatical terminology of Terentianus Maurus.

The difference is that in Greek the mere existence of a conjunct constitutes heaviness and can induce hyperbaton. In English, if a postponed subject conjunct is not heavy, it suggests an afterthought

> Jack came and Arthur.

Greek conjunct hyperbaton is not normally an afterthought construction but a more systematically available strategy for syntactically encoding coordination. (An afterthought analysis is in any case excluded for instances with τε... καὶ.) We shall take up the analysis of conjunct hyperbaton in chapter 4. There we shall argue that object conjunct hyperbata originate neither as syntactically discontinuous coordinate phrases nor as elliptical conjoined clauses, but as expansions that are semantically integrated into the nuclear X-phrase. We shall also argue for a strong structural similarity between conjunct hyperbaton and regular modifier Y2 hyperbaton. This is theoretically important, since it points to there being a single general explanation for both these types of hyperbaton. For the purposes of this chapter, the above preliminary data analysis will be sufficient.

Clitic hyperbaton

In one type of clitic hyperbaton, the clitic is simply hosted by an adjective or genitive which is itself in Y1 hyperbaton

(109)   δεινός τις ἐνέστακτο ἵμερος Her 9.3 (v.l.)
         δαιμονίη τις γίνεται ὁρμή Her 7.18
         αἱμασιῆς τις περιθέει κύκλος Her 6.74.

---

(107) Of evil and unrighteous men (Pl *Laws* 899d). With large slippery stones (Xen *An* 4.3.6).
(108) Having both suffered and inflicted many losses (Aesch 2.172).
(109) Some strange desire had come over him (Her 9.3). There is a heaven-sent impulse (Her 7.18). A circular stone wall surrounds it (Her 6.74).

In a second type, the clitic is raised to second position after a coordinating or subordinating conjunction, thereby stranding a noun in Y2 position

(110)   ἔνθα γάρ τι δεῖ ψεῦδος λέγεσθαι Her 3.72
        μή τί τοι ἐξ αὐτῆς γένηται βλάβος Her 1.9
        καίτοι τινὰ ἤδη ἤκουσα λόγον ἄλλον Her 4.77
        εἴ τινα τῆς Ἀττικῆς λῃσταὶ τόπον καταλάβοιεν Dem 7.4 (Y2V).

The clitic can be raised out of a prepositional phrase

(111)   εἴ τινα πρὸς ἄλλον δέοι Thuc 5.37.2.

When the clitic is an adjective modifying the stranded Y2 noun, the structure is a type of Y1 hyperbaton. When the stranded Y2 noun is a genitive, then the clitic is unequivocally a pronoun rather than an adjective, and the result is a type of Y1 genitive hyperbaton

(112)   μή κοτέ τις κατὰ ταῦτα ἀναβαίη ἀνθρώπων Her 8.53
        εἴ τις βούλοιτο Λακεδαιμονίων Her 7.134
        αἰεὶ ὅκως τινὰ ἴδοι τῶν ἀσταχύων ὑπερέχοντα Her 5.92ζ
        καί τινας διώκοντες εἷλον τῶν Φωκέων Her 8.33.

If a noun is topicalized or otherwise moved to a preverbal slot, it is the clitic that can get stranded in Y2 position: both are illustrated by a single passage from Plato

(113)   γυναῖκα δὲ γαμετὴν ἐὰν ἀνὴρ δι' ὀργὴν κτείνῃ τινά τις
        Pl *Laws* 868d.

When clitic movement within the noun phrase is allowed, it is to a position following the determiner

(114)   τῶν τινα προβοσκῶν Her 1.113
        ἐς τῶν τινα κωμέων Her 1.185,

and this type can occur with hyperbaton

(115)   τῶν τις δοκίμων ἄλλος Μήδων Her 1.124 (clitic hyperbaton plus
        Y1 hyperbaton).

(110) Where a lie has to be told (Her 3.72). That some harm may come to you from her (Her 1.9). I have heard some other story (Her 4.77). If pirates were to seize some area of Attic teritory (Dem 7.4).

(111) Towards anyone else necessary (Thuc 5.37.2).

(112) That any person would ever climb up that way (Her 8.53). If anyone of the Spartans wanted (Her 7.134). Every time he saw one of the ears of corn sticking up above the others (Her 5.92ζ). They pursued and captured some Phocians (Her 8.33).

(113) If a husband kills his wedded wife in anger (Pl *Laws* 868d).

(114) An assistant herdsman (Her 1.113). At one of the villages (Her 1.185).

(115) Some other of the notable Medians (Her 1.124).

In clitic hyperbaton, the posthead position of the Y2 noun is due to the usual factors; it is mostly presentational or tail material. This latter condition is particularly clearly illustrated in the following passage

(116)   εἰ γάρ τις πόλις πλουτεῖ ξύλοις... τί δ' εἴ τις σιδήρῳ... πλουτεῖ πόλις;
        Xen *Ath Pol* 2.11.

The clitic, on the other hand, is not pragmatically comparable to anything permitted in Y1 position in canonical hyperbaton, since clitics are incompatible with focus. This is a theoretically important observation. It is the clearest demonstration that Y1 hyperbaton is an autonomous syntactic phenomenon: Y1 hyperbaton is licensed by the syntax whenever a left branch is allowed to raise. Y1 hyperbaton cannot be explained purely in terms of pragmatically driven serial word order. Clitics and focused modifiers raise to different syntactic positons for entirely different reasons. In fact, the hyperbaton data cited for the indefinite τις after a conditional or temporal conjunction may have a semantic explanation in the same spirit (but different from) recent semantically based approaches to the clitic raising of definite pronouns (Jelinek 1996). Consider again examples like the following

> ἐκόλουε αἰεὶ ὅκως τινὰ ἴδοι τῶν ἀσταχύων ὑπερέχοντα Her 5.92ζ
> εἴ τινα... λῃσταὶ τόπον καταλάβοιεν Dem 7.4.

These are both variants of the notorious "donkey" sentences that have played a central role in the study of anaphora for the past twenty years. Mercifully, for our purposes the precise semantics of such sentences is not relevant. The point is that each example begins with some sort of quantifier or quantifier complex (irrespective of the precise theory chosen: $\forall x$, Always$_x \exists x$, $\forall e \exists x$, etc.) which introduces the variable associated with YP. For instance, here is one possible, rough and informal, paraphrase of our two examples: 'It is always the case for x if there is an entity x such that he sees x and x is one of the stalks and x is taller that he cuts x'; 'It is always the case for x if there is an entity x and x is a place and pirates capture x...'. The indefinite pronominal τινα seems to correspond to the introduction of the variable associated with the quantification and to have raised to join the initial quantifier complex stranding the noun. If this is actually the case, then hyperbaton with indefinite clitics shares with Y1 focus hyperbaton the property of encoding logical form or semantic structure overtly in the surface syntax.

In interrogative hyperbaton (already illustrated in chapter 1), the interrogative, which is an accented form of the indefinite, moves to the sentence initial interrogative operator position, stranding the Y2 element.

---

(116) If some city is rich in timber... what if some city is rich in iron? (Xen *Ath Pol* 2.11).

Specifier hyperbaton

We illustrate this type of hyperbaton with examples of πολύ moving from the specifier position of a comparative adjective to the specifier position of a higher projection

(117)   πολὺ εὐκαταλυτωτέρα Xen *Hell* 3.5.15 (Spec AP)
πολὺ γὰρ νομίζω κρεῖττον εἶναι Xen *Oec* 17.6
πολὺ γάρ τῶν ἵππων ἔτρεχον θᾶττον Xen *An* 1.5.2
πολὺ ἄλλους ἐμοῦ δεινοτέρους Xen *Oec* 2.16
πολὺ γάρ ὁ λόγος ἦν μοι ἰσχυρότερος Dem 33.29.

Nonhead X hyperbaton

One of the most evident regularities of hyperbaton is the fact that the intervening X element is the head of a superordinate phrase including YP, as amply illustrated in chapter 1. This is probably not just a reflex of the way hyperbaton is defined, since a superordinate head constraint like that in Greek is typologically supported. It applies to discontinuous noun phrases in Fox (Dahlstrom 1987), where in postpositional phrases the intervening X is the postposition, in possessor phrases it is the possessed noun, and in argument phrases it is the verb. Similarly, both Luiseño (Steele 1989) and Polish (Siewierska 1984) allow a discontinuous object phrase with intervening verb but not with intervening indirect object. In Kayardild (Evans 1995), hyperbaton can only have the structure Y1VY2, that is it always straddles the verb.

Exceptions to the superordinate head constraint in Greek fall into three main classes. In one small group, an initial verb is followed by two arguments, one of them in hyperbaton

(118)   ἔδωκε Γοργίᾳ ἀργύριον τῷ Λεοντίνῳ Xen *An* 2.6.16.

This seems to be the same structure we find in verse examples with Y2 hyperbaton like

(119)   πλήξας ξίφει αὐχένα κωπήεντι *Il* 16.332
καί μιν βάλε μηρὸν ὀϊστῷ | δεξιόν *Il* 11.583
λίσσεσθαι ἐπεέσσιν ἀποσταδὰ μειλιχίοισι *Od* 6.146.

(117) Far easier to overthrow (Xen *Hell* 3.5.15). I think that it is much better (Xen *Oec* 17.6). They ran much faster than the horses (Xen *An* 1.5.2). Others much more skilled than me (Xen *Oec* 2.16). My argument would have been much stronger (Dem 33.29).

(118) He paid money to Gorgias of Leontini (Xen *An* 2.6.16).

(119) Striking him on the neck with his hilted sword (*Il* 16. 332). Struck him on the right thigh with an arrow (*Il* 11.583). Keeping his distance to implore her with gentle words (*Od* 6.146).

Conjunct hyperbaton can also show this arrangement

(120)   ἀπολύω καὶ ὑμᾶς τῆς αἰτίας καὶ Ἀγασίαν Xen *An* 6.6.15.

More intricate is the treaty language in the following example

(121)   σπονδὰς ἐποιήσαντο ἑκατὸν Ἀθηναῖοι ἔτη καὶ Ἀργεῖοι
        Thuc 5.47.1;

here there is a Y₁ hyperbaton in addition to the conjunct hyperbaton; the Y₁ numeral has been fronted ahead of the first postverbal subject.

In a second group, the universal quantifier is stranded or floats and has an adverbial flavour

(122)   τοὺς δὲ δούλους οἱ Σκύθαι πάντας τυφλοῦσι Her 4.2 (v.l.)
        (δούλους is topicalized)
        σκεύεσιν ἰδίοις τὴν ναῦν ἅπασι κατεσκεύασα Dem 50.7 (v.l.)
        εἰρήσεται γάρ, ἄνδρες Ἀθηναῖοι, πᾶσα πρὸς ὑμᾶς ἡ ἀλήθεια
        Dem 32.26.

The third group is more interesting

(123)   τόνδε Αἰγύπτιοι λόγον λέγουσι Her 2.54
        τοιαύτην διὰ τέλους γνώμην ἔχω Lys 25.17
        ὅπου πλείστη εὐκοσμία ἐστί, ταύτην ἄριστα τὴν πόλιν οἰκησομένην
        Aesch 1.22.
        ὁ νομοθέτης οὐδεμίαν ὀργῇ συγγνώμην δίδωσιν Lys 10.30
        φέρω | τὰ τῆς πόλεως ἅπαντα βαρέως πράγματα Ar *Eccl* 174.

Significantly, there are some examples of this type with distributive universal quantifiers

(124)   ἔχει γυναῖκας ἕκαστος πολλάς Her 5.5 (Y₂)
        πολλὰς ἑκάτεροι ἐλπίδας εἴχομεν Lys 12.53
        μνησθέντες... τῶν ἰδίων ἕκαστος δυστυχημάτων Lys 13.48.

The effect of the distributive pronoun in these examples is to set up a binary relation (called a pair list) between each member of the subject set and each member of the object set. For instance, for each member of the Thracian tribe

(120) I absolve you and Agasias of the accusation (Xen *An* 6.6.15).
(121) The Athenians and the Argives made a treaty for a hundred years (Thuc 5.47.1).
(122) The Scythians blind all their slaves (Her 4.2). I equipped the ship entirely with my own equipment (Dem 50.7). The whole truth, men of Athens, will be told to you (Dem 32.26).
(123) The Egyptians give this account (Her 2.54). I have consistently held these principles (Lys 25.17). That that city where there is the most law and order is governed in the best manner (Aesch 1.22). The lawmaker makes no allowance for loss of selfcontrol (Lys 10.30). I am upset with the entire political situation (Ar *Eccl* 174).
(124) They each have many wives (Her 5.5). We both had high hopes (Lys 12.53). Each remembering his personal misfortunes (Lys 13.48).

in the Herodotus passage there is a corresponding batch of wives; and for each person in the Lysias 13 passage there is a corresponding batch of ill fortunes. Note that when the object phrase has broad scope, no binary relation results. A sentence like

Each student read a play of Euripides

allows a reading in which each student read a different play and one in which they all read the same play. Now one way of thinking about the informational structure of Y₁ hyperbaton is in terms of the implicit questions it answers. This involves abstracting away from the exclusivity and treating strong focus on a par with weak focus, but the procedure is useful with this qualification. Regular Y₁ hyperbaton corresponds to a simple question with a single queried constituent

(125)   τίνι χρώμενος τεκμηρίῳ; Dem 20.115
         τῷ αὐτῷ... χρησόμεθα τεκμηρίῳ Pl *Symp* 195e.

The Y₁ interrogative and, respectively, the Y₁ focus are new information, and the rest belongs to the presupposition. However, when a pair list is involved, the situation is more complex. The question

What did each student read?

can be answered functionally (intensionally)

His assigned play of Euripides

or it can be answered extensionally with a list pairing different students with different plays, often with gapping of the repeated verb

Jack read the *Hecuba,* Sue the *Bacchae,* and Arthur the *Medea.*

This amounts to an answer to the question

Which student read which play?

(not in the context of a singleton pair) and takes the form of a function mapping each element in the domain of students to its appropriate value in the range of plays; pragmatically, the domain can be compared to a contrastive topic, the range to a contrastive focus. When we look again at an example of nonhead X hyperbaton like Her 2.54 just cited, we find that it is actually a pair list structure relating different accounts to different authorities

τόνδε Αἰγύπτιοι λόγον λέγουσι... τάδε δὲ Δωδωναίων φασὶ αἱ
προμάντεις Her 2.54-5: 'THIS is the account given by the
EGYPTIANS... but THIS is what the prophetesses of DODONA say.'

(125) Using what evidence? (Dem 20.115). We will use the same evidence (Pl *Symp* 195e).

The following verse example is even clearer

(126)   ὁρῶ δὲ θιάσους τρεῖς γυναικείων χορῶν, | ὧν ἦρχ᾽ ἑνὸς μὲν Αὐτονόη, τοῦ δευτέρου | μήτηρ Ἀγαύη σή, τρίτου δ᾽ Ἰνὼ χοροῦ *Bacch* 680

bijectively pairing Bacchant bands with their leaders. Such a pair list appears as the answer to a multiple interrogative question in the grasshopper story in the *Phaedrus*

(127)   ἀπαγγέλλειν τίς τίνα αὐτων τιμᾷ τῶν ἐνθάδε. Τερψιχόρᾳ... τοὺς ἐν τοῖς χοροῖς... τῇ δ᾽ Ἐρατοῖ τοὺς ἐν τοῖς ἐρωτικοῖς... τῇ δὲ... Καλλιόπῃ... τοὺς ἐν φιλοσοφίᾳ διάγοντας Pl *Phaedr* 259c.

So the reason why the third group of hyperbaton examples violates the superordinate head constraint is that they involve two foci (rather than just one, as in ordinary Y1 hyperbaton); they enter into a pair list relationship with each other, one being a focused topic and the other a straight focus. While the Herodotus passage is explicitly contrastive, the other passages have an implicit contrast with other actually occurring or theoretically possible pairs. For instance, in Aeschines 1.22 different cities are governed with different grades of efficiency; the passage excludes some other city being governed best and this city being governed second best. In Lysias 10.30, different excuses are associated with different degrees of mitigation; the passage excludes some allowance being made for anger, and implicates that some allowance does get made for certain other excuses. Nonhead X hyperbaton is found with argument pairing when Y1 belongs to the first argument of the pair. When YP is the second argument and the first is a contrastive topic, regular Y1 hyperbaton can be used, as for instance with μεγάλας in the following examples

(128)   τῷ μὲν διώκοντι ἐλάττω ἐποίησαν τὰ ἐπιτίμια..., τῷ δὲ φεύγοντι μεγάλας ἐπέθηκαν τιμωρίας Dem 47.2;

the nonhead X hyperbaton pattern would have given

μεγάλας δὲ τῷ φεύγοντι τιμωρίας ἐπέθηκαν.

Since Y1 can be either focus or topic, it can belong either to the range element or to the domain element of the functional map; for nonhead X hyperbaton to result, it has to belong to whichever is the serially preceding element (which does not depend on argument ranking). Even the corresponding multiple interrogatives should not show absolute superiority effects, since the Y2 nouns support a closed set of alternates.

(126) I see three bands of female dancers, of which one band was led by Autonoe, the second by your mother Agave, and the third by Ino (*Bacch* 680).

(127) To announce which one of those here on earth honours which one of them. To Terpsichore those in the dances, to Erato those in love, to Calliope those passing their lives in philosophy (Pl *Phaedr* 259c).

(128) They made the penalty less for the prosecution, but for the defendant they imposed a heavy punishment (Dem 47.2).

Whether the paired arguments and/or adjuncts in nonhead X hyperbaton could in any sense be said to form a constituent is a question we shall not address beyond the following very brief remarks. Sequences of pairs with verb ellipsis (gapping) as in the *Bacchae* example are obviously constituents if a missing verb is syntactically represented, but the status of socalled nonconstituent coordination

He gave his wife a cardigan and his mother a flat in Mayfair

is less clear. In the phrase punctuating *Lex Opuntiorum*, conjoined paired phrases are punctuated as prosodic constituents

(129)   : τον Λοϙρον τὸπιϝοιϙοι : και τον επιϝοιϙον τοι Λοϙροι : *Locr* 34.

Some theories assign direct plus indirect object to a single constituent of one type or another; the pair of arguments combine with the verb as a single unit (Kayne 1984; Dowty 1988; Steedman 1996). According to one idea, multiple interrogatives can be "absorbed" into a single binary interrogative operator at logical form (Higginbotham & May 1981). It has also been suggested that a form of constituency unites argument pairs which undergo long scrambling in Japanese (Kitahara 1997:122)

Sono hono Bill-ni John-ga Mary-ga   kinoo watasita-to
that book-ACC Bill-DAT John-NOM Mary-NOM yesterday handed-COMP
omotteiru (koto)
think   (fact)
'John thinks that Mary handed that book to Bill yesterday.'

Double hyperbaton

Double hyperbaton can arise when there are two branching noun phrases, each of which is a candidate for some type of hyperbaton. Again, double hyperbaton is just one of the various possible outcomes in this situation. The simplest outcome is for the two phrases to be kept serially separate

(130)   ὁ δ' ἄδικος λόγος | ...φαρμάκων δεῖται σοφῶν *Phoen* 471;

here the first noun phrase, a contrastively focused topic, is continuous, the second is in hyperbaton. More complex is the outcome in which one phrase is in hyperbaton and the other is continuous but nested inside the hyperbaton

(131)   ταύτην μὲν οὖν εἰς τὸν μέλλοντα χρόνον ἀνέγραψαν τὴν πολιτείαν,
ἐν δὲ τῷ παρόντι καιρῷ τήνδε Arist *Ath Pol* 31.1;

(129) One of the Locrians for the colonist and one of the colonists for the Locrian (*Locr* 34).

(130) The unjust argument needs clever doctoring (*Phoen* 471).

(131) They drew up this constitution for the future, but the following one for the present crisis (Arist *Ath Pol* 31.1).

here ταύτην, topicalized in hyperbaton, is explicitly contrastive with τήνδε, and μέλλοντα in the nested continuous noun phrase with παρόντι. This nested double focus structure can also occur with external verb

(132)   δυοῖν γε πάντες ἄνθρωποι λόγοιν | τὸν κρείσσον᾽ ἴσμεν
         Eur *Suppl* 486.

The third possible outcome is double hyperbaton, where both noun phrases (YP and ZP) are discontinuous and intersected. The order last in last out predominates over the nested order last in first out

(133)   λέπτ᾽ ἐπ᾽ ὀμμάτων φάρη | βαλοῦσα τῶν σῶν Eur *Suppl* 286
         (last in last out)
         ὀλολύγματα παννυχίοις ὑπὸ παρθένων ἰαχεῖ ποδῶν κρότοισιν
         Heracl 782 (last in first out).

Not all languages that allow single hyperbaton also allow double hyperbaton. For instance, Warlpiri does but Luiseño does not. Here is an example of double genitive hyperbaton from Polish (Giejgo 1981)

Jacka Marysi poleciłem ciotce kolegę
'I recommended Jack's friend to Mary's aunt.'

In Latin verse, double hyperbaton is almost a mannerism

inrita ventosae rapiebant verba procellae (Statius *Achilleid* 1.960)

but in Greek it is relatively rare, particularly in prose. This suggests that its rarity is not a matter of pragmatics, which should not vary greatly from one language to the next in comparable styles of discourse, but that there is a syntactic constraint in Greek. In the *Supplices* example just cited, the verb occurs between Y2 and Z2; similarly

(134)   πεδία δὲ πάντα... | ὠκεῖα μάργοις φλὸξ ἐδαίνυτο γνάθοις
         Phrynichus 5.3 Snell
         οὐδεμίαν πω... ἀγαθοὶ πόλιν ὤλεσαν ἄνδρες Theognis 43.

The verb can also stand between Z1 and Y2

(135)   ἐν οὐδὲν οὕτω δύναμιν ἔχει παίδειον μάθημα μεγάλην Pl *Laws* 747b

or outside the intersected noun phrase

(136)   ὃς μεγα πᾶσιν | ἕρκος Ἀχαιοῖσιν πέλεται πολεμοῖο κακοῖο *Il* 1.283

(132) All of us humans know the stronger of two arguments (Eur *Suppl* 486).
    (133) Putting a fine veil over your eyes (Eur *Suppl* 286). Shouts resound to the night-long beating of maiden feet (*Heracl* 782).
    (134) The swift flame devoured the whole plain with greedy jaws (Phrynichus 5.3). Upright men never destroyed any city (Theognis 43).
    (135) No single instructional discipline has as much influence (Pl *Laws* 747b).
    (136) Who is a great protection against evil war for all the Achaeans (*Il* 1.283).

(137)   ὡς Αἴας ἐπὶ πολλὰ θοάων ἴκρια νηῶν | φοίτα *Il* 15.685
          ἐπιβαλλομέναν χαίταισιν εὐώδη ῥοδέων πλόκον ἀνθέων *Med* 842
          φανήσεταί τι τῆσδε φάρμακον νόσου *Hipp* 479 (clitic hyperbaton).

The following prose examples have the same pairing structure as the nonhead
X hyperbaton discussed in the preceding section, but with an added Z_2

(138)   τοῦτον ἁπάσας τὸν τρόπον εἰληφέναι τὰς βουλάς Dem 22.6
          τὴν πόλιν ἅπαντες ἡμῶν Ἕλληνες ὑπολαμβάνουσιν ὡς φιλόλογός τέ
          ἐστι καὶ πολύλογος, Λακεδαίμονα δὲ... Pl *Laws* 641e;

in the Demosthenes passage the verb is inside the intersective double hyperbaton; in the Plato passage it is outside, πόλιν is topicalized and ἡμῶν is contrastively focused. This impression of pairing is reinforced by various types of
figura etymologica that characterize a number of instances, probably actually
licensing the prose ones (the following examples belong to the verb external
type)

(139)   δημιουργεῖν σύνθετα ἐκ μὴ συντιθεμένων εἴδη γενῶν Pl *Polit* 288e
          μηδὲν... ἧττον ἑτέραν ἑτέρας ψυχὴν ψυχῆς εἶναι Pl *Phaedo* 93d.

The special syntax of word pair structures is reminiscent of English *arm in arm,
face to face.* Here are some similar examples from verse

(140)   παρὰ φίλης φίλῳ φέρειν | γυναικὸς ἀνδρί *Cho* 89
          κραυγὴ δ᾽ ἐν εὐφήμοισι δύσφημος δόμοις | πέτραισιν ἀντέκλαγξ᾽
          Andr 1144
          ἕτερα δ᾽ ἀφ᾽ ἑτέρων κακὰ κακῶν κυρεῖ *Hec* 690.

Compare also καλὸς κ[αλ]ô on a nonconfigurational Boeotian cup (Morpurgo-
Davies 1968).

Attribute YP hyperbaton

In ordinary Y_1 hyperbaton, YP is prototypically an argument of the superordinate head X; Y_1 is a modifier of Y_2 and the discontinuity of Y_1 from Y_2 represents a prima facie violation of the left branch constraint. Attribute hyperbaton
involves a different distribution of categories. In attribute hyperbaton, the

(137) So did Ajax range over the many decks of the swift ships (*Il* 15.685). Putting on
her hair a fragrant wreath of rose blossoms (*Med* 842). Some remedy for this disease will
turn up (*Hipp* 479).
(138) That all the councils have received it in this way (Dem 22.6). All the Greeks
think that our city is fond of talk and full of talk, while Lacedaemon... (Pl *Laws* 641e).
(139) To manufacture composite products from noncomposite materials (Pl *Polit*
288e). That one soul is no less a soul than another (Pl *Phaedo* 93d).
(140) That I bring them from a dear wife to a dear husband (*Cho* 89). In the holy halls
an unholy clamour echoed from the rocks (*Andr* 1144). One evil follows another (*Hec*
690).

modifier relationship is between YP and X, while the argument (or adjunct) relationship is between the two Y elements. Consequently, the discontinuity of Y₁ and Y₂ is discontinuity between head and complement rather than between modifier and modified, and no left branch violation ensues. We will begin by illustrating how the system works with adjectives; as the "translations" demonstrate, Greek is much less constrained than English (where discontinuity is found mainly with comparatives, superlatives and infinitival complements of *tough* adjectives).

When an adjective is used attributively in prenominal position, in both definite and indefinite noun phrases, its complement or adjunct can be stranded postnominally

(141) ἀγνῶτος ἀνθρώπου τοῖς ῞Ελλησιν Lyc 14: 'an unknown man
            to the Greeks'
         τοὺς διαφανέας λίθους τῷ πυρί Her 4.75: 'the red-hot stones
            with fire'
         τραχύτερα πράγματα τῶν τότε γενομένων Isoc 7.18: 'harsher
            circumstances than those before'
         τὰ βέλτιστα σιτία τῷ σώματι Pl *Gorg* 464d: 'the best foods
            for the body.'

When the information in the complement of the adjective is more salient, an adjective can get stranded postnominally

(142) τὰ τῶν παρόδων τῶν εἰς Πύλας χωρία κύρια Aesch 2.132:
            'the approaches to Thermopylae places controlling.'

Note that there is no determiner doubling: τὰ τῶν παρόδων... χωρία is not a constituent at all, and so the adjective cannot be a separate complete adjective phrase but only the head of a discontinuous adjective phrase. The same applies when an attributive improper prepositional phrase is made discontinuous

(143) τὴν μεταξὺ πόλιν ῾Ηραίας καὶ Μακίστου Xen *Hell* 3.2.30:
            'the between city Heraea and Macistus.'

If τὴν μεταξὺ πόλιν τὴν ῾Ηραίας καὶ Μακίστου means anything at all, it is something quite different from the Xenophon example. Finally, as happens in ordinary hyperbaton, a further superordinate head is allowed to separate the adjective from its complement

(144) τῇ δὲ προτεραίᾳ ἡμέρᾳ ξυνέβη τῆς μάχης ταύτης Thuc 5.75.4:
            'on the previous day it happened to this battle.'

(141) A man unknown to the Greeks (Lyc 14). The stones red-hot with fire (Her 4.75). Harsher circumstances than those before (Isoc 7.18). The best foods for the body (Pl; *Gorg* 464d).
(142) The places controlling the approaches to Thermopylae (Aesch 2.132).
(143) The city between Heraea and Macistus (Xen *Hell* 3.2.20).
(144) On the day before the battle it happened that... (Thuc 5.75.4).

Since participles are more likely to have complements than adjectives, it is not surprising that attribute hyperbaton is particularly well attested with attributively used participles. On the other hand, since attributive participles pattern like attributive adjectives with complements, there is no need to appeal to the specifically bicategorial nature of participles. Sometimes attributive participles have no complement or adjunct, for instance if they are intransitive or passive or have implicit arguments

(145) ἐπὶ τοὺς παρατεταγμένους ἱππέας Xen Hell 3.4.23
       τοὺς δάκνοντας κύνας Xen Hell 2.4.41 (v.l.)
       ἐπὶ τοὺς παρεσκευσμένους ἵππους Xen Hell 6.4.32.

The rearticulated postnominal type is also found

(146) εἰς τὰς χώρας τὰς προσηκούσας Xen Oec 9.8
       ἐν ταῖς πόλεσι ταῖς στασιαζούσαις Xen Ath Pol 3.10.

When there is a complement or adjunct, it can appear adjacent to the participle both in the postnominal type

(147) μετὰ τοὺς ὅρκους τοὺς ἐν Λακεδαίμονι γενομένους Xen Hell 6.4.1
       κατὰ τὰς πύλας τὰς εἰς τὴν ἄκραν φερούσας Xen An 5.2.23

and in the prenominal type

(148) κατὰ τὰς ἐπὶ τὸ τεῖχος φερούσας κλίμακας Xen Hell 7.2.7
       τοὺς ἐπὶ κέρως πορευομένους λόχους Xen Hell 7.5.22
       τοὺς ὑπὸ τῶν λῃστῶν ἁλισκομένους βαρβάρους Xen Hell 3.4.19
       ἐν ταῖς πρὸς μεσημβρίαν βλεπούσαις οἰκίαις Xen Mem 3.8.9.

The participle precedes the complement in the following broad scope example

(149) τὰς πολεμούσας πρὸς ἀλλήλας πόλεις Xen Vect 5.8.

Note that the interpretation of prenominal adjectives as heads or coheads is thought to require adjacency of the adjective and the noun and consequently to preclude intervening complements. Even two noun phrases can join the participle in prenominal position, their order being pragmatically determined

(145) Against the cavalry drawn up opposite (Xen Hell 3.4.23). Dogs that bite (Xen Hell 2.4.41). Onto the horses which they had ready (Xen Hell 6.4.32).
(146) Into their proper places (Xen Oec 9.8). In the cities undergoing political strife (Xen Ath Pol 3.10).
(147) After the oaths that had been sworn at Lacedaemon (Xen Hell 6.4.1). Towards the gates that led into the citadel (Xen An 5.2.23).
(148) By the steps that led to the wall (Xen An 7.2.7). The squads stretching out to the wing (Xen Hell 7.5.22). The barbarians captured by the patrols (Xen Hell 3.4.19). In the houses facing south (Xen Mem 3.8.9).
(149) The cities fighting against each other (Xen Vect 5.8).

(150) τοῖς διὰ τῶν εἰκότων τὰς ἀποδείξεις ποιουμένοις λόγοις
Pl *Phaedo* 92d
τὴν ἐξ ἅπαντος τοῦ αἰῶνος συνηθροισμένην τῇ πόλει δόξαν Lyc 110.

However, it is also possible for either the complement or the participle to be stranded postnominally, depending on the pragmatic status of the complement phrase. When it is the participle that is prenominal, the postnominal complement of the participle is usually not focused but predictable tail material

(151) τὰς προσηκούσας ὄχθας ἐπὶ τὸν ποταμόν Xen *An* 4.3.23
(the river is part of the previously described scene)
τοὺς γευομένους κύνας τῶν προβάτων Dem 25.40
(second mention of the sheep)
τὸν ῥέοντα ποταμὸν διὰ τῆς πόλεως Xen *Hell* 5.2.4 (cp. τὸν
παρὰ τὴν πόλιν ῥέοντα ποταμόν *ibid.* 5.3.3)
τὸν ἐφεστηκότα κίνδυνον τῇ πόλει Dem 18.176
τὸν κατειληφότα κίνδυνον τὴν πόλιν Dem 18.220.

When it is the complement that stands before the noun, it is often focused

(152) τοῖς ἀπὸ τῶν θεῶν σημείοις γενομένοις Antiph 5.81
(contrast ἐκ τῶν ἀνθρωπίνων τεκμηρίων preceding)
τὰ ἐν τοῖς παραδείσοις θηρία τρεφόμενα Xen *Cyr* 8.1.38
(contrastive with hunting expeditions away from home)
κατὰ τὸν πᾶσι νόμον καθεστῶτα Thuc 3.56.2 (usual focus
on the universal quantifier)
τοῖς γε ἐκ τῆς γνησίας θυγατρὸς παισὶ γεγονόσιν Isae 3.50
(the case concerns illegitimacy)
τὰς μετὰ τοῦ Δημοσθένους ναῦς ἐπελθούσας Thuc 7.55.1
(contrasts with the original fleet).

The following examples clearly illustrate the difference between the two structures

(153) τὰς κατὰ τοὺς πρότερον κυρίους νόμους κρίσεις γεγενημένας
Dem 24.72
τῶν τεταγμένων χρόνων ἐν τοῖς νόμοις Dem 24.26;

(150) Arguments that make use of probability as proof (Pl *Phaedo* 92d). The glory that has been accumulated by the city from all time (Lyc 110).
(151) The steep banks that reached down to the river (Xen *An* 4.3.23). Dogs that taste sheep (Dem 25.40). The river flowing through the city (Xen *Hell* 5.2.4). The danger that hangs over the city (Dem 18.176). The danger that had overtaken the city (Dem 18.220).
(152) The signs coming from the gods (Antiph 5.81). The animals kept in parks (Xen *Cyr* 8.1.38). According to the law applying to everyone (Thuc 3.56.2). The children born of the legitimate daughter (Isae 3.50). The ships that had come later with Demosthenes (Thuc 7.55.1).
(153) Judgements handed down according to the previously applicable laws (Dem 24.72). The times prescribed in the laws (Dem 24.26).

in the first example (24.72) the previously applicable laws are being contrasted with newly proposed laws, in the second example (24.26) there is no modifier and the laws are simply tail material supporting the interpretation of τεταγμένων.

Although both types of attribute YP hyperbaton seem at first sight to be simple extrapositions, they actually involve two separate mechanisms. The prenominal complement type results from the fronting of focus to the specifier position of the superordinate head, which is a general feature of hyperbaton. The prenominal participle type reflects the tendency, which is particularly strong in definite noun phrases, for attributive modifiers to become prenominal. This is why the movement metaphor we have used for this type of hyperbaton entails stranding, after movement of the determiner plus participle or of the complement.

Multiple arguments and adjuncts can be distributed between pre- and postnominal positions

(154)   τοῖς ἀπὸ ὑμῶν χρήμασι φερομένοις παρ᾽ Ἀθηναίους Thuc 4.87.3
         οἱ δ᾽ ἐκ τῶν Συρακουσῶν τότε μετὰ τὴν τοῦ Πλημμυρίου ἅλωσιν
         πρέσβεις οἰχόμενοι ἐς τὰς πόλεις Thuc 7.32.1.

In the following more complex example, the participle has an infinitival complement clause which is split between pre- and postnominal positions

(155)   τῇ μελλούσῃ τοῦ ὄντος ἱκανῶς τε καὶ τελέως ψυχῇ μεταλήψεσθαι
         Pl *Rep* 486e.

NONFINITE CLAUSES

Adjunct participial clauses

Hyperbaton within a participial clause is well attested

(156)   τὴν ἀγαθὴν προβαλλομένους ἐλπίδα Dem 18.97 (Y₁)
         αἰτίαν λέγοντες ψευδῆ Dem 20.133 (Y₂).

It can occur in genitive absolutes

(157)   οὐδεμίαν ἐκείνου περὶ τούτων ποιησαμένου διαθήκην Isae 8.40
         ἐμοῦ ἅπαντας διδόντος τοὺς θεράποντας Lys 7.43.

---

(154) The money paid by you to the Athenians (Thuc 4.87.3). The envoys who at that time after the capture of Plemmyrium went from Syracuse to the cities (Thuc 7.32.1).

(155) The spirit that is going to partake of reality sufficiently and completely (Pl *Rep* 486e).

(156) Shielding themselves with a positive attitude of optimism (Dem 18.97). Giving a false reason (Dem 20.133).

(157) Although he had made no will concerning these matters (Isae 8.40). When I offered all the servants (Lys 7.43).

It sometimes happens that continuous phrases are scrambled within a superordinate clause containing a participial clause; in other words, the participial clause is not an independent domain or an island for scrambling. Here are a couple of striking verse examples

(158)   ἐγώ τε γὰρ λέξασα κουφισθήσομαι | ψυχὴν κακῶς σε *Med* 472
ἑκὰς δὲ φρυκτοῦ φῶς ἐπ᾽ Εὐρίπου ῥοὰς | Μεσσαπίου φύλαξι
σημαίνει μολόν *Ag* 292.

The following passage illustrates genitive hyperbaton with fronting of a contrastive topic out of a participial phrase

(159)   ταύτης τῆς πρεσβείας οὐ κατηγόρεις μου διδόντος τὰς εὐθύνας
Aesch 2.96.

Modifier hyperbaton is attested with auxiliaries and when participle and main verb share the same object

(160)   οὐδὲν γὰρ ἔμοιγέ ἐστι τοιοῦτον πεπραγμένον Lys 4.19
τὴν στολὴν ἐκδὺς ἔδωκε τὴν Μηδικήν Xen *Cyr* 5.1.2,

but most cases involve a verb of motion plus participle. This construction has two main types. In one, the participle ἔχων is used in the sense of 'together with'

(161)   μηχανὰς ὅτι οὐκ ἀνῆλθεν ἔχων Thuc 5.7.5 (nonbranching)
τὴν ἱερὰν ἀπὸ τῆς χώρας ᾤχετ᾽ ἔχων τριήρη Dem 4.34
(cp. Theocr 2.8) (X = ᾤχετ᾽ ἔχων)
δέκα ναῦς ἀπεστείλατ᾽ ἔχοντα κενὰς Χαρίδημον Dem 3.5
(X = ἀπεστείλατ᾽ ἔχοντα).

Note that in οὐκ ἀνῆλθεν ἔχων, the participle is inside the scope of negation: 'he came not having any siege engines,' rather than 'he did not come, having some siege engines.' In a second type, a verb of motion is used in a semiauxiliary way; the hyperbaton may be confined to the participial clause

(162)   ἥκει ψευδῆ συντάξας καθ᾽ ἡμῶν κατηγορίαν Aesch 2.183,

or it may apply in a unified clausal domain

(158) I shall be relieved in my heart by speaking ill of you (*Med* 472). The light of the beacon signals its coming from afar over the waters of Euripus to the guards of Messapium (*Ag* 292).
(159) You do not accuse me when I render my account of that embassy (Aesch 2.96).
(160) Nothing of this sort has been done by me (Lys 4.19). He took off and gave his Median robe (Xen *Cyr* 5.1.2).
(161) Because he came without siege engines (Thuc 5.7.5). He made off from the land with the sacred trireme (Dem 4.34). You sent Charidemus with ten unmanned ships (Dem 3.5).
(162) He comes having concocted a false charge against us (Aesch 2.183).

(163)   ἐξ ἑτέρας ᾤχετο πρεσβεύων πόλεως Dem 19.147
      ποίαν τίν᾽ οὖν χρὴ εἰρήνην πρεσβεύοντας ἥκειν; Andoc 3.23
      ἐγὼ δὲ ἑτέραν ἀπελθὼν ὁδὸν ᾠχόμην Lys 3.35 (cp. ἑτέραν
         ὁδὸν ᾠχόμην ἀπιών ibid. 13)
      τόνδε δ᾽ ἔρχομαι τρίτον | ἀγῶνα πώλοις δεσπότῃ τε συμβαλών
         Alc 504
      τοὺς Ἡρακλείους ἦλθε δουλώσων γόνους *Heracl* 817.

Complement clauses

As we saw in chapter 2, it is possible that finite complement clauses are islands for hyperbaton in Greek: they allow hyperbaton within the complement clause (short hyperbaton) but not as a rule in a domain including both the complement and the matrix clause (long hyperbaton). The situation with nonfinite clauses could not be more different: here any modifier eligible for short hyperbaton is also eligible for long hyperbaton

(164)   ἅπαντας μὲν οὖν χρὴ νομίζειν μεγάλους εἶναι τοὺς δημοσίους
         ἀγῶνας Lyc 7 (object of M, subject of I)
      μεγίστην ἡγοῦμαι περὶ ἐμαυτοῦ τῇ δημοκρατίᾳ πίστιν δεδωκέναι
         Lys 25.17 (object of I)
      ἅπασι συνοίσειν ὑμῖν μέλλει Dem 3.36: indirect object of I
      πολλῆς δεῖ με συγγνώμης τυχεῖν παρ᾽ ὑμῶν Isae 10.1 (oblique
         complement of I)
      τοὺς δ᾽ ἐν ἁπάσῃ καθεστάναι δοκοῦντας εὐδαιμονίᾳ Dem 20.49
         (prepositional complement of I)
      ἅπαντες δήπου δουλεύειν συγχωρήσουσιν οἱ ἄλλοι Dem 9.70
         (subject of M and I)

A schema in which long and short hyperbaton in nonfinite complement clauses is derived by cyclical raising of Y₁ is illustrated in Figure 3.4.

Long hyperbaton also occurs out of participial clauses associated with raising verbs

(165)   οὐδεμίαν πώποτε φανήσεται πρεσβείαν... καλέσας Aesch 3.76.

(163) He went on an embassy from another city (Dem 19.147). What sort of a peace should they come as negotiators of? (Andoc 3.23). I made off leaving by another street (Lys 3.35). I come to engage in this my third contest against horses and master (*Alc* 504). Has he come to enslave the children of Heracles? (*Heracl* 817).

(164) One ought to think that all public trials are important (Lyc 7). I believe that I have given the democracy the greatest assurance about myself (Lys 25.17). It is likely to benefit all of you (Dem 3.36). I ought to receive great understanding on your part (Isae 10.1). Those who seem to be in a state of complete prosperity (Dem 20.49). All the others will agree to be slaves (Dem 9.70).

(165) He will be found not to have ever invited a single embassy (Aesch 3.76).

In the following example with genitive hyperbaton, the matrix verb of a complement clause is itself the participle in a raising construction

(166)   τὴν ἑτέρου ζητῶν ἐπιτιμίαν ἀφελέσθαι φαίνεται Dem 18.15.

As in simple sentences, interrogatives can pattern grosso modo like Y₁ hyperbaton modifiers

(167)   τίνα αὐτοὺς οἴεσθε γνώμην ἕξειν Andoc 1.104, cp. Lys 13.46
τίνας αὐτοὺς οὐκ οἰόμεθ᾽ ὑπερβολὰς ποεῖσθαι βδελυρίας Aesch 1.70
τίνος ἂν ὑμῖν ὁ τοιοῦτος ἀποσχέσθαι δοκεῖ πονηρίας; Lys 24.2
τίνα χρὴ ἐλπίδα ἔχειν σωτηρίας Lys 27.3
τίς ἂν ἀποκρύψαι χρόνος δύναιτ᾽ ἂν Aesch 3.222 (v.l.).

A hyperbaton like

(168)   πλεῖστα ἔμελλον πράγματα ἕξειν Lys 3.32

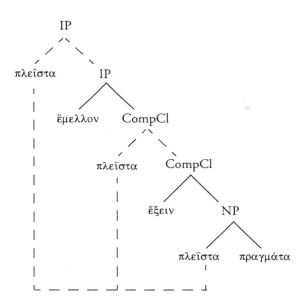

Figure 3.4
Short and long Y₁ hyperbaton with infinitival complement clause
πλεῖστα [ἔμελλον — πράγματα ἕξειν] Lys 3.32

(166) He seems to be trying to take away the civil rights of someone else (Dem 18.15).
(167) What opinion do you think they will have (Andoc 1.104). What excesses of disgusting behaviour are we not to think that they commit (Aesch 1.70). From what wicked conduct does it seem to you that such a man would refrain? (Lys 24.2). What hope of safety ought we to have (Lys 27.3). What length of time could conceal them (Aesch 3.222).
(168) I was likely to get into the most trouble (Lys 3.32).

evidently answers the question

   (169)   πόσα ἔμελλες πράγματα ἕξειν;

similarly

   (170)   πόσον ἂν οἴει γέλωτα ὀφλεῖν; Pl *Alc* 1.121b
           ὁπόσα ἂν ἕκαστος δύναιτο πορίσαι μοι χρήματα Xen *Cyr* 8.2.16.

Complement clause hyperbaton in Greek is typically Y_1 hyperbaton. However, the Y_2 type can also occur, not only in the more topic oriented style of Herodotus but also in the orators

   (171)   γυναῖκας δὲ νομίζοντες πολλὰς ἔχειν ἕκαστος Her 4.172 (topic Y_1)
           τούτοις ἐξῆν ἅπασι χρῆσθαι Dem 18.14 (topic Y_1)
           λοιδορίαν εἶναί τις ἂν φήσειε κενὴν Dem 2.5 (focus Y_1).

The basic elements of infinitive complement clause hyperbaton, namely Y_1, Y_2, M(atrix verb), and I(nfinitive), can surface in any of six different serial orders

MY_1IY_2	IY_1MY_2	Y_1MIY_2
Y_1IY_2M	Y_1MY_2I	Y_1IMY_2

In the lefthand column, the noun phrase straddles the infinitive, with the matrix verb preceding or following the hyperbaton. In the middle column, the noun phrase straddles the matrix verb, with the infinitive preceding or following the hyperbaton. In the righthand column, the noun phrase straddles both matrix verb and infinitive, in either order. The following examples illustrate these different orders

   (172)   ἡγούμενος τὴν μεγίστην αὐτοῖς ὀφείλειν χάριν Lys Frag 8.1.3
           Albini: (MY_1IY_2)
           ἐν πολλῇ ἂν ἔχεσθαι ὑμᾶς ἀπορίᾳ δοκῶ Antiph 5.65 (Y_1IY_2M)
           ἐὰν ὑμῖν εἰπεῖν ἅπαντα δυνηθῶ τὰ πεπραγμένα Lys 1.5 (IY_1MY_2)
           μεγάλα τούτων οἶμαι σημεῖα δείξειν ὑμῖν Aesch 3.177 (Y_1MY_2I)
           οὐ προσήκοντας ἐμαυτῷ δόξω προῃρῆσθαι λόγους Dem 18.129
           (Y_1MIY_2)
           ἐκ τούτου τὴν μορίαν ἀφανίζειν ἐπεχείρησα τοῦ χωρίου Lys 7.28
           (Y_1IMY_2).

(169) How much trouble were you likely to get into?.
(170) How much ridicule do you expect to incur? (Pl *Alc* 1.121b). How much money each person could provide me with (Xen *Cyr* 8.2.16).
(171) Having the custom each to have many wives (Her 4.172). It was possible to use all these (Dem 18.14). One might say was empty insult (Dem 2.5).
(172) Believing that I owed them the greatest thanks (Lys Frag 8.1.3). I think that you would be in great difficulty (Antiph 5.65). If I can tell you everything that was done (Lys 1.5). I think that I will show you great proof (Aesch 3.177). I will seem to have chosen topics not appropriate to myself (Dem 18.129). I tried to remove the sacred olive from this plot of land (Lys 7.28).

The various hyperbaton orders correspond to two types of nonhyperbaton orders. In one YP stands between the two verbs in either order; in the other it stands after them in either order

$$MY_1Y_2I \rightarrow Y_1M—Y_2I$$
$$IY_2M \rightarrow Y_1I—M$$
$$MIY_1Y_2 \rightarrow MY_1I—Y_2, Y_1MI—Y_2$$
$$IMY_1Y_2 \rightarrow IY_1M—Y_2, Y_1IM—Y_2.$$

Where a single nonhyperbaton structure corresponds to two hyperbaton structures, it is because, as in the phrasal domain, the modifier can dock in a lower or a higher specifier slot, e.g. $(Y_1)M(Y_1)I—Y_2$.

At first sight, the temptation is to dismiss these data as a morass: any theoretically possible order for M, I and Y is permitted without constraint. In a Finnish sentence ('I did not intend to start to play tennis in these ⟨clothes⟩'), scrambling from out of the complement clause generates 42 possible variant word orders, none of which is unequivocally ungrammatical (Karttunen 1989). However, the fact that all orders are permissible does not necessarily entail that all orders are equivalent. We shall suggest that they may not be equivalent, either syntactically or pragmatically, or even perhaps semantically. Let us start with the syntax. Complement clauses of various types have been found to join together with the matrix clause into a single domain for rules such as scrambling (Japanese: Matsumoto 1992) and clitic raising (Italian: Rosen 1990; Monachesi 1998). We will call such structures monoclausal. Biclausal structures, in which each clause is a separate domain for the rule in question, can appear alongside the monoclausal type. Consider the following Italian examples

Mario ci sarebbe proprio voluto andare
Mario avrebbe proprio voluto andarci
'Mario would really have liked to go there.'

The first sentence has clitic climbing (*ci sarebbe*) and the choice of the auxiliary verb (*essere*) depends on the complement infinitive (*andare*). The second sentence has no clitic climbing (*andarci*) and the choice of the auxiliary verb (*avere*) depends on the matrix verb (*volere*). If such a distinction applies to our hyperbaton structures, then those in the first column, where the hyperbaton is internal to the complement clause preceded or followed by the matrix verb

$$M[Y_1IY_2]$$
$$[Y_1IY_2]M$$

could be interpreted as biclausal, while the scrambled structures of the other two columns could be monoclausal: $[Y_1MY_2I]$ etc.

The status of the verbs under clause union seems to vary. As the morphology indicates, they are not actually incorporated into a single word, but sometimes they function as a syntactic unit known as a verbal complex, in other cases they retain a greater degree of syntactic independence. For instance, while in Italian they can be separated by adverbs and in Korean by arguments (Chung 1998), in the Urdu indirect command construction known as the instructive they cohere (Butt 1997)

> Anjum-ne Saddaf-ko likhne-ko kahaa citthii
> Anjum   to Saddaf   to write   said   letter
> *Anjum-ne Saddaf-ko likhne-ko citthii kahaa
> 'Anjum told Saddaf to write a letter.'

These and similar examples indicate that the two verbs behave as a unit. Perhaps in some languages the verb complex and the independent types could coexist in competition: that would provide a basis other than coincidence for the appearance in Greek of the orders in the third column

$$Y_1[[M][I]]Y_2$$
$$Y_1[[I][M]]Y_2.$$

in addition to the nonadjacent type in the second column.

Turning now to the pragmatic structure, we note the following interesting fact. The most common order is not, as might be expected from the clausal structure, that in which the noun phrase straddles the infinitive only, $(M)Y_1IY_2(M)$, but that in which it straddles the matrix verb only, with the infinitive to the right: Y_1MY_2I. This is initially counterintuitive, since it seems to violate the superordinate head constraint by excluding its own immediately superordinate infinitival head from inside the YXY hyperbaton structure. A purely mechanical derivational explanation is available for this phenomenon: since the matrix verb usually appears initially in the underlying structure, the common order arises when Y_1 is fronted ahead of the matrix verb

$$MY_1Y_2I \rightarrow Y_1M—Y_2I.$$

However, it may not be coincidental that the most common order also directly encodes what is arguably the appropriate informational structure. Early transformational grammar had syntactic operators used to derive questions and commands from declarations, and declarations themselves could be marked by an operator of assertion. When these operators were endowed with lexical substance, the result was the socalled "performative hypothesis," according to which all simple sentences were derived from underlying indirect statements, indirect commands or indirect questions (Sadock 1974; Lewis 1976; Levinson 1983). Nowadays, linguists would be reluctant to use the syntax to do so much semantic work. However, it is not unreasonable to associate overt interrogative and imperative particles in a complementizer position with illocutionary operators

(173)   ὅπως οὖν ἔσεσθε ἄνδρες ἄξιοι τῆς ἐλευθερίας ἧς κέκτησθε
         Xen *An* 1.7.3.

(173) Be men worthy of the freedom which you possess (Xen *An* 1.7.3).

The focus operator ASSERT mentioned in chapter 2 could be seen as a focus sensitive version of a sentential declarative operator, meaning something like 'I assert that for x = focus...'. For instance

πολλὴν ἔχει πρόνοιαν ὑπὲρ εὐσεβείας

would mean 'I assert that, for Q = much, he pays Q amount of attention to piety (rather than some other potentially applicable amount).' When assertions with narrow scope focus are reported in indirect speech, the focus is associated with an overt illocutionary verb

(174)   πολλὴν ἔφη πρόνοιαν ὑπὲρ εὐσεβείας ἔχειν, cp. οὐδένα φησὶν
         Ἀρχιάδῃ γενέσθαι υἱὸν Dem 44.49.

This idea can be generalized to Y₁M... complement clause hyperbata with other matrix verbs. The following are among the matrix verbs attested with this type of hyperbaton

(175)   ἡγέομαι, οἶμαι, δοκέω, φαίνομαι, νομίζω, ὑπολαμβάνω, αἰσθάνομαι,
         πειράομαι, μέλλω, ζητέω, βούλομαι, δεῖ, δύναμαι, ἔξεστι,
         ἐπιχειρέω, προσήκει, συμφέρει.

This list includes verbs of perception, supposition, permission, subject raising verbs, and subject control verbs. What it involves, taking a modal approach to propositional attitudes, is epistemic, volitional or deontic modality: it relates to belief, desire, intention, ability, duty. Instead of asserting that the infinitival clause is a fact in the real world, they attribute it to some epistemically or deontically possible world. With regular focus, the excluded alternatives belong to possible worlds and the asserted focus belongs to the actual world. In these sentences with modal verbs, the focus itself can belong to a possible world

(176)   πολλὴν προσήκει πρόνοιαν ὑπὲρ εὐσεβείας ἔχειν Aesch 2.114;

of the various degrees of care one could have about piety, a high degree is attributed to appropriate worlds. From a semantic point of view, what is believed, desired, intended etc. is the complete situation described by the complement clause, but from a pragmatic point of view it is just the difference between the presupposed situation and the new situation. This latter relationship is what Y₁M... hyperbaton reflects, as is particularly clear when the matrix verb is formalized as a sentential operator. For instance, consider again the example already cited from Lysias 25.17

μεγίστην ἡγοῦμαι περὶ ἐμαυτοῦ τῇ δημοκρατίᾳ πίστιν δεδωκέναι.

The speaker—we do not know his name, so let us call him A—believes that he has given the democracy the greatest assurance of his loyalty. *Believe* can be

(174) He says that no son was born to Archiades (Dem 44.49).
(175) believe, think, seem, appear, consider, suppose, perceive, try, intend, seek, wish, ought, can, is possible, attempt, is appropriate, is useful.
(176) He ought to have much consideration for piety (Aesch 2.114).

treated as a sentential operator BEL applying to the proposition expressed by the complement clause φ, in symbols $BEL_A φ$, where A is the speaker-believer and φ is the proposition, in our case

περὶ ἐμαυτοῦ τῇ δημοκρατίᾳ μεγίστην πίστιν δέδωκα.

From a semantic point of view BEL_A is a one place operator with scope over φ: translating this into syntactic scope, we get

BEL_A [περὶ ἐμαυτοῦ τῇ δημοκρατίᾳ μεγίστην πίστιν δεδωκέναι].

From a pragmatic point of view, it is (or combines with) a two place operator which requires φ to be decomposed into the focus (μεγίστην) and the presupposition (φ less μεγίστην) and triggers further raising of the focus into contact with the focus operator as hypothesized in chapter 2

[μεγίστην] BEL_A [περὶ ἐμαυτοῦ τῇ δημοκρατίᾳ πίστιν δεδωκέναι].

These Y₁M... structures occur already in Homer

(177)   μὴ δὴ πάντας ἐμοὺς ἐπιέλπεο μύθους | εἰδήσειν *Il* 1.545
        οὕτω που Διὶ μέλλει ὑπερμενέϊ φίλον εἶναι *Il* 14.69.

Their prima facie similarity to examples in which Y₁ is an argument of the matrix verb

(178)   τὰ μὲν οὔ τι καταθνητοῖσιν ἔοικεν | ἄνδρεσσιν φορέειν *Il* 10.440
        πολέες τέ μιν ἠρήσαντο | ἱππῆες φορέειν *Il* 4.143

suggests the speculation that for some cases there may originally have been a proleptic-type syntax in which Y₁ or YP formed a constituent with the matrix verb and the infinitive was an amplifying adjunct. As already noted, in Hungarian a focus can be raised from a finite complement clause into the matrix focus position; when the raised focus is the subject of its own clause, it is case marked accusative by the matrix verb as in Greek prolepsis (Kenesei 1994)

Anna Petert akarja hogy megnyerje a versenyt
Ann Peter-ACC wants that he win the race
'It is Peter who Ann wants that he should win the race.'

Our mention of prolepsis leads us to consider a final question, namely whether there could be properly semantic or truthconditional differences between Y₁M... and MY₁... orders. Complement clauses easily give rise to scopal ambiguities

Caligula declared that the female centurions had been put to death
Sulla only ordered the troops to attack THIS city.

The Caligula example is restricted to a de dicto reading; the de re reading ('Let me tell you about the female centurions: Caligula said that they had been put

(177) Do not hope to know everything that I say (*Il* 1.545). It is likely to be the pleasure of almighty Zeus that... (*Il* 14.69).
(178) It is not suitable for mortal men to wear them (*Il* 10.440). Many horsemen prayed to wear it (*Il* 4.143).

to death') would require a narrator as crazy as Caligula. The Sulla example includes the following readings

> 'This was the only city for which Sulla issued attack-orders'
> 'Sulla issued orders that there not be an attack on any city
> other than this one.'

Prolepsis induces an overt syntactic difference that corresponds to the semantic scopal difference: 'Caligula declared about the female centurions that they had been put to death,' or discontinuously 'he declared about the female ones that they had been put to death centurions.' Prolepsis is a topic raising construction which in most contexts induces a broad scope reading. The raised noun phrase is syntactically part of the speaker's assertion, not part of the reported speech; so it is natural for the existential presupposition coming with a definite to hold for the former rather than just for the latter. Our little discourse cannot continue 'but, as you know, there are none.' What about Y_1 hyperbaton? Do $Y_1M...$ sentences in hyperbaton likewise allow only broad scope readings or do they allow both broad and narrow scope readings? Is it coherent to say 'the female he said centurions to have been put to death, but, as you know, there are none'?

Consider again the Sulla example. The question is what readings are available for

> Hanc solam iussit oppugnari urbem
> Iussit hanc solam oppugnari urbem.

The following Greek examples are comparable

> ἔδοξε δὲ τοῖσι πατρίοισι μοῦνον χρᾶσθαι θεοῖσι Her 1.172
> ταύτας δὲ μόνας ἀναγκασθεὶς τὰς λῃτουργίας λειτουργῆσαι
> Isae 5.36
> τοῦτον μόνον ἔφη γνῶναι τῶν παιόντων αὐτούς Antiph 2a.9.

The Herodotus passage has MY_1 syntax and a narrow scope reading: 'they decided to worship only their ancestral gods.' A broad scope reading such as 'their decision to worship gods (rather than be atheists) applied only to their ancestral gods' is illicit. Conversely, the Isaeus passage has Y_1M syntax and a broad scope reading: 'these were the only public services that he was compelled to undertake.' A narrow scope reading such as 'he was compelled not to undertake any public services other than these' is illicit. Finally, the Antipho passage has Y_1M syntax, but a narrow scope reading is the most natural: 'he said that this was the only one of the assailants that he recognized.' A broad scope reading such as 'it was only this assailant that he admitted recognizing, although he may well have in fact recognized others' is illicit. ἔφη may have a stronger syntactic propensity to be postposited than other matrix verbs, which could affect its scopal possibilities. Nevertheless, this example is preliminary evidence that Y_1 hyperbaton allows narrow scope readings, in other words that overt movement for pragmatic reasons can result in inverse scope.

4 Licensing Hyperbaton

In chapters 1 and 2 we developed an account of prose Y1 hyperbaton in terms of overt syntactic movement of a modifier with strong narrow focus. However, as the analysis was extended in chapter 3 to Y2 hyperbaton, to hyperbaton in verse, and to various other classes of hyperbaton, it became increasingly clear that strong focus movement was just an explanation for one type of hyperbaton. It could not be a general theory of hyperbaton, because other types of hyperbaton involved other pragmatic structures. Y2 hyperbaton and genitive hyperbaton often had simple weak focus on the modifier; demonstratives and possessives in Y2 hyperbaton could be low in informational content; and Y1 hyperbaton in verse was even permitted for descriptive adjectives, which might be emphatic but were unable to bear focus since they did not restrict reference. Clitic hyperbaton depends on the absence of focus, and interrogative hyperbaton involves more than just focus. Conjunct hyperbaton too seemed to have only a weak basis in focus, since at best it involved the fronting of the more salient of two foci. So we are left still looking for an explanation to cover these other types of hyperbaton which did not involve strong focus. In principle, each type of hyperbaton could have its own explanation, in which case their formal similarity would be coincidental. That would not give a particularly elegant or satisfying account. But if the various types of hyperbaton share some common property which accounts for their shared formal structure, then, given what we have just said, that property must involve not the syntax of focus but rather the syntax of modification itself and the syntax of coordination. Different types of hyperbaton seem to split different types of constituents under different pragmatic conditions, and we would like to know if there is some shared underlying syntactic principle that in general accounts for this sort of disruptive behaviour and licenses modifiers and conjuncts in hyperbaton positions. It is often pointed out that the way to understand the use of the subordinating conjunctions *ut, ne* and *quin* is in terms of an earlier paratactic clausal syntax. We shall cite evidence that there is a phrasal analogue to this type of syntax, and that hyperbaton is licensed in this syntactic typology.

NONCONFIGURATIONALITY

Hyperbaton is not a syntactic characteristic that is randomly distributed among languages of different types across the world. Rather, it tends to be implicationally related to a set of other syntactic characteristics that cooccur to various degrees in socalled "nonconfigurational" languages. The term nonconfigurational implies that the language has a rather flat (as opposed to hierarchical) phrase structure. In the most highly nonconfigurational languages, there is little or no evidence for the verb phrase as a syntactic constituent, and there are no subject-object asymmetries that require a structural explanation. Nonconfigurational languages come in two basic types, those that are primarily head marking and those that are primarily dependent marking. In the latter type, grammatical functions like subject and object are mostly marked by inflectional affixes on nominals (as in Latin and Greek), although there may also be verbal agreement morphemes. In the head marking type, nominals are often uninflected, and there is a rich system of verbal agreement morphemes. These crossreference the nominal arguments and are open to interpretation as being (either themselves or via null pronominals) the true syntactic actuation of the argument structure—leaving the nominals as extranuclear adjuncts. Such languages are called pronominal argument languages. Although these classifications raise a variety of problems and overlay a finer-grained typology, they provide convenient labels to apply to the cluster of syntactic properties of which discontinuity is often, but not always, one.

Some of the most notoriously nonconfigurational languages are Australian dependent marking languages like Warlpiri and Kalkatungu. There are also Australian pronominal argument languages, Mayali and Nunggubuyu for instance, but the Amerindian ones are more familiar, including Mohawk, Southern Tiwa and Nahuatl. When reading analyses of such languages, the Classicist is liable to experience an eerie feeling of *déjà vu*, because many features typical of this type of syntax are familiar features of Greek syntax. This is particularly true of Homeric Greek, with its paratactic proclivities. Much of what might at first sight seem to be archaic epic style or properties of spoken discourse turns out also to be archaic syntactic typology, reminiscent of, though not necessarily identical to, features of nonconfigurational languages. It is a reasonable hypothesis that these features of Greek represent the historical residue of a much earlier stage when the syntax had a more pronounced nonconfigurational character than it has in the classical period. It is not our purpose here to pursue this suggestive hypothesis (which has Indo-European rather than specifically Greek implications: many of the same features are found in Vedic and in Old Norse), but merely to interpret hyperbaton in an appropriate typological perspective. To this end, we present a very brief, even allusive overview of a complex of ten syntactic features found in various nonconfigurational languages (Allen et al. 1984; Heath 1984; Payne & Payne

1990; McGregor 1990; Simpson 1991; Baker 1992, 1996; Faltz 1995; Vieira 1995; Nordlinger 1997) and cite arguably related phenomena from Greek, some of which are still productive in the classical period, while others are historical relics even in Homer. Although some of these features also occur in other types of languages, they cluster in nonconfigurational languages, and their occurrence seems to be more systematic in such languages.

Some nonconfigurational properties

1. Free word order. Nonconfigurational languages of all types usually have free word order: this is hardly surprising, since nonconfigurationality is a theorization of free word order. "Free" of course means grammatically free, not (necessarily) pragmatically free. However, not all free word order languages need be literally nonconfigurational. For instance, free word order could arise as a result of pragmatically driven movement from an underlying configurational structure; if the resulting surface structure is hierarchical, it can be called discourse configurational. Some pronominal argument languages, like Lakhota and Navajo, have fairly stable word order. Free word order is commonly associated with a rich morphology, involving either case marking or verbal agreement markers or both, although not all languages having a rich morphology have particularly free word order. Greek has a fairly rich inflectional system and relatively free word order.

2. Null anaphora. Omission of pronominal arguments is common

Warlpiri:	Nya-nyi ka
	see-TNS AUX
	'[He] sees [it]'
Mohawk	Ra-núhwe'-s
	AGR-likes-ASP
	'[He] likes [it].'

Whereas in English the only pronominal argument we normally omit is the subject of an imperative ('[You] come here!'), in Greek omission of subject pronouns is systematic and instances of object pronoun omission are not difficult to find, particularly in dialogue

Φοίνικες δ'ἄγον ἄνδρες *Il* 23.744 'Phoenician men brought [it]'
Θησεὺς ἤγαγεν Ar *Frogs* 142 'Theseus brought [them]'
ἀράττω Ar *Clouds* 1373 '[I] assail [him]'
ἀποδώσειν Ar *Clouds* 1227 'to pay [them] back'.

3. Adjunct lexical arguments. A noticeable feature of various dialects of northern Italy and of Catalan, for instance, is that under certain conditions (particularly when they are topics or tail material) arguments are dislocated from and

adjoined to the nuclear clause and replaced by clitic pronouns. Here are some examples from the dialect of Conegliano, north of Venice (Saccon 1993)

> La è rivada, la Maria 'She has arrived, Maria'
> I fiori, li a portadi la Maria 'The flowers, Maria brought them'
> Li ha portadi la Maria, i fiori 'Maria brought them, the flowers.'

It is rare in transitive clauses for both subject and object to remain in the nuclear clause. One way of interpreting languages with pronominal verbal agreement morphemes is to treat these morphemes (or null pronouns co-indexed with them) as the real arguments, and the nominals, including even indefinites, as adjuncts comparable to the dislocated Italian arguments just cited. Here is a Lakhota example

> John Mary waŋyaŋke
> 'John, Mary, he sees her.'

It is interesting that Lakhota (and Navajo) speakers sometimes write commas after nominals in sentences like

> John, śkate
> 'John, he is playing.'

This treatment of nominals is broadly reminiscent of Homeric nominals which are appositional to independent pronouns (Sławomirski 1988)

(1)   δὴ γάρ μιν ἔφαντ' ἐπιδήμιον εἶναι, | σὸν πατέρ' *Od* 1.194
      ἥ μιν ἔγειρε | Ναυσικάαν εὔπεπλον *Od* 6.48
      ἡμεῖς δ' ἐνθάδε οἱ φραζώμεθα λυγρὸν ὄλεθρον | Τηλεμάχῳ *Od* 16.371.

ὁ δέ, perhaps a reanalyzed particle (Dunkel 1990), is used as an independent pronoun for change of subject or for contrasted predicates

(2)   ὣς ἔφαθ', αἱ δ' ἐπέμυξαν Ἀθηναίη τε καὶ Ἥρη *Il* 4.20
      ὁ δ' ἐπέδραμε φαίδιμος Αἴας *Il* 5.617
      ἡ δὲ διαπρὸ | ἤλυθεν ἐγχείη *Il* 7.260, cp. 4.502
      τοὺς δὲ κατὰ πρύμνας τε καὶ ἀμφ' ἅλα ἔλσαι Ἀχαιοὺς *Il* 1.409
      τὰ δ' ἐπέρρεον ἔθνεα πεζῶν *Il* 11.724
      τοῦ δ' ἐκράαινεν ἐφετμὰς | Φοίβου Ἀπόλλωνος *Il* 5.508.

4. Failure of agreement. Certain types of number and case agreement lapses are less a matter of conversational anacolouthon and more a systematically

---

(1)   They said that your father was among the people (*Od* 1.194). And she awakened the beautifully dressed Nausicaa (*Od* 6.48). But let us here devise a miserable death for Telemachus (*Od* 16.371).

(2)   So he spoke, but Athena and Hera muttered in protest (*Il* 4.20). Noble Ajax ran up (*Il* 5.617). The spear went right through (*Il* 7.260). To confine the Achaeans to the ships around the sea (*Il* 1.409). The squads of infantry kept passing (*Il* 11.724). He carried out the orders of Phoebus Apollo (*Il* 5.508).

licensed feature of the syntax in nonconfigurational languages. Mohawk constructions (Baker 1992) like

> *The friends, he came in*

call to mind Homeric

(3) τῇ ῥα παραδραμέτην φεύγων, ὁ δ᾽ ὄπισθε διώκων *Il* 22.157

and the socalled partitive apposition

(4) οἱ δὲ δύω σπόπελοι, ὁ μὲν οὐρανὸν εὐρὺν ἱκάνει *Od* 12.73
Νεστορίδαι δ᾽, ὁ μὲν οὕτασ᾽ Ἀτύμνιον ὀξέϊ δουρὶ *Il* 16.317.

The pronominal subject of the first following clause is included in, but does not exhaust, the referents of the lexical topic. Failure of agreement is related to lack of syntactic integration: nouns which are separated from the nuclear clause by an intonation break can appear in a default case in Jingulu, and hanging topics in Modern Greek can appear in a default nominative case (Anagnostopoulou 1997). Failure of case agreement between a pronominal argument and a participle is well attested in Homer (Chantraine 1953:322)

(5) τῆς δ᾽... ἀναγνούσῃ *Od* 23.205.

The famous vocative plus nominative coordination

(6) Ζεῦ πάτερ... Ἠέλιός θ᾽ *Il* 3.276

also appears in Vedic (Schmitt 1967:269).

5. Noun incorporation. Some but not all languages of this type have productive noun incorporation, a special type of compounding in which a noun, typically the internal complement of the verb, is morphologically integrated into the verb

> Mohawk Wa'-k-hnínu-' ne ka-nákt-a'
>   I bought the/a bed
>
>   Wa'-ke-nakt-a-hnínu-'
>   I bed-bought.

Noun incorporation is taken up in chapter 6.

6. Prepositional phrases. Although the details are not always clear, a number of reports point to a restricted use of syntactic prepositional phrases in these languages. Adpositions can be morphologically joined to their complements

---

(3) There they ran by, one fleeing, the other pursuing from behind (*Il* 22.157).

(4) But on the other side are two cliffs, one of which reaches up to wide heaven (*Od* 12.73). One of the sons of Nestor struck Atymnius with his sharp spear (*Il* 16.317).

(5) her-GEN... recognizing-DAT (*Od* 23.205).

(6) O Father Zeus... and Sun (*Il* 3.276).

(Mohawk), to the verb (Cree) or can act suspiciously like floating adverbs (Lakhota). The oldest stratum of Homeric prepositional syntax is interpretable as involving a null pronominal argument and a specifying noun phrase with locative inflectional marking (Horrocks 1980)

(7)   ἀμφὶ δὲ χαῖται | ὤμοις ἀΐσσονται *Il* 6.509.

We may compare the following examples from Yagua (Payne 1986)

> jу̧muñu-viimú
>   canoe-inside
> 'inside the canoe'

> rá-viimú
> PRO-inside
> 'inside it'

> rá-viimu jу̧muñú
> PRO-inside canoe
> 'inside the canoe' (literally 'inside it, the canoe').

7. Articles. Although these languages have demonstrative adjectives, they mostly do not have a system of determiners, and in particular they mostly lack a definite article

Mohawk	Érhar te-wak-atʌhutsóni
	dog I want
	'I want a/the dog'
Southern Tiwa	Seuanide ti-mū-ban
	man I saw
	'I saw a/the man.'

The embryonic status of the definite article in Homer is one of the clearest differences between Homeric Greek and classical prose.

8. Noun phrase coordination. In some languages like Dyirbal (Dixon 1972) noun phrase coordination is simply disallowed. In others like Yagua, simple juxtaposition is the normal method of coordinating phrases. In some other languages comitative coordination (Aissen 1989; Schwartz 1985; McNally 1993) is used as an alternative to noun phrase coordination, giving sentences like the following from Lakhota

> *The boy with his father, they will read the newspaper*

and from Navajo

> Shí ashkiiké biɬ ndaashnish
> I   boys   with we-work
> 'The boys and I are working.'

(7)   His mane streams on his shoulders (*Il* 6.509).

Comitative adpositions can be a diachronic source for syntactic conjunctions (Mithun 1988). Various related constructions are documented for Indo-European languages (Krause 1924). Also interesting is the following Homeric line

(8)   ἦλθ' ὁ γέρων Δολίος, σὺν δ' υἱεῖς τοῖο γέροντος *Od* 24.387.

The pronominal type seen in Old Icelandic *Vit Halldórr* 'We two, Halldórr [and I]' can cooccur with split coordination (Liberman 1990)

> Þeir Ormr sátu í öndvegi... ok hans menn (Vatnsdœla saga 44.8)
> 'They, Orm, sat-PL in the highseat, and his men.'
>
> Ásbjörn mælti hann undan, ok þeir Einarr (Sturlunga saga)
> 'Asbjörn wanted to pardon him, and they, Einar ⟨and his men⟩'

This socalled subsuming pronominal occurs in a number of Australian languages (Heath 1986); here is an example from Gooniyandi (McGregor 1990:286)

> ngidi David-jooddoo
> we two David-DUAL
> 'We two, David [and I].'

Compare also the Indo-European elliptical duals (Wackernagel 1875).

9. Adverbial quantification and deixis. A feature of these languages that has attracted some interest is that, just as they tend not to have determiners, so they may avoid adnominal quantification and make greater use of adverbial quantification and verb affixes with quantificational meaning. The quantifier scopes over the nuclear clause with its pronominal argument, while the noun phrase is an adjunct and not quantified. The universal quantifier in hyperbaton often has a rather adverbial flavour in Homer. An interesting correlate is the observation that in Asurini (Vieira 1995), in place of demonstratives like *this* and *that*, locative adverbials are used meaning *here, there*. In Hixkaryana (Derbyshire 1985), the distinction between adjective and adverb is unclear, and words of this class are not used as adnominal modifiers in noun phrases.

10. Parataxis. At the phrasal level, there may be a penchant for juxtaposed noun phrases. Gooniyandi, for instances, uses phrasal juxtaposition for conjunction and disjunction (there are no words for *and, or*) and for various types of amplification serving to identify, clarify or attribute additional properties to a noun phrase. Much the same applies in Hixkaryana, where not only the lexical arguments but also prepositional phrases and other modifying material can appear as intonationally dislocated adjuncts

(8)   The old man Dolius came and the sons of that old man (*Od* 24.387).

nomokno Nonato, Manawsɨ hoye, thetx yakoro
he came Nonato, Manaus from, his-wife with
'Nonato has come from Manaus with his wife.'

The Hixkaryana have a noticeable propensity to talk in Homeric hemistichs. At the clausal level, these languages seem to have a dislike for at least some types of subordination (Baker 1996). Nunggubuyu, for instance, has no infinitival complements and no indirect statements. Hixkaryana has no indirect statements, questions or commands, and no finite subordinate clauses. Juxtaposition or coordination tends to be used in place of subordination in Tuscarora, Otomi and Wichita (Gil 1983). Relative clauses can be clausal adjuncts rather than noun phrase constituents (Hale 1976; Larson 1983). This is generally reminiscent of the paratactic character of Homeric syntax. In prolepsis

(9)   αὐτὸν δ᾽ οὐ σάφα οἶδα, πόθεν γένος εὔχεται εἶναι *Od* 17.373
      Τυδεΐδην δ᾽ οὐκ ἂν γνοίης ποτέροισι μετείη *Il* 5.85,

the second clause is a paratactic amplification of the first clause, an adjunct rather than a clausal complement of the main verb. In these examples, prolepsis caters to the pragmatic needs of the strong topic, it provides a (pro)nominal complement as opposed to a clausal complement, and it lightens the structure of the adjoined clause by externalizing one argument. It is also possible that linguistic (rather than epigraphical) parataxis is responsible for some peculiarities of Linear B (Duhoux 1968). Paratactic structure is a characteristic of Vedic and Germanic heroic poetry too. In nonconfigurational languages, such structure is licensed by the syntax: it is not confined to the context of oral literary composition, although it may certainly be exploited for artistic purposes.

Hyperbaton and nonconfigurationality

Some languages allow the arguments of the verb to appear in any order but require the subconstituents of the noun phrase to be contiguous to one another. Other languages also allow what are from a configurational perspective the subconstituents of noun phrases to be interspersed with other elements of the clause (hyperbaton), and even the subconstituents of two noun phrases to be interspersed with each other (double hyperbaton). Hyperbaton with quantifiers, demonstratives and sometimes restrictive adjectives is reported for quite a number of languages with nonconfigurational tendencies, including Cree, Fox, Ojibwa, Mohawk, Pima, Tzotzil, Kalkatungu, Nyangumarda, Yidin; not all types of hyperbaton are licensed in all these languages. Here are some examples (Baker 1996; Dahlstrom 1987) illustrating some of the types of Yı hyperbaton that also occur in Greek

(9) I do not know clearly where he claims to come from as regards his family (*Od* 17.373). You couldn't tell which side the son of Tydeus belonged to (*Il* 5.85).

Southern Tiwa   Shimba bi-mū-ban seuan-nin
               all   I saw   men
               πάντας   εἶδον   τοὺς ἄνδρας

               Yede ti-mū-ban seuan-ide
               that   I saw   man
               ἐκεῖνον εἶδον   τὸν ἄνδρα

               Yoadeu a-mū-ban seuan-ide
               which   you saw   man?
               τίνα   εἶδες   ἄνδρα;

Nahuatl   Miyaqu-intin Ø-huîtze-' in tlaca
               a lot   came   people
               πολλοὶ   ἦλθον   ἄνθρωποι

Fox   nekoti mehteno·hi e·h=ne·wačči neniwani
               one   only   he saw   man
               ἕνα   μόνον   εἶδεν   ἄνδρα.

The examples seem to translate quite naturally into Greek. The following are the rules for the use of Y₁ hyperbaton in Fox, which is a pronominal argument language. In this language, discontinuous noun phrases are interrupted by their superordinate head and so have the familiar Y₁XY₂ structure. X may be a verb, a postposition or a noun, the latter with a possessor YP. Other syntactic material may intervene between Y₁ and V or V and Y₂, and Y₂ may be a branching constituent. If there are two modifiers, both may be placed in the Y₁ slot or, more commonly, one modifier is Y₁ and the other goes in the Y₂ slot with the noun. Double hyperbaton is rare or nonoccurring. A parenthetical may interrupt the hyperbaton structure. (The language also has a type of pre-verb "tmesis.") These rules closely mirror the analysis of Greek hyperbaton presented in chapter 1; the speaker of Fox would, it appears, be a natural in a Greek prose composition class.

So it is not unreasonable to think that Greek preserves a progressively weakening residue of (presumably early Indo-European) nonconfigurational features, and that hyperbaton is one of those features. The ten features of nonconfigurationality sketched in the preceding section, plus hyperbaton, represent an at first sight rather diverse collection of syntactic properties. As already noted, some of them can be found in other types of languages. The point is that in nonconfigurational languages they cluster and their occurrence is more systematic. It follows that there should be some general linguistic principle underlying part or all of this complex of diverse properties. Various intriguing theories have been proposed in this regard (Hale 1983; Jelinek 1984; Faltz 1995; Baker 1996; Russell & Reinholtz 1997; Pensalfini 1996). The general property that these languages in particular share, and manifest to various degrees, is an avoidance of lexical arguments and adnominal modifiers, a sort of *horror dependentis*. Instead of the familiar syntax of government and embedding, they prefer a syntax of juxtaposition. The former is characterized by hierarchical structural complexity, the latter by comparatively simple and lean phrase structure. Let us see how this principle could relate to our set of ten syntactic features. Free word order is obviously encouraged by a type of syntax in which nominals are coreferenced and simply equated with pronominal arguments rather than themselves entering into a hierarchical structural relationship with a head. Modifiers are in one way or another more independent of the modifiee than in languages with a more structured syntax. Some failure of number and case agreement is not unexpected when nominals are adjuncts. Noun incorporation simplifies the syntax of the head-complement relation, reducing it from a syntactic relationship to a more morphological one. Syntactic prepositional phrases involve head-argument structure. Articles and adnominal quantifiers build a hierarchically structured noun phrase in configurational languages, and coordinated nominals build complex noun phrases: all of which can be construed as at odds with the sort of flat paratactic structures that these languages prefer.

The more nonconfigurational a language is, the leaner its nuclear phrase structure and the more systematically it conforms to that structure. Less strongly nonconfigurational languages admit richer phrase structures and/or treat lean phrase structure as a preference or option rather than as a requirement. In a pure pronominal argument language, even simple nonbranching lexical noun phrase arguments are informationally too heavy to join with a functor into a phrase. In principle, the arguments are projected into a single phrase by the head, but only the head can be lexical. Consequently, the arguments are pronominal, and lexical noun phrases appear as adjuncts external to the core phrase. This syntax is one in which all arguments have been raised or lowered out of the nuclear clause. The mechanics of the projection of argument positions has been separated from the process of enhancing them with lexical information. Think of a car in which the body panels are not attached directly to the frame but separated from the frame by foot-long connector rods. Modification also tends to work differently. It is much more likely to be paratactic than in a configurational language. By paratactic we mean that it is a separate secondary predication rather than an integrated component of the noun phrase (rather as posited for deep structure by early transformational [Chomsky 1957] and generative semantic [Carden 1968] theories). This difference emerges quite nicely when speakers of a configurational language like English try to elicit modified noun phrases from speakers of a nonconfigurational language like Kalkatungu (Blake 1983). When asked to translate a sentence such as *The big dog bit the snake* into Kalkatungu, informants are apt to respond with two separate sentences (*Dog bit snake. That dog [is] big.*) This sort of effect recurs in some types of syntactically impaired aphasia when patients are asked to repeat modified noun phrases (Devine & Stephens 1994:299).

Similar reports can be found for coordination. In Diegueño "informants are typically uncomfortable when asked to translate English sentences with conjoined nouns" (Langdon 1970). In Maricopa (Gil 1982) they respond either with juxtaposition

> *John, Bill, they will come,*

or with a verbal construction something like

> *John, Bill, he accompanies him, they will come.*

Comitative verbs are another diachronic source of syntactic conjunctions (Mithun 1988).

Extreme versions of this sort of syntax contrast rather dramatically with the syntax of configurational languages, in which modifiers are integrated into noun phrases and arguments are hierarchically projected by the head and directly encoded by lexical noun phrases. However, it is often wrong to conclude that nonconfigurational languages do not have phrase structure or that they do not have configurations of any sort. Rather, their structures are different and their configurations less hierarchical. Moreover, it is often the case that more and less complex structures coexist in nonconfigurational languages. This also seems to have been the case in prehistoric Greek. What we can reconstruct from survivals in Homer is probably a not so extreme version of nonconfigurationality, in which some arguments are admitted into the nuclear phrase and others are adjuncts, and some modifiers are integrated and others are paratactic

(10)   ἵνα μιν παύσειε πόνοιο | δῖον Ἀχιλλῆα *Il* 21.249.

It is a very reasonable assumption that, at this intermediate stage at which lexical arguments begin to be admitted into the nuclear clause, there is a preference for arguments that are light, i.e. that do not branch. A single noun could easily form a phrase with the verb, but a more complex structure like noun plus adjective or noun plus noun (coordination) would run into greater resistance. One way of handling a modified lexical argument in a single sentence would be to allow the noun to form a phrase with the verb and leave the paratactic modifier in adjunct position. When applied to a possessive genitive, this strategy would result in a structure like

(11)   ἡ δ' ἐν γούνασι πῖπτε Διώνης, δῖ' Ἀφροδίτη *Il* 5.370;

here the branching subject phrase is an adjunct to the topic changing pronominal argument, the complement ἐν γούνασι is phrased with the verb, and the genitive modifier of the complement is paratactic; it does not form a surface phrase with the complement noun. The result is a genitive hyperbaton. When the modifier is placed after the adjunct branching subject phrase, it is even more clearly paratactic and amplificatory

(10) To restrain the noble Achilles from his labour (*Il* 21.249).
(11) The beautiful Aphrodite fell at the knees of Dione (*Il* 5.370).

(12)   αὐτὰρ ὁ βοῦν ἱέρευσεν ἄναξ ἀνδρῶν Ἀγαμέμνων | πίονα *Il* 2.402.

The language provides for the option of joining complement nouns with their heads, leaving paratactic modifiers unintegrated. This strategy preserves some degree of constraint on the informational complexity of the minimally configurational X′ structure. Specifically, it allows a phrase to be formed such that no further functional application (modification or complementation) is embedded inside the argument, and in which neither the argument nor the head is coordinated. An additional level of hierarchical complexity cannot be built up within XP by allowing any of the ordinary structure building operations to apply: Y cannot be transitive (take its own complement), it cannot be modified (subset creation: ⊆), and neither Y nor X can form a conjunction (∧) or a disjunction (∨)

$$*X[Y\ Z] \qquad *X[Y_1 \vee Y_2]$$
$$*X[Y_1\ Y_2] \qquad *[X_1 \wedge X_2]Y$$
$$*X[Y_1 \wedge Y_2] \qquad *[X_1 \vee X_2]Y.$$

We shall refer to these conditions on phrase formation as the complexity constraint. Even in more complex situations, as when the noun has two modifiers, hyperbaton reduces the overall complexity, whether the first modifier is integrated or not

(13)   πίονα μηρία καῖε βοὸς *Il* 11.773
       Δαναῶν νέες ἤλυθον ἀμφιέλισσαι *Il* 13.174.

So instead of

(14)   [[πόλιν αἰπὴν] ὤλεσα]

with branching object phrase, there was the option of saying

       [[πόλιν ὤλεσα] [αἰπὴν]]

with simply nonbranching object phrase and external modifier. Instead of

(15)   [[πόλιν Κιλίκων] ὤλεσα]

there was the option of saying

       [[πόλιν ὤλεσα] [Κιλίκων]]

with external possessive modifier. Instead of

(16)   [[πόλιν καὶ ἄστυ] ὤλεσα]

with coordinated object phrase, there was the option of saying

(12) But Agamemnon, the king of men, sacrificed a fat ox (*Il* 2.402).
(13) He was burning the fat thighs of an ox (*Il* 11.773). The curved ships of the Greeks came (*Il* 13.174).
(14) I destroyed the lofty city.
(15) I destroyed the city of the Cilicians.
(16) I destroyed the inhabitants and the city.

[[πόλιν ὤλεσα] [καὶ ἄστυ]].

Finally, instead of

(17)   [[ἔπραθον καὶ ὤλεσα] πόλιν]

with coordinated head, there was the option of saying

[[ἔπραθον πόλιν] [καὶ ὤλεσα]].

Here are some real examples from Homer

(18)   ἐπὶ δ' ἄλφιτα λευκὰ πάλυνε *Il* 11.640 (NAV)
        ἐπὶ δ' ἤπια φάρμακα πάσσε *Il* 11.830 (ANV)
        ἐπὶ δὲ ῥίζαν βάλε πικρὴν *Il* 11.846 (Y2 hyperbaton)
        ἐπὶ δ' αἴγειον κνῆ τυρὸν *Il* 11.639 (Y1 hyperbaton).

The coexistence of discontinuous, integrated continuous and even paratactic continuous nominal structures is illustrated by the notoriously nonconfigurational Warlpiri, which has all three types (Laughren 1989):

[A]-AUX [N] V   [AN]-AUX V   [A]-AUX V [N].

The nonconfigurationality of modified and coordinated nominals feeds hyperbaton and constitutes its essential basis. On the other hand, hyperbaton is probably not simply the pragmatically conditioned arrangement of autonomous nominals in a flat syntactic structure. Conjunct hyperbaton, as well as some types of Y2 hyperbaton, pretty clearly involve a nuclear phrase plus adjunct and not a single flat structure. But granted that there is phrasing in hyperbaton, then it follows that there is some form of complexity constraint to keep the adjunct out of the core phrase and thereby preserve a degree of nonconfigurationality. We tend to associate such constraints more with the morphological level, for instance the avoidance of free syntactic modes of modification and coordination in compounds (ἱπποδάμος, *μεγαλιπποδαμος, *ἱπποκαιλεοντοδαμος) or the prima facie stranding of inherited complements (*believer in Aeschylean authorship*) and of modifiers in bracketing paradoxes (*Faliscan epigrapher*). So even in the absence of overt incorporation, the nuclear phrase in these languages has some wordlike properties.

ORIGINS OF HYPERBATON

In the following sections we will try to account for various categories of hyperbaton in terms of the schema just developed. Since our objective here is not theory construction but just understanding hyperbaton, we feel free to proceed

(17) I sacked and destroyed the city.
(18) She sprinkled white barley over it (*Il* 11.640). Sprinkle soothing medications on it (*Il* 11.830). He applied a bitter herbal remedy to it (*Il* 11.846). She grated goat cheese over it (*Il* 11.639).

eclectically, choosing a simple and informal descriptive framework. We shall think of phrases as constructed by variable merging of their components; so what is merged in one way in a configurational language can be merged in a different way, or not be merged at all, in a nonconfigurational language, or both strategies can coexist in one and the same language in different syntactic or pragmatic contexts. The sensitivity of Greek word order to pragmatic factors (Dik 1995) calls for some form of discourse configurational approach; most importantly, we need a crosscategorial phrase peripheral focus position. For ease of exposition, we shall assume with the usual disclaimers that this position is filled by movement from an underlying directionally uniform structure in which complements and adjuncts follow the head. This is a simple, convenient and familiar way of thinking and talking about focus positions. The aim is to express a relationship between sentences with narrow focus on some constituent and broad scope focus sentences, not to make the claim that the former start out as the latter in the speech production process. Of course, from a maximally nonconfigurational perspective, the concept of movement at this level tends to be vacuous, because, one might claim, there is no basic word order and, definitionally, there are no phrasal configurations for an element to move out of. But in languages like Greek, heads do project phrases with lexical arguments, though not necessarily of the same degree of hierarchical complexity as in configurational languages, and these phrases have a specifier-like focus position. From this perspective, what is loosely termed configurationality involves three potentially independent parameters: first the complexity permitted in the nuclear clausal projection, second the degree to which word order is pragmatically rather than grammatically determined, and third the degree to which the nuclear and adjunct structures are flat as opposed to hierarchical.

Practically everything we lay hands on in this analysis is a topic of vigorous contention, even abstracting away from what might seem to be strictly sectarian questions. In addition to the range of issues relating to phrase structure and movement in different types of language, the syntax and semantics of coordination, of ellipsis and of secondary predication are themselves subjects of ongoing dispute. To avoid getting hopelessly bogged down in theoretical issues, we shall need to make various assumptions without justifying them or exploring alternatives.

Focus in ditransitive structures

Instead of proceeding directly to hyperbaton, we start with a preliminary analysis of weak focus movement in simple verb phrases with two complements. In such ditransitive clauses, when the verb phrase has broad scope focus both complements follow the verb in classical Greek, giving the order (S) V O_1 O_2, at least for nonthetic clauses

(19) ἡ δὲ Λαδίκη ἀπέδωκε τὴν εὐχὴν τῇ θεῷ Her 2.181
      Λύσανδρος δὲ... ἀπέδωκε τὴν πόλιν Αἰγινήταις Xen *Hell* 2.2.9
      ἔδωκε χρήματα Ἀνταλκίδα Xen *Hell* 4.8.16.

We will represent this with a traditional binarily branching structure in which the indirect object asymmetrically c-commands the direct object, or vice versa, as in Figure 4.1. A flat VP would imply that there were no structurally significant effects of either grammatical or pragmatic properties of the arguments, which is probably too cautious; a ditransitive VP-shell would be too abstract for our purposes. If one of the complements is a weak focus, it is placed to the left of the verb

(20) ξένια ἔδωκαν τῇ στρατιᾷ Xen *An* 5.5.14.

If, additionally, one of the complements is a strong topic, it is placed to the left of the focus

(21) Κλεισθένης δὲ χοροὺς μὲν τῷ Διονύσῳ ἀπέδωκε, τὴν δὲ ἄλλην
         θυσίην Μελανίππῳ Her 5.67
      τούτοις δὲ χώραν καὶ οἴκους ἔδωκε Xen *Cyr* 8.4.28
      τοῖς ναύταις τὸν ὀφειλόμενον μισθὸν ἀπέδωκε Xen *Hell* 2.1.12
      τοῖς μὲν ἄλλοις ἑρπετοῖς πόδας ἔδωκαν... ἀνθρώπῳ δὲ καὶ χεῖρας
         Xen *Mem* 1.4.11.

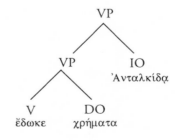

Figure 4.1
Broad scope verb phrase focus
ἔδωκε χρήματα Ἀνταλκίδα Xen *Hell* 4.8.16

(19) Ladice fulfilled her vow to the goddess (Her 2.181). Lysander gave the city back to the Aeginetans (Xen *Hell* 2.2.9). He gave money to Antalcidas (Xen *Hell* 4.8.16).

(20) They gave hospitable gifts to the army (Xen *An* 5.5.14).

(21) Cleisthenes gave the choruses back to Dionysus, and the other worship to Melanippus (Her 5.67). He gave these land and houses (Xen *Cyr* 8.4.28). He paid the sailors their outstanding wages (Xen *Hell* 2.1.12). They gave feet to the other beasts but hands as well to man (Xen *Mem* 1.4.11).

The phrase punctuating inscriptions indicate that the weak focus phrases very easily with the verb

(22)   : οσια λανχανειν : *Locr* 2

τον χρεματον κρατειν : τον επιϝοιϟον *Locr* 31

αι κα hυπ' ανανκας απελαονται : ε Ναυπακτο : *Locr* 8.

This points to a rather local inversion around the head, as illustrated in Figure 4.2; as usual, the empty DO position serves to indicate where the direct object would be in the broad scope focus version of the sentence, it does not necessarily make the claim that weak focus movement leaves a trace in the technical sense. On the other hand, for the topics, movement to a position c-commanding the whole phrase is appropriate, as in

(23)   εν Ναυπακτοι : καρυξαι εν τἀγοραι : *Locr* 20.

More generally, in classical prose complements and adjuncts that have weak (informational) or strong (exclusive, contrastive) focus normally precede the verb, while complements and adjuncts that are tail material or part of a broad scope phrasal focus usually appear after the verb in main clauses

ἀπὸ λόφου τινὸς καταθεωμένους τὰ γιγνόμενα Xen *An* 6.5.30

this means 'watching the goings on and doing it from a hill' and not 'watching from a hill and doing it to the goings on.' So we shall assume that weak focus moves to a specifier position in the verb phrase. This leftward movement fits well both with focus movement in various other languages and more generally

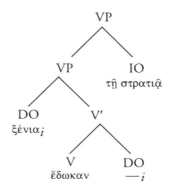

Figure 4.2
Weak focus on direct object
ξενία ἔδωκαν τῇ στρατιᾷ Xen *An* 5.5.14

(22) To receive portions of the sacrifice (*Locr* 2). The colonist shall take possession of the property (*Locr* 31). If they are expelled by force from Naupactus (*Locr* 8).
(23) He should announce it in the marketplace at Naupactus (*Locr* 20).

with scrambling and object shift. The often observed relationship of scrambling to definiteness and specificity (Mahajan 1990; Rapoport 1995; de Hoop 1996) does not apply in Greek, since it seems to reflect topicality and Greek scrambling is not so predominantly topic oriented. To cite just one parallel, Yagua has VSO order with a left peripheral position for pragmatically marked constituents (Payne 1993). We have assumed a head-initial XP in Greek on the basis of the evidence cited (quite apart from any theoretical assumptions about linear precedence of heads), although a grammatically defined Object–Verb word order is commonly stipulated for Indo-European. The posited Greek structure could be derived directly from a prehistoric pronominal argument framework with pragmatically controlled word order, simply by reanalyzing the adjuncts as lexical arguments. Then ἔδωκε χρήματα Ἀνταλκίδᾳ would ultimately derive from a structure like 'He gave it to him, money, Antalcidas'; and χρήματα ἔδωκε Ἀνταλκίδᾳ from 'money, he gave it to him, Antalcidas.' As already suggested in chapter 2, a sentence with a preposed narrow focus and a postverbal grammatical subject can be considered a simple spellout of the sentential structure posited by the predicational theory of focus; this is less abstract than a verbal head movement analysis.

Subject conjunct hyperbaton

Although we shall sometimes use the convenient term "split coordination," we shall argue that, from a diachronic perspective at least, it is misleading to think of conjunct hyperbaton in terms of splitting a coordinated noun phrase. Consider first the question of number agreement. Languages vary in the rules they have for number agreement. In addition to the familiar type where two noun phrases join together into a single coordinated noun phrase that triggers plural agreement ('Jack and Jill sing'), there are languages that allow or require agreement with the linearly nearest conjunct ('The children and Jill sings'), and even languages that allow agreement with the farthest conjunct (van Oirsouw 1987; Johannessen 1998). There is some variation in classical Greek, as already noted in chapter 3; we will concentrate on Homeric Greek, which has both agreement with the conjoined noun phrase

(24)   τῶν αὖ Φείδιππός τε καὶ Ἄντιφος ἡγησάσθην *Il* 2.678 (SV)

and agreement with the nearest constituent

(25)   πρὸ γὰρ ἧκε πατὴρ ἄλλοι τε γέροντες *Od* 21.21 (VS);

ἧκε is singular and agrees with πατὴρ only. This latter type is asymmetrical; agreement is with the first subject phrase only; another term for this is "analytic" (McCloskey 1986). The asymmetrical type seems to be favoured when the verb precedes the subject, as in Czech (Corbett 1983), Palestinian Arabic

(24) Phidippus and Antiphus led these (*Il* 2.678).
(25) His father and the other elders sent him out (*Od* 21.21).

and Portuguese (Munn 1993). Asymmetrical coordination is evidently a type of adjunction. Particularly in a paratactic and nonconfigurational syntax, adjunction is possible not only to the first conjunct in a coordinated noun phrase but also to the nuclear clause, as is clear from other examples of agreement failure where the first conjunct precedes the verb

(26) [Ἕκτωρ τε προέηκε] [καὶ ἄλλοι Τρῶες ἀγαυοί] *Il* 10.563
[δοιὼ δ' Ἀτρεΐδα μενέτην] [καὶ δῖος Ὀδυσσεύς] *Il* 19.310
[γαῖα δ' ἔτι ξυνὴ πάντων] [καὶ μακρὸς Ὄλυμπος] *Il* 15.193.

Formally these could be called conjunct hyperbata. But one would be justifiably suspicious of an analysis which started by constructing a coordinated noun phrase, then applied agreement with the first conjunct only, and finally deconstructed the noun phrase via hyperbaton. Note that split coordinates with a singular verb can control a plural participle

(27) ταχέως δ' Ἄδματος ἷκεν καὶ Μέλαμπος, εὐμενέοντες ἀνεψιόν
Pindar *Pyth* 4.126 (see app. crit.).

In the socalled schema Alcmanicum, one of the subject noun phrases precedes the verb, but the verb is plural or dual, indicating an integrated interpretation

(28) ἦ μὲν δὴ θάρσος μοι Ἄρης τ' ἔδοσαν καὶ Ἀθήνη *Od* 14.216
Τροίην ἷξον ποταμώ τε ῥέοντε | ἧχι ῥοὰς Σιμόεις συμβάλλετον
ἠδὲ Σκάμανδρος *Il* 5.774.
εἰς Ἀχέροντα Πυριφλεγέθων τε ῥέουσιν | Κώκυτός θ' *Od* 10.513.

From a configurational point of view, these lines involve the fronting of the first conjunct ahead of the plural verb which shows number agreement with the conjoined noun phrase: Ἄρης τ' [ἔδοσαν — καὶ Ἀθήνη]. Ἄρης would be reconstructed back into its original position for semantic interpretation (or καὶ Ἀθήνη raised to join Ἄρης). Diachronically, one might think at first sight that the number agreement was adjusted when the structure was reanalyzed as derived from a coordinated noun phrase rather than as involving coordinated clauses

(29) τοῦτο τὸ σχῆμα καλεῖται προδιεζευγμένον καὶ καθ' ὑπέρβατον,
ὑπ' ἐνίων δὲ Ἀλκμανικόν Schol. on *Od* 10.513.

(26) Hector and the other noble Trojans sent him out (*Il* 10.563). The two sons of Atreus and the noble Odysseus remained (*Il* 19.310). The earth and high Olympus are still common to all (*Il* 15.193).
(27) Admetus and Melampus came quickly, with kindly feelings for their cousin (Pi *Pyth* 4.126).
(28) Ares and Athena gave me courage (*Od* 14.216). They came to Troy and the two flowing rivers where the Simois and the Scamander join their streams (*Il* 5.774). Pyriphlegethon and Cocytus flow into Acheron (*Od* 10.513).
(29) This construction is called *prodiezeugmenon* and *cath' hyperbaton*, but by some *Alcmanicon* (Schol on *Od* 10.513).

However, the construction goes back to Indo-European (Krause 1924), occurring in Vedic

> Indraś ca yad yuyudhāte ahiś ca
> Indra and when they fought snake and
> 'When Indra and the snake fought one another.'

In our view, the construction originated at a pronominal argument stage, with the noun phrases as adjuncts to a null pronominal subject: 'the two rivers, where, the Simois, they merge their streams, and the Scamander.' This approach would also make sense of a disputed disjunctive example

(30) εἰ δέ κ᾽ ῎Αρης ἄρχωσι μάχης ἢ Φοῖβος ᾽Απόλλων *Il* 20.138.

In Maricopa, which has no conjunctions, juxtaposition serves for both conjunction and disjunction; the latter is distinguished by use of a subjunctive-like suffix on the verb (Gil 1991). Mohawk can say

> *Paul together they (DUAL) swim Peter*
> *Jim they (DUAL) danced Mary*

for 'Paul swims with Peter,' 'Jim danced with Mary,' which seems to be the same sort of construction. Instead of being simply juxtaposed, the conjuncts are pragmatically distributed around the nuclear clause. There is a clear relation between the schema Alcmanicum and various types of comitative coordination: discontinuous pronominal coordination, continuous comitative coordination and lexical comitative coordination. Compare the following examples from Tera (Newman 1970), where the schema Alcmanicum is the preferred form for subject coordination

> tem wà ɗə Kanu ndə Dala
> we have gone to Kano and Dala
> 'Dala and I went to Kano'

> Ali wà ɗə Kanu ku ndə Dala
> Ali have gone to Kano PLURAL and Dala
> 'Ali and Dala went to Kano.'

In light of the evidence presented in this section, it is unlikely that subject conjunct hyperbaton originated from the splitting of a coordinated noun phrase either in regular conjunct hyperbaton with a singular verb or in the schema Alcmanicum with a plural verb. In fact, more than any other single piece of evidence, the schema Alcmanicum requires us to take seriously the idea that in its prehistory Greek was not only a nonconfigurational language but one that made at least some use of pronominal arguments.

(30) If Ares or Phoebus Apollo start to fight (*Il* 20.138).

Object conjunct hyperbaton

For object coordination, there is no number agreement in Greek to guide the analysis, but we can extrapolate from what has been established for subject coordination. So a line like

(31)   οὐρῆας μὲν πρῶτον ἐπῴχετο καὶ κύνας ἀργούς *Il* 1.50

is assumed to have originated as a type of adjunction structure, as depicted in Figure 4.3. (For the same of simplicity, VP is used to mark the nuclear projection of the verb in a nonconfigurational language; nothing is necessarily implied about the syntactic status of the subject argument.) οὐρῆας is a weak focus that has moved to (nonderivationally, is placed in) the specifier position. This movement does not violate Ross's Coordinate Structure Constraint (a coordinate version of the Left Branch Condition) because οὐρῆας does not enter into a coordinate noun phrase with κύνας ἀργούς at this stage of the language. At the same time, it can phrase with the verb, because, not being coordinated, it does not violate the complexity constraint. Of course, if there ever was a stage of the Greek language at which objects too were adjuncts to pronominal arguments, then the construction ultimately goes back to an object version of the schema Alcmanicum: 'the mules*i*, he attacked them*ik*, and the swift dogs*k*.' A parallel fronting accounts for instances with a nominal head

(32)   Διὸς ἄγγελοι ἠδὲ καὶ ἀνδρῶν *Il* 7.274
         ἀρνῶν κνίσης αἰγῶν τε τελείων *Il* 1.66.

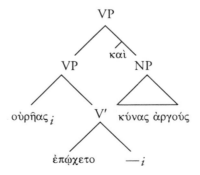

Figure 4.3
Object conjunct hyperbaton:
adjunct analysis

(31) First he went after the mules and the swift dogs (*Il* 1.50).
(32) Messengers of Zeus and men (*Il* 7.274). The aroma of sacrificed sheep and unblemished goats (*Il* 1.66).

In historical Greek, conjunct hyperbaton might conceivably have been reanalyzed as a discontinuous coordinated noun phrase, as depicted in Figure 4.4, but there are good arguments against this view. For subject conjunct hyperbaton, the verb agreement rule has to be ordered after extraction, which is not convincing. Norwegian examples like

> Per så jeg og Ola i går
> 'I saw Per and Ola yesterday'

are equally problematic, because the adverbial can only be taken with the second conjunct (Johannessen 1998). The independence of conjuncts in nonconfigurational languages is illustrated by examples like the following from Warlpiri

> Kuyu-rna ngarnu, manu Napaljarri-rli-yijala
> meat-AUX (1sg) ate, and   Napaljarri-ERG-also
> 'Napaljarri and I ate meat'

> Kuyu-rna purraja, manu miyi
> meat-AUX   cooked,   and   bread
> 'I cooked meat and bread.'

The first Warlpiri example is a split agent coordination with singular agreement on the auxiliary, the second is a split patient coordination.

Y2 hyperbaton

The analysis of object conjunct hyperbaton just presented generalizes easily to Y2 hyperbaton with adjectives and genitives. Consider the following

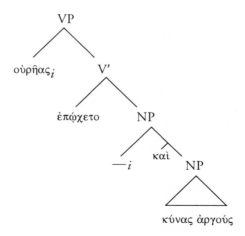

Figure 4.4
Object conjunct hyperbaton:
discontinuous noun phrase analysis

(33)   πόλιν αἱρήσομεν εὐρυάγυιαν *Il* 2.329
         ἐκ δὲ πόλιν πέρσεν Κιλίκων *Il* 6.415.

For the sake of brevity, we will collapse these two examples. Given the potentially independent status of modifiers in nonconfigurational languages, we are
not limited to a structure in which the modifier is syntactically integrated into
the noun phrase. We can start with a structure in which the noun is phrased
with the verb and the modifier is a secondary predicate and syntactic adjunct
external to the nuclear verbal projection. Both structures are depicted in Figure
4.5. The latter structure conforms to the complexity constraint, and Y2 hyperbaton is simply derived by regular fronting of the weak focus noun to a specifier position (or, nonderivationally, simply by placing the noun in the focus
position). When a structure would permit both Y2 hyperbaton and conjunct
hyperbaton, either the specifier is allowed to branch, giving conjunct hyperbaton

(34)   ἔνθ’ ἀλοχόν τε φίλην ἔλιπον καὶ νήπιον υἱόν *Il* 5.480

or the complexity constraint can block branching in the specifier position and
trigger Y2 hyperbaton rather than simple conjunct hyperbaton

(35)   μῆλα φυλασσέμεναι πατρώϊα καὶ ἕλικας βοῦς *Od* 12.136;

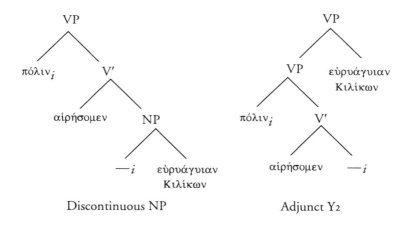

Figure 4.5
Movement analyses of Y2 hyperbaton
πόλιν αἱρήσομεν εὐρυάγυιαν / Κιλίκων

(33) We will capture the city with its broad streets (*Il* 2.329). He destroyed the city of
the Cilicians (*Il* 6.415).
(34) Where I left my dear wife and infant son (*Il* 5.480).
(35) To look after their father's sheep and curved oxen (*Od* 12.136).

similarly with a possessive structure

(36)   τόν ῥ' Ἠοῦς ἔκτεινε φαεινῆς ἀγλαὸς υἱός *Od* 4.188.

One might object that modifiers and conjuncts are different things, and that one cannot extrapolate from an analysis of conjunct hyperbaton to an analysis of Y₂ hyperbaton. On this view, the parallel structure of

(37)   ...χλαῖναν καλὴν βάλεν ἠδὲ χιτῶνα *Od* 10.365
       ...χλαῖναν βάλε φοινικόεσσαν *Od* 14.500 v.l.

is only superficial, a question of serial order, not of structure. However, note how the Y₂ modifier can be delayed until after the completion of the nuclear verb phrase

(38)   καί μιν βάλε μηρὸν οἰστῷ | δεξιόν *Il* 11.583 (VY₁ZY₂).

In any case, this objection has less basis in a nonconfigurational language than in English, since the independent and autonomous status of modifiers is one of the distinguishing features of nonconfigurational languages. The structural parallelism between object conjuncts and postmodifiers is very close. As illustrated in Figure 4.6, in the continuous structure they are both adjoined to NP, while in the discontinuous structure they are both adjoined to what we have been calling VP. There is empirical evidence from historical Greek that directly supports the proposed analysis, and actually indicates that the VP adjunction analysis can be correct even in some cases of apparently continuous NP structures. It comes from a few cases of inscriptional phrase punctuation (which

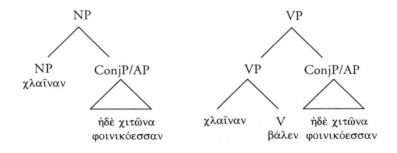

Figure 4.6
NP adjunct and VP adjunct
χλαῖναν (βάλε(ν)) ἠδὲ χιτῶνα / φοινικόεσσαν

(36) Whom the glorious son of bright Dawn killed (*Od* 4.188).
(37) She put on a beautiful cloak and a tunic (*Od* 10.365). He threw off his purple cloak (*Od* 14.500).
(38) And he hit him with an arrow on the right thigh (*Il* 11.583).

encodes prosodic phrasing and so indirectly provides evidence for syntactic phrasing). There are a couple of cases in the Locrian *Lex Opuntiorum* where a noun is phrased with a preceding verb and its articulated modifier is phrased separately, even though the noun and the modifier are contiguous

(39)   : διομοσαι hορϙον : τον νομιον : *Locr* 45

       : επιϝοικους Λοϙρον : τον Ηυποκναμιδιον : *Locr* 5.

These punctuations are unlikely to be purely prosodically motivated; in particular, there is no pairing effect to motivate splitting a constituent. The phrasings correspond roughly to English

       *[he sacked the ministers] $_\varphi$ [responsible] $_\varphi$

rather than to a paired structure like

       [he sacked the ministers] $_\varphi$ [responsible for the leaks] $_\varphi$.

So these punctuations support the underlying structure assumed for independent modifiers at the posited prehistorical nonconfigurational stage. Y_2 hyperbaton is generated by weak focus fronting of the noun entirely inside the nuclear verbal projection, leaving the modifier in its separate phrase as before. It happens that the resulting structure, this time with a prepositional phrase complement and independent articulated participial modifier, is preserved in a phrase punctuated inscription from Olympia

(40)   εν τἐπιαροι κ᾽ ενεχοιτο : τοι ᾽νταυτ᾽ εγραμενοι *LSAG* Pl. 42.6

       (punctuation worn but clearly visible).

The separation of definite Y_2 receives further support from a punctuated subject Y_2 hyperbaton from Argos

(41)   hα δε βολα ποτελατο : hαντιτυχονσα IG IV.554.

Y_2 hyperbaton can also be punctuated as a single phrase, which reflects the superordinate VP node

(42)   : ϙωι βασιλευς εδωϙ᾽ ωιγυπτιος : Masson et al. 1988.3

       : τελος με φαρειν μεδεν : *Locr* 10.

However, given the more articulated punctuations just cited, there is little to be said for positing a flat structure such as that found with strings of unconnected right dislocated arguments. The structures are branching (hierarchical), just not in the way an English speaker would expect

(39) They should swear the prescribed oath (*Locr* 45). The colonists of the Hypocnemidian Locrians (ibid. 5).

(40) He should be liable to the penalty here written (*LSAG* Pl. 42.6).

(41) The council that is in office shall enforce it (IG IV.554).

(42) The Egyptian king gave to him (Masson 1988). They shall pay no taxes (*Locr* 10).

*[διομοσαι] [ho϶϶ον] [τον νομιον]
*[διομοσαι] [ho϶϶ον τον νομιον]
[διομοσαι ho϶϶ον] [τον νομιον]
[ho϶϶ον διομοσαι] [τον νομιον].

Distributed modifiers and complements

There are a number of examples, mainly in tragedy, where a modifier or a complement that semantically belongs to two conjuncts appears syntactically internal to one conjunct only

(43)   ἀνδρῶν τε παλαιῶν ἠδὲ γυναικῶν *Hymn to Apollo* 160
λιπὼν δὲ λίμνην Δηλίαν τε χοιράδα *Eum* 9
φράζων ἅλωσιν Ἰλίου τ' ἀνάστασιν *Ag* 589
ἢν δ' ἐς λόγους τε καὶ τὰ τῶνδ' οἰκτίσματα | βλέψας πεπανθῇς
   Heracl 158
οὔθ' ἥδομαι τοῖσδ' οὔτ' ἐπάχθομαι κακοῖς *Hipp* 1260
ἐζημίωσε πατέρα κἀπέκτειν' ἐμόν *Orest* 578
ἀλλ' ἀπερύκοι καὶ Ζεὺς κακὰν καὶ Φοῖβος Ἀργείων φάτιν *Ajax* 186.

There are even some prose examples

(44)   λαβὼν χλανίδα καὶ περιβαλόμενος πυρρὴν Her 3.139
ἐξηγησάμενος πᾶσαν καὶ ἐπιδέξας τὴν Ἑλλάδα Her 3.135.

These structures seem to cry out for syntactic reconstruction of a configurational coordinate phrase

[ἀνδρῶν τ' ἠδὲ γυναικῶν] παλαιῶν
Δηλίαν [λίμνην χοιράδα τε]
Ἰλίου [ἅλωσιν ἀνάστασίν τε]
ἀπερύκοι [καὶ Ζεὺς καὶ Φοῖβος] [κακὰν Ἀργείων φάτιν].

But note the singular verb agreement in the *Ajax* example. If this type of syntax has a nonconfigurational origin, it is less perverse, and in fact falls out quite naturally from the typical nonconfigurational amplifying strategy, the mechanics of which were discussed in the preceding section: for instance 'announcing the/its capture, and the destruction of Troy'; 'I am not pleased at these, nor am I displeased at (them,) the evils'; 'let him avert it, Zeus the evil one; and Phoebus, the rumour; of the Argives.' This is not intended to claim that the syntax

(43) The men and women of old (*Hymn to Apollo* 160). Leaving the rock and the lake of Delos (*Eum* 9). Indicating the capture and destruction of Troy (*Ag* 589). If you become softhearted considering their words and lamentations (*Heracl* 158). I am neither happy nor sad at these misfortunes (*Hipp* 1260). She punished and killed my father (*Orest* 578). May both Zeus and Phoebus ward off the evil rumour of the Argives (*Ajax* 186).
(44) Taking and putting on a red cloak (Her 3.139). Having given them a guided tour of the whole of Greece (Her 3.135).

of tragedy is or can be nonconfigurational to this degree, but merely that it permits structures which are easier to motivate in terms of such nonconfigurational origins.

Even though the modifiers could usually be interpreted as originally separate adjuncts, there is an evident pairing effect

[φράζων ἅλωσιν] [᾿Ιλίου τ᾿ ἀνάστασιν]
[οὔθ᾿ ἥδομαι τοῖσδ᾿] [οὔτ᾿ ἐπάχθομαι κακοῖς]
[λαβὼν χλανίδα] [καὶ περιβαλόμενος πυρρὴν].

The *Ajax* example seems at first sight similar to regular gapping

(45)   τοὺς ἴρηκας ἀπάγουσι ἐς Βουτοῦν πόλιν, τὰς δὲ ἴβις ἐς ῾Ερμέω πόλιν
       Her 2.67
       αἱ συμφοραὶ τῶν ἀνθρώπων ἄρχουσι καὶ οὐκὶ ὥνθρωποι τῶν
       συμφορέων Her 7.49.

However, the object arguments are coindexed and the structure need not be biclausal; it is probably derived from a conjunct hyperbaton with the subject conjuncts straddling the branching object phrase: $S_1O_1O_2S_2 \rightarrow S_1O_1S_2O_2$. The examples with coordinated verbs seem to work the same way: $V_1O_1O_2V_2 \rightarrow V_1O_1V_2O_2$.

Y₁ hyperbaton

In languages having consistently configurational noun phrases, two factors have been identified as particularly important for adjective location. The first is head relative directionality, the position of the complement relative to the head and of the modifier relative to the modifiee. Such considerations played an important role in discussions of Indo-European syntactic typology in the 1970s (Friedrich 1977). The second is the distinction between attributive and adnominal predicative adjectives. The former have a fixed serial order, the latter do not. In the Romance languages, attributive adjectives are said to be generated in prenominal position; fixed order in postnominal adjectives is thought to be evidence for noun raising (Cinque 1994). Both factors are conceived of in terms of a hierarchical noun phrase, and so would not apply as stated to nonconfigurational languages, in which modifiers were often more independent of the nouns they are associated with. Some differences, for instance the availability of intensional readings for adjectives might crucially hinge on the availability of configurational adnominal modification. But other differences between pre- and postnominal location of adjectives in nonconfigurational languages may reflect the same sort of semantic factors that are ultimately

(45) They take hawks away to the city of Buto, ibises to the city of Hermes (Her 2.67). Circumstances govern men not men circumstances (Her 7.49).

involved in configurational languages, as well as the pragmatic factors that are so important in free word order languages.

An intriguing property of hyperbaton is that it "preserves" the word order of the corresponding continuous noun phrase. Y_1 hyperbaton is found with modifiers that would also be prenominal in the corresponding continuous YP, and Y_2 hyperbaton with those that would be postnominal. Moreover, whenever strings of adjectives in hyperbaton are split by the intervening head X, the order of the adjectives in hyperbaton regularly corresponds to what the order would be in the corresponding continuous structure, as can be verified in the examples cited in earlier chapters. This feature of discontinuity is not a peculiarity of Greek but has been noted in other languages, for instance in Kalkatungu (Blake 1983) and in the German split topic construction (van Riemsdijk 1989). From a configurational perspective, this suggests that Y_1 hyperbaton is derived from a continuous noun phrase with a prenominal adjective, or at least that the adjective passes through the prenominal position on its way to the Y_1 slot. From a nonconfigurational perspective, such assumptions may be superfluous; it is simply a matter of the same factors applying to both discontinuous and continuous sequences, and modifier movement may be mostly unnecessary.

For the sake of highlighting the difference between Y_1 and Y_2 hyperbaton, let us choose an example in which a modifier movement analysis would not be inappropriate. Adjectives in -εις tend to appear after their nouns in Homer, as in the common formula

(46)   ἔπεα πτερόεντα προσηύδα.

This fact is presumably related to the status of the suffix -ϝεντ- 'richly endowed with' (Risch 1974:151). However, they can also appear as premodifiers

(47)   θυόεν νέφος *Il* 15.153,

and there are a few cases of such adjectives in Y_1 hyperbaton

(48)   ῥοδόεντι δὲ χρῖεν ἐλαίῳ *Il* 23.186.

If an -εις adjective moves to the left from a postulated basic postnominal position, being still independent of the noun ('she anointed him with oil which was rose-scented'), it can move to the left of the whole nuclear XP, rather than simply to the left of the noun as in a configurational language. This option avoids a violation of the complexity constraint. In other words, the modifier moves around the nuclear XP from postadjunct to specifier position. This seems to make pragmatic sense, since while ἐλαίῳ is fairly predictable from the

(46)   Addressed winged words.
(47)   A fragrant cloud (*Il* 15.153).
(48)   She anointed him with rose-scented oil (*Il* 23.186).

verb, ῥοδόεντι specifies which of the various perfumes was chosen for the oil. Compare with appositional nouns

(49)   ἀνὴρ χαλκεὺς *Od* 9.391
   τὴν χαλκῆες κάμον ἄνδρες *Il* 4.187, 216.

A comparison of Y1 and Y2 hyperbaton based on this analysis is given in Figure 4.7. Whereas the Y2 modifier is treated as an adjunct to XP, the Y1 modifier is interpreted as a specifier of XP. Hence movement of an adjective from Y2 to Y1 position shows up as a lowering; the adjective changes from being outside XP to being inside XP. Similarly when continuous postmodifiers become pre-modifiers, they move from outside NP to inside NP (Figure 1.5). This is the inverse to the (for us) more familiar right-raising movements like extraposition and heavy noun phrase shift. The latter create adjunct structures out of basic hierarchical ones by moving a constituent out of XP and raising it to a right adjunct position. Our movement creates a hierarchical structure out of a basic adjunct structure by lowering an adjunct into specifier position. This distinction applies quite independently of the derivational framework in which we have chosen to present it. Both Y1 and Y2 adjectives have the property of being "transportable" to higher positions in the tree. Y2 adjectives belong outside (adjoined to) the maximal projection of the modified noun and rise to higher adjoined positions. Y1 adjectives belong inside the maximal projection of the modified head noun and rise to higher positions inside maximal projections that dominate the head noun. This distinction, or some other equivalent piece of formalism, is not entirely stipulative and does not depend on whether the theory makes a distinction between specifiers and adjuncts. As we shall see,

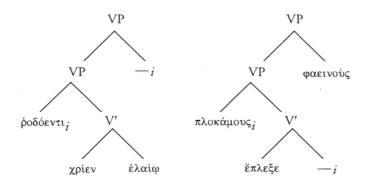

Figure 4.7
Comparison of Y1 and Y2 hyperbaton (movement analyses)
ῥοδόεντι... χρῖεν ἐλαίῳ (*Il* 23.186), πλοκάμους ἔπλεξε φαεινοὺς (*Il* 14.176)

(49) A man who is a smith (*Od* 9.391). Which men who were smiths made (*Il* 4.187).

there is empirical evidence from enjambement in Homer to support it. Intuitively, left moved constituents (other than left dislocated topics) are more specifier-like and right-moved constituents often more adjunct-like; left-moved constituents seem to scope over the nuclear clause, while right-moved constituents often seem to be just added to it. This distinction can be reflected in the prosody in some languages; a clear case is Haya (Tenenbaum 1977). In the following paragraphs we will survey the main types of Y₁ hyperbaton in Homer, in order to get some idea of the conditions that favour the Y₁ position.

The first type corresponds very well with Y₁ hyperbaton in classical prose; modifiers include quantifiers, pronominals and superlatives

(50) πᾶσαν ἐπιφρασσαίμεθα βουλήν *Il* 13.741
πλεῖσται κλονέοντο φάλαγγες *Il* 11.148
πεντήκοντα δ' ἕλον δίφρους *Il* 11.748
ἄλλας δ' ἀλεγύνετε δαῖτας *Od* 2.139
πύματον δ' ὡπλίσσατο δόρπον *Od* 2.20.

Focused restrictive adjectives are less common

(51) εὐρὺ γὰρ ἀμφ' ὤμοισιν ἔχει σάκος *Il* 11.527
σὺ δ' ἄξια δέξαι ἄποινα *Il* 11.131.

The difference between a possessive pronoun in Y₁ hyperbaton as a focused topic and the same pronoun as a subsidiary specification in Y₂ hyperbaton is nicely illustrated by the following example

(52) ὣς ἄρ' ἔφαν ἀπιόντες, ἐμὸν δ' ἐγέλασσε φίλον κῆρ | ὡς ὄνομ' ἐξαπάτησεν ἐμὸν *Od* 9.413.

A second category involves descriptive adjectives; as already pointed out in chapter 3, it has no prose counterpart

(53) ξανθὴν ἀπεκείρατο χαίτην *Il* 23.141
πολιῆς ἐπὶ θινὶ θαλάσσης *Il* 4.248
λευκοὺς δ' ἐπέρησεν ὀδόντας *Il* 5.291.

Descriptive adjectives are not excluded from higher positions in the clause

(54) χρύσεια πατὴρ ἐτίταινε τάλαντα *Il* 8.69.

(50) We could consider all sorts of counsel (*Il* 13.741). The most troops were thrown into disarray (*Il* 11.148). I seized fifty chariots (*Il* 11.748). Find your meals elsewhere (*Od* 2.139). He made himself his last meal (*Od* 2.20).
(51) He has a broad shield around his shoulders (*Il* 11.527). Receive a worthy ransom (*Il* 11.131).
(52) So they spoke as they left. I smiled to myself at how my name had been deceptive (*Od* 9.413).
(53) He cut off a lock of golden hair (*Il* 23.141). On the shore of the grey sea (*Il* 4.248). It pierced his white teeth (*Il* 5.291).
(54) The Father held up his golden scales (*Il* 8.69).

Quite a few instances, particularly subject phrases, are open to a predicative interpretation ('the water ran cool,' etc.)

(55)   ἀδακρύτω ἔχεν ὄσσε *Od* 4.186
        λισσὴ δ' ἀναδέδρομε πέτρη *Od* 5.412
        ἀσβέστη κέχυτο φλόξ *Il* 16.123
        κατὰ δὲ νότιος ῥέεν ἱδρὼς *Il* 11.811
        κατὰ δὲ ψυχρὸν ῥέεν ὕδωρ *Od* 17.209.

Rather like adverbs, these depictive secondary predicates c-command and take scope over following the verb plus argument complex, and they are interpreted relative to the event or situation described by the main predicate: the water is cool in the flowing event. The property does not necessarily hold of the entity to which it is ascribed either prior to or subsequent to the event. Regular adnominal ornamental epithets are often individual level and consequently not event particular (Parry 1971:120), irrespective of whether they are in hyperbaton or not

(56)   ταχέες δ' ἔκπιπτον ὀϊστοί *Il* 21.492.

The secondary predicate also seems to be the salient information in the clause. When we say

        Jack arrived angry,

it is usually not the fact that Jack arrived, but the state he was in on arrival that is important. Contrast

        Jack arrived, angry;

here the adjective is less of a restriction on the type of arrival, and both the arrival and the angriness are salient items of information. Similarly, in

(57)   ταρφειαὶ νιφάδες Διὸς ἐκποτέονται | ψυχραί *Il* 19.357

the quantifier ταρφειαὶ is preverbal and event-related, the postverbal adjective ψυχραί is also probably event-related and predicative but amplificatory. Contrast the preverbal ψυχρὴ in

(58)   αὔρη δ' ἐκ ποταμοῦ ψυχρὴ πνέει *Od* 5.469

which amounts to an adverbial restriction on the nuclear clause.

More generally, while the main function of restrictive adjectives is to narrow down the possible referents of the noun phrase, descriptive adjectives simply express an additional property; consequently they can often be paraphrased as

(55) He kept his eyes free of tears (*Od* 4.186). The rock runs up sheer (*Od* 5.412). The flame enveloped it unquenchable (*Il* 16.123). The sweat ran down wet (*Il* 11.811). The water flowed down cold (*Od* 17.209).
(56) The swift arrows fell out (*Il* 21.492).
(57) The cold snowflakes fly down from heaven in thick clouds (*Il* 19.357).
(58) A breeze blows cold off the river (*Od* 5.469).

an adjunct participle or subordinate clause—relative, causal or concessive according to the context. So a number of Y₁ complement hyperbata could easily be expanded by the insertion of the participle ἐών

(59) νεουτάτου ⟨ἐούσης⟩ ἔρρεε χειρός *Il* 13.539
χαλεπὴν ⟨ἐοῦσαν⟩ ἐδείσατε μῆνιν *Il* 13.624
βαθέης ⟨ἐούσης⟩ ἐξάλλεται αὐλῆς *Il* 5.142;

the blood ran down from his arm which was/inasmuch as it was newly wounded; you did not fear the anger of Zeus, harsh though it is; and so on. Compare the secondary predicate participle in continuous structures like

(60) ἔπεμψαν... ἐστεφανωμένους δύο κήρυκας Xen *Hell* 4.7.3.

Warlpiri has temporal enclitics like *-lku* 'then' and *-wiyi* 'before' which can be attached to adjectives in hyperbaton and favour a secondary predicative as opposed to attributive reading (Simpson 1991:200; Bittner & Hale 1995:86). This general approach to descriptive adjectives in Y₁ hyperbaton rests on the idea that a radically nonconfigurational correlate of

He kissed the beautiful Miss Jones

would be

Beautiful as she was, he kissed her, Miss Jones.

Finally, it is a reasonable hypothesis that one of the factors governing the choice between Y₁ and Y₂ hyperbaton should be the salience of the information in Y₁ relative to that in Y₂. There may be a tendency for the noun in these Y₁ hyperbata to be either a postverbal predicate internal subject ('there gushed blood') or actually tail material (as in prose Y₁ hyperbaton)

(61) κυάνεος ἐλέλικτο δράκων *Il* 11.39
μέλαν δ' ἀνεκήκιεν αἷμα *Il* 7.262
εὐεργέος ἔκπεσε δίφρου *Il* 5.585, 13.399.

δράκων and αἷμα are presentational and so postverbal. In both passsages cited for ἔκπεσε δίφρου, the fall guy, so to speak, is the charioteer; consequently the δίφρος is predictable. The following progression is also suggestive

(62) ἠέρι δ' ἔγχος ἐκέκλιτο καὶ ταχέ' ἵππω *Il* 5.356
χρυσάμπυκας ἤτεεν ἵππους ib. 358
δῶκε χρυσάμπυκας ἵππους ib. 363;

(59) It ran down from his newly-wounded arm (*Il* 13.539). You feared the harsh anger (*Il* 13.624). Jumps out of the high-walled enclosure (*Il* 5.142).

(60) They sent two heralds garlanded (Xen *Hell* 4.7.3).

(61) A blue enamel serpent was entwined (*Il* 11.39). The dark blood gushed out (*Il* 7.262). He fell out of the well-built chariot (*Il* 5.585).

(62) His spear and his swift horses were leaning on a cloud (*Il* 5.356). She asked for his horses with golden frontlets (*Il* 5.358). He gave her his horses with golden frontlets (*Il* 5.363).

in line 356 the horses are new information in a conjunct hyperbaton; in line 358 the horses are old information and we get a Y1 hyperbaton; in line 363 the whole noun phrase is repeated and is placed after the verb. In chapter 6 we suggest that the noun in prose Y1 hyperbaton is nonreferential, and that this may be the case for certain types of Y1 hyperbaton in verse too. Modification and predictability can by themselves be sufficient to induce nonreferentiality, even in the absence of the strong narrow focus that is additionally required in prose.

Other Y1 hyperbata

In genitive Y1 hyperbaton, the genitive is usually less predictable than the Y2 noun, as in later Greek

(63)   Τρώων ῥήγνυντο φάλαγγας *Il* 13.718
       Τρώων εἴποντο φάλαγγες *Il* 11.344
       Ὀδυσσῆος φθῖσαι γόνον *Od* 4.741.

In two remaining types of Y1 hyperbaton, clitic hyperbaton and interrogative hyperbaton, there is unequivocal movement to a higher clausal position. However, both types may go back to a null head pronominal adjective (chapter 6) with a specifying tail noun ('Which one did you buy, car?'). Here are some examples with clitics

(64)   ἦ τίς σφωε πόρεν θεὸς ἀντιβολήσας *Il* 10.546
       ὅσσον τίς τ’ ἔρριψε καλαύροπα βουκόλος ἀνήρ *Il* 23.845.

Interrogative instances include a couple in the old heroic greeting formula

(65)   τέων δ’ ἐξ εὔχεται εἶναι | ἀνδρῶν; *Od* 20.192
       ποίης δ’ ἐξ εὔχεται εἶναι | γαίης…; *Od* 1.406
       τίνα δ’ αὐτῷ μήσατ’ ὄλεθρον | Αἴγισθος δολόμητις…; *Od* 3.249.

Domain of hyperbaton

As established in earlier chapters, in classical Greek hyperbaton has a cross-categorial phrasal domain. The same applies for Homer. The following examples are of Y1 hyperbaton, where X is some category other than a verb

(63) They proceeded to break the ranks of the Trojans (*Il* 13.718). The battalions of the Trojans followed (*Il* 11.344). To destroy the offspring of Odysseus (*Od* 4.741).
(64) Or did some god meet you and give them to you? (*Il* 10.546). As far as a herdsman throws his staff (*Il* 23.845).
(65) From what men does he claim descent? (*Od* 20.192). From what land does he claim to be? (*Od* 1.406). What destruction did the cunning Aegisthus devise for him? (*Od* 3.249).

(66) NOUN PHRASE

μεγάλων ἐπιίστορα ἔργων *Od* 21.26

ἀναιδέος ἔχματα πέτρης *Il* 13.139

πολυφόρβου πείρατα γαίης *Il* 14.200

(67) PREPOSITION PLUS NOUN PHRASE

ἱερῆς εἰς ἄστυ Ζελείης *Il* 4.103

ἱερῆς παρὰ πυθμέν᾽ ἐλαίης *Od* 13.372

(68) ADJECTIVE PHRASE

θοῷ ἀτάλαντος ᾿Άρηϊ *Il* 13.295

κακῶν ἐπίληθον ἁπάντων *Od* 4.221 (Y₂)

δεινῆς ἀκόρητοι ἀϋτῆς *Il* 13.621

(69) PREPOSITIONAL PHRASE

δεξιτερὸν δ᾽ ὑπὲρ ὦμον *Il* 10.373

μελαινάων ἀπὸ νηῶν *Il* 24.780.

We have already suggested in relation to strong focus that there could be a connection between the phrasal domain of hyperbaton and nonconfigurationality, and the suggestion generalizes easily to other types of hyperbaton. The relatively independent status of argument and adjunct phrases—the fact that they are paratactic rather than integrated into a larger and more complex hierarchical structure—leads to a situation in which each phrase has its own pragmatically sensitive word order which replicates in miniature the word order of the clause. [X YP] phrases are pragmatic small clauses, if you will, particularly in terms of the predicational theory of focus. So the independent status of the modifier and the independent status of the [X YP] phrase conspire to permit modifiers to be located in phrases in much the same way that phrases are located in clauses. Classical prose is beginning to unload some of this nonconfigurational heritage, restricting Y₁ hyperbaton to strong narrow focus and eliminating most types of prepositional phrase hyperbaton.

Conclusion

Phrasal discontinuity in configurational languages is a particularly recalcitrant problem, which has elicited a whole range of competing descriptive devices, some of which will be mentioned briefly at the beginning of chapter 6. The

(66) One with much experience of great deeds (*Od* 21.26). The support of the shameless rock (*Il* 13.139). The ends of the bountiful earth (*Il* 14.200).

(67) To the city of holy Zelea (*Il* 4.103). By the trunk of the sacred olive tree (*Od* 13.372).

(68) Equal to the swift Ares (*Il* 13.295). Inducing forgetfulness of all misfortunes (*Od* 4.221). You who can never get enough of the terrible battle cry (*Il* 13.621).

(69) Over his right shoulder (*Il* 10.373). From the black ships (*Il* 24.780).

essential point here is that, if our analysis of the origins of hyperbaton is on the right track, hyperbaton initially had little if anything to do with phrasal discontinuity.

According to the analysis we have presented, movement generates discontiguity, not discontinuity. Discontinuous constituency can be interpreted derivationally and nonderivationally. In derivational terms, it means that there is a semantic constituent actuated by an underlying syntactic constituent that can be syntactically discontinuous in some of its surface manifestations. In nonderivational terms, it means that there is a semantic constituent that is, in one of its actuations, syntactically discontinuous. Either of these definitions might be appropriate for some stage of classical Greek, but neither is relevant for the origins of hyperbaton. The autonomous modifiers of hyperbaton may be coindexed with the noun, but they do not form either a semantic or a syntactic constituent with it to the exclusion of all other material. Syntactically, the Y-modifier does not form a constituent with the Y-noun but with the whole of the rest of XP. So the term discontinuous constituency is misleading in a nonconfigurational context: what is not a constituent can be neither a continuous constituent nor a discontinuous constituent, and what does not branch cannot have a left branch. Discontinuous constituency of this type implies not the dismembering of a syntactic constituent, but the failure to merge into a syntactic constituent.

THE MEANING OF Y₂ ADJUNCTS

With the concept of the nonconfigurational adjunct we may have solved a syntactic problem, but we have created a semantic problem. How are these adjunct modifiers and conjuncts interpreted semantically? Consider, for instance

ἀμφὶ δὲ ποσσὶ πέδας ἔβαλε χρυσείας *Il* 13.36.

If we assume that hyperbaton is semantically irrelevant, we might think of positing a fully integrated noun phrase reading with an English type attributive adjective: 'he put gold fetters around their feet.' In that case, one would like to know what sort of interpretive mechanisms are required to get from the discontinuous syntax to the integrated semantics. On the other hand, we might posit a completely unintegrated reading, such as 'he put fetters around their feet, gold ones/which were gold.' This certainly caters to the syntactic discontinuity, but are such unintegrated readings actually supported by the way Y₂ hyperbaton is used in the texts, or at least by the way it might have been used in a prehistoric nonconfigurational syntax? A similar story applies to object conjunct hyperbaton

Ἄβαντα μετῴχετο καὶ Πολύειδον *Il* 5.148.

With a fully integrated noun phrase reading, this means 'he went after Abas and Polyidus.' With a maximally unintegrated reading, it would be 'he went after Abas, and Polyidus too.' A third possibility, which we shall argue for, is that neither of the obvious English paraphrases just given is appropriate, and that Y2 hyperbaton involves a third reading intermediate between the two. In addition to finding appropriate English paraphrases, we need to specify just what is entailed by the different readings and whether they are truthconditionally or merely compositionally different. The further question of whether more than one reading is available for Y2 hyperbaton in Greek, as it is in some other languages, will be taken up later.

Unintegrated interpretation

Let us start with conjunct hyperbaton. The problems here are aggravated by the long history of scholarly disagreement about the best analysis of ordinary (continuous YP) noun phrase conjunction (Lasersohn 1995). Many noun phrase conjunctions are logically equivalent to clausal conjunctions

> Jack and Mary passed the test
> Jack passed the test, and Mary passed the test.

However others, particularly in clauses with a symmetrical or a reciprocal predicate, are obviously not (nonboolean coordination)

> Jack and Mary met ≠ Jack met and Mary met
> Jack and Mary are alike ≠ Jack is alike and Mary is alike.

According to one approach, conjoined noun phrases are semantically monoclausal and conjoined clauses are semantically biclausal. According to another, noun phrase conjunction is interpreted as clausal conjunction whenever possible. According to a third approach, it remains noun phrase conjunction at logical form but is expanded into a clausal conjunction for the semantic computation of truth values. We will assume that the first approach is correct. The important point to note is that the other two approaches tend to neutralize potential distinctions between continuous coordination and conjunct hyperbaton at some point in the interpretation.

   To test for the unintegrated interpretation, we will compare conjunct hyperbaton with an English construction that clearly has unintegrated readings, namely stripping, also known as bare argument ellipsis. In this construction, as its name implies, material identical to that in the antecedent clause is stripped away leaving one constituent, often a bare argument, and in many cases a particle like *too* or a negative

> The students read Aeschylus last night, and Sophocles too
> The students read Aeschylus last night, but not Sophocles.

Addition of the adverbial *last night* ensures a canonical example of stripping as opposed to some form of subclausal conjunction (*Aeschylus and Sophocles too*). In stripping sentences, indefinites are normally interpreted without coreference

> Menelaus attacked a warrior, and Diomedes too.

The natural interpretation is distributive, with two events of attacking and two different warriors. The indefinite *a warrior* can be interpreted as a predicate modifier or as a specific indefinite with broad scope within its conjunct, but, typically, not as a specific indefinite with broad scope over both conjuncts: in symbols (using typographically differentiated variables x and z) $\exists x[\text{warrior}(x) \wedge \text{attack}(M,x)] \wedge \exists z[\text{warrior}(z) \wedge \text{attack}(D,z)]$ ('There is a warrior such that Menelaus attacks him, and there is a warrior such that Diomedes attacks him'). The less readily available collective interpretation, $\exists x[\text{warrior}(x) \wedge \text{attack}(M \oplus D,x)]$ ('There is a warrior such that Menelaus and Diomedes attack him collectively'), requires cancelling this strong implicature

> Menelaus attacked a warrior, and Diomedes did too. It was the same warrior and they attacked him together.

As far as we know, conjunct hyperbaton does not have this implicature, although we have not found any strongly collective examples with "once only" or "piano-carrying" predicates

> Menelaus killed a warrior and Diomedes
> Menelaus carried a piano upstairs and Diomedes,

where not only are both subjects involved in the same event with the same object, but neither subject individually performs the action described by the verb phrase. Note however with a definite object and Y1 hyperbaton within the first conjunct

> (70)   ὃν κορυνήτης | γείνατ' Ἀρηΐθοος καὶ Φυλομέδουσα βοῶπις *Il* 7.10
>   (cp. *Il* 21.141, *Od* 7.57).

The definite by itself guarantees identity of the direct object but not of the event. Where a more reciprocal meaning is involved, we find one clear and one possible case of continuous YP coordination and plural agreement

> (71)   Πηνέλεως δὲ Λύκων τε συνέδραμον *Il* 16.335
>   οἱ δὲ δὴ ἄλλοι | Τρῶες καὶ Δαναοὶ σύναγον κρατερὴν ὑσμίνην
>   *Il* 16.763.

Regular conjunct hyperbaton would presumably be illicit, as it would be with plural reflexive and reciprocal pronouns

---

(70) Whose parents were the macebearer Areithous and the ox-eyed Phylomedusa (*Il* 7.10).
(71) Peneleus and Lycon rushed at each other (*Il* 16.335).

Hector praises themselves and Achilles
Peneleus attacks each other and Lycon.

This assumption is supported by number agreement evidence from Lebanese
and Moroccan Arabic (Standard Arabic works differently), where singular
agreement with postverbal conjuncts is illicit for reflexives, reciprocals and collective predicates like *meet* and *share* (Aoun & Benmamoun 1999). However,
the schema Alcmanicum with its plural verb agreement is licensed with this
type of predicate

(72)   ἧχι ῥοὰς Σιμόεις συμβάλλετον ἠδὲ Σκάμανδρος *Il* 5.774.

Like comitative coordination in Slavic (McNally 1993), the schema Alcmanicum is particularly suited to situations in which the conjoined subjects are
either intrinsically connected like Simois and Scamander, Pyriphlegethon and
Cocytus (*Od* 10.513), Castor and Pollux (Alcman Frag. 2 Calame: appositional) (Fraser 1910) or at least collectively associated in the event. Pairing
seems to be a particularly strong manifestation of the general requirement for
semantic compatibility between coordinates

the cup and saucer
?the cup and saucepan
the cup and the saucepan.

In languages that do not have conjunctions but simply juxtapose conjuncts,
intonation is used to encode the distinction between paired and independent
items (Mithun 1988).

Similar distinctions can be made for object conjunct hyperbaton. In an
English stripping sentence like

He mixed martinis last night, and margheritas

there are two separate mixing subevents. You cannot say

*He mixed martinis last night, and margheritas; and the result was
a weird mixture.

This restriction does not apply to conjunct hyperbaton in Greek

(73)   οἶνον ἔμισγον ἐνὶ κρητῆρσι καὶ ὕδωρ *Od* 1.110.

A distributive reading with separate mixing episodes is hardly possible, but
given the normal usage of μείγνυμι and κεράννυμι in Homer, the line might go
back to a nonconfigurational structure in which the (etymologically unclear)
καὶ meant 'and together with it.'

(72) Where the Simois and the Scamander join their streams (*Il* 5.774). But the others,
the Trojans and the Greeks joined in fierce combat (*Il* 16.763).
(73) They were mixing wine and water in bowls (*Od* 1.110).

Another difference between English stripping and Greek conjunct hyperbaton involves the scope of adverbials. In the following examples, the second elliptical clause is either a correction to the first or outright impossible

> He only read Aeschylus, and Sophocles too
> He first read Aeschylus, and Sophocles too
> War together destroyed the Achaeans, and pestilence too
> He held the arrow notches together, and the string too.

But there is no problem with comparable types of conjunct hyperbaton in Greek

> (74)   τὸ ἐγγὺς μόνον ὁρῶν καὶ τὸ παραχρῆμα Pl *Crat* 395d
> οὐρῆας μὲν πρῶτον ἐπῴχετο καὶ κύνας ἀργούς *Il* 1.50
> εἰ δὴ ὁμοῦ πόλεμός τε δαμᾷ καὶ λοιμὸς Ἀχαιούς *Il* 1.61
> ὁμοῦ γλυφίδας τε λαβὼν καὶ νεῦρα βόεια *Il* 4.122.

The adverbs in these examples scope over both conjuncts. For instance, in the Plato example, μόνον has scope over Y2 just as it does in a similar structure not interrupted by a superordinate X

> (75)   ἁρμονίᾳ μόνον καὶ μήκει Pl *Crat* 416b.

The same result is achieved if we test with negation. In Kru (Hyman 1975), split object coordination is regularly associated with an intonation break after the verb

> *He not fish buy, and rice*
> 'He did not buy fish and rice.'

Despite the intonation break, the negative has scope over both conjuncts, as it does in Greek

> οὐ τόξοισι μαχέσκετο δουρί τε μακρῷ *Il* 7.140;

'it is not the case that he fought with arrows and with the long spear.' (It is interesting that Nunggubuyu has developed a system of morphological indexing that explicitly marks the scope of negation in paratactic structures [Heath 1986].)

Whatever levels of phrase structure are being coordinated in Greek conjunct hyperbaton, they are evidently lower ranked than those involved in English stripping, and conjunct hyperbaton is a more local construction: stripping is more like a clausal coordination, object conjunct hyperbaton is more like a phrasal coordination. Extrapolating from the evidence of nonconfigurational

---

(74) Only seeing what was near and immediate (Pl *Crat* 395d). First he went after the mules and the swift dogs (*Il* 1.50). If war and pestilence together are going to tame the Achaeans (*Il* 1.61). Holding together the arrow notches and the bowstring of ox sinew (*Il* 4.122).

(75) Only in tone and duration (Pl *Crat* 416b).

Australian languages like Nunggubuyu and Warlpiri, one can posit three different strategies of object coordination corresponding to simple noun phrase coordination in English

(1) NOUN PHRASE COORDINATION WITH PLURAL AGREEMENT
   I ate-3PL [the meat and the fish]

(2) ADJUNCT (INCLUDING HYPERBATON)
   The meat I-ate-3SG and the fish

(3) CONJOINED CLAUSES
   I ate-3SG the meat and I ate-3SG the fish.

The adjunction strategy should probably not be reduced to one of the other two strategies: (2) is not a discontinuous version of (1) as the object agreement rule shows, nor is it simply a gapped version of (3).

The same sort of scopal differences that we found for conjunct hyperbaton are relevant for modifier hyperbaton too. We can use an example with a relative clause to illustrate the effect

She finally found a boyfriend who was Italian.

If the relative clause is nonrestrictive and so adpositive ('who turned out to be Italian'), she was looking for a boyfriend of any nationality; perhaps she was lonely. If the relative clause is restrictive and so integrated, she was specifically looking for an Italian boyfriend; perhaps she wanted to study unaccusatives. When used in this sense, the verb *find* is partly intensional. The intensional phase (equivalent to *look for, try to find*) is drawn out by *finally* on its most natural reading; the extensional phase is the punctual telos of finding. This is why *find* gives mixed results with some recently proposed intensionality tests (Moltmann 1997)

She finally found what/*who Sue had found the year before,
   namely an Italian boyfriend
She finally found a boyfriend. He was Italian
She was looking for a boyfriend. *He was Italian (nonspecific reading).

Now consider the relative clause in the original example. The restrictive relative clause is in one way or another internal to the nuclear noun phrase and so inside the scope of the intensional verb. But the adpositive relative clause is outside its scope; it is like a conjoined clause, and its antecedent is the same as that for socalled E-type intersentential pronominal anaphora ('and he was Italian'), namely the boyfriend that was actually found. Now it is intuitively obvious that texts are interpreted in incremental stages, and that certain update operations are performed at the boundaries between stages. For instance, in narrative the reference time is moved forward with each stage, allowing the correct interpretation of iconically sequenced sentences like ἦλθον. εἶδον. ἐνίκησα. (Plutarch *Caesar* 50). Discourse referents introduced at one stage can remain active and be picked up by anaphoric pronouns at a subsequent stage.

Prototypically, the boundaries between these dynamic semantic update stages correlate with the boundaries between syntactic simple sentences. But, as we have just seen, adpositive relative clauses behave like independent update stages. The first stage says that she was looking for a boyfriend and was ultimately successful in finding someone who became her boyfriend as a result of being found; the second stage adds the information that he (the found boyfriend) was Italian. The same sort of distinction applies to the following

> She finally found an Italian boyfriend
> She finally found a boyfriend, an Italian one.

The appositional *an Italian one* again involves anaphoric reference. Negation interferes with this type of anaphora (Iatridou 1991)

> She didn't find an Italian boyfriend
> *She didn't find a boyfriend, who was Italian
> *She didn't find a boyfriend, an Italian one.

The starred sentences are bad to the extent that it is difficult to get a specific (referential) reading of the indefinite noun phrase ('It is not the case that she found a particular boyfriend, who was waiting for her at the station'), and one does not specify additional restrictions on an unavailable referent. Since no boyfriend was found, there is no referent of whom Italian nationality could be predicated. It would be like saying

> *Noone came in. He was wearing a red shirt

where the antecedent of the pronoun is a negative quantifier phrase. (This is obviously different from 'Noone came. They were all at the game.') In general, negation (but not double negation) blocks the normal "dynamic potential" of indefinites

> *She didn't find a boyfriend. He was Italian.

We have already used negation as a test for conjunct hyperbaton, and we can use it here too as a test for the integrated reading of indefinites in Y_2 hyperbaton. The negative test confirms the availability of the integrated reading

> (76) συνεβούλευε... γυναῖκα μὴ ἄγεσθαι τεκνοποιὸν ἐς τὰ οἰκία Her 1.59
>   εἰ μισθόν γε μὴ 'φερες πολύν Ar *Ach* 137.

The first example does not mean 'he advised him that he should not bring a wife into his house, and that the wife he didn't bring into his house should be able to have children'; note also that syntactically the Y_2 modifier precedes the goal complement. Likewise, the second example does not mean 'if you weren't getting a payment, and if the payment you weren't getting was large.' Rather

(76) He advisd him not to marry and bring home a woman capable of having children (Her 1.59). If you weren't getting very well paid (Ar *Ach* 137).

these examples have the same sort of integrated meaning typically required for
Y₂ hyperbata like

(77)   ἐπ' ἄνδρας στρατευόμεθα ἀγαθούς Her 7.53
       ἐς γῆν ἔπλευσε Τρῳάδ' Eur *El* 3.

The Herodotus example does not mean 'we are waging war against men, valiant ones,' i.e. 'we are waging war against men ⟨rather than women⟩, and they
are valiant,' but, as noted in chapter 3, 'the men we are waging war against are
valiant.' Similarly, in the *Electra* example the verb phrase is vacuous without
the modifier. We shall return to examples like this at the end of the next section.

Integrated readings are common in Homer too, but some form of less integrated reading also seems to be available, as in the following examples where
the Y₂ modifiers come in addition to earlier adjective and possessive modifiers

(78)   ἥ με κέλεαι σχεδίῃ περάαν μέγα λαῖτμα θαλάσσης | δεινόν τ'
       ἀργαλέον τε *Od* 5.174 (Y₁Y₂)
       καὶ τῷ νήδυμος ὕπνος ἐπὶ βλεφάροισιν ἔπιπτε | νήγρετος, ἥδιστος,
       θανάτῳ ἄγχιστα ἐοικώς *Od* 13.79 (Y₁ZXY₂).

The matter is discussed in more detail later.

The recurrent conclusion in the analysis we have just conducted was that Y₂
and conjunct hyperbaton are not comparable to unintegrated English constructions of the type 'he put on fetters, gold ones' or 'he went after Abas, and
Polyidus too.' These English constructions are clausal adpositives, whereas
hyperbaton is basically phrasal.

Integrated interpretation

On the other hand, there are also problems with the idea that hyperbaton is
equivalent to the fully integrated structures with which we are familiar in configurational languages like English. The normal clause internal constructions
in English involve attributively modified noun phrases ('he put on [gold fet-
ters]') and coordinate noun phrases ('he went after [Abas and Polyidus]'). Note
that such integrated noun phrase readings would effectively neutralize nonconfigurationality. They reconstruct just those hierarchically structured meanings that are overtly encoded in a configurational syntax like that of English.
Hyperbaton would be reduced to a semantically and probably even compositionally irrelevant piece of syntactic machinery. One obvious way to account
for such posited integrated noun phrase readings is simply to reconstruct the

---

(77) We are waging war against valiant men (Her 7.53). He sailed to the Trojan land
(Eur *El* 3).
(78) Who order me to cross on a raft the great gulf of the sea, awe-inspiring and challenging (*Od* 5.174). Pleasant sleep fell on his eyelids, sound, very sweet and very closely
resembling death (*Od* 13.79).

(modified or conjunct) noun phrase at logical form. Various versions of this approach are conceivable. The Y2 element might be supposed to move into a trace position marking the site from which it had been extraposed (we did not adopt an extraposition analysis above)

(79)   [πέδας χρυσείας$_i$]$_{NP}$ ἔβαλε —$_i$
       [Ἄβαντα καὶ Πολύειδον$_i$]$_{NP}$ μετῴχετο —$_i$

or to move into an empty base generated modifier position next to Y1 (Bittner 1998), or simply to be adjoined to Y1 (Reinhart 1991). Alternatively, the Y1 element could be thought to move into a trace position from which it had been raised (as in Figures 4.3 and 4.5)

       —$_i$ ἔβαλε [πέδας χρυσείας$_i$]$_{NP}$
       —$_i$ μετῴχετο [Ἄβαντα καὶ Πολύειδον$_i$]$_{NP}$.

Note that, for subject hyperbaton, the schema Alcmanicum requires plural number agreement, and regular Y2 conjunct hyperbaton requires singular agreement. τε... καὶ examples (Il 5.300) permit but do not require reconstruction. For object conjunct hyperbaton, we have already pointed out that reconstruction is not possible when a language has object agreement and it is singular in the hyperbaton structure.

The general idea of reconstructing Y2 hyperbata into a single noun phrase at logical form is open to two basic criticisms: first, that it tends to underestimate the potential differences between attributive and predicative types of adjective; and second, that it is glossocentric and insensitive to the general principles of informational structure and organization that underly the phenomenon of nonconfigurationality. Obviously, it makes a huge difference to one's general understanding of hyperbaton whether one posits reconstruction as a step in the process of interpretation. So we need to look at both of these criticisms in greater detail.

The semantics of modification (which was briefly discussed in chapter 1) has been a topic of some debate over the years for both adjectives and adverbs (Reichenbach 1947; Bartsch 1975; Siegel 1976; Parsons 1980, 1990; Hoepelman 1983; Keenan & Faltz 1985; Bierwisch 1989; Sproat & Shih 1991; Pustejovsky 1993, 1995; Kamp & Partee 1995). We have argued that prenominal attributive adjectives are normally functions from one common noun to another (so extensionally a function from one set to a different set), while postnominal adjectives in Greek are functions from one noun phrase or determiner phrase to another (p. 29). These rather open-ended characterizations need to be supplemented and constrained by certain generalizations about how the meanings of the adjective and the noun can be combined to compute the ultimate meaning of the whole modified noun phrase.

(79) He put on gold fetters. He went after Abas and Polyidus.

The most straightforward case is that of intersective adjectives. These are simple extensional predicates like *four-legged, speckled, circular, married, indivisible.* By and large, an entity just either has four legs or it does not, irrespective of what entity it is and without regard to the context. So when such an adjective attributively modifies a nominal predicate, the result simply amounts to the intersection of the two sets. The ultimate meaning is just the conjunction of the adjective property and the noun property, simultaneously predicated of the same individual: in symbols $\lambda x[\text{N}(x) \wedge \text{A}(x)]$.

Scalar adjectives (both dimensional and evaluative) are a bit more complicated. These are adjectives like *large, good, fast.* They can be used in a fairly absolute way ('large as entities go'), but often need to be interpreted relative to some comparison set based on the noun and the context, in which case they can be called relative adjectives. If Achilles kills a tall warrior, he is tall qua warrior rather than tall qua person (and the standard of enemy warrior tallness depends on whether Achilles was fighting against Trojans, Pygmies or Vikings). The point becomes obvious when one starts to compare tall dwarfs with tall basketball players. What is important here is that the attributive adjective can access the noun for its interpretation. Even intersective adjectives may have some degree of relational sensitivity, since what counts as *white* for chocolate might not count as *white* for paint or paper. Obviously the comparison class cannot be identical to the denotation of the noun phrase, or the comparison would be vacuous. This leads to an interesting difference between restrictive and descriptive adjectives and between regular and generic sentences

> The huge elephant was trampling the grass
> The rose is beautiful.

If *huge* is restrictive, the comparison class is other elephants; if it is descriptive, it is other animals. If the rose sentence is situation specific, the comparison class is other roses; if it is generic, it is other flowers.

Adjectives of the socalled subsective class have already been exemplified in chapter 1: *beautiful soprano, eloquent pianist.* The adjective here modifies not the person who is a soprano but the event associated with performing the function of a soprano: a *beautiful soprano* is someone who sings soprano beautifully (even if she weighs 300 pounds). *Beautifully* is interpreted relative to the standard set by the performance of other sopranos. *Beautiful soprano* also has an extensional reading ('physically attractive'), but adjectives like *skillful* are difficult to interpret in purely extensional terms without reference to some contextually determined domain of evaluation, since most people are skillful at some things and unskilled at others. In one way or another (Moltmann 1997b), the meaning of the predicate has to be restricted to the particular property that is contextually relevant: of the various functions that Prof. Jones performs, he is skillful qua textual critic but unskilled qua violinist. This contextual dependency is reduced but not eliminated by appealing to events: in one and the same event, our soprano could give a dramatically riveting performance which was horribly off pitch. Comparison classes are still required: a beautiful soprano in Miss Marple's village choir might not be a beautiful soprano at the Scala theatre. The comparison classes themselves may require intensional definition: for instance, it could be that all soccer players both dribble and kick the ball across the field, but some individual players are lousy dribblers and great kickers or vice versa.

Finally, intensional adjectives of the negativizing (*fake, phony*) and modalizing (*alleged, possible*) classes are unequivocal property modifiers and cannot be used extensionally. There is hardly a set of alleged, supposed or ostensible things. As for the nouns that such adjectives modify, the English Patient's rule ("a thing is still a thing no matter what you place in front of it") crashes as badly as his plane. While intersective adjectives create subsets of the denotation of the modified noun (*red shirts*), negativizing adjectives create sets that are actually, and modalizing adjectives sets that are potentially, disjoint from the denotation of the noun (*fake fibula, alleged Modigliani*), even if good fake fibulae have significantly fibular properties. Whereas intersective adjectives have simple denotations (the set of red things, etc.), these adjectives are more like modal or tense (*former*) operators. For instance, *alleged* relates to the propositional attitude of alleging and to the possible world alleged to be the real world. An alleged Modigliani is something that would be a real Modigliani in a world in which the art dealer had a better reputation. Similarly, a former chair is something that used to be a chair and is now firewood.

Many adjectives can be used either with an extensional or with an intensional (including subsective) or relative reading. Most adjectives can also be used either predicatively or attributively. So one would like to know if and how the two distributions correlate. There is no one-to-one mapping. For instance, it is not the case that all predicative uses are extensional, while all attributive uses are intensional or relative. Uniformity could be achieved for the attributives if apparently extensional cases could be reanalyzed as intensional without losing the generalizations just discussed. But there is no parallel way of getting rid of the intensional readings for the predicatives. However, a weaker but still instructive claim can be made: when the syntax does discriminate between the two readings, the intensional and relative readings are normally more accessible from the (prenominal) attributive position.

We will start by comparing prenominal attributive adjectives with simple main predicate adjectives. The property modifiers, which are fully intensional, are mostly illicit as predicates

> *The prime minister is former
> *This Modigliani is alleged.

When an adjective has both intensional and extensional uses, intensional readings can be unavailable in predicative position, as in the following French and Italian examples

un furieux menteur 'a compulsive liar'
Le menteur est furieux 'The liar is angry'

un alto ufficiale 'a highranking official'
L'ufficiale è alto 'The official is tall.'

In Russian, the short form of adjectives occurs only in predicative position and has an extensional reading; the long form has access to an intensional reading and is used attributively; it can also occur predicatively a bit like a null head modifier (Siegel 1976). In English, a sentence such as

The epigrapher is good

is more likely to get an intensional reading involving Prof. Jones' excellence as an epigrapher than an extensional reading which, if it exists, would relate to his goodness as a person. Also, if Prof. Jones is both a baritone and an epigrapher, a richer context is needed to give the reading in which the epigrapher sings excellently. On the other hand, in its attributive use

Prof. Jones is a good epigrapher

the adjective can hardly refer to his qualities as a baritone (context-driven intensional reading) or to his general goodness as a person (extensional reading) at all except in very specific and contrived contexts. For the most part, coordination of Y2 nouns seems to be acceptable for all classes of adjective

large [mice and elephants]
fake [cups and fibulae]
skillful [dancers and typists]
beautiful [singers and dancers].

Now we are ready to look at postnominal (Y2) adjectives. To the extent that Y1 and Y2 adjectives can access different meanings, it is the Y2 adjectives rather than the Y1 adjectives that tend to agree with the predicative type. Going back to our French and Italian examples, we find

un menteur furieux 'an angry liar,' not *'a compulsive liar'
un ufficiale alto 'a tall official,' not *'a highranking official.'

In English, when there is a difference between temporary and permanent properties, the temporary meaning is usually associated with the Y2 adjective

the only navigable river
the only river navigable (scil. on that occasion)

They used the handy tools
They used the tools handy.

The Y1 adjective contributes directly to the identification of the nominal, the Y2 adjective predicates information about its temporary state as a secondary restriction. Nominal properties are prototypically more stable and predicate properties more transitory, so it makes sense that Y1 modification should be more compatible with the noun in this feature (whether modification is thought of as complex property formation or as property conjunction). It seems to be a question of how information is structured, which recalls the distinction made in cognitive grammar between "summary scanning" and "sequential scanning" (Langacker 1987). The temporary-permanent distinction can also occur with Russian long and short form adjectives; in two of Siegel's (1976) examples it is the predicative short form adjective that has the temporary meaning: *zanjatoj* 'generally busy,' *zanjat* 'occupied at the moment'; *bol'noj* 'suffering from ill health,' *bolen* 'ill at the moment.' In Hungarian, attributive adjectives are prenominal, but under certain pragmatic conditions they can be used in Y2 positions including typical Y2 hyperbaton. In Hungarian Y2 hyperbaton, adjectives lose direct access to the noun, which can lead to illicit structures with both intensional and relative adjectives. For instance, the following Y2 hyperbata are impossible, even though the corresponding sentences with regular prenominal attributive adjectives are perfectly acceptable (Marácz 1989)

> *Mari   elnököt   látott   előzőt
> Mary president-ACC saw   former-ACC
> 'Mary saw the former president'

> *Mari bolhát látott nagyot
> Mary flea-ACC saw big-ACC
> 'Mary saw a big flea.'

The problem is that in Hungarian the Y2 position forces a purely extensional reading, which is unavailable for *former* and inappropriate for *big* (since fleas are all small entities). Hungarian Y2 hyperbaton also fails to access the more local of two readings associated with superlatives under certain conditions (Szabolcsi 1986). It is not clear whether Greek, even a hypothetical more non-configurational prehistoric Greek, had any extensionality constraints on Y2 adjectives, although the prototypical Y2 modifier in classical Greek seems to be restrictive, concrete and extensional. Figuratively used Y2 adjectives occur in Homer

> (80) ὄπα χάλκεον *Il* 18.222
> ἐπέεσσι καθάπτεσθαι μαλακοῖσιν *Il* 1.582
> μένεος δ' ἐμπλήσατο θυμὸν | ἀγρίου *Il* 22.314
> ἄτη ἐνέδησε βαρείῃ *Il* 9.18.

ψευδής can be used as a Y2 adjective with or without hyperbaton in the orators, but it has an extensional meaning ('forged, untrue'). Even ψυχρός 'vain' can be used predicatively (Herodotus 6.108). On the other hand, the fact that scalar adjectives tend to prenominal position in Greek follows directly from the

---

(80) Brazen voice (*Il* 18.222). Engage with soft words (*Il* 1.582). He filled his heart with wild rage (*Il* 22.314). He has entangled men in heavy infatuation (*Il* 9.18).

greater access of Y1 adjectives to the nominal comparison class. Another possible source of evidence is the neuter predicative adjective

(81)   θήλεια δ' ἵππος καλὴ οὐ καλόν... ; Pl *Hipp Mai* 288b.

The neuter can also be used as a gender resolution strategy

(82)   λίθοι τε καὶ πλίνθοι καὶ ξύλα καὶ κέραμος ἀτάκτως μὲν ἐρριμένα
       οὐδὲν χρήσιμά ἐστιν Xen *Mem* 3.1.7.

A gender resolution neuter plural is attested in nonconfigurational structures in Homer, both when the nouns are appositional

(83)   ἔπειτα δὲ χίλι' ὑπέστη | αἶγας ὁμοῦ καὶ ὄϊς *Il* 11.244

('a thousand head' cp. *Il* 5.140) and significantly with amplifying Y2 adjectives, which are presumably predicated of the same inanimate individuals as the nouns they modify

(84)   ἀμφὶ δέ μιν ῥάκος... βάλεν ἠδὲ χιτῶνα | ῥωγαλέα ῥυπόωντα
       Od 13.435.

Attributive Y1 neuters are not allowed

       *θήλεια ἵππος καλὸν οὐ καλὴ
       *χρήσιμα λίθοι τε καὶ ξύλα καὶ κέραμος
       *ῥωγαλέα ῥάκος ἠδὲ χιτῶνα.

At all events, the upshot is that we have three different syntactic positions and three different readings, even if the degree of correlation between them is open to dispute and may vary from one language to another. Syntactically we have Y1, Y2 and adpositive Y2; semantically we have the operator type (which builds modified properties), the independent predicate type and the adpositive type. For the sake of concreteness, we will illustrate these types with approximate English paraphrases and informal symbolic representations (that are vague about the logical status of nonspecific indefinites).

(1)   OPERATOR
      Jack met an old girlfriend
      $\exists x[A(N)x \land V(y,x)]$

At least on its intensional reading of 'former' as opposed to 'aged' ('This young lady is Jack's old girlfriend'), A(N) is not "cashed out" intersectively. What is modified is not the person (call her Phoebe) but the state of Phoebe being in a girlfriend relation to Jack

(81) Isn't a beautiful mare a beautiful thing? (Pl *Hipp Mai* 288b).
(82) Stones, bricks, timber and tiles thrown together any old how are quite useless (Xen *Mem* 3.1.7).
(83) Then he promised a thousand goats and sheep (*Il* 11.244).
(84) She put around him a cloak and a tunic which were torn and filthy (*Od* 13.435).

(2) SECONDARY PREDICATE

Jack met a girlfriend ⟨who was⟩ old

$\exists x[N(x) \wedge A(x) \wedge V(y,x)]$

(3) APPOSITIVE

Jack met a girlfriend, ⟨and she was⟩ old

$\exists x[N(x) \wedge V(y,x)] \wedge [A(x^{DYN})]$, with dynamic variable (or E-type anaphora).

In addition, adjectives appear as main predicates ('She was old') and as null head or pronominal head modifiers ('an old one,' 'one which was old'). It can be argued that both syntactically and semantically class (1), the operator type, is more complex and hierarchical than class (2), the secondary predicate type. The latter often just predicates a simple property in a separate adjoined phrase. It should be particularly favoured in nonconfigurational languages. Hence the interesting tendency, already noted, for speakers of nonconfigurational Kalkatungu to translate English attributive modifiers with class (3) modifiers in their own language: 'The big dog bit the snake' → 'Dog bit snake. That dog ⟨is⟩ big.' So one might think that the development of configurational structure over time should involve a progressive increase in the frequency of class (2) and then class (1) modifiers, entailing both a reanalysis of unchanged discontinuous syntax and a trend towards attributive Y_1 modifiers at the expense of the Y_2 type. For instance, the difference in the frequency of Y_2 adjectives between Herodotus and Attic prose (Table 1.4) could reflect the development of a more progressive and hierarchical phrase structure in Attic.

The association of Y_1 adjectives with hierarchical structure is corroborated by the evidence of multiple adjectives. These can be stacked or conjoined (Gil 1983; Crain & Hamburger 1992)

> a small powerful engine (stacked)
> a powerful small engine (stacked)
> a small and powerful engine (conjoined).

The conjoined type has a parallel interpretation, 'an engine that is both small and powerful relative to engines in general.' This interpretation is also available for the stacked types, particularly when pronounced with a prosodic phrase boundary between the two adjectives ("comma intonation"): *a small, powerful engine*. Taking the intersective approach to relative adjectives, we can say that the three sets are simultaneously intersected, and the noun by itself provides or contributes to the comparison set. The stacked types additionally have hierarchical interpretations, namely 'small relative to powerful engines' and 'powerful relative to small engines,' respectively. Here the intersection proceeds in two stages, and the set generated by the initial intersection of the noun and the internal adjective provides the comparison set; powerful small engines need not be powerful engines. Inverse scope readings are not available. In English the stacked hierarchical type can also be used for postnominal adjectives and relative clauses

> engines small in size powerful enough to run a scooter
> engines which are small in size which are powerful enough to run
>   a scooter

but not predicatively without a pronominal head. Some languages, like Hebrew, disallow hierarchical interpretations for stacked adjectives; there has also been some discussion of the availability of the hierarchical interpretation in child language (Matthei 1982; O'Grady 1997). Hungarian allows both parallel and hierarchical readings for Y_1 stacked adjectives, but only allows a parallel reading when the adjectives are stacked in Y_2 hyperbaton (Marácz 1989). This is a further indication that the mechanisms of adjective interpretation in Y_1 position are different from the simple predication associated with the Y_2 position.

Most of the distinctions between Y_1 and Y_2 adjectives just described might conceivably be dismissed as purely a matter of syntax, of the degree to which the adjective can locally access the noun to build an interpretive context. For instance, subsective adjectives have to be able to get inside the semantic representation of the noun to modify an eventive component of its meaning. Alternatively, one might be tempted to suppose that the class of adjectives subsumes two semantically distinct subclasses, an attributive type which on its default reading forms modified properties out of simple properties (Komlósy 1994) and a predicative type which on its default reading just predicates independent properties. This type of semantics would underpin syntactic analyses that draw a distinction between prenominal adjectives as heads and postnominal adjectives as full phrasal projections licensing their own complements (*fond of chocolate*) and postmodifiers (*polite in manner*). There is a particularly tight fit with the head-to-head adjunction theory (p. 29). If one does not want to make such an explicit semantic claim, one could use the more descriptive terms "direct" and "indirect" modification (Sproat & Shih 1991).

However this question is ultimately resolved, the consequences for the reconstruction of hyperbaton are fairly clear. The temptation was, under the impetus of English paraphrases like *golden fetters*, to reconstruct a logical form with English style attributive modification: [NV]A → [AN]V, V[AN]. But this implicitly changes secondary predicates into attributive adjectives prior to semantic interpretation, and a whole range of evidence just cited from Y_2 hyperbaton in Hungarian shows that such a move is in principle illicit. We still have the option of reconstructing a Y_2 modified noun phrase ([NV]A → [NA]V, V[NA]), if we are willing to make the assumption that Y_2 hyperbaton and continuous Y_2 adnominal modification are interpreted identically. However, at least for reconstructed VNA, there is evidence that movement at logical form would be pointless, since it would not necessarily produce the intended noun phrase structure. If we can generalize from the articulated modifiers in the inscriptional examples already cited, even in the surface syntax of historical Greek the constituent structure could be [VN]A rather than V[NA] (διομοσαι hopϑον : τον νομιον).

In any case, there are also more general grounds for objecting to the idea of reconstruction. This is where our second basic criticism comes in to play. Reconstruction treats the complexity constraint as a purely surface syntactic phenomenon, not a constraint on structure that applies equally to the overt syntax and to logical form. Consequently, nonconfigurational syntax is seen not as a less hierarchical way of structuring and packaging meaning, but as an inefficient, flat and paratactic attempt at encoding the hierarchically structured meanings with which we are familiar. However, in point of fact, nonconfigurational syntax has a very "semantic" flavour to it. The nuclear clause with its pronominal arguments is reminiscent of a formula in predicate logic with no content assigned to the variables; the identity of the variables is established in a separate operation. Adjunct adverbials are reminiscent of event modifiers; for instance, a prepositional phrase might predicate a spatial or temporal relationship between the event and the complement of the preposition. Adnominal modification and coordination also involve separate semantic predications. The simplest logical representations do not use devices like lambda abstraction or group formation to create complex argument structures. A sentence like

A boy kissed a blonde girl in the park

can be represented (omitting the existential quantifiers) as: $girl(x) \wedge blonde(x) \wedge boy(y) \wedge kissed(x,y,e) \wedge in\text{-}the\text{-}park(e)$. Apart from the overt logical coordinators, this bears an unmistakable resemblance to a nonconfigurational version of the same sentence (in a language allowing multiple adjuncts): 'A boy, a girl, he kissed her, blonde, in the park.' It is unlikely to be a concidence that this syntax encodes meaning in a way that mimics the atomic formulae of predicate logic (using the term "atomic" for each minimal predicative semantic relationship). Now, the shortest distance between an atomic syntax and an atomic semantics is a straight line and not a zigzag in which nonconfigurational representations are first reconstructed into configurational structures at logical form and then deconstructed into atomic semantic predications. Such a system would only be appropriate in a world in which the syntax of nonconfigurational languages could not be semantically interpreted without first being translated into English. It is much easier to assume that nonconfigurational languages prefer to bypass those hierarchical relations that they do not express in their syntax, many of which are also bypassed by the simplest forms of predicate logic. Whether this affects the ultimate computation of semantic values is arguable and leads to rather deep questions about the conceptualization of meaning and the universality of semantics (Sasse 1991; Gil 1991; Croft 1993; Faltz 1995), but it surely affects the compositional semantics.

So the Y₁ noun is not replaced by a modified or conjoined version of itself prior to semantic combination with the verb. First the Y₁ noun combines with the verb, and then the resulting structure is expanded by the Y₂ modifier or conjunct. We can speculate a little about the nature of this expansion. Consider again our example of object conjunct hyperbaton with broad scope negation

οὐ τόξοισι μαχέσκετο δουρί τε μακρῷ *Il* 7.140.

Instead of reconstructing a coordinated noun phrase

He didn't fight with [arrows and the long spear]

perhaps we could supply a (semantic) copy of the verb within the scope of the negation

He didn't [with arrows fight] and [with the long spear ⟨fight⟩].

In that case, the expansion would be interpreted semantically as the equivalent of an elliptical verb phrase. As for Y₂ adjectives, they are probably secondary predicates which are less constrained than English depictives, in that they are not necessarily event-related or temporary (stage level) properties (Rapoport 1992); unlike in English, Russian and Icelandic (Schein 1995), they are also allowed to occur with Y₁ nouns governed by prepositions or in an oblique case. Typical English depictives like *hot* in

He ate half his soup hot

can only be interpreted relative to the event of eating or to its time of occurrence. The meaning is not 'he ate half of his hot soup' but 'he ate half of his soup such that it was hot during the event of its being eaten.' The other half he ate cold. Similarly for the resultative 'He hammered the nail flat,' what is flat is the nail after being successfully hammered. If we factor out the simultaneity component from 'the soup while it got eaten,' we are left with 'the soup which got eaten.' If we factor out the sequentiality from 'the nail after it got hammered,' we are left with 'the nail which got hammered.' So maybe it is not the denotation of the complement [N] but the denotation of [NV] that is modified by the Y₂ adjective. This would fit particularly well with the pragmatic structure of topic-type Y₂ hyperbaton, in which the adjective is in effect predicated of the topic phrase [Y₁X], as proposed in chapter 3

ἐπ' ἄνδρας στρατευόμεθα ἀγαθούς Her 7.53
ἐσθῆτι δὲ χρεωμένους Μηδικῇ Her 5.9;

'the men-we-are-waging-war-against are valiant,' 'the-clothes-they-use are in the Median style.' That [NV] can form a constituent in Y₂ hyperbaton is suggested by the following example with a subject intervening between [NV] and Y₂

(85)   ἐσθῆτα δὲ φορέουσι οἱ ἱρέες λινέην μούνην Her 2.37,

as well as by the failure of definiteness to spread to the noun in

(85) The priests wear only linen clothing (Her 2.37).

(86)   εἵματά τε ἐφόρεον τὰ κάλλιστα Her 3.27.

Here the syntax transparently encodes a tripartite focus structure in which the restriction is the topic [εἵματα (x) ∧ ἐφόρεον (x)] or [εἱματοφόρεον (x)] and the nuclear scope is the focus [τὰ κάλλιστα (x)]. This is not the case for all types of Y₂ hyperbaton, particularly not in Homer where descriptive Y₂ adjectives are common too

(87)   χεῖρ᾽ ἕλε δεξιτερὴν *Od* 1.121 (restrictive)
θύρας ἐπέθηκε φαεινάς *Il* 14.169 (descriptive).

But so long as what is modified by the Y₂ adjective is not an interclausal antecedent, adverbs and negatives can scope over the adjective

> He didn't eat a steak raw
> *He didn't eat a steak, a raw one

and the Italian boyfriend problem will not arise. In any case, there is a clear difference between proposals of this sort and reconstruction. One way of thinking about this difference is in terms of the scope of coordination and modification. Reconstruction gives narrow scope to both, while proposals like the above extend scope in a way that reduces the syntax-semantics mismatch. For reconstruction, what is coordinated is one Y element with the other, and what is modified is one Y element by the other. On the competing approaches, what is coordinated and modified is not [Y] but [XY]. (For coordination the head of [XY] is the silent X, for postadjunct modification it is Y; in chapter 6 we shall suggest an analysis of Y₁ hyperbaton in which the head of [XY] is X.) Another way of thinking about the difference is that reconstruction imposes uniform adnominal modification, whereas the above proposal allows adjunct modifiers to find their modifees from preceding material by a sort of E-type strategy that is internal to the clause.

FROM VERSE TO PROSE

Let us take this opportunity to recapitulate briefly what has been proposed so far. Hyperbaton originates in a flatter, less configurational type of syntax than that familiar to us from modern western European languages. Although Homeric syntax has developed considerably from the posited prehistoric typology, it still permits us to reconstruct a system in which the nuclear phrase XP consists prototypically of just the head X plus a preferably nonbranching complement Y. A position adjoined to the right of XP can host a variety of (at this stage) adjunct material. For instance, a nuclear phrase like πόλιν ὤλεσα could be fol-

(86)   They put on their best clothes (Her 3.27).
(87)   He took her right hand (*Od* 1.121). She closed the shining doors (*Il* 14.169).

lowed in the adjunct position by a Y_2 adjective (αἰπὴν), or a Y_2 genitive (Κιλίκων), or a Y_2 conjunct (καὶ ἄστυ), or an adverbial phrase (ἤματι κείνῳ), originally probably also a complement coindexed with a nuclear phrase internal pronominal argument. A modifier may also appear to the left of the nuclear XP, in Y_1 hyperbaton. Just as postnominal adjectives are sisters of NP and prenominal adjectives are sisters of N', so the postadjunct Y_2 is a sister of XP and the preadjunct Y_1 is a sister of X'.

Many things in language turn out on detailed analysis to be more complicated than they seemed to be at first sight. So it will probably not come as a surprise if the analysis of hyperbaton just presented involved some oversimplification. In particular, we will reexamine the presupposition that Y_1 and Y_2 hyperbaton are syntactically uniform, in the sense that all cases of Y_1 (and respectively Y_2) hyperbaton are supposed to involve the same structural position. The results of this exercise are not only interesting for themselves, they also lead to a clearer understanding of the difference between prose hyperbaton and verse hyperbaton. We will also look for empirical evidence to support the claim that Y_2 modifiers are more loosely attached to XP than Y_1 modifiers.

The evidence we shall adduce involves the correlation between syntactic constituency and metrical constituency, more specifically line end, in Homer. The material is familiar from literary analyses of enjambement (Higbie 1990; Clark 1997). It is important to realize that enjambement is not first order but second order evidence for syntactic constituency. Enjambement operates via the medium of prosodic constituency. It is intuitively obvious that, ontologically, metrical units are prosodic domains, and that the hemistich is prototypically a prosodic minor phrase and the stichos a prosodic major phrase. We have recently set out in detail the theoretical and empirical bases for this assumption (Devine & Stephens 1994). What concerns us here is that, while the metrical units reflect prosodic domains, the prosodic domains in turn reflect syntactic structure (with some degree of adjustment). So, ultimately, metrical structure reflects syntactic structure. Consequently, metrical structure can be adduced as evidence for the syntax. Here is an extremely simple illustration of this principle. In English nursery rhymes like

> [Doctor Foster] [went to Gloucester]
> [Humpty Dumpty] [sat on a wall]

the line is a prosodic major phrase and the caesura splits the line into two prosodic minor phrases. Such lines would hardly support the thesis that English had syntactic structures like [Doctor] [Foster went] or [Humpty] [Dumpty sat] (nor, for that matter, the thesis that syntax is unstructured). Enjambement in Homer indicates that a prosodic boundary is allowed to occur at that point in the syntax where the line ends. Note that it does not indicate that a prosodic boundary is necessarily disallowed between line internal words.

Y2 hyperbaton positions

In this section we revisit the question of integrated and unintegrated readings for Y2 hyperbaton. We will start with some typological data. On the basis of a range of evidence from the nonconfigurational languages of Australia, particularly Warlpiri, one can posit three possible syntactic structures for the "noun phrase": continuous YP, nuclear clause internal discontinuous YP, nuclear clause internal nominal plus independent extranuclear amplification (Hale 1981, 1994; Simpson 1991; Pensalfini 1992; Bittner & Hale 1995). The last is normally set off by an intonational break of some kind. Correspondingly, there are different possible semantic interpretations, which do not correlate perfectly with the three different syntactic structures. There is a merged interpretation and an unmerged interpretation. The unmerged interpretation might possibly be further differentiated into a relatively integrated type and a fully external afterthought. The continuous YP gets the merged interpretation, while the discontinuous YP (i.e. hyperbaton) can have either the merged or the unmerged interpretation. The merged interpretation is comparable to an English noun phrase like 'the small children.' The unmerged interpretation gives readings for the modifier like 'and they are small,' 'who are small,' 'the small ones, that is.' The details are still under investigation. There are also two readings for Y2 hyperbaton in Hungarian according as it is, or is not, prosodically integrated (Marácz 1989)

> Mari biciklit látott kettőtt
> Mary bikes saw two.

The prosodically integrated version of this sentence means roughly 'It was bikes that Mary saw two of.' But if the sentence is uttered with a prosodic break between the verb and Y2, it means 'It was bikes that Mary saw, two of them.'

The potentially string vacuous distinction between integrated and amplifying adjectives is familiar from languages having postnominal adjectives like Italian

> Ho visto una ragazza bionda
> 'I saw a blonde girl'
>
> Ho visto una ragazza,... bionda
> 'I saw a girl,... ⟨she was⟩ blonde'

and Modern Greek (Androutsopoulou 1996)

> ena kalo vivlio 'a good book'
> ena vivlio kalo 'a book ⟨which is⟩ good'
> ena vivlio, ena kalo 'a book, a good one' (has a prosodic break
>   at the comma).

The typological evidence just cited from Australian and other languages fits fairly well with the conclusions of our earlier theoretical analysis, where we posited three main classes—Y₁, Y₂ and adpositive Y₂. In principle, it should be possible for some or all of these categories to cooccur. We can again illustrate with relative clauses

> She finally found a boyfriend who was Italian, tall, dark and
>   handsome (those were the qualities she was looking for)
> She finally found a boyfriend who was Italian, who was bald,
>   nearsighted and a bit overweight.

It is a natural intuition for the reader of Homer that some Y₂ adjectives are more integrated than others, but the details are difficult to nail down. If the intuition is wellfounded, it would mean that Y₂ adjectives could be attached at different hierarchical levels of structure. The null hypothesis, on the other hand, would be that Y₂ adjectives are simply added in a flat, replicating string to the right of X along with other adjunct material, and that our intuitions about integrated versus unintegrated readings are an effect of prosodic phrasing unrelated to the syntax, or of some type of additional syntactic pairing mechanism. The null hypothesis is more economical in the structures that it assumes, but the typological evidence just cited suggests that this could be a false economy. Consider the following progression

(88)   πέδας ἔβαλε χρυσείας *Il* 13.36
   περὶ κουλεὸν ἦεν | ἀργύρεον *Il* 11.30
   κρητῆρα φέρειν Μεγαπένθε᾽ ἄνωγεν | ἀργύρεον *Od* 15.103
   ὁ δ ἄρα κρητῆρα φαεινὸν | θῆκ᾽ αὐτοῦ προπάροιθε φέρων κρατερὸς
     Μεγαπένθης | ἀργύρεον *Od* 15.121
   δώσω τοι κρητῆρα τετυγμένον· ἀργύρεος δὲ | ἐστὶν ἅπας *Od* 15.115.

Line 115 is overtly anaphoric. Despite the mention of silver in line 103, ἀργύρεον is fairly clearly adpositive in line 121, more like 'the butler finally found a clean dish, which was silver' than 'the butler finally found a clean silver dish.'

Dionysius of Halicarnassus already drew attention to the phenomenon (Parry 1971:252) citing the first lines of *Odyssey* 14

(89)   ἔνθα οἱ αὐλὴ | ὑψηλὴ δέδμητο περισκέπτῳ ἐνὶ χώρῳ | καλή τε
   μεγάλη τε, περίδρομος.

(88) He put on gold fetters (*Il* 13.36). Around it was a silver scabbard (*Il* 11.30). He told Megapenthes to bring a silver mixing bowl (*Od* 15.103). But the mighty Megapenthes brought the shining silver mixing bowl and placed it in front of him (*Od* 15.121). I will give you a beautifully made mixing bowl; it is entirely of silver (*Od* 15.115).

(89) Where his courtyard was built with a high wall, visible on all sides, beautiful and large, with open space around it (*Od* 14.5).

Dionysius notes the amplificatory character of the Y₂ modifiers following the prepositional phrase

(90)   ἐπιθεὶς γὰρ ʻπερισκέπτῳ ἐνὶ χώρῳʼ πάλιν ἐποίσει ʻκαλή τε
        μεγάλη τεʼ... εἶτα ʻπερίδρομοςʼ *De Comp Verb* 26.

The question is whether, and if so how, the syntax correlates with Parry's compositional features [± enjambed] and [± periodic] (Parry uses Dionysius' term) with respect to Y₂ modifiers.

Pairs of Y₂ adjectives can appear at the beginning of the next line after that containing the verb

(91)   Τρῶες δ᾽ ἐπὶ δούρατ᾽ ἔχευαν | ὀξέα παμφανόωντα *Il* 5.618
        ἐπὶ δὲ νεφέλην ἕσσαντο | καλὴν χρυσείην *Il* 14.350.

This is preferable to splitting the adjectives between lines (when no relative follows)

(92)   κόρυθι δ᾽ ἐπένευε φαεινῇ | τετραφάλῳ *Il* 22.314.

Strings of three adjectives in Y₂ hyperbaton (without conjunctions) are usually arranged so that the first is in the same line as the Y₁ noun, and the last two are placed in the following line, giving N V A₁ | A₂ A₃ rather than N V A₁ A₂ | A₃

(93)   ἀμφὶ δ᾽ ἄρα χλαῖναν περονήσατο φοινικόεσσαν | διπλῆν ἐκταδίην
        Il 10.133
        ἀμφὶ δὲ ποσσὶ πέδας ἔβαλε χρυσείας | ἀρρήκτους ἀλύτους *Il* 13.36
        πλοκάμους ἔπλεξε φαεινούς | καλοὺς ἀμβροσίους *Il* 14.176.

This arrangement suggests that the first adjective is part of an integrated Y₁XY₂ structure, and the last two are an amplificatory pair. The rule could simply be a reflex of prosodic phrase formation. However the prosodic explanation is less likely for the following example, in which other material intervenes between A₁ and A₂-A₃

(94)   θάμνος ἔφυ τανύφυλλος ἐλαίης ἕρκεος ἐντός | ἄκμηνος θαλέθων
        Od 23.190.

Sometimes all Y₂ modifiers appear in the verse following that of the Y₁ noun, strung out probably with some sort of internal pairing structure

(90) After adding περισκέπτῳ ἐνὶ χώρῳ he further subjoins καλὴ τε μεγάλη τε and then περίδρομος (*De Comp Verb* 26).

(91) The Trojans rained spears on him, sharp and gleaming (*Il* 5.618). They were cloaked in a beautiful gold cloud (*Il* 14.350).

(92) He nodded with his bright helmet with four bosses (*Il* 22.314).

(93) Around him he fastened a large purple double cloak (*Il* 10.133). Around their feet he put golden fetters not to be broken or loosened (*Il* 13.36). She plaited her glossy hair, beautiful and divine (*Il* 14.176).

(94) A long-leaved olive bush grew inside the courtyard, fullgrown and flourishing (*Od* 23.190).

(95) λίθον εἵλετο χειρὶ παχείῃ | κείμενον ἐν πεδίῳ μέλανα τρηχύν τε
μέγαν τε *Il* 21.403

ἀμφὶ δὲ οἱ κυνέην κεφαλῆφιν ἔθηκε | ταυρείην ἀφαλόν τε καὶ ἄλλοφον
Il 10.257.

In general, Y₂ is attracted to line initial position by any sort of pairing including juxtaposition or coordination with another adjective (as just illustrated), an
adjunct relative clause, comparison or explanatory clause

(96) ἔντεα δύω | καλὰ τὰ Πατρόκλοιο βίην ἐνάριξα κατακτάς *Il* 17.187

ἐπὶ δὲ Τρῶες κελάδησαν | νήπιοι· ἐκ γὰρ σφεων φρένας εἵλετο
Παλλὰς Ἀθήνη *Il* 18.310

ἐπὶ δὲ πτόλεμος τέτατό σφιν | ἄγριος ἠΰτε πῦρ *Il* 17.736

αὐτὰρ ἔπειτά σε δαιτὶ ἐνὶ κλισίης ἀρεσάσθω | πιείρῃ ἵνα μή τι δίκης
ἐπιδευὲς ἔχῃσθα *Il* 19.179.

Note that the explanatory clause, as in *Iliad* 18.310 just cited, does not give a
reason for the preceding clause but only for the modifier, which consequently
cannot be semantically attributive and has to be amplificatory. Finally, a second argument or adjunct can intervene between Y₁ and Y₂ to the left or the
right of X

(97) παρδαλέῃ μὲν πρῶτα μετάφρενον εὐρὺ κάλυψε | ποικίλῃ *Il* 10.29

ἐγκέφαλος δὲ παρ᾿ αὐλὸν ἀνέδραμεν ἐξ ὠτειλῆς | αἱματόεις
Il 17.297.

Y₁ hyperbaton positions

The idea that in the YXY template, Y stands for more than one position is
much easier to substantiate for Y₁ hyperbaton than it is for Y₂ hyperbaton,
even though it is less apparent to the cursory reader. The evidence, which again
comes from enjambement in Homer, has long been available: it was collected
(along with the Y₂ evidence) in the "rainy [Austrian] summer" of 1866 (La
Roche 1867) and reviewed and supplemented exactly a century later (Edwards
1966).

(95) With her strong hand she seized a stone lying on the ground, black, rough and
massive (*Il* 21.403). Around his head he put a helmet of oxhide without metal plates or
plume (*Il* 10.257).
(96) I put on the beautiful armour which I stripped from the mighty Patroclus after
killing him (*Il* 17.187). The Trojans applauded thereat, foolish because Pallas Athena
took away their good sense (*Il* 18.310). They were opposed by intense fighting, wild as
fire (*Il* 17.736). Afterwards let him make amends to you with a rich feast in his hut, so
that you may not have anything lacking that you deserve (*Il* 19.179).
(97) First he covered his broad back with a spotted leopard skin (*Il* 10.29). His brain
ran out all bloody along the spear socket (*Il* 17.297).

Not all prenominal adjectives (whether in prima facie continuous YPs or in Y₁ hyperbaton) can be separated from their nouns by line end. The following classes of Y₁ adjectives allow intervening line end:

(98)   QUANTIFIERS
ἔνθα δὲ πολλαὶ | ψυχαὶ ἐλεύσονται *Od* 10.529
οὕνεκα πᾶσι | Φαιήκεσσιν ἄνασσε *Od* 7.10
ἥ οἱ ἁπάσας | ἔσχ᾽ ὀδύνας *Il* 11.847 (YXY)
ἀκοντίζουσι θαμειὰς | αἰχμὰς *Il* 12.44

(99)   DEMONSTRATIVES, PRONOMINAL ADJECTIVES
ἔξοχον ἄλλων | ᾽Αργείων *Od* 4.171
πὰρ δέ οἱ ἄλλοι | ναῖον Βοιωτοί *Il* 5.710 (YXY)
ὀϊζύος ἦν ἐν ἐκείνῳ | δήμῳ ἀνέτλημεν *Od* 3.103

(100)   SUPERLATIVES
ὅς κεν ἀρίστην | βουλὴν βουλεύσῃ *Il* 9.74 (predicative?)
μέγιστον | τέκμωρ *Il* 1.525

(101)   FOCUSED POSSESSIVE PRONOUNS
ὅς κεν ἐμῆς γε | χοίνικος ἅπτηται *Od* 19.27
οὐδέ πω ἀμῆς | γῆς ἐπέβην *Od* 11.166

(102)   FOCUSED RESTRICTIVE ADJECTIVES
ἦ μάλα λυγρῆς | πεύσεαι ἀγγελίης *Il* 18.18 (YXY)
ἦ καὶ πατρώϊός ἐσσι | ξεῖνος *Od* 1.175 (YXY).

Possessive pronouns and restrictive adjectives, except for a few that are focused, and, significantly, descriptive adjectives are never or hardly ever allowed with enjambement when they are prenominal. This observation is unlikely to be merely a reflex of the relative frequency of the different types of adjective in Homer. καλός is a very common adjective in Homer, appearing in prenominal as well as postnominal positions: καλὰ πρόσωπα, καλὰ ῥέεθρα, καλὰς στεφάνας, καλὰ πέδιλα, etc. Of the only two examples of enjambed prenominal καλός, one at least is an unequivocally focused restrictive adjective (if it is adnominal)

(103)   οὕνεκα καλὸν | εἶδος ἔπ᾽ *Il* 3.44;

(98) Then many ghosts will come (*Od* 10.529). Since he was king of all the Phaeacians (*Od* 7.10). Which stopped all his pain (*Il* 11.847). They rain down javelins (*Il* 12.44).

(99) More than the other Argives (*Od* 4.171). Beside him lived other Boeotians (*Il* 5.710). The sorrow that we endured in that land (*Od* 3.103).

(100) Whoever gives the best advice (*Il* 9.74). The greatest guarantee (*Il* 1.525).

(101) Whoever shares my food (*Od* 19.27). I have not yet set foot on my land (*Od* 11.166).

(102) You will learn some really miserable news (*Il* 18.18). Or if you are a friend of my father (*Od* 1.175).

(103) Because he has a handsome appearance (*Il* 3.44).

in the other, the noun also has a postmodifier (*Il* 13.611; cp. *Od* 24.228). Y₁ descriptive or restrictive adjectives can sometimes be placed before the caesura

(104)   χρυσέοισιν / ἀορτήρεσσιν *Il* 11.31
           χρυσέῃσιν / ἐθείρῃσιν *Il* 8.42, 13.24
           ἀργυρέοισιν / ἐπισφυρίοις *Il* 3.331 et alibi.

However, they do not normally appear before line end:

(105)   ἱεροῖο δόμοιο | *Il* 6.89 ·

is fine, but

      *ἱεροῖσι | δώμασι

is not. There is no problem with such adjectives in Y₂ position at the beginning of the line

(106)   κορώνη | ἀργυρέη *Od* 1.441
           τραπέζας | ἀργυρέας *Od* 10.354
           κώπη | ἀργυρέη *Od* 8.403.

It is just that the order cannot be reversed, with or without hyperbaton

      *ἀργυρέῃσιν (X) | (X) κώπῃσιν.

When formulae with Y₁ modifiers like

(107)   ἡδὺς ὕπνος
           χάλκεον ἔγχος
           χρύσεον ὅρμον
           ἄγριαι αἶγες

are split between lines, the order is reversed from Y₁ modifier to Y₂ modifier, usually with hyperbaton (Hainsworth 1968)

(108)   ὕπνον | ἡδὺν *Od* 1.364
           ἐξ ὕπνου μ' ἀνεγείρεις | ἡδέος *Od* 23.16.

The Homeric enjambement evidence points to a number of conclusions, most importantly the following: (1) prenominal adjectives are structurally different from postnominal adjectives, and (2) prenominal descriptive and ordinary restrictive adjectives are also structurally different from prenominal quantifiers and strongly focused restrictive adjectives. The first distinction amounts to, or is related to, the observation, first mentioned in chapter 1, that

(104) With golden rings (*Il* 11.31). With golden manes (*Il* 8.42). With silver ankle-pieces (*Il* 3.331).
(105) Of the holy house (*Il* 6.89).
(106) With its silver handle (*Od* 1.441). Silver tables (*Od* 10.354). A silver hilt (*Od* 8.403).
(107) Sweet sleep. Bronze spear. Gold necklace. Wild goats.
(108) Sweet sleep (*Od* 1.364). You are waking me out of sweet sleep (*Od* 23.16).

prenominal adjectives tend to be more closely attached to the noun than post-nominal adjectives. The former are simply attributive, the latter have a more predicative character; they are more comparable to reduced relative clauses. Potential semantic implications of this distinction were analyzed earlier in this chapter. In prima facie continuous noun phrases, a Y1 noun can be phrased with the verb, allowing a line initial adjective to stand as a separate phrase, whence VN | A enjambement

(109)   εὗρε δὲ φώκας | ζατρεφέας *Od* 4.450
        ἐτίταινε τραπέζας | ἀγυρέας *Od* 10.354,

like the inscriptional διομοσαι ηορϘον : τον νομιον already cited. VA | N enjambement with an ordinary adjective is not possible, because an ordinary prenominal adjective has to be phrased with the noun and cannot phrase with the verb to the exclusion of the noun. One way of capturing this difference structurally for YPs is to treat prenominal adjectives as coheads or as specifiers of N′ and postnominal adjectives as phrasal sisters of NP, as in Figure 1.5. In hyperbaton, the difference was captured by making Y1 modifiers specifiers of X′ and Y2 modifiers adjuncts to XP, as we did in Figure 4.7. Hence AV | N enjambement is illicit for ordinary adjectives, while NV | A enjambement occurs: a Y1 noun can, under certain conditions, phrase with a following verb, often when the Y2 adjective is an emphatic amplification

(110)   ὁμοφροσύνην ὀπάσειαν | ἐσθλήν *Od* 6.181
        ἐπὶ δεσμὸν ἴηλεν | ποικίλον *Od* 8.447.

Conversely, N | VA enjambement occurs mostly with subject and/or strong focus nouns

(111)   τῷ ἔνι νύμφη | ναῖεν ἐϋπλόκαμος *Od* 5.57
        ἀλλά με δεσμῷ | δήσατ᾽ ἐν ἀργαλέῳ *Od* 12.160
        αἱ μὲν λεπτὰς ὀθόνας ἔχον, οἱ δὲ χιτῶνας | εἵατ᾽ ἐυννήτους
        Il 18.595.

The second distinction, that between regular adjectives on the one hand and quantifiers, focused adjectives, etc. on the other, strongly suggests that the two categories belong in separate structural positions in Homer, an internal premodifier position for regular adjectives and one or more external positions for focused adjectives, quantifiers, demonstratives, etc.

(109) He found the fat seals (*Od* 4.450). She drew up silver tables (*Od* 10.354).
(110) May they grant you the blessing of harmony (*Od* 6.181). He tied an intricate knot (*Od* 8.447).
(111) In which the nymph with beautiful hair lived (*Od* 5.57). But bind me in a strong bond (*Od* 12.160). The girls had fine linen dresses and the boys wore well-woven tunics (*Il* 18.595).

(112)   πολλὰς [ἰφθίμους ψυχὰς] *Il* 1.3
       [ἰφθίμους ψυχὰς]
       πολλὰς [ψυχὰς]

       πάντα [περήσαμεν εὐρέα πόντον] *Od* 24.118
       [εὐρέα περήσαμεν πόντον]
       πάντα [περήσαμεν πόντον].

The focus position could be in a separate focus functional projection or it could be an adjoined position or a second specifier position (Koizumi 1994); the theoretical status of this distinction is not entirely clear (Kayne 1994). As far as the univeral quantifiers and demonstratives are concerned, apart from the fact that these attract focus, there is an evident connection with the situation in the classical language, where these categories probably project their own phrases and are sisters of DP (whereas regular prenominal adjectives are sisters of N′ or NP). Some of the enjambed examples also have the flavour of adverbial quantifiers, predicative adjectives or null head modifiers.

In continuous YPs, movement to (location in) the focus position is string vacuous

       [λυγρῆς ἀγγελίης] → μάλα λυγρῆς [— ἀγγελίης].

This may seem unnecessarily abstract, but a very similar case for string vacuous movement can be made for Tangale, also on the basis of phonological evidence (Tuller 1992). This language has strict Subject–Verb–Object word order in neutral sentences; the focus position is after the object; an unfocused object forms a phonological minor phrase with the preceding verb on the evidence of vowel apocope, but a focused object does not. This suggests that under focus the object has been string vacuously moved into the focus slot outside V′. The alternative in such situations is to assume that the separate phrasing of focused words is a process internal to the phonology. On this view, focus assigns additional prosodic prominence to the focused word, one or more of the following: pitch obtrusion, increased intensity, increased duration. This prosodic salience, so the theory goes, would overload the minor phrase and so directly blocks the application of the phrasing algorithm. The durational component of this argument needs to be presented in a much more sophisticated framework, since as it stands it is wrong: a short quantifier like πολλά can appear with enjambement, but a long regular Y₁ adjective like ἀργυρέοισιν cannot, despite the fact that it presumably has greater overall duration than focused πολλά. Moreover, overt focus movement is needed anyway, not only for ordinary hyperbaton with focused adjectives (XYY → YXY) but also for the perhaps cyclical movement to higher clausal operator positions

(112) Many great souls (*Il* 1.3). We crossed all the wide sea (*Od* 24.118).

(113)   εὐρὺ γὰρ ἀμφ᾽ ὤμοισιν ἔχει σάκος *Il* 11.527
κακὰ δὲ φρεσὶ μήδετο ἔργα *Il* 23.176
μέγα γάρ μιν Ὀλύμπιος ἔτρεφε πῆμα *Il* 6.282.

From verse to prose

We are now in a position to give a more properly syntactic (rather than simply pragmatic) account of the difference between hyperbaton in Homer and hyperbaton in classical prose. Nonconfigurational syntax is quintessentially a syntax of adjunction, and modification has access to an elastic system of adjunct predication. In the more hierarchical configurational syntax, on the other hand, modification tends to be attributive and secondary predication is constrained. This typological difference underlies the greater constraints on hyperbaton in prose. As far as Y_2 hyperbaton is concerned, prose retains the short range integrated type and makes less use of the long range amplificatory type. In structural terms, the difference probably involves the level at which the Y_2 adjective is attached to the preceding material. Both prose and verse allow adjunction of Y_2 to NP and VP, whereas clausal adjunction is typically Homeric. For Y_1 hyperbaton, the difference can be stated quite specifically, since the categories of adjective that are illicit in enjambement are also illicit in Y_1 hyperbaton in prose. The rule for adjectives is that prose retains the Y_1 hyperbaton focus position but disallows the ordinary Y_1 hyperbaton modifier position (which is still acceptable in tragedy). Recall that a Y_1 hyperbaton such as

(114)   ἐΰτριχας ὡπλίσαθ᾽ ἵππους *Il* 23.351

in verse means that he prepared his horses which had beautiful manes; but in prose it would presumably mean that he prepared (the) horses that had beautiful manes while omitting to prepare (the) mangy ones, and that the main point was which ones he prepared, not the fact that he prepared, equipped or harnessed them. So Simonides writes

(115)   τοῦτ᾽ ἔχοι γέρας *LGS* 370.14,

but Plato paraphrases his words with

(116)   τοῦτο γέρας ἀπένειμε Pl *Prot* 341e.

The move to a more configurational noun phrase, as also evidenced by the development of the definite article, brings with it the requirement that prenominal adjectives cannot be separated from their noun by a superordinate head unless they are in a strong focus operator position. The operator position

(113)   He has a wide shield around his shoulders (*Il* 11.527). He intended evil deeds in his heart (*Il* 23.176). The Olympian one reared him as a great woe (*Il* 6.282).
(114)   He prepared his horses with beautiful manes (*Il* 23.351).
(115)   Could have this privilege (*LGS* 370.14).
(116)   He attributed this privilege (Pl *Prot* 341e).

for strong narrow focus provides a syntactic-semantic rationale that protects this type of Y1 hyperbaton and licenses its continued use. No such raison-d'être is available for the simple unfocused internal modifier position in Y1 hyperbaton, and it is consequently eliminated as incompatible with the basically configurational noun phrase of classical prose.

If we step back and consider our conclusions about hyperbaton in a broad evolutionary perspective, what emerges is a suggestive, if somewhat speculative, scenario. When we compare the prehistoric nonconfigurational syntax that partly survives in Homer with the Greek of the New Testament, we observe a complete typological shift from a freely nonconfigurational to a principally configurational style of noun phrase syntax. Classical verse still preserves Y1 hyperbaton in a recognizably nonconfigurational form, whereas the more restricted usage of classical prose represents a transitional stage between the two types of syntax. Hyperbaton survives quite well in modern Greek: an account has just come out (Androutsopoulou 1998), which provides welcome direct corroboration for some of the philologically based assumptions we make in this book (although the analysis is more abstract than what we propose in chapter 6). Hyperbaton could conceivably have been restructured through three very different typologies: a pronominal argument stage, a nonconfigurational stage with lexical arguments, and a largely configurational stage with a residue of discontinuous noun phrases — quite a lesson in the difference between word order and syntax. The familiar modern western European languages have a mostly rather configurational syntax, although, for instance, German is notorious for scrambled word order (Choi 1996) and Catalan has detached clitic-bound nonfocal phrases. The Slavic languages are, on many counts, much more conservative, and some allow hyperbaton; the situation reported for hyperbaton in literary and colloquial modern Polish is somewhat reminiscent of that for classical Greek verse and prose respectively (p. 115). (Our own Polish informant accepted conjunct hyperbaton but expressed dissatisfaction with examples of modifier hyperbaton presented out of context.) One might even speculate that configurationality was the basic linguistic component of the Greek legacy to modern western culture, if it spread, along with lexically filled functional projections (articles, auxiliaries [Coleman 1975]), via the Greek lingua franca of the Roman slave population; but that is another story.

5 Phonological Garden Paths

According to a perception of hyperbaton quite different from that suggested in this work, it is not a syntactic phenomenon at all, but phonologically motivated. There are a number of possible variations on this idea. E. Norden, for instance, emphasized the desire to avoid hiatus and to achieve a good rhythmic clausula (Norden 1958:65). Here we shall consider first phonological interpretations of nonconfigurationality which have implications for, and can be generalized to, hyperbaton; and then clitic theories of hyperbaton and of prepositional phrase hyperbaton.

PROSODIC PHRASE THEORY

As discussed in chapter 4, in a highly nonconfigurational pronominal argument language, instead of 'The noble Ajax wounded the Trojan with his spear,' one might say something like 'The noble one, he wounded him, Ajax, the Trojan, with his spear.' The assumption was that there is a very strong complexity constraint applying to phrase formation. In particular, lexical noun phrases do not form phrases with governing heads. The motivation was supposed to be a desire to keep the syntactic mechanism of function-argument application as simple as possible, separate from and unencumbered by the added weight of lexical information. This incidentally results in prosodically simpler and less hierarchical minor phonological phrases, given that prosodic phrasing is in principle mapped from syntactic structure. There is more of a one-to-one relationship between words and phrases in pronominal argument languages. It has been suggested that the cause and the effect should be reversed, that the syntactic complexity constraint is an incidental reflex of a phonological requirement for prosodically simple minor phrases. The idea is that there should be a flat one-to-one mapping between syntactic phrases and phonological phrases (Russell & Reinholtz 1996). Informally, nouns and verbs (and nouns and modifiers) have to be mapped to separate minor phrases. Since prosody is quintessentially hierarchical in all its actuations, presumably there should be no reason why these minor phrases could not be joined into a hierarchically structured superordinate phrase. However, for the rather appositional noun phrases of Nunggubuyu, "even when two NP segments are contiguous, no clear phrasal prosody is observed" (Heath 1986). So the crucial point is the basic complexity constraint that prevents head and complement or head and modifier from forming a single minor phrase. In a framework with copresent syntax and phonology, this sort of "downstairs-upstairs" effect is not a problem. The idea could apply mutatis mutandis also to the weaker complexity constraint we have posited for the nonconfigurational stage of Greek. In fact, verbal clisis could be a factor licensing the verb plus lexical complement structure that distinguishes the type of nonconfigurationality posited for prehistorical Greek from straight pronominal argument nonconfigurationality (where verbal complements are mainly adjuncts).

It is certainly true that the phonology can modulate the syntax in quite subtle ways: for instance, intrinsic and allophonic vowel duration can affect word order (Devine & Stephens 1994:49). However, in principle one thinks of the phonology serving to encode informational packaging rather than information being systematically packaged to conform to phonological exigencies. Intuitively, what is at stake is the way in which information is conveyed in the different syntactic typologies. In northern Italian dialects having strong propensities for pronominal argument structure, quite short and light topic and tail arguments can be taken out of the nuclear clause for pragmatic reasons (not merely to create a prosodically light nuclear clause), while quite long and heavy adverbials can remain as focus material inside the nuclear clause

> *Maria, the perfume, she sent it to her immediately without even trying it, to the contessina.*

At the other end of the scale, the Australian language Jingulu has been analyzed as having the lexical component of the verb in some way separate from the agreement markers and tense morphemes, giving structures of the type 'drink, they did it, the students, the coffee' (Pensalfini 1996). If we understand this report correctly, it represents a further delexicalization of the core predicate-argument structure, going beyond the familiar "AUX" structure, which is presumably not phonologically motivated. That is not to say that phonological weight is irrelevant to the complexity constraint. In Greek, for instance, pronominal arguments occur more easily in Homer when the coindexed lexical phrase is branching. It is just that phonological weight is unlikely to be the principal motivation for pronominal argument structure. In these languages, information is presented in equipollent serial chunks, like beads on a string and not like bricks in a pyramid, with the phonology serving to keep the beads separate. This slows down the rate at which new information is communicated. It has been noted that these languages are also rather redundant by our standards. Such redundancy is obviously related to the density of new information in the message and cannot be understood as a reflex of its segmentation into prosodic units.

ORALITY

It is well known that there are significant differences between spoken and written language (as well as differences from one style of spoken language to another, and from one style of written language to another) (Tannen 1982, 1984; Chafe 1985; Halliday 1989). Some studies found that spoken language uses fewer embedded structures and less clause internal constituent coordination. It tends to present information at a lower rate per clause, and is more repetitive and redundant, and less coherent and integrated, than written language. These properties of spoken language were long ago linked to the paratactic characteristics of the syntax of Homeric Greek, and to the way they interact with the binary prosodic structures of the hexameter. The intuition was clearly expressed by Giseke (1864:37): "Neben ihm machen die versen der Alexandriner den eindruck als seien perioden von Thucydides und Demosthenes in hexameter umgeformt, und diesen dichtern ist der vers ein fessel, bei Homer scheint er von der sprache unzutrennlich zu sein." We shall call such interpretations of Homeric syntax "orality theories."

Although they are sometimes expressed phonologically (in terms of intonational phrases), orality theories actually appeal in one way or another to differences between spoken and written language. So they are concerned with the differences between two types of syntax, the syntax of spoken language and the syntax of written language. It does not necessarily follow that the peculiarities of the former are phonologically motivated. For instance, they could simply be due to the general demands of processing syntax in a real time conversational context, rather than to the specific demands of producing and perceiving syntax in the acoustic medium. In the following, we will briefly characterize the main possible variants of this approach to Homeric syntax.

The first theory, the *Modality Theory*, sees a direct link between the properties of casual, spontaneous conversation and the literary context of oral tradition. Reference is made to "the fragmented organization of oral discourse in idea units" (Bakker 1990). The physical context of oral literary production is thought to preclude the sort of integrated, hierarchical syntax found in written language. A second theory, the *Register Theory*, would be a little more abstract. It would appeal to the difference between formal and informal registers on the assumption that the syntax of the informal register is more pragmatically oriented. This is particularly obvious in a language like French, where there is a far stronger tendency to dislocate lexical arguments in the colloquial language. According to the register theory, the physical context of oral literary production requires it to access that register which is primarily associated with spoken language, namely the informal register. It may be that both the modality theory and the register theory overemphasize the parallel with spontaneous conversation, and that a parallel with the less informal style of oral narration would be more appropriate. It is also important not to assume that correlation entails causation. After all, child language too is structurally simpler and less coherent than written language, but it would not follow that Homeric syntax originated in the kindergarten; the same applies to some types of aphasia. In fact, a problem with both these theories is that they fail to take account of the most obvious correlation of them all. Much as nineteenth-century Homeric studies, not being familiar with the concept of oral tradition, were basically confined to two options — either Homer was a single literary text or it was a conflation of literary texts, so, if you start out with the premise that all languages are configurational in the way English is, then you are inevitably led to attribute departures from configurationality in Homeric syntax either to conversational fragmentation or to register differences. But the point about nonconfigurational languages is that, while they may have some associated register variation, in principle they are systematically nonconfigurational in every register. Features which, if they are allowed at all, are pragmatic options in other languages, are grammaticalized in nonconfigurational languages. All literature in a nonconfigurational language, oral or otherwise, has nonconfigurational syntax simply because that is the only way the language can be used. The syntactic typology does not depend on whether you are extemporizing oral poetry or typing an article on neuroscience with two fingers. To cite just one example, in Hixkaryana (Derbyshire 1985), the normal way to encode a prepositional phrase or a conjunct is as a paratactic adjunct phrase, usually intonationally separate from the nuclear clause; that is the way the language is. It follows that many of the differences in syntax between Homer and classical Greek are not, from the point of view of their origin, purely matters of literary genre and style. Rather, they reflect the fact that in Homer there survives a strong residue of a stage in the history of Greek when the syntax of the language was typologically quite different. Simply put, the characteristic flavour of Homeric syntax is ultimately a question not of style but of grammar.

It may seem that this is all that needs to be said about nonconfigurational syntax and orality; but it is not. Far from it. The configurational languages with which we are most familiar are spoken in societies with widespread literacy and a longstanding tradition of abstract, scientific and intellectual discourse. On the other hand, the best-known nonconfigurational languages, particularly the pronominal argument languages, are spoken by aboriginal peoples having, at least until recently, a primarily oral culture. This distribution is the basis for the *Cultural Relativity Theory*. The slogan of this theory is "writing restructures consciousness" (Ong 1982); literacy is claimed to have profound effects on social organization and culture (Goody 1986, 1987). Additionally, syntactic typology is supposed by this theory to be determined by cultural practice, a sort of cultural relativity (Gumperz & Levinson 1996) working in the inverse direction, from culture back to language. It follows that "literacy restructures syntax," a manifestation of the more general proposition that syntactic typology is associated with sociological complexity (Givon 1979). Oral culture is supposed to grammaticalize the syntactic propensities of spoken language and literate culture is supposed to grammaticalize the syntactic propensities of written language. For those who subscribe to this view, it would not be surprising if Homeric syntax has a residue of nonconfigurationality, because nonconfigurationality is particularly associated with oral cultures. It would further not be surprising if later Greek becomes configurational, because configurationality is particularly associated with literate cultures. Obviously, the categories invoked will have to be explicitly defined and the extent of the implicational relations between them empirically investigated. For instance, what is the incidence of fully configurational languages having an oral culture? The cultural claims too need to be made more precise. When the languages of oral cultures come into contact with European languages, they can borrow elements which, from our point of view, are missing in their languages. Quite a number of Australian and Mexican languages which lack conjunctions borrow them from English and Spanish respectively (Mithun 1988), and the Hixkaryana borrow all numerals above three from Brazilian Portuguese. Yet it would be factually (as well as politically) incorrect to think that nonconfigurational languages are simply impoverished. Take the Papuan language Yimas (Foley 1991). It is nonconfigurational and allows hyperbaton. It is furthermore polysynthetic and has intricate and complex rules of word formation. From the point of view of the patterning of surface elements, Yimas has simple syntax and complicated morphology. There is a trade-off between the simplicity of the patterns generated by syntactic embedding and the internal complexity of the constituent elements of those patterns. We also suggest in chapter 6 that there can be a greater diversity of category and type in nonconfigurational languages.

The last theory, the *Null Hypothesis*, takes the apparent correlation between nonconfigurational languages and oral culture to be coincidental (Baker 1996) and the purported causative relation between literacy and configurational syntax to be unproven. For the null hypothesis, modern western literate and scientific culture just happened to develop in an area (Western Europe) that does not have strongly nonconfigurational languages. In fact, it just happened to develop in the same place and at very approximately the same time (Thomas 1992) as configurational syntax, which is a more striking coincidence and makes it a bit more difficult simply to dismiss the cultural relativity theory as another piece of Classical eurocentric romanticism. Whether in the end it turns out to be no more than that depends on the results of future research. In the present state of our knowledge, two possibilities remain. Either orality theory, in so far as it concerns hyperbaton, is a glossocentric misinterpretation of an unfamiliar syntactic typology, or it involves a more far-reaching and profound phenomenon than what is envisaged by many of its proponents.

Finally, a brief note specifically about hyperbaton. In Warlpiri, discontinuous noun phrases are more common in the spoken language and continuous ones in the written language (Andrews 1985). If this is not due to influence of English on the written language, it supports the orality theory. More precisely, it suggests that if there is a difference, it will be in the direction predicted by the orality theory and not in that predicted by Denniston (1952), who thought that hyperbaton is a purely literary artificiality. That is just what it probably is in the style of the sixth century hagiographer Theodorus, where hyperbaton appears at a rate of 146 per thousand lines of text (Lindhamer 1908). Here is a sample passage

(1)   τοῦτον αὖθις ὁ μακάριος περιπτυξάμενος Μαρκιανὸς ἐπὶ τὸ τοῦ
σίτου ἀπήγαγε καταγώγιον, "Εὐλόγησον" λέγων "πάτερ, ὥστε
τὰς τῆς ἀποθήκης ἀνεῷξαι θύρας ἡμᾶς καὶ ἐκ τῶν ἀγεωργήτων
δρέψασθαι καρπῶν (Usener 75).

On the other hand, in the New Testament, which reflects the simple, everyday spoken Greek of its period, hyperbaton is comparatively rare: according to the same count, Matthew has only two examples per thousand lines of text.

CLITIC THEORY

It is fairly well established that verbs can manifest less salient prosodic properties than nouns. They may tend to have weaker stress or less salient pitch excursions, or they may exhibit more restricted tonal patterns (as in Greek). This property seems to be ultimately related to the nature and salience of their informational content relative to that of nouns. In Vedic, finite verbs in main clauses were clitic unless they stood at the beginning of the clause or the verse line. General verb clisis is also reconstructed for prehistoric Greek, and it is argued that in both languages the verb can move to second position rather than being in the posited final position.

Enclitics can certainly appear in the X position of hyperbaton

(2)   τούτων τις τῶν τεχνῶν Pl Gorg 451a
ταύτην ποτὲ τὴν χώραν κατῴκησαν Κιρραῖοι Aesch 3.107
πολλήν μοι ἀπορίαν παρέχει Lys 19.1
μέγιστόν ἐστι σημεῖον Dem 32.21
ταῦτα ἐπ᾽ εὐνοίᾳ φασὶ τῇ ὑμετέρᾳ παρανομῆσαι Lys 22.13.

So at a time when verbs in general were clitic, they might have moved into the X position at least of clause initial YP qua clitics, and the YXY word order

(1) The blessed Marcianus, having embraced him, led him again to the granary, saying "Grant your blessing, Father, so that we may open the doors of the storehouse and pluck of the uncultivated harvest."

(2) One of those arts (Pl Gorg 451a). The Cirrhaeans once inhabited this area (Aesch 3.107). It puts me in a very difficult position (Lys 19.1). It is the strongest proof (Dem 32.21). They saw that they committed these illegal acts as a favour to you (Lys 22.13).

could then have been preserved when verbs later acquired a word accent. Here is a minimal pair to illustrate

(3) μεγάλα ἐκτήσατο χρήματα... μεγάλα οἱ χρήματα ἀναθεῖναι
      Her 2.135.

Furthermore prepositions remain "proclitic" in classical Greek, and so they too might move to the X position in the prepositional phrase qua clitics. On this approach, it is not the modifier but the superordinate head that moves to create hyperbaton; informational content does not generate hyperbaton as a direct reflex of factors like focus and amplification but as an indirect consequence of its phonologization in the accentual system.

For prepositions, and for the more restricted varieties of verb hyperbaton, the domain of the posited clisis is phrasal rather than clausal. This is not a problem per se, although the details might not be completely compatible with what we know about clitic location. In any case, the fact that hyperbaton is licensed with any phrasal head means that the theory lacks generality, since nominal heads were not clitic. Besides

(4) οὐδ'... δολίης ἐπελήθετο τέχνης Od 4.455

we find

(5) κακῶν ἐπίληθον ἁπάντων Od 4.221
      θεῶν χόλον αἰὲν ἐόντων Od 4.583.

Many other examples have been cited in earlier chapters. The same line of reasoning applies to conjunct hyperbaton. When the head is verbal, it is possible to posit a simple "clitic inversion" operating on the first conjunct only

(6) Ἄβαντα$_k$ μετῴχετο —$_k$ καὶ Πολύειδον Il 5.148
      δόρυ τ'$_k$ ἔσχε —$_k$ καὶ ἀσπίδα Il 5.300.

However, conjunct hyperbaton is well attested with nonfinite verb forms too

(7) Διί τ' εὐχόμενοι καὶ Ἀθήνῃ Il 11.736
      χείρεσσι πεποιθότες ἠδὲ βίηφι Il 12.135

and with nominals

(8) δόλων ἆτ' ἠδὲ πόνοιο Il 11.430

(3) She obtained great wealth... to ascribe to her great wealth (Her 2.135).
(4) He did not forget his deceitful ways (Od 4.455).
(5) Inducing forgetfulness of all misfortunes (Od 4.221). The anger of the immortal gods (Od 4.583).
(6) He went after Abas and Polyidus (Il 5.148). He held his spear and his shield (Il 5.300).
(7) Praying to Zeus and Athena (Il 11.736). Trusting in their hands and their strength (Il 12.135).
(8) You who have an insatiable liking for guile and for the toil of battle (Il 11.430).

(9) ἠνορέη πίσυνοι καὶ κάρτεϊ χειρῶν *Il* 11.9
Διὸς ἄγγελοι ἠδὲ καὶ ἀνδρῶν *Il* 7.274
ἀρνῶν κνίσης αἰγῶν τε τελείων *Il* 1.66.

So again the theory crashes, unless one posits a system in which all heads are clitic in branching phrases. It is also unsatisfactory from an informational point of view. YPs interrupted by clitics behave like YPs interrupted by particles

(10) μεγάλη γὰρ ῥοπή Dem 2.22
ὀλίγοι γὰρ δὴ στόλοι Thuc 6.33.5
ὑστέρῳ δὲ χρόνῳ Lys 2.48.

The Y1 modifier may have strong narrow focus or it may not. (If it does, it is a specifier of N′ rather than of X′ because particles do not project phrases in the way lexical heads do.) The restriction of Y1 to strong narrow focus, which defines Y1 hyperbaton in prose, is found just when X is the superordinate head of YP, a generalization that associates verbs with nouns and adjectives rather than with clitics and particles.

PREPOSITIONAL PHRASE HYPERBATON

The clitic theory of verb phrase hyperbaton has no synchronic validity (verbs were not clitic in classical Greek) and fails to capture the fact that hyperbaton is a structural phenomenon and insensitive to the category of the head. For prepositional phrase hyperbaton, the other candidate for a clitic theory of hyperbaton, neither objection applies with the same force. Prepositions do have accentual reduction, and the distribution of prepositional phrase hyperbaton in Greek texts is sufficiently different from that of other types of hyperbaton for us to consider seriously that the posited categorial insensitivity may be limited to lexical heads. For these reasons, the status of prepositional phrase hyperbaton demands more detailed analysis.

In previous chapters, we simply took it for granted that prepositional (adpositional) phrases participated in the crosscategorial application of hyperbaton, as they do in Fox for instance (Dahlstrom 1987)

ayo·h=iši wi·ki·ya·peki
this-LOC to house-LOC
'to this house.'

The encliticization of the postposition is optional in Fox, and hyperbaton can occur without cliticization; consequently, it is real hyperbaton and not simply

(9) Trusting in their valour and in the strength of their hands (*Il* 11.9). Messengers of Zeus and of men (*Il* 7.274). The aroma of sacrificed sheep and unblemished goats (*Il* 1.66).
(10) For great weight (Dem 2.22). For indeed few expeditions (Thuc 6.33.5). But at a later time (Lys 2.48).

clitic movement that looks like hyperbaton. In Greek verse, prepositional hyperbaton seems to work very much like other types of hyperbaton

(11)   Σκύθην ἐς οἶμον, ἄβατον εἰς ἐρημίαν *PV* 2 (v.l.)
χλωραῖς ὑπ᾽ ἐλάταις ἀνορόφοις ἧνται πέτραις *Bacch* 38
ἀλώμενος | ξένην ἐπ᾽ αἶαν λυπρὸν ἀντλήσει βίον *Hipp* 897.

The *Prometheus* line has a prepositional phrase hyperbaton in each hemistich, the *Bacchae* and *Hippolytus* lines have a prepositional phrase hyperbaton in the first hemistich and a verb phrase hyperbaton in the second hemistich. The prima facie structure of all six hemistichs is identical, namely a prosodic minor phrase consisting of Y_1XY_2, X being any superordinate head, in these lines either a verb or a preposition. In the following Homeric line, the pattern is repeated for proper and improper prepositions

(12)   κρουνῶν ἐκ μεγάλων κοίλης ἔντοσθε χαράδρης *Il* 4.454.

Similarly, in the case of conjunct hyperbaton, coordinate complements of prepositions seem to pattern just like coordinate complements of verbs

(13)   νηῶν ἄπο καὶ κλισιάων *Il* 13.723
ἐπέων κεχολωμένος ἠδὲ καὶ ἔργων *Il* 11.703.

However, it is not the case that prepositional heads have the same distribution as nominal, adjectival or verbal heads. Disregarding serial order within YP, there are three logically possible orders for head plus branching noun phrase: continuous posthead noun phrase (X YP), continuous prehead noun phrase (YP X), and discontinuous (hyperbaton: YXY). For instance, with an adjectival head

(14)   μεστῇ πολλῶν ἀγαθῶν Xen *An* 3.5.1 (X YP)
πολλῶν ἀγαθῶν μεσταί Xen *Cyr* 4.1.9 (YP X)
πολλῶν μεστὸν ἀγαθῶν Pl *Laws* 906a (YXY).

The incidence of hyperbaton varies from one style to another and from one modifier to another, but in prose the continuous types are far more common than hyperbaton. All three logically possible orders are also attested for the prepositional head, both in prose and in verse (tragedy)

(15)   μετ᾽ ἄλλων μυρίων *Andr* 697 (X YP)

(11) To the Scythian country, to an untrod desert (*PV* 2). Under green pine trees they sit on roofless rocks (*Bacch* 38). Wandering over foreign land he will drag out a miserable life (*Hipp* 897).
(12) From great springs inside a hollow gorge (*Il* 4.454).
(13) From the ships and the huts (*Il* 13.723). Enraged at words and at deeds (*Il* 11.703).
(14) Full of many supplies (Xen *An* 3.5.1). Full of many good things (Xen *Cyr* 4.1.9). Full of many good things (Pl *Laws* 906a).
(15) With countless others (*Andr* 697).

(16) χειρὸς ἀσιδήρου μέτα *Bacch* 736, cp. *Phoen* 1326(YP X)
πολλῶν μετ᾽ ἄλλων *Andr* 1152, *Hipp* 835 (YXY).

But the relative frequency of the three types in prepositional phrases is quite different from that found with other heads. Hyperbaton with prepositions is very common in verse, but prepositions following a branching noun phrase are not nearly so common. In prose, a few examples of a preposition following a branching noun phrase are found with περί, mostly in Plato

(17) ἀλλοτρίας γῆς πέρι Thuc 3.13.5
πασῶν ὡρῶν πέρι Pl *Laws* 899b
τούτων δὴ πάντων πέρι Pl *Laws* 870d
πολλῶν νεῶν πέρι Pl *Rep* 488a
κλοπῆς πάσης πέρι Pl *Laws* 859b
τῶν παλαιῶν ἀνδρῶν πέρι Pl *Gorg* 519b,

but hyperbaton is more than twice as common as postposition

(18) τῶν δ᾽ ἄλλων περὶ βλάψεως Pl *Laws* 932e
τοῦ γυναικείου περὶ νόμου Pl *Rep* 457b,

and is also found rarely with prepositions other than περί and in prose authors other than Plato

(19) οὐδενὶ ξὺν νῷ Pl *Crito* 48c
τοιᾷδ᾽ ἐν τάξει Pl *Criti* 115c
χρόνον ἔπι μακρὸν Her 1.81
χρόνον ἐπ᾽ ὀλίγον Her 5.46.

Note that the adjectives are nonlexical or high frequency core adjectives, while the nouns are with one exception phonologically and semantically light: these examples do not license structures like

(20) (*)τῶν τολμηροτάτων μετὰ λοχαγῶν.

So for prepositional heads the data indicate the following hierarchy for the location of branching YP in prose:

$$X\ YP > YXY > YP\ X$$

(16) With unarmed hand (*Bacch* 736). With many others (*Andr* 1152).

(17) For a foreign country (Thuc 3.13.5). About all the seasons (Pl *Laws* 899b). About all of these (Pl *Laws* 870d). About many ships (Pl *Rep* 488a). About all types of theft (Pl *Laws* 859b). About the men of old (Pl *Gorg* 519b).

(18) About the other injuries (Pl *Laws* 932e). With respect to the regulation for women (Pl *Rep* 457b).

(19) Without any rationale (Pl *Crito* 48c). In the following sort of arrangement (Pl *Criti* 115c). For a long time (Her 1.81). For a short time (Her 5.46).

(20) With the boldest company commanders.

or in words, continuous posthead is more common than hyperbaton which is more common the continuous prehead. By contrast, for the other head categories, as just noted, the hierarchy is

X YP, YP X (continuous) > YXY (hyperbaton).

Postposed prepositions after a nonbranching YP (simple anastrophe) are far less constrained than after a branching YP, amounting to six percent of all prepositional phrases in Euripides (Mommsen 1895)

(21)   δεμνίων ἄπο Orest 44, 278
       ἀπορίας ὕπο Orest 232
       πολεμίων πάρα Orest 875.

(For clarity of exposition, anastrophic accent is uniformly written, even after an intervening word.) Simple anastrophe is found in prose with περί only, in tragedy predominantly with disyllabic prepositions taking the genitive; in Homer these restrictions do not apply.

Prepositions are notorious for not conforming to otherwise applicable rules governing the relative order of head and complement, and the data just cited seem in general to reflect a more rigidly head initial order for prepositions than for other heads. In prose, prepositions other than περί, that is prepositions that cannot be postpositions, are simply required to be phrase initial: the specifier position in the prepositional phrase can no longer be filled either by a complement of the preposition or by a modifier of the complement of the preposition. The only permissible prehead item is a specifier of the preposition itself

(22)   εὐθὺς ἐξ ἀρχῆς Xen Cyr 7.2.16
       πολὺ πρὸ τῶν ἄλλων Thuc 2.91.2

or a specifier of an adjective modifying the complement of the preposition

(23)   πολὺ σὺν φρονήματι μείζονι Xen An 3.1.22.

Word order changes from pragmatic to grammatical earlier in prepositional phrases. Regular hyperbaton is for reasons explained later (p. 222) completely blocked. Verse appears to require some form of optimality computation. The preposition preferentially precedes at least one subconstituent of its complement. The additional constraint that only disyllabic prepositions are allowed in absolute phrase final position is prosodic rather than syntactic. This suggests that the whole rule could be reformulated in prosodic terms: the preposition should preferably be proclitic to some subconstituent of the prepositional phrase and monosyllabic prepositions may not be postpositive at all. This for-

---

(21) From his bed (Orest 44). Because of their helplessness (Orest 232). From enemies (Orest 875).

(22) Right from the beginning (Xen Cyr 7.2.16). Well ahead of the others (Thuc 2.91.2).

(23) With far greater confidence (Xen An 3.1.22).

mulation is complicated by the problem of anastrophe in disyllabic prepositional phrase hyperbaton. Monosyllabic prepositions seem to have been
proclitic (even in the NPA order)

(24)   χθόνα | εἰς τήνδ' Eur *Suppl* 1191
   Τιρυνθίαν | πρὸς κλιτύν *Trach* 270
   βάθρων | ἐκ τῶνδε *OC* 263
   μίαν | καθ' ἡμέραν *Ant* 170.

By contrast, disyllabic prepositions in hyperbaton are fine in the metrically
convenient line end position

(25)   ὑψηλῶν δ' ἔπι | ναῶν Eur *El* 6
   μιᾶς ὕπο | χλαίνης *Trach* 539
   τοξικῆς τ' ἄπο | θώμιγγος *Pers* 460.

In brief, prepositions are generated in phrase initial position and they are proclitic. In verse, they permit material to be fronted to their left in hyperbaton,
with the consequence that the surface order of the phrase is not head initial. In
prose, apart from περί, they are rigidly head initial, and fronting in hyperbaton
is, with very few exceptions, forbidden.

Clitic theory

The clitic theory of prepositional phrase hyperbaton takes a quite different
approach. It is a wellknown property of phrase initial clitics that some of them
are in absolute initial position and others in socalled second position. The
enclitics, as their name implies, need to lean on something to their left large
enough to host them, usually a prosodic word. One could think that syntactically they were generated at the beginning of the phrase and then inverted to
second position for purely prosodic reasons (Halpern 1995): [καὶ ἵππους], but
[τε ἵππους] → [ἵππους τε]. The prepositions are proclitic and vary between initial and second position, so it is natural to think that this variation is due to
optional inversion. This theory, which in one form or another is quite popular,
was originally proposed to account for the Homeric data (Golston 1988). It
rests crucially on two assumptions: first, that it is the prepositional head that
moves for prosodic (or at least clisis-related) reasons, not its complement for
pragmatic reasons; and second, that the only positions available to the preposition are the initial position and the second position. We will analyze both of
these claims in the following discussion. For proponents of the clitic theory,
the parallel between prepositional phrase hyperbaton and other hyperbata is a
trompe d'oeil: pairs like

(24) Into this land (Eur *Suppl* 1191). At the hill of Tiryns (*Trach* 270). From this seat
(*OC* 263). In a single day (*Ant* 170).
(25) On the high temples (Eur *El* 6). Under a single blanket (*Trach* 539). From the
string of the archer's bow (*Pers* 460).

(26)   μελαινάων ἀπὸ νηῶν *Il* 16.304

μελαινέων ἔρμ᾽ ὀδυνάων *Il* 4.117 (see app. crit.)

δεξιτερὸν κατὰ μαζὸν *Il* 5.393

δεξιτερῆς ἕλε χειρός *Il* 7.108

κοίλῃς ἐνὶ νηυσὶν *Il* 7.389

πολέες δ᾽ἔνι μῦθοι *Il* 20.248

are deemed to be derived by quite unrelated processes and only superficially parallel. Although the status of verbs is less clear (as discussed earlier in this chapter), there is no way that the clitic theory of prepositional hyperbaton could be generalized to cover hyperbaton with nominal heads.

Clitic theory in tragedy

For tragedy, the clitic theory is on the face of it empirically inadequate. Prepositions are securely attested after branching noun phrases, even if this is not a favoured location

(27)   ποντίας ἀκτῆς ἔπι *Hec* 778

ἐλατίνων ὄζων ἔπι *Bacch* 1070

χειρὸς εὐσεβοῦς ἄπο *Hipp* 83

ποταμίων ῥείθρων ἄπο Eur *El* 794

βασιλικῶν δόμων ὕπερ *Phoen* 1326

ἐλπίδων καλῶν ὕπο *Hec* 351

κισσίνου βάκτρου μέτα *Bacch* 363.

Prepositions can also stand in nonfinal third position when an additional adjective modifies the hyperbaton structure from a higher left branch position, as in the following lyric examples

(28)   Ἰλιάσιν τοῖσδ᾽ ἐν κορυφαῖς *Troad* 1256

λάβροις ὀλεθρίοισιν ἐν κύμασιν *Orest* 343

οὐράνιον ὑψιπετὲς ἐς μέλαθρον *Hec* 1100

εὐάχητόν θ᾽ ἁλμυρὸν ἐπὶ πόντον *Hipp* 1272.

In these more complex examples, it could be argued that the additional adjective stands outside the hyperbaton structure, just as it could stand outside the continuous prepositional phrase in the following example

(26) From the black ships (*Il* 16.304). Carrier of black pains (*Il* 4.117). On the right breast (*Il* 5.393). He took him by the right hand (*Il* 7.108). In hollow ships (*Il* 7.389). There are many speeches in it (*Il* 20.248).

(27) On the sea shore (*Hec* 778). On the pine branches (*Bacch* 1070). From a pious hand (*Hipp* 83). From a flowing stream (Eur *El* 794). For the royal palace (*Phoen* 1326). By high hopes (*Hec* 351). With your ivy wand (*Bacch* 363).

(28) On these heights of Ilium (*Troad* 1256). In the furious destructive waves (*Orest* 343). To the lofty hall of heaven (*Hec* 1100). And over the roaring salty sea (*Hipp* 1272).

(29) πολυάνορι δ᾽ ἐν ξενόεντι θρόνῳ *IT* 1282.

This sort of nonconfigurational analysis could in principle be extended to the simpler ANP and NAP examples: [ποντίας] [ἀκτῆς ἔπι], etc. Consider an example with a clausal topic like

(30) ἔτεα μὲν ἐς εἴκοσι καὶ ἑκατὸν τοὺς πολλοὺς αὐτῶν ἀπικνέεσθαι
     Her 3.23;

'as for years, up to 120.' On this approach, [ἐλπίδων] [καλῶν ὕπο] would be a phrasal counterpart of this structure: 'hopes, with fine ones'; similarly, with hyperbaton

     λιμένας ἦλθες εἰς εὐηνέμους *Andr* 749;

'harbour, you have come to a sheltered one.' However, it would remain unclear why Homer, who does not allow such structures, is more configurational than tragic dialogue which does.

Another consequence of the clitic theory is that one loses the relationship between regular hyperbaton and interrogative hyperbaton

(31) τίν᾽ ἐς χρόνον; *HF* 143
     τίνος γ᾽ ὑπ᾽ ἄλλου *Hec* 774
     τίν᾽ ἀνὰ χεῖρα; *Ion* 1455
     τίν᾽ ἐς ταραγμὸν; *HF* 533.

If such examples are ascribed to interrogative subextraction, then, on the clitic theory of prepositional phrase hyperbaton, they cannot be parallel in some way to noninterrogative prepositional hyperbata, which are assumed to arise by clitic placement

(32) ξενικοῖς ἐπ᾽ ὄχοις *Troad* 569
     ἁγνοῖς ἐν ἱεροῖς *Andr* 1065
     παύρων μετ᾽ ἄλλων *Heracl* 327.

Or, if interrogative prepositional hyperbata are parallel to regular prepositional hyperbata, then they cannot be parallel to interrogative hyperbata where X is not a preposition

(33) τίν᾽ εἶδον ὄψιν; *Hel* 72
     τίνα βοᾷς λόγον; *Hipp* 571,

nor to verb phrase interrogative hyperbata where YP is a prepositional phrase

(29) At the throne frequented by many foreign visitors (*IT* 1282).
(30) The majority of them live to be up to 120 years old (Her 3.23).
(31) To what point in time (*HF* 143). By who else? (*Hec* 774). On what hand? (*Ion* 1455). To what confusion? (*HF* 533).
(32) On a foreign cart (*Troad* 569). In the holy shrine (*Andr* 1065). With few others (*Heracl* 327).
(33) What sight did I see? (*Hel* 72). What words are you crying out? (*Hipp* 571).

(34)   τίν' ὑπάγεις μ' ἐς ἐλπίδα; *Hel* 826
      ποίας ὄλλυμαι πρὸς αἰτίας; *Andr* 1126.

A similar loss of generality occurs when an intervening verb separates a post-posed preposition from its complement

(35)   τοῦ θεοῦ πάρα *OT* 95 (YP Prep)
      παιδὸς τοῦδ' ἐμάνθανον πάρα *Ant* 1012 (YP V Prep)
      ὃ τοῦδε τυγχάνω μαθὼν πάρα *Trach* 370 (YP V Ptcple Prep).

Clitic theory in Homer

The Homeric data are more equivocal. Hyperbaton is common with prepositions (about 15% of all prepositional phrases, so a much higher percentage of prepositional phrases having branching complements). Simple anastrophe occurs with monosyllabic as well as disyllabic prepositions, but the preposition is said not to be allowed in absolute phrase final position after a branching phrase

(36)   ἀπὸ νηῶν
      νηῶν ἄπο

      ἀπὸ κρήνης μελανύδρου *Il* 16.160
      μελαινάων ἀπὸ νηῶν *Il* 16.304
      *μελαινάων νηῶν ἄπο.

Lines like

(37)   κραναὴν Ἰθάκην κάτα κοιρανέουσι *Od* 1.247

are not clear exceptions, and there does appear to be a constraining factor in Homer that is absent in tragedy. There are also said to be no instances of a preposition in third position preceding a phrase final adjective or noun

(38)   ἐν νήεσσι κορώνισι ποντοπόροισι *Il* 2.771
      *νήεσσι κορώνισιν ἐν ποντοπόροισι (NAPA)

      κοίλῃ παρὰ νηὶ μελαίνῃ *Od* 3.365
      *κοίλῃ νηὶ πάρα μελαίνῃ (ANPA)

      πολλὴν ἐπ' ἀπείρονα γαῖαν *Od* 15.79
      *πολλὴν ἀπείρον' ἐπὶ γαῖαν (QAPN).

(34) To what hope are you leading me? (*Hel* 826). For what reason am I being killed? (*Andr* 1126).

(35) From the god (*OT* 95). I learned from this boy (*Ant* 1012). Which I have just learned from this man (*Trach* 370).

(36) From the ships. From a dark spring (*Il* 16.160). From the black ships (*Il* 16.304).

(37) They rule over rocky Ithaca (*Od* 1.247).

(38) In the curved seagoing ships (*Il* 2.771). By the hollow black ship (*Od* 3.365). Far over the boundless lands (*Od* 15.79).

An instructive exception is

(39)   ἄστυ περιπλομένων δηΐων ὕπο θυμοραϊστέων *Il* 18.220

where the first modifier branches and probably constitutes a separate paratactic phrase outside the core hyperbaton structure. When we compare the distribution of prepositions with that of verbs, we find that the starred types of hyperbaton cited above do occur with verbal X

(40)   νῆας ἐϋσσέλμους ἅλαδ᾽ ἑλκέμεν ἀμφιελίσσας *Il* 9.683 (NAVA)
        πορφυρέοις πέπλοισι καλύψαντες μαλακοῖσιν *Il* 24.796 (ANVA)
        μὴ δὴ πάντας ἐμοὺς ἐπιέλπεο μύθους | εἰδήσειν *Il* 1.545 (QAVN).

However, these types are quite rare with verbs too. The type with the quantifier is the only one with the head preceding the noun, but this is because the adjective is focused (cp. *Il* 1.22), and the normal order for this type of verb phrase hyperbaton is QVAN (*Od* 10.289, *Il* 9.387). As far as we can tell, the evidence is not strong enough to treat prepositional hyperbaton in Homer as essentially different from prepositional hyperbaton in tragedy.

Clitic theory in prose

For prose, the clitic theory is superfluous for almost all cases of all prepositions except περί, since they are syntactically initial in their phrases and second position is almost uniformly disallowed. The exceptional status of περί allows us to test the other basic assumption of the clitic theory, namely that movement is driven by the prosody (rather than by pragmatics). Specifically, the clitic theory attributes the appearance of prepositions in second position to prosodic inversion or simply to the rules governing the location of clitics at the margins of their domain. The syntactic theory attributes second position not to the clitic properties of the preposition but to whatever causes a complement or its modifier to appear to the left of any head in Greek syntax in general. In prose this frequently means weak or strong focus for a simple complement and strong focus for a modifier in hyperbaton. Consequently, the two theories make different predictions for those prepositional phrases which do show variation between first and second position in prose, namely περί initially, with simple anastrophe, and with hyperbaton. The syntactic theory predicts that the distribution will be pragmatically motivated, the clitic theory that it will be motivated by whatever motivates variation in clitic placement (presumably not just the pragmatics, or the clitic theory does not contribute anything to the account, since clisis is not needed to account for pragmatic movement in Greek). Let us try and test these predictions with περί in Plato.

(39) By life-destroying enemies surrounding a town (*Il* 18.220).
(40) To drag the well-benched curved ships to the sea (*Il* 9.683). Covering them with soft purple robes (*Il* 24.796). Do not hope to know everything that I say (*Il* 1.545).

Nonlocal περί is semantically similar to the improper prepositions ἕνεκα and χάριν. χάριν almost always follows its complement, ἕνεκα and περί may precede or follow their complement. It is often difficult to quantify partly subjective decisions about informational structure; furthermore, since focus fronting is optional, περί may precede or follow a focused constituent. However, it is clear that Plato's use of postposed πέρι is more strongly associated with focus than his use of preposed περί. As an initial observation, postposed πέρι is rare with the anaphoric pronoun

(41)   αὐτῶν πέρι *Soph* 226b

but preposed περί is common enough

(42)   περὶ αὐτῶν *Euthyph* 6b, *Phaedo* 61d, 62b, etc.

This distribution evidently reflects the fact that in Greek demonstratives are usually used for focused anaphoric pronouns. Demonstratives by contrast are fairly well represented with postposed πέρι

(43)   τούτων πέρι *Meno* 92c
       ἐκείνων πέρι *Rep* 510d.

Postposition is also found with interrogatives, which are related to focus and are extracted

(44)   τοῦ πέρι; *Soph* 222d, *Polit* 257c, *Laws* 658b,

also with intervening focus particle or parenthetical

(45)   τοῦ δὴ πέρι; *Soph* 233a
       τίνων δὴ πέρι *Laws* 809d
       ποίων δὴ πέρι *Laws* 812b
       τίνος δέ, ἦ δ᾽ ὅς, πέρι λέγεις; *Rep* 410c.

Postposed πέρι also occurs with words which associate with focus like *only*, *rather*

(46)   ἡδονῆς πέρι μόνον *Laws* 658a
       τῶν ἀγαθῶν πέρι μᾶλλον ἢ τῶν κακῶν *Tim* 87c,

---

(41) About them (*Soph* 226b).
(42) About them (*Euthyph* 6b).
(43) About these things (*Meno* 92c). About THOSE things (*Rep* 510d).
(44) In what respect? (*Soph* 222d).
(45) In what respect? (*Soph* 233a). About what? (*Laws* 809d). About what sort of things (*Laws* 812b). "In what respect do you mean?," he said (*Rep* 410c).
(46) Only about pleasure (*Laws* 658a). About good things rather than about bad things (*Tim* 87c).

and with different types of topicalization

(47) ταύτης δὴ πέρι... τῆς μεταβολῆς *Laws* 676c
      εὐθύνων δὴ πέρι, τίς ἡμῖν λόγος ἂν εἴη πρέπων *Laws* 945b.

A number of instances of postposited πέρι are associated with explicit μέν... δέ contrasts

(48) τὰ μὲν οὖν δὴ τῶν ἀρχαίων πέρι... τὰ δὲ τῶν νέων *Laws* 886d
      τῶν μὲν τοίνυν ἄλλων πέρι... περὶ δὲ ὧν μεγίστων *Rep* 599b
      τὰ μὲν δὴ λόγων πέρι... τὸ δὲ λέξεως *Rep* 392c;

such contrasts can cooccur with hyperbaton

(49) τὰ μὲν θανάσιμα... τῶν δ' ἄλλων περὶ βλάψεων *Laws* 932e

or with postverbal stranding of the preposition after focus fronting of its complement

(50) τῶν μὲν οὖν νικητηρίων... τῶν δὲ δευτερείων ὁρᾶν καὶ σκοπεῖν
      χρὴ πέρι *Phil* 22c
      τῶν τε οὖν ἄλλων εὐλαβεῖσθαι πέρι πλημμελεῖν εἰς δίκην,
      διαφερόντως δὲ... *Laws* 943e (v.l.).

Stranded postpositions also occur with relatives, another category that is extracted

(51) ὧν εἴρηκεν πέρι *Laws* 814d
      ὧν ἂν ἐρεῖν πέρι μέλλη *Phaedr* 259e
      ὧν ἔφραζον δεῖν πέρι λέγειν *Laws* 887a
      ὧν ἐγὼ οὐδὲν οὔτε μέγα οὔτε μικρὸν πέρι ἐπαΐω *Apol* 19c.

Although conjuncts and disjuncts can certainly occur with preposed περί

(52) περὶ τοῦ ὁσίου καὶ τοῦ ἀνοσίου *Euthyph* 9d (contrast previously
      established in the discourse, cp. 4e)
      ἢ περὶ φόνους ἢ περὶ ἱερῶν κλοπὰς *Euthyph* 5d,

(47) About this change (*Laws* 676c). What would be an appropriate statement for us to make about examiners (*Laws* 945b).
(48) As far as those of the ancients are concerned... as for those of the moderns (*Laws* 886d). About other matters... but about the most important things which... (*Rep* 599b). As far as subject matter is concerned... but as for diction (*Rep* 392c).
(49) Those instances that are fatal... but about other injuries (*Laws* 932e).
(50) About first prize... but we must look and see about second prize (*Phil* 22c). To take care not to offend against justice about other matters, but particularly... (*Laws* 943e).
(51) About which it has spoken (*Laws* 814d). Of those things about which he is going to speak (*Phaedr* 259e). The things about which they said one ought to speak (*Laws* 887a). Things about which I have nothing whatsoever to say (*Apol* 19c).
(52) Concerning the pious and the impious (*Euthyph* 9d). Either with respect to murder or with respect to sacrilegious theft (*Euthyph* 5d).

postposited πέρι is quite well represented in this context, since there is often some degree of implicit or explicit contrast involved which leads to fronting of the noun

(53) τοῦ ὁσίου τε πέρι καὶ τοῦ ἀνοσίου *Euthyph* 4e
 εὐδαιμονίας τε πέρι καὶ τοῦ ἐναντίου *Rep* 472c
εἴτε πολλῶν νεῶν πέρι εἴτε μιᾶς *Rep* 488a.

Y₁ hyperbaton with περί has the typical strong focus on the modifier

(54) τῶν ἄλλων περὶ νομέων *Polit* 268b
αὐτομάτου περὶ βίου *Polit* 271e
πάντων περὶ τῶν ἄλλων *Rep* 353b
περὶ Δημοκράτους... καὶ πάντων περὶ τῶν προγόνων *Lysis* 205b
τοῦ γυναικείου περὶ νόμου *Rep* 457b.

Here is a similar example from a Thucydides speech

(55) τῶν μεγίστων περὶ κινδύνων Thuc 1.75.5.

In Y₂ hyperbaton with πέρι, the noun is often a focused topic, not surprisingly given the meaning of the preposition

(56) ἰατρῶν δὲ πέρι πάντων *Laws* 865b
ἄστρων δὴ πέρι πάντων *Laws* 899b.

The evidence just cited points to the following account. Περί is proclitic, just like παρά for instance. The difference is that in its nonlocal meaning, unlike παρά, it does not block movement of a complement noun or of a strong focus Y₁ modifier to a prehead position. Such movement is conditioned by the same factors that condition it for other heads. For the clitic theory, on the other hand, the correlation of second position πέρι with focus would be coincidental.

Now we can return to the question why there is such a discrepancy between verse and prose. For hyperbaton where X is a verb, prose rejects the old style paratactic ːnodifiers and accepts the focus operator modifier; but where X is a preposition, prose rejects the operator type too. As compared with verbs, prepositions are defective heads: they fail to license extraction of a focus in prose. This is not surprising, since prepositional phrases are known to be islands for extraction in various languages. The improper prepositions, being semantically closer to oblique cases of nouns, have a greater tolerance of hyperbaton. Given the conclusions of chapters 1–4, the data fall rather neatly into place.

(53) Concerning the pious and the impious (*Euthyph* 4e). With respect to happiness or its contrary (*Rep* 472c). About many ships or just one (*Rep* 488a).

(54) About the other herdsmen (*Polit* 268b). About the spontaneous life (*Polit* 271e). About all the other things (*Rep* 353b). About Democrates... and about all the ancestors (*Lysis* 205b). With respect to the regulation for women (*Rep* 457b).

(55) In the matter of the greatest dangers (Thuc 1.75.5).

(56) About all doctors (*Laws* 865b). About all the stars (*Laws* 899b).

6 The Syntax of Y₁ Hyperbaton

Representation of hyperbaton in classical Greek

The problem of the status of hyperbaton in classical Greek is quite different from the problem of the origin of hyperbaton. Hyperbaton starts out in a relatively nonconfigurational typology, but what sort of structures does it presuppose in the classical language? Consider the case of a tragic actor, say the notorious Hegelochus. His everyday speech has configurational noun phrases, and his use of Y₁ hyperbaton is restricted to cases with focused modifiers. On the other hand, the poetic language he declaims in the theatre has an earlier, less constrained type of hyperbaton without these restrictions. So there are two questions, one involving the representation of hyperbaton in a language which has systematically configurational noun phrases, the other relating to the coexistence of earlier and later syntactic typologies associated with the spoken and the poetic language respectively. This chapter is concerned with the first of these questions.

It would be a reasonable assumption that once Greek develops a consistently configurational noun phrase, hyperbaton will be interpreted as a deviation from the normal configurational structure

(1)   λέξεων... ἐκ τοῦ κατ᾽ ἀκολουθίαν κεκινημένη τάξις *De Sublimitate* 22;
       Transgressio est quae verborum perturbat ordinem (Auctor
       ad Herennium 4.44).

On this view, the language develops syntactic configurations before generalizing the continuous word order that overtly encodes them. YP would now be seen as a discontinuous constituent. The term as applied to our canonical Y₁XY₂ is intended to convey that, although Y₁ and Y₂ are normally both syntactically related to X, they are syntactically related to each other in a way that excludes X. However, they are not adjacent, because X intervenes between them in the linear order. There is no requirement for YP to show surface struc-

---

(1) An arrangement of expressions disturbed from its natural sequence (*De Sublimitate* 22).

tural integrity. Discontinuous constituency is a recalcitrant problem in syntactic theory, and various devices have been proposed for its representation (Bach 1981; Pullum 1982; Zwicky 1986; Huck & Ojeda 1987; Blevins 1990; Bunt & van Horck 1997). We will briefly review some of them and apply them to Y_1 hyperbaton, since that is the most integrated type of hyperbaton. That way, the advantages and disadvantages of this general line of analysis will become apparent.

The cleanest approach is simply to construct a tree appropriate to the pragmatic structure; the morphology serves as an overt coindexing system that guides unification of the discontinuous Y elements into a single semantic constituent. This is illustrated for

(2)   τὴν ἄλλην διεξῆλθον πρεσβείαν Aesch 2.48

in Figure 6.1. In a few rare cases, the morphology might fail as a precise coreferencing system. For instance, in a sentence like

τὴν καλὴν ἐδίδαξε γυναῖκα ἐργασίαν

the interpretation could conceivably be ambiguous between 'he taught a woman the NOBLE profession' (cp. Dem 18.129) and 'he taught the BEAUTIFUL woman a trade.' Then interpretation would have to rely on word order, argument ranking, and inferential reasoning from knowledge of the context and knowledge of the world. Similarly, in Warlpiri, the dative case can encode both indirect object and benefactive, and the ergative case can encode both subject and instrumental: in sentences having both types of dative or both types of ergative, a discontinuous modifier could theoretically be taken with either. Some sentences of this type are reported as remaining ambiguous, at least out of context (van Riemsdijk 1982)

Maliki-rli ka wita-ngku kurdu yalki-rni kartirdi-rli
dog-ERG AUX small-ERG child   bite-NPST teeth-ERG
'The small dog bites the child with its teeth'
'The dog bites the child with its small teeth.'

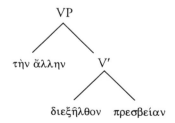

Figure 6.1
Nonderivational Y_1 hyperbaton structure
τὴν ἄλλην διεξῆλθον πρεσβείαν Aesch 2.48

(2) I gave an account of the rest of the embassy (Aesch 2.48).

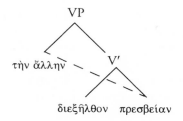

Figure 6.2
Hyperbaton with crossing lines
τὴν ἄλλην διεξῆλθον πρεσβείαν Aesch 2.48

If, given the slight potential for ambiguity, some structural indication of the constituency of YP were felt to be indispensable, this could be achieved by allowing the lines of the tree to cross (Figure 6.2). Another approach is to use a trace or slash mechanism to encode in the syntax the fact that from a semantic point of view the X′ is missing an element. Traces (Figure 6.3) are usually interpreted derivationally as indicating the source position from which an element has been moved. This system is suitable for prose Υ1 hyperbaton in the framework of a movement theory of focus. However, if it is generalized to other types of hyperbaton, it may be necessary to distinguish different types of traces or gaps and different types of landing sites, since not all hyperbaton involves the sort of operator-variable relationship posited for strong focus. The question has been the topic of much discussion (Saito 1992; Deprez 1989; Webelhuth 1992; Müller & Sternefeld 1993; Corver & van Riemsdijk 1994).

If hyperbaton is assigned a flat, ternary syntax, then X can be thought of as inserted into YP or YP as wrapped around X (Figure 6.4). The idea of infixing and wrapping relations originated in categorial grammar (Morrill 1995) where,

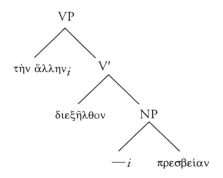

Figure 6.3
Hyperbaton with trace
τὴν ἄλλην διεξῆλθον πρεσβείαν Aesch 2.48

in the absence of a derivation, simple concatenation of adjacent expressions is inadequate for bona fide cases of discontinuity. For instance, the notation B↑A might be used for a verb with tmesis that wraps itself around its complement A to form a verb phrase B, and A↓B for a head that infixes itself into its complement A to form a superordinate phrase B. Alternatively, constituency and linear precedence can be unhitched, either by liberating grammatical constituents within a superordinate domain, or by assuming that, within that domain, the linear ordering required to encode constituency fails to overcome the pragmatic forces working in the opposite direction; consequently the words never get into the order appropriate to their constituency. Applying this to hyperbaton, we get the XP as the pragmatically required domain and YP as the constituent that fails to get its words into adjacency. Within the domain, different pragmatic requirements can produce different word orders (so that the relative order of adjective and noun turns out the same as in the continuous YP)

[YP X]
[X YP]
[A X N]
[N X A].

These schemata all start from the premise that words which belong together semantically (and in one sense or another also syntactically) have been syntactically separated: the way the words are composed semantically is different from the way they are arranged in the surface syntax. This perspective is almost automatic for a speaker of English. As we saw in chapter 4, it turned out to be an obstacle when we tried to develop a theory of the origins and licensing of hyperbaton. Nevertheless, there is no question that phrases have discourse configurational peripheral position(s) in Greek, and it is reasonable to assume that, from the point of view of the classical language, there could be discontinuity between head and complement

(3)   τοὺς γευομένους κύνας τῶν προβάτων Dem 25.40,

Figure 6.4
Wrap analysis of hyperbaton
τὴν ἄλλην διεξῆλθον πρεσβείαν Aesch 2.48

(3) Dogs that taste sheep (Dem 25.40).

between specifier and head

(4)   πολὺ ἄλλους ἐμοῦ δεινοτέρους Xen *Oec* 2.16,

and between head and external modifier

(5)   ἡ στρατία ἥξει τῶν Ἀθηναίων Thuc 4.42.3.

Discontinuity arises when compositionality is violated. Compositionality prescribes that semantic constituents should be encoded by continuous syntactic constituents. When some syntactic requirement conflicts with and overrides compositionality, a possible outcome is that semantic constituency is not respected and syntactic discontinuity results. Semantic constituency then has to be read off syntactically discontinuous subconstituents. Take participial attribute hyperbaton for instance. When the participle is attracted to the prenominal attributive position

(6)   τοὺς δάκνοντας κύνας Xen *Hell* 2.4.41 (v.l.),

it can strand a tail complement in hyperbaton, as in the example just cited

τοὺς γευομένους κύνας τῶν προβάτων Dem 25.40.

The complement τῶν προβάτων then has to be composed with its head γευομένους across the superordinate head κύνας. Some apparent violations of compositionality might turn out to involve a less usual order of semantic composition: our participle and noun would in that case disharmonically compose into a functor category meaning 'canine tasters.' But for most theories participle hyperbaton and external genitive hyperbaton are bona fide cases of discontinuity. However, they are not left branch violations: rather the head is discontinuous with a complement or external modifier phrase; consequently they are less serious infractions. Even specifier hyperbaton might not be a true left branch violation, if specifiers like πολύ and οὕτως (Xen *Symp* 4.40, *Hiero* 1.1) are more comparable to English phrases like 'by a large degree,' 'to such an extent' than to single degree words like 'very,' 'so.'

But what about Y1 hyperbaton? This seems to be a quintessential left branch violation. In fact, for definite YPs (other than those with a demonstrative or universal quantifier) discontinuity involves splitting off two left branches (the determiner and the prenominal adjective), which is a particularly grave left branch violation, since the two left branches do not on the face of it form a constituent to the exclusion of the noun but appear to be simply stranded disiecta membra. The problem with the discontinuous constituent theory is that this particularly nasty variety of constituent busting is treated like common garden discontinuity. But if Y1 hyperbaton is as innocuous as other types of hyperbaton, why is verse type Y1 hyperbaton with restrictive lexical and non-lexical adjectives illicit in prose, whereas ordinary Y2 hyperbaton with restric-

(4) Others much more skilled than me (Xen *Oec* 2.16).
(5) That the enemy of the Athenians would come (Thuc 4.42.3).
(6) Dogs that bite (Xen *Hell* 2.4.41).

tive adjectives is licit in both verse and prose? and what is it about strong narrow focus that rescues Y_1 hyperbaton in prose and makes it acceptable? Something else must be going on. As things stand at present, we are restricted to two options for Y_1 hyperbaton in classical prose: either we can say it is a nonconfigurational relic in a sea of configurational Y_1 noun phrases ("layering" theory), or we can say it is a configurational noun phrase with a discontinuous structure like one of the structures just reviewed ("reanalysis" theory). Neither of these approaches is particularly explanatory. While they are both plausible diachronic scenarios, they presuppose the continued acceptability of Y_1 discontinuity without offering any syntactic motivation for it (nor for its restriction to strong focus modifiers). So it is worth trying to look for an interpretation of Y_1 hyperbaton that is compositionally more faithful to its surface syntax. The task, then, is not so much to devise mechanisms that allow the words to get out of order as to find structures that explain why the words are in order.

One way of doing this is to try and "typeshift" the Y elements. The two theories we will examine in this chapter are designed to do just that. The null head modifier theory allows adjectives to be reinterpreted as noun phrases. From a syntactic point of view, the effect of changing *red* into *the red one*, for example, is to change Y_1 from an adjectival phrase (or cohead) into a determiner phrase. From a semantic point of view, *red* denotes the set of entities having the property of redness, in symbols $\lambda x[\mathrm{red}(x)]$, while *the red one* is the unique Y_2 having that property, after resolution of the anaphora in the null head $\iota x[\mathrm{red}(x) \wedge Y_2(x)]$. The second theory, the complex predicate theory, allows a noun to be reinterpreted as a type of predicate modifier, with the consequence that syntactically it is not a determiner phrase but rather an appositional bare noun, and semantically it does not directly refer to Y_2 and is not an ordinary individuated argument. One might expect this to lead, at some level of interpretation to a change in valence, in symbols $\lambda y \lambda x[V(x,y)] \rightarrow \lambda x[V^y(x)]$, but this is not the case because the "stranded" modifier takes over the argument function. The effect of the null head modifier theory is to remove the left branch violation by categorial reanalysis: Y_1 is no longer a left branch but a complete determiner phrase. The effect of the complex predicate theory is to save compositionality, at least in the sense that Y_2 is no longer a discontinuous subconstituent of a regular premodified YP. Since the operation of both theories is more tangible when the hyperbaton includes an overt article, we will concentrate the analysis on hyperbata in which YP involves definiteness, and then consider to what extent the conclusions can be generalized to other types, including indefinite YPs.

NULL HEAD MODIFIER THEORY

As its name suggests, a null head modifier is a modifier that can stand by itself in place of a noun phrase without the support of a noun or an overt pronoun. Null head modifiers are syntactic entities, and distinct from nominalizations of adjectives, which are morpholexical entities. Note further the accentual difference in the following examples

> λευκός, λευκή ' white one'
> λεῦκος 'white fish,' λεύκη 'white poplar.'

The difference is modelled in Figure 6.5, where we use a headless projection (Chao 1988) in preference to an empty pronominal with its own syntactic node (Lobeck 1995). Compare also Italian *uno povero* 'a poor one,' *un povero* 'a poor man' (Bernstein 1993). Particularly relevant is the distinction between Latin *quid* 'what' and *quod* 'which (one)': it is *quod* that appears in hyperbaton

> Vide quod inceptet facinus. Terence *Heaut* 600
> 'Look what a lousy thing she's doing'
>
> Quod excogitabitur in eum supplicium...? Cicero *Rab Perd* 27
> 'What punishment will be dreamed up for that man...?'.

A similar distinction applies in Mohawk (Baker 1996). In one type of null head modifier, the null head is "arbitrary," simply denoting any person or entity

> (7)   ὀλίγοι ἔμφρονες Pl *Symp* 194b
>   ἀγαθῷ Pl *Tim* 29e
>   ἱππικὸν οὐκ εἶχεν Xen *Ag* 1.15
>   τοὺς αἰτίους Dem 3.17
>   τὸ ἀληθὲς Pl *Gorg* 473b.

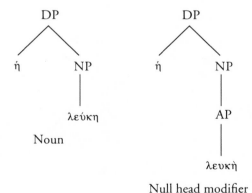

Figure 6.5
Nominalization and null head modifier
ἡ λεύκη / ἡ λευκὴ

(7) A few sensible people (Pl *Symp* 194b). In a good man (Pl *Tim* 29e). He had no cavalry (Xen *Ag* 1.15). Those responsible (Dem 3.17). The truth (Pl *Gorg* 473b).

In general, English does not require a proform with definite phrases of this type: *the good, the wise, the guilty*. In a second type, the null head may be a noun predictably associated with the adjective

(8)   ἡ ὑστεραία
      ἡ εὐθεῖα

or a predictably selected noun, either an internal accusative or derived from a fairly fixed expression, as in *have a good one, pick a ripe one*

(9)   ὡς ὀλίγας παίσειεν Xen *An* 5.8.12 (scil. πληγάς)
      τὴν αὐτὴν ἐσκευασμένοι Her 7.84 (scil. σκευήν)
      ναυμαχήσαντας μίαν Ar *Frogs* 693 (scil. ναυμαχίαν)
      λοῦνται... ψυχρῷ Her 2.37 (scil. ὕδατι)
      ἐρήμην κατηγοροῦντες Pl *Apol* 18c (scil. δίκην).

In the third type, which is the one that mainly concerns us here, the null head is available from the syntactic or pragmatic context

(10) ἐκ δέ οἱ ταύτης τῆς γυναικὸς οὐδ᾽ ἐξ ἄλλης παῖδες ἐγίνοντο
      Her 5.92
      ὅπως δ᾽ ἐκείνω τὼ λόγω μαθήσεται, | τὸν κρείττον᾽, ὅστις ἐστί, καὶ
      τὸν ἥττονα, | ὃς τἄδικα λέγων ἀνατρέπει τὸν κρείττονα· | ἐὰν δὲ
      μή, τὸν γοῦν ἄδικον πάσῃ τέχνῃ Ar *Clouds* 882.

With count nouns, English requires the proform *one* for this type. With mass nouns, the noun has to be repeated

      red roses and yellow ones
      ripe fruit and unripe fruit.

The rule does not apply to determiners (*these*) nor to superlatives and ordinals (*the ripest, the fourth*), which are akin to determiners in their function of specifying referents. If attributive adjectives are taken to be (co)heads of modified noun phrases, then there may be a parallel between these Greek null heads and covert pronominal object arguments of verbs. It is more difficult in Greek than in English to draw the line between null head modifiers and coordinating or right node raising constructions in which an adjective is separated from its noun by some interrupting material with no independent noun phrase resulting. The following examples include both types

(8)   The following day. Straight line/nominative case.
(9)   That he had struck too few blows (Xen *An* 5.8.12). Equipped in the same way (Her 7.84). Having fought a single naval engagement (Ar *Frogs* 693). They wash with cold water (Her 2.37). Prosecuting an undefended case (Pl *Apol* 18c).
(10) No children were born to him by this wife nor by another (Her 5.92). See to it that he learns those two arguments, the stronger one, in any given case, and the weaker one, which by an unjust plea overturns the stronger; and if not, at least the unjust one by all means (Ar *Clouds* 882).

He wrote both a short and a long paper
He wrote a short instead of a long paper
He wrote a short paper instead of a long one
*He wrote a short

(11)   πῆ διαφέρει ὁ τυραννικός τε καὶ ὁ ἰδιωτικὸς βίος; Xen *Hiero* 1.2 (v.l.)
        κενῇ προφάσει ταύτῃ κατεχρῶ καὶ ψευδεῖ Dem 18.150 (adjective
        phrase conjunct hyperbaton)
        προφάσεις ἀντὶ τῶν ἀληθῶν ψευδεῖς μεταθέντα Dem 18.225
        ἐπιδείξαντες... τὰς ὑμετέρας παρὰ τὰς ἡμετέρας ᾠδάς Pl *Laws* 817d.

Although null head modifiers occur in many different types of language, there appears to be a correlation between null head modifiers and discontinuous phrase structure. This suggested the idea that in hyperbaton the discontinuous modifiers were not adjectives at all but null head modifiers, that is noun phrases. The null head was thought of as bound by the other Y element (Fanselow 1988). In pronominal argument languages, consequently, hyperbaton was licensed by simply allowing both Y elements to be coindexed in parallel with the pronominal argument as independent adjunct noun phrases (Jelinek 1984). In languages like Greek, the theory might offer a licensing mechanism for hyperbaton and go some way towards explaining why Greek could have hyperbaton but English could not. It also fits better with the currently popular solution to the island problem. Recall that covert focus movement of modifiers was suspect because it violates island constraints. Yı hyperbaton, being overt movement of just this type, seems to provide empirical evidence for the reality of modifier movement under focus, in defiance at least of the left branch constraint. To solve the island problem it was suggested that covert focus movement involves complete noun phrases (focus phrases) rather than just the focused modifier embedded within them. Then why does overt focus movement in hyperbaton move just the modifier? If, in languages allowing hyperbaton, the modifier moved under focus is actually a complete noun phrase, this difficulty is eliminated and crosslinguistic uniformity restored.

Various further factors seem to support the null head modifier theory. Firstly, discontinuity in noun phrases is particularly characteristic of some Australian languages, and it is just in many Australian languages that the categorial distinction between noun and adjective tends to be indeterminate, making it difficult to distinguish *the big man* from *the male adult* (Heath 1986). Thus the same Warlpiri nominals are used attributively and referentially, and can either trigger agreement in the auxiliary complex like nouns or themselves show adjective-like agreement with another nominal when used as secondary predi-

(11) How the royal life and the private life differ (Xen *Hiero* 1.2). You used this empty and false pretext (Dem 18.150). Substituting false reasons for the true ones (Dem 18.225). Showing your songs alongside ours (Pl *Laws* 817d).

cates (Bittner & Hale 1995). So again, there seems to be a correlation between discontinuity and nounlike properties of adjectives. Further evidence comes from demonstrative doubling, as in examples of the following type from Jingulu

> *Those ones scolded us, those two old men,*

and from cases where there is an intonational break before the Y₂ noun, as in this example from Martuthunira (Pensalfini 1992:47)

> Nguhu kuyilwa-lalha-rru, warruwa
> that-NOM spoil-PASS-NOW, devil
> 'That one spoiled it all, devil.'

In Hungarian (Marácz 1989; Kester 1996) attributive modifiers are uninflected, but a null head modifier (or the last in a string of null head modifiers) is inflected

> Láttam a zöld autókat
>   saw   the green car-PL-ACC
> 'I have seen the green cars'

> Láttam a piros autókat és a zöldeket
>   saw   the red car-PL-ACC and the green-PL-ACC
> 'I have seen the red cars and the green ones.'

Discontinuous modifiers are also inflected

> Láttam nagy bicikliket
>   saw   big bike-PL-ACC
> Bicikliket   láttam nagyokat
> bikes-PL-ACC saw big-PL-ACC
> 'I saw big bikes.'

Another consideration was that discontinuity was thought to arise due to movement, but theories of movement had been developed for languages that had a left branch condition, and tended to exclude some or all of the movements presupposed by hyperbaton. Very briefly, it was believed that movement (both substitution and adjunction) should preserve structure, that the source and the landing site should be structurally compatible (Baltin 1982, 1991), and that movement was restricted to minimal and maximal projections (heads and full phrases). From an English point of view, these constraints were not conducive to a straightforward analysis of structures like *a large he bought shirt* in terms of movement. If *shirt* was N′, it could not be moved at all; and if it was N°, it should be moved to a head position. *A large* was not a constituent of any sort, however it was labelled, and in any case if movement was to a specifier position, what was moved should be a complete phrase. These difficulties seemed to be alleviated if in languages with hyperbaton *a large shirt* was actually two full noun phrases, or if *a large* was allowed to "grow back" into a full noun phrase when it was moved (van Riemsdijk 1989). One interesting application of null head modifier theory involved hyperbaton in Dutch child language (p. 35). It was suggested that hyperbaton comes to be disallowed in adult language as the child learns to reanalyze the posited Y1 paratactic noun phrase as a determiner (Hoekstra & Jordens 1994).

The general idea of these approaches is that analyzing modifiers as null head noun phrases helps to license hyperbaton. The argument is not as strong as it appears, because it is also possible to analyze modifiers as nonconfigurational secondary predicates, in which case they would still be adjectives, but adjectives with the same sort of freedom as null head modifiers. So there are not two but three ways in which we could interpret an indefinite Y2 hyperbaton such as

ναυμαχία γίγνεται ἐπ᾽ Αἰγίνῃ μεγάλη Thuc 1.105.2:

(1) an integrated attributive reading 'There took place a big sea battle at Aegina'; (2) a null head modifier reading (an apposition, i.e. a noun phrase secondary predication) 'There took place a sea battle at Aegina ⟨which was⟩ a big one'; (3) an adjectival secondary predicate reading 'There took place a sea battle at Aegina which was big.'

In its strongest form, the null head modifier hypothesis claims that hyperbaton can only occur in languages having null head modifiers independent of hyperbaton, and that in such languages only those modifiers can occur in hyperbaton that can also occur independently as null head modifiers. The latter claim may have to be restated in such a way as to allow different categories of modifier to behave differently in hyperbaton. Swampy Cree (Russell & Reinholtz 1996) has universal distributive quantifiers (*each, every*) which occur in hyperbaton but not as independent null head modifiers. In Kayardild (Evans 1995) there are some adjectives like *jungarra* 'big' that can be used adjacent to their noun or in hyperbaton

> ngada jungarra-wu karna-ju kaburrba-wu
> I   big   light   fire
> 'I want to light a BIG fire'

but not as independent null head modifiers

> jungarra dangkaa dalija
>   big   man   came
> 'The big man came'

> *jungarra dalija
> 'The big one came.'

However, the independent null head modifier is allowed under strong contrastive focus, which suggests that strong focus can trigger the shift from adjective to noun phrase. This is an intriguing observation, both for the general problem of focus movement from left branch positions and for the specific question of the difference between prose and verse hyperbaton in Greek.

Turning now to Greek, the first thing to note is that hyperbaton is found with appositional nouns in Homer

(12) τὴν χαλκῆες κάμον ἄνδρες *Il* 4.187, 216
    πατὴρ ἐπετέλλετο Πηλεὺς *Il* 9.252
    τὸν Χρύσην ἠτίμασεν ἀρητῆρα *Il* 1.11
    Πηλεὺς μὲν ᾧ παιδὶ γέρων ἐπέτελλ' Ἀχιλλῆϊ *Il* 11.783 (double hyperbaton).

This substantiates an assumption of the null head modifier theory, namely that hyperbaton can (or at least could originally) occur with appositional noun phrases, but it does not follow that all hyperbaton must involve appositional noun phrases. Just as the occurrence of

(13) αἰπόλοι ἄνδρες *Il* 2.474

does not mean that ἄλκιμον is necessarily a noun phrase in

(14) ἄλκιμον υἱόν *Il* 6.437,

although this was just the proposal of Rosén (1967) for all Y₁ adjectives in Homer, so the occurrence of

    πατὴρ ἐπετέλλετο Πηλεὺς

does not mean that ἐμὸς and πελώριος are necessarily noun phrases in

(15) πατήρ οἱ δῶκεν ἐμὸς *Od* 1.264
    ὡς Αἴας ἐπέτελλε πελώριος *Il* 17.360.

Nevertheless, particularly in view of the Australian situation, one wonders whether the categorial distinction between noun and adjective was as clearcut in prehistoric Greek as it is at later periods. It is also true, even in the classical language, that in many cases if the noun in a hyperbaton were ellipsed, the resulting structure would be perfectly acceptable Greek with a null head modifier interpretation

(16) ἐν τοῖς δημοσίοις ἀναγέγραπται ⟨γράμμασι⟩ Aesch 2.58
    τάς τ' ἰδίας δίκας καὶ τὰς δημοσίας Dem 18.210 (anaphoric)

    ἐν τοῖς φονικοῖς γέγραπται ⟨νόμοις⟩ Dem 9.44
    ἔστι μὲν οὐκέτι τῶν φονικῶν ὅδ' ὁ νῦν ἀνεγνωσμένος νόμος
    Dem 23.86 (cataphoric).

(12) Which men who were smiths made (*Il* 4.187). Your father Peleus ordered (*Il* 9.252). He dishonoured Chryses, his priest (*Il* 1.11). The old man Peleus instructed his son Achilles (*Il* 11.783).
(13) Men who are goatherds (*Il* 2.474).
(14) The valiant son (*Il* 6.437).
(15) My father gave it to him (*Od* 1.264). So mighty Ajax instructed them (*Il* 17.360).
(16) They are registered in the public archives (Aesch 2.58). Private cases and public ones (Dem 18.210). It is written in the homicide laws (Dem 9.44). The law that has just now been read out is not, like the others, one of the homicide ones (Dem 23.86).

In the following sections we shall review the evidence for null head modifiers in a broad range of different contexts.

Definites

Greek offers an intricate variety of structures in this category. The noun may precede or follow the modifier; in the former condition, the noun may or may not be articulated; the article never stands between an attributive adjective and its noun. The modifier may be an adjective or a possessive genitive (inter alia). The following data sets present the continuous YP structure, the corresponding YXY hyperbaton structure, and the corresponding ellipsed structure for each subcategory. The ellipsed structure (DA) repeats itself from one category to another: this is not entirely trivial, as becomes clear if one inserts overt syntactic empty positions. When a Y2 noun is contextually ellipsed, the null head and the site of the ellipsis are identical (DA∅), but when a Y1 noun is contextually ellipsed, they are not (∅DA∅). However, no attempt is made to draw this distinction in the following data sets; the DA examples cited mostly seem to belong to the first type.

1. ARTICLE NOUN ARTICLE ADJECTIVE
   (17)   DNDA (διέφθειρε τὴν πόλιν τὴν μεγάλην)
   ὑπὸ τῆς μητρυιᾶς τῆς ἐμῆς ἐξαπατωμένη Antiph 1.19

   DNVDA (τὴν πόλιν διέφθειρε τὴν μεγάλην)
   ὑπὸ τῶν ἐχθρῶν πεισθεὶς τῶν ἐμῶν Lys 7.39

   DA (τὴν μεγάλην)
   ὁμολογουμένων δὲ τῶν σημείων καὶ παρὰ τῆς τούτου γυναικὸς καὶ παρὰ τῆς ἐμῆς Dem 41.21

2. NOUN ARTICLE ADJECTIVE
   (18)   NDA (διέφθειρε πόλιν τὴν μεγίστην)
   ἡ πόλις ἐν κακοῖς τοῖς μεγίστοις ἐγίγνετο Andoc 1.58

   NVDA (πόλιν διέφθειρε τὴν μεγίστην)
   τὴν δὲ πόλιν ἐν κακοῖς οὖσαν τοῖς μεγίστοις Andoc 1.51

   DA (τὴν μεγίστην)
   τῶν μὲν τοῖς ἐχθροῖς ὑπαρχουσῶν δυνάμεων τὰς μεγίστας ἀφελεῖν
   Dem 18.302

(17) That she had been deceived by my stepmother (Antiph 1.19). Persuaded by my enemies (Lys 7.39). The seals being acknowledged both by this man's wife and by mine (Dem 41.21).

(18) The city was getting into a desperate situation (Andoc 1.58). The fact that the city was in a desperate situation (Andoc 1.51). To eliminate the most important of the enemy's strengths (Dem 18.302).

3. ARTICLE ADJECTIVE ARTICLE NOUN
>   DADN: not used
>   DAVDN: not used
>   DA: see previous examples

4. ARTICLE ADJECTIVE NOUN
>   (19)   DAN (διέφθειρε τὴν μεγάλην πόλιν)
>   τοὺς ἰδίους πολέμους ἐπανορθῶσαι Dem 14.5
>
>   DAVN (τὴν μεγάλην διέφθειρε πόλιν)
>   τὰς ἰδίας κατεσκευάκασιν οἰκίας Dem 23.208
>
>   DA (διέφθειρε τὴν μεγάλην)
>   τὰς ὅλης γε τῆς πατρίδος σπονδάς... οὐ μόνον τὰς ἰδίας Dem 19.191

5. (ARTICLE) NOUN ARTICLE POSSESSIVE
>   (20)   (D)NDPoss (διέφθειρε (τὴν) πόλιν τὴν Κροίσου)
>   λέγε καὶ τὴν ἐπιστολὴν τὴν τοῦ Βηρισάδου Dem 23.174
>
>   (D)NVDPoss ((τὴν) πόλιν διέφθειρε τὴν Κροίσου)
>   τῆς ἐπιστολῆς ἠκούετε τῆς Προξένου Aesch 2.134
>   ἐπὶ σκηνὴν ἰόντες τὴν Ξενοφῶντος Xen An 6.4.19
>
>   DPoss (διέφθειρε τὴν Κροίσου)
>   κατὰ τὸ Κλεωνύμου ψήφισμα... κατὰ δὲ τὸ Πεισάνδρου Andoc 1.27

6. ARTICLE POSSESSIVE NOUN
>   (21)   DPossN (διέφθειρε τὴν Κροίσου πόλιν)
>   ἰασόμενοι τὸ Δημοσθένους δωροδόκημα Aesch 3.69
>
>   DPossVN (τὴν Κροίσου διέφθειρε πόλιν)
>   τὸ Δημοσθένους ἐπιγράφειν ὄνομα Aesch 3.159
>
>   DPoss (διέφθειρε τὴν Κροίσου)
>   εἰς τὰς λητουργίας ἀποχωρήσεται. τὰς πότ᾽ ἢ ποῦ γεγονυίας;
>   τὰς τοῦ πατρός; Dem 25.78

7. COMPLEX TYPES
>   (22)   DNDADA: τὸ τεῖχος τὸ μακρὸν τὸ νότιον Andoc 3.7
>   DADAN: ἐν τῇ ἀρχαίᾳ τῇ ἡμετέρᾳ φωνῇ Pl Crat 398b

(19) To fix their private wars (Dem 14.5). They have built their private homes (Dem 23.208). Their obligations to the entire country, not only their personal ones (Dem 19.191).

(20) Read also the letter of Berisades (Dem 23.174). You heard the letter of Proxenus (Aesch 2.134). Coming to Xenophon's tent (Xen An 6.4.19). According to Cleonymus' decree... according to Pisander's (Andoc 1.27).

(21) To remedy Demosthenes' bribery (Aesch 3.69). To write Demosthenes' name (Aesch 3.159). He will have recourse to public services. Those which were performed when or where? Those of his father? (Dem 25.78).

(22) The south long wall (Andoc 3.7). In the archaic stage of our language (Pl Crat 398b).

(23)   DADPossN: ὁ μὲν δὴ ναυτικὸς ὁ τῶν βαρβάρων στράτος Her 7.196
       (D)NDAVDPoss: τριήρης ἡ στρατηγὶς ἤδη ἐξώρμει ἡ Λαμάχου
       Andoc 1.11
       DN(Dem)VDADA: τὴν λίθον | ταύτην ἑόρακας τὴν καλὴν
       τὴν διαφανῆ Ar *Clouds* 766.

We can make the preliminary generalization that the same rules apply to all types in each of the data sets 1–7. When the adjective is Y₂, the article may be omitted before the Y₁ noun (particularly with superlatives and possessive pronouns) both in continuous phrases and in hyperbaton. When the adjective is Y₁, a second article never appears with the Y₂ noun, either in continuous phrases or in hyperbaton. So Y₁ hyperbaton never triggers rearticulation of the noun. If it did, there would have been overt evidence for null head modifier status of the adjective in Y₁ hyperbaton.

One might want to argue that everything in these data sets looks very parallel and that they ought to have a uniform analysis. Y₂ hyperbaton ((D)NVDA) is just like the ellipsed type (VDA) but with the noun retained preceding the verb, and the continuous type (VDNDA) is like Y₂ hyperbaton but with the noun adjacent to the adjective rather than to the left of the verb; derivationally

$$\text{VDNDA} \rightarrow \text{VDA} / \text{DNVDA}.$$

Since the ellipsed type involves a null head modifier, so should the other two. However, to be consistent, this logic also has to be applied to Y₁ hyperbaton, which exhibits the same parallelism: VDA (ellipsed) – DAVN (hyperbaton) – VDAN (continuous); derivationally

$$\text{VDAN} \rightarrow \text{VDA} / \text{DAVN}.$$

Again it would follow that DA has a null head in all three types. The problem is that this logic crashes, because we know perfectly well that in classical Greek the continuous type is an integrated noun phrase with an overt nominal head ([DAN] and not a paratactic structure consisting of two noun phrases, one with a null head ([[DA][N]])). The other way to get a uniform analysis is to reverse the above logic. Since the continuous type VDAN does not involve a null head modifier, neither should the entirely parallel Y₁ hyperbaton; null head modifiers would then be restricted to the cases when the head is physically absent, that is to the ellipsed type. Again, to be consistent, the same logic has to be applied to Y₂ hyperbaton. This leads to the conclusion that the continuous structure DNDA is a single integrated noun phrase, and that Y₂ hyperbaton is a discontinuous version of an integrated noun phrase. The problem with this is that each determiner seems to belong to its own phrase: [[DN][DA]] 'the city, the big one.' It has been suggested for modern Greek (Androutsopoulou 1994) and for modern Hebrew (Ritter 1991) that these

(23) The naval force of the barbarians (Her 7.196). Lamachus' flagship was already out of harbour (Andoc 1.11) Have you seen that beautiful transparent stone (Ar *Clouds* 766).

iterated determiners are just a sort of morphological agreement marker to indicate definiteness, and that they have mechanically spread from the nominal head; other approaches are also available (Tredinnick 1992; Alexiadou & Wilder 1998). Determiner spreading in modern Greek is not allowed with nonpredicative adjectives. Presumably, these iterated determiners start out in separate appositional noun phrases and, if the analysis is correct, progressively weaken into definiteness morphemes as the two separate phrases are progressively integrated into a single modified noun phrase. At all events, determiner spreading seems inappropriate for the ancient Greek data. It would be perverse to argue that in the NDA, NVDA type

(24)   ἥδιον γὰρ ἂν κωμῳδίας τῆς φαυλοτάτης... ἀκούσαιεν Isoc 2.44
       εἵματά τε ἐφόρεον τὰ κάλλιστα Her 3.27

underlyingly there was no article where there is one and there was an article where there is none, particularly as the NDA type can be semantically distinct from the DNDA type. We conclude that a uniform, across the board analysis of DA is not feasible. The various structures in the data sets need to be evaluated separately.

As usual, it is instructive to view the problem in a diachronic perspective. Fortunately, we can catch the article in its incipient stages in Homer (Michelini 1987). The fact that the examples cited may cluster in books or passages suspected by some of being relatively late (Shipp 1972) is of course irrelevant for our purposes. Whatever the actual status of the articles in these passages, they clearly reflect their demonstrative origins. To the extent that the weakened demonstrative or embryonic article occurs with modified nouns in Homer, it occurs only once, either with the adjective or, less commonly, with the noun. When it occurs with the noun, the modifier is descriptive

(25)   καὶ πρὸς τοῦ βασιλῆος ἀπηνέος Il 1.340
       τὸν ξεῖνον δύστηνον Od 17.10
       τοῦ παιδὸς ἀγαυοῦ Od 11.492
       τὰ τεύχεα καλά Il 21.317.

This type presumably originates with the structure [Demonstrative Noun] [Modifier], for instance 'this stranger ⟨who is⟩ wretched.' When the demonstrative occurs with the adjective, the adjective is usually restrictive

(26)   πατὴρ οὑμὸς Il 8.360
       τοίχου τοῦ ἑτέροιο Il 9.219
       ἠοῖ τῇ προτέρῃ Il 13.794

(24)   They would sooner listen to the most low-brow comedy (Isoc 2.44). They put on their most beautiful clothes (Her 3.27).
(25)   And before that harsh king (Il 1.340). That wretched stranger (Od 17.10). That noble child (Od 11.492). That beautiful armour (Il 21.317).
(26)   My father (Il 8.360). The other wall (Il 9.219). The morning before (Il 13.794).

(27) ἤματι τῷ προτέρῳ *Il* 21.5
      ἤματι τῷ αὐτῷ *Od* 7.326.

One might wonder whether the null head modifier is the adjective ('the day, that previous one') or the demonstrative ('the day, that one ⟨which was⟩ previous'). That the latter interpretation is correct is indicated by instances (with and without noun) in which the modifier is an adverb or possessive

(28) τά γ' ὄπισθε *Il* 11.613
      τῶν ὄπιθεν *Od* 11.66
      ἀνδρῶν | τῶν τότε *Il* 9.558
      τοῖσιν Ὀδυσσῆος *Od* 22.221
      τοὺς Λαομέδοντος *Il* 23.348
      υἱεῖς οἱ Δολίοιο *Od* 24.497.

So two conclusions emerge at this stage of the analysis. First, originally in the type (τὴν) πόλιν τὴν μεγάλην if there was a null head modifier, it was not the adjective but the demonstrative: 'that one which is big,' not 'that big one.' Secondly, the type πόλιν τὴν μεγάλην is earlier than the type τὴν πόλιν τὴν μεγάλην. From a diachronic perspective, the determiner does not spread from the noun to the modifier.

We can even see the beginnings of articulated Y₂ hyperbaton in the following passages

(29) μακάρεσσι θεοῖς ἀντικρὺ μάχεσθαι | τοῖς ἄλλοις *Il* 5.819,
         cp. *Il* 5.130
      θεοὺς δ' ὀνόμηνεν ἅπαντας | τοὺς ὑποταρταρίους *Il* 14.279.

In these structures, the demonstrative pronoun plus modifier is a restrictive apposition, adjoined to the nuclear VP. Later, when the demonstrative came to be perceived as an article, the structure was reanalyzed as article plus null head modifier in Y₂ hyperbaton.

Turning to Y₁ modifiers, we find superlatives and 1st or 2nd person pronominal possessives particularly well represented, because they are categories strongly associated with definiteness

(30) τὸν ἄριστον Ἀχαιῶν *Il* 5.414
      οὐ... ὁ κάκιστος Ἀχαιῶν | ...ἀλλ' ὤριστος *Od* 17.415
      τὰ μακρότατ' ἔγχε' *Il* 14.373

(27) The day before (*Il* 21.5). That same day (*Od* 7.326).
(28) From behind (*Il* 11.613). Those left behind (*Od* 11.66). Of the men of that time (*Il* 9.558). With those of Odysseus (*Od* 22.221). Those of Laomedon (*Il* 23.348). The sons of Dolius (*Od* 24.497).
(29) To fight opposite the other blessed gods (*Il* 5.819). He named all the gods under Tartarus (*Il* 14.279).
(30) The best one of the Achaeans (*Il* 5.414). Not the worst of the Achaeans but the best (*Od* 17.415). The longest spears (*Il* 14.373).

(31)   τὸ σὸν γέρας *Il* 1.185
       τὸν ἐμὸν χόλον *Il* 4.42
       τῷ σῷ ἐπὶ μαζῷ *Od* 19.483.

These categories correspondingly have the strongest tendency in the classical language to resist the articulation of the noun in the NDA word order. The antecedents of articulated Y1 hyperbaton are discernible in a set of Homeric appositional structures. In the simplest type, a contrastive demonstrative pronoun by itself is the Y1 element; originally it may have been coindexed with a pronominal object argument, leaving the Y2 noun as a specifying amplification

(32)   τοὺς δ' εὗρ' εἰν ἀγορῇ Δαναοὺς θεράποντας Ἄρηος *Il* 7.382
       τοὺς δὲ κατὰ πρύμνας τε καὶ ἀμφ' ἅλα ἔλσαι Ἀχαιοὺς *Il* 1.409
       τοὺς δ' ἄρ' ὑπὸ τρόμος εἷλεν Ἀχαιούς τε Τρῶάς τε *Il* 5.862.

Compare without a Y2 noun

(33)   τοὺς μὲν λίπεν αὐτοῦ *Il* 4.364.

The Y1 pronoun can be additionally modified by a Y1 adjective

(34)   τοὺς μὲν ἑοὺς ἠρύκακε μώνυχας ἵππους *Il* 5.321
       τὰ μέγιστα παρ' αὐτόθι λείπετ' ἄεθλα *Il* 23.640
       τὴν ὀλοὴν μὲν ὑπεκπροφύγοιμι Χάρυβδιν *Od* 12.113
       ὁ κλυτὸς ἦεν Ἀχιλλεύς *Il* 20.320
       σὺν δ' ὁ θρασὺς εἵπετ' Ὀδυσσεύς *Od* 10.436.

All the examples have some type of narrow focus on the Y1 complex; most are contrastive topics: with the postulated original pronominal argument structure 'those ones which were his own, he held them back, single-hooved horses.' Later, when the demonstrative was perceived as an article, the structure with a restrictive adjective was reanalyzed as a regular Y1 hyperbaton. In the examples with proper names, the modifiers are restrictive relative to the class of persons but descriptive relative to the denotation of the Y2 noun; consequently this type is not open to reanalysis as Y1 hyperbaton in the classical language. Whether, at this later stage, the Y1 complex was interpreted as a null head modifier or as the first segment of a discontinuous noun phrase is a question

(31)   That prize of yours (*Il* 1.185). My anger (*Il* 4.42). At your breast (*Od* 19.483).
(32)   He found the Greeks, attendants of Ares, in the meeting place (*Il* 7.382). To hem in the Achaeans among the ships and next to the sea (*Il* 1.409). Terror came over both the Achaeans and the Trojans (*Il* 5.862).
(33)   He left them there (*Il* 4.364).
(34)   He held back his own single-hooved horses (*Il* 5.321). The biggest prizes remained right there (*Il* 23.640). I might escape destructive Charybdis (*Od* 12.113). The famous Achilles was (*Il* 20.320). The rash Odysseus followed with them (*Od* 10.436).

we shall take up below. Meanwhile, note that in discontinuous Y1 prolepsis, a null head modifier analysis is required by the case difference

(35)   ὁρᾷς τὸν εὐτράπεζον ὡς ἡδὺς βίος Eur Frag 1052.3 Nauck
        ἐπιδεῖξαι... τὴν δικαίαν ἥτις ἐστὶν ἀπολογία Dem 19.203
            (see app. crit.)
        τοὺς σοὺς ἐλέγξω, μῆτερ, εἰ σαφεῖς λόγοι Eur *Phaeth* 62 Diggle
        τῆς γὰρ ἐμῆς εἰ δή τίς ἐστιν σοφία... μάρτυρα Pl *Apol* 20e.

So we have to take seriously the possibility of a parallel analysis for

        τὸν εὐτράπεζον ὁρᾷς βίον
        τὴν δικαίαν ἐπιδεῖξαι ἀπολογίαν.

Similarly, besides genitive Y1 hyperbata like

(36)   τὴν τῆς παρανοίας γράφεσθαι δίκην Pl *Laws* 929d
        τὴν τῆς εἱμαρμένης βίᾳ ἀποστερῶν μοῖραν Pl *Laws* 873c

we find prolepsis

(37)   γνῷ μὲν τὸν Ἥρας οἷός ἐστ᾽ αὐτῷ χόλος *HF* 840.

Indefinites

The distribution of modifiers in indefinite phrases is parallel to that of the definites set out in the preceding section

1. Y2 MODIFIER
    (38)   NA (διέφθειρε πόλιν μεγάλην)
            πρᾶγμα γὰρ... μέγα καὶ λαμπρόν... ἀνείλετο Dem 10.47

            NVA (πόλιν διέφθειρε μεγάλην)
            πρᾶγμα ηὑρηκέναι μέγα καὶ πολλοῦ ἄξιον Lys 12.68

            A (διέφθειρε μεγάλην)
            πῶς ἡμῖν ἡ πόλις οἵα τ᾽ ἔσται πολεμεῖν... ἄλλως τε κἂν πρὸς μεγάλην
            τε καὶ πλουσίαν ἀναγκασθῇ πολεμεῖν Pl *Rep* 422a

---

(35) You see how sweet is a life of luxury (Eur Frag 1052.3). To demonstrate what is the just defence (Dem 19.203). I shall test if your words are true, mother (Eur *Phaeth* 62). Witness of any wisdom I may have (Pl *Apol* 20e).

(36) To bring a charge of insanity against him (Pl *Laws* 929d). Depriving himself by force of his destined lifespan (Pl *Laws* 873c).

(37) He may learn what Hera's anger is like for him (*HF* 840).

(38) He has carried off a great and glorious prize (Dem 10.47). That he had discovered something of great importance and value (Lys 12.68). How will our city be able to fight a war... particularly if it is forced to fight against a great and rich city (Pl *Rep* 422a).

2. Y₁ MODIFIER

(39)   AN (διέφθειρε μεγάλην πόλιν)
πολλὰ καὶ μεγάλα πράγματα Pl *Meno* 99d

AVN (μεγάλην διέφθειρε πόλιν)
τοὺς μὲν πολλὰ καὶ μεγάλα ποιήσαντας ὑμᾶς ἀγαθὰ Dem 26.7

A (μεγάλην διέφθειρε)
μὴ σμικρὸν μόριον ἕν πρὸς μεγάλα καὶ πολλὰ ἀφαιρῶμεν
Pl *Polit* 262a.

This parallelism is not by itself sufficient to motivate a null head modifier interpretation for the continuous (NA, AN) and hyperbaton (NVA, AVN) structures. In the definite type, the adjective originally modified a demonstrative pronoun coindexed with the noun (ἤματι τῷ προτέρῳ), but in the indefinite type it presumably modified the noun directly. This is probably true even for amplificatory Y₂ postmodifiers

(40)   ὁ καλὸν ἄλεισον ἀναιρήσεσθαι ἔμελλε | χρύσεον ἄμφωτον *Od* 22.9

'⟨which was⟩ golden and two-handled,' rather than 'a golden and two-handled one.' At a later stage, the Y₂ definites came under structural pressure to provide a null head for what was now interpreted as a determiner plus adjective sequence. But there would presumably be no similar pressure on the Y₂ indefinites, which might continue to modify the noun directly rather than being independent noun phrases with null syntactic heads and perhaps covert (semantic) indefinite determiners.

On the other hand, the ellipsed type clearly has to be interpreted as a null head modifier. Adjectives in Y₂ hyperbaton that are unequivocally arguments rather than modifiers, most obviously objects of prepositions which unambiguously govern to the right

(41)   λιμένας ἦλθες εἰς εὐηνέμους *Andr* 749

seem to require either a null head or a trace for interpretation. A trace would entail some form of left branch movement or stranding. If we posit a null head modifier in this example with topic Y₁ noun, that would suggest doing the same for the inverse structure with tail Y₂ noun (εἰς εὐηνέμους ἦλθες λιμένας), which in turn could generalize to regular Y₁ hyperbaton without prepositions.

Descriptive Y₂ adjectives

The fact that Y₂ adjectives in Homer can be descriptive seems to lend support to the claim in the preceding section that not all discontinuous Y₂ adjectives

(39) Many great things (Pl *Meno* 99d). Those who have done you many good deeds (Dem 26.7). Let us not contrast one small separate part with many large ones (Pl *Polit* 262a).
(40) He was about to raise a beautiful, gold, two-handled cup (*Od* 22.9).
(41) You came to a harbour sheltered from the wind (*Andr* 749).

are null head modifiers. Because null head modifier phrases are typically restrictive, it is difficult to find satisfactory null head modifier readings for descriptive Y2 adjectives. For count nouns, one would have to posit something like 'the elephant, that huge entity' for definites and 'an elephant, a huge entity' for indefinites; 'a huge one' would presumably be restrictive within the class of elephants rather than within the class of entities. The situation with mass nouns is if anything even less clear. Consider the following examples

(42) πίθοι οἴνοιο παλαιοῦ ἡδυπότοιο *Od* 2.340 (continuous)
κύπελλα οἴνου πινέμεναι μελιηδέος *Il* 4.346
οἶνον ἐκίρνα | ἡδὺν *Od* 10.356

ἐκ πόντου βὰς ἰοειδέος *Od* 5.56
ἐν πόντῳ πάθετ᾽ ἄλγεα ἰχθυόεντι *Od* 10.457.

The wine examples could be restrictive, allowing for different degrees of sweetness, but there is hardly a contrast intended between purple and nonpurple submasses of the sea. So a null head modifier reading would apparently amount to 'that notoriously purple substance' (as contrasted with other substances like the land). A directly adjectival reading seems much more straightforward. Finally, it is worth noting that in the rather rare double hyperbaton, one noun can be mass and the other count

(43) οἶνον ἔχουσ᾽ ἐν χειρὶ μελίφρονα δεξιτερῆφι *Il* 24.284.

It is not clear whether this can be taken as an indication of categorial uniformity for the Y2 modifier phrase.

Universal quantifier

Adnominal πάντες occurs in Homer

(44) ἵνα πάντες Ἀχαιοὶ | ὀφθαλμοῖσιν ἴδωσι *Il* 19.173,

but a pre- or postverbal position is more common. This latter type has an adverbial character comparable to the English floated quantifier (though not necessarily with its distributive meaning)

(45) θεοὶ δ᾽ ὑπὸ πάντες ἄκουον *Il* 8.4
οἳ δὲ τρίτῳ ἤματι πάντες | ἦλθον *Il* 11.707
οὐ... πάντες βασιλεύσομεν ἐνθάδ᾽ Ἀχαιοί *Il* 2.203
οὔ τοι πάντες ἐπαινέομεν θεοὶ ἄλλοι *Il* 4.29.

---

(42) Jars of old sweet wine (*Od* 2.340). To drink cups of honey-sweet wine (*Il* 4.346). Mixed the sweet wine (*Od* 10.356). Coming from the purple sea (*Od* 5.56). You have suffered hardships on the sea teeming with fish (*Od* 10.457).
(43) Holding delicious wine in her right hand (*Il* 24.284).
(44) So that all the Achaeans may see them with their eyes (*Il* 19.173).
(45) All the gods paid attention (*Il* 8.4). On the third day they all came (*Il* 11.707). We Achaeans will not all be kings here (*Il* 2.203). We other gods do not all approve (*Il* 4.29).

Examples like

(46)   οἱ δ᾽ ἄρα πάντες ἀκὴν ἐγένοντο σιωπῇ *Il* 7.398

are less clear. When they have a noun in the Y₂ position, it is probably amplificatory

(47)   οἱ δ᾽ ἄρα πάντες ἐπίαχον υἷες Ἀχαιῶν *Il* 7.403
       οἱ δ᾽ ἄρα πάντες ἐπήνησαν βασιλῆες *Il* 7.344.

This analysis may generalize to Y₁ hyperbata of the type

(48)   τὸν πάντες ἀναστενάχουσιν Ἀχαιοί *Il* 23.211
       ὅθι πάντες ἐπιρρέζεσκον ὁδῖται *Od* 17.211,

going back to an original structure like 'they used to all sacrifice, the travellers,' with a null subject pronominal argument.

In classical prose, the noun is often articulated in Y₁ hyperbaton with the universal quantifier

(49)   ἅπαντες γὰρ ἀπαγορεύουσιν οἱ νόμοι Aesch 3.50
       ταῦτα πάντες ἴσασιν οἱ ἱππεῖς Dem 21.174.

In theory, there are four possible interpretations of such structures: a progressive configurational one 'all the knights know this,' a floated quantifier one 'the knights all know this'; a conservative pronominal argument one, 'they all know this, the knights'; and an appositional null head modifier one, 'all of them know this, the knights.'

It is not apparent that a null head modifier analysis is helpful for these nominative quantifiers at any stage of their development. In contrast to ordinary adjectives, *all* appears in the socalled predicative position, that is it is followed, not preceded, by the article; we do not find

       *οἱ πάντες ἴσασιν ἱππεῖς

with the meaning 'all the knights know' any more than we find

       *οἱ οὗτοι ἴσασιν ἱππεῖς,

nor of course their continuous YP counterparts. As already noted, they probably project their own quantifier and demonstrative phrases

       ₀ₚ[πάντες ₀ₚ[οἱ ἱππεῖς]]
       Dₑₘₚ[οὗτοι ₀ₚ[οἱ ἱππεῖς]].

(46) They all became quiet in silence (*Il* 7.398)..
(47) All the sons of the Achaeans shouted in applause (*Il* 7.403). All the kings approved (*Il* 7.344).
(48) Whom all the Achaeans mourn for aloud (*Il* 23.211). Where all travellers would offer sacrifices (*Od* 17.211).
(49) All the laws forbid (Aesch 3.50). All the knights know this (Dem 21.174).

When a restrictive adjective is used in a definite noun phrase (*the red shirts*), it contributes the information which, given the discourse context, uniquely identifies the set. When a strong quantifier like *all, both* or a partitive is used with a definite noun phrase (*all the shirts, some of the shirts*), it quantifies over an independently established contextually fixed set (whereas in the indefinite *all shirts* the quantifier ranges over whatever entities meet the description of *shirt* in a contextually inferred domain). So in τοίχου τοῦ ἑτέροιο, definiteness is attracted to the restrictive phrase, whence the null head modifier structure. In the case of πάντες, there is no restrictive phrase for definiteness to migrate to. Perhaps the structures start out as 'the knights in their entirety' and 'knights, the richest ones,' respectively. However, when quantification or deixis is applied to a subset, definiteness is attracted to the adjective and the universal quantifier or demonstrative can appear to the right of the article in the surface string

(50)   τοῖς ἄλλοις ἅπασιν ἀνθρώποις Din 1.106
        τοῦ κοινοῦ τούτου βίου Pl *Phil* 22d.

Since the quantification and the deixis are applied to the modifier rather than to the noun ('all the others,' not 'all the men'), the original structure may have been [[τοῖς ἄλλοις] ἅπασιν] [ἀνθρώποις] 'men, all those other.'

Restrictive adjectives and demonstratives do not permit a pronominal head

        *τοὺς μεγίστους αὐτούς
        *τούτους αὐτούς

but the universal quantifier, like predicative adjectives, is external to the determiner phrase and less strictly adnominal in character and consequently permits a pronominal

(51)   πάντας ἀπεκτόνεσαν αὐτούς Xen *Hell* 7.2.4
        πάντας αὐτοὺς ἀποθανεῖν Dem 20.42 (subject)
        κατάστησον αὐτὰς τελευταίας Xen *Cyr* 6.3.30.

Predicative adjectives

Modifiers in hyperbaton can be ordinary depictive secondary predicates. This type occurs in Homer

(52)   αἴ κε νέκυν περ Ἀχιλλῆϊ προφέρωμεν | γυμνόν *Il* 17.121
        νέκυος δὲ δὴ ἀμφιμάχονται | γυμνοῦ *Il* 18.20
        γαστέρα τύψε μέσην *Il* 4.531
        μέσῳ ἐνὶ οἴνοπι πόντῳ *Od* 5.132.

(50) To all other men (Din 1.106). Of this combined type of life (Pl *Phil* 22d).
(51) They had killed them all (Xen *Hell* 7.2.4). That they should all die (Dem 20.42). Place them at the rear (Xen *Cyr* 6.3.30).
(52) If we can carry his body to Achilles without armour (*Il* 17.121). They are fighting around his corpse stripped of its armour (*Il* 18.20). He struck him in the middle of the belly (*Il* 4.531). In the middle of the wine-dark sea (*Od* 5.132).

A null head modifier interpretation is impossible here. γυμνόν does not mean 'a/the stripped one' but 'being stripped.' If μέσος were not predicative and meant 'the middle one,' the implication would be that there were three stomachs and three seas; this seems to exclude even 'while being a stripped one' for γυμνόν. Predicative Y₁ hyperbaton in prose has the article preceding the noun rather than preceding the adjective. This conforms to the corresponding continuous structures and confirms the distinction between the two types of Y₁ hyperbaton

(53)   γλυκὺν γεύσας τὸν αἰῶνα Her 7.46
       μετεώρους ἐξεκόμισαν τὰς ἁμάξας Xen *An* 1.5.8
       διὰ πολεμίας πορεύσονται τῆς χώρας Xen *An* 5.4.2
       ἀνωμότοις πιστεύσαντας τοῖς μαρτυροῦσι Antiph 5.12
       μισθωτοῖς χρώμεθα τοῖς στρατοπέδοις Isoc *Pax* 47
       ἃ μὲν ἐκ κοινῶν ἐλῃτούργεις τῶν χρημάτων Dem 36.39.

Again, null head modifier interpretation is highly improbable in these examples, and was not be expected for secondary predicates of these types anyway. We do not say 'He ate the steak a raw one' (depictive) or 'He hammered the nail a flat one' (resultative) in English either, even though there is nothing wrong with temporary qualities as null or pronominal head modifiers (*buy a raw one*). An example like the following indicates that different syntactic positions are involved

(54)   τὸ τῶν συμμάχων ἄκυρον πεποιηκὼς δόγμα Aesch 2.62.

Note that in the examples cited the secondary predicate adjective is consistently in immediately preverbal position.

Partitives

For partitive genitive hyperbaton with adjective Y₁, a null head modifier analysis is natural. The quantifier is taken to be a noun phrase in all of the following

(55)   πολλοὶ ἀπέθανον Xen *Hell* 4.8.29
       πολλοὶ αὐτῶν ἀπέθανον Xen *Hell* 5.2.42
       πολλοὶ ἀπέθανον αὐτῶν Thuc 3.108.3
       πολλοὶ ἐπείσθησαν τῶν μαρτύρων Lyc 20

(53) Having given us a taste of the sweetness of life (Her 7.46). They lifted the wagons clear of the mud (Xen *An* 1.5.8). Whether they would be marching through the country as a hostile one (Xen *An* 5.4.2). Trusting the witnesses without their having taken the oath (Antiph 5.12). Use armies on hire (Isoc *Pax* 47). The public services you performed out of funds held in common (Dem 36.39).

(54) Having made void the decree of the allies (Aesch 2.62).

(55) Many died (Xen *Hell* 4.8.29). Many of them were killed (Xen *Hell* 5.2.42). Many of them were killed (Thuc 3.108.3). Many witnesses are typically persuaded (Lyc 20).

(56)   πολλοὺς ἔχων τῶν ἐπιτηδείων Lys 3.38

       ἄλλους πολλοὺς σεσώκατε τῶν πολιτῶν Hyper 4.38

       οἱ δὲ πολλοὶ... κακοὶ γίγνονται τῶν δυναστῶν Pl *Gorg* 526b.

Note also the parallel null head modifier in the second clause of the following example

(57)   πολλὰ μὲν ἔσωσε τῶν χρημάτων τοῖσι Πέρσῃσι, πολλὰ δὲ καὶ αὐτὸς

       περιεβάλετο Her 8.8.

Corresponding English partitives like *many of the soldiers* are also commonly thought to involve a null head modifier (Jackendoff 1977; Olsen 1987; Lobeck 1995).

COMPLEX PREDICATE THEORY

Given the wide use of null head modifiers in general and the fact that they are required for prolepsis, a construction related to hyperbaton, there are obvious advantages to the null head modifier theory of hyperbaton. On the downside, it raises problems of analysis that do not arise for the discontinuous theory. If hyperbaton is simply syntactically discontinuous, the categories of the phrase and their structural relation to each other are the same as they would be in the continuous version, and the phrase is presumably reconstructed into a single continuous noun phrase at some level of semantic interpretation. For the null head modifier theory, the situation is quite different. The insertion of the null head means that we no longer have a single discontinuous phrase, but in one sense or another two separate phrases. We no longer need a semantic operation to recombine the fragments of a single phrase (although the option remains of recombining the two separate phrases into a complex phrase), but we have to come up with a satisfactory account for why there are now two separate noun phrases implementing a single grammatical function. For instance, in

(58)   τὰς ἰδίας κατεσκευάκασιν οἰκίας Dem 23.208

the direct object should on the face of it be either [τὰς ἰδίας Ø] or [οἰκίας] but not both. In what follows, we will consider how this sort of structure could be syntactically licensed. This is a technically more challenging task than drawing a line to join two fragments of a discontinuous constituent, but there are two reasons for making the effort. First, the null head modifier theory helps to integrate hyperbaton coherently into the historical development of Greek syntax, while the discontinuous theory treats it in purely synchronic terms as some-

(56) Having with me many of my friends (Lys 3.38). You have saved many others of the citizens (Hyper 4.38). The majority of powerful men become evil (Pl *Gorg* 526b).

(57) He saved many precious objects for the Persians and appropriated many for himself too (Her 8.8).

(58) They have built their private homes (Dem 23.208).

thing of a freak structure. Secondly, the null head modifier theory seeks to provide a semantic-pragmatic rationale for the apparent discontinuity, and thereby a closer fit between the syntax and the compositional semantics. The advantage of this can be illustrated by another discontinuous structure, namely quantification at a distance in French (Doetjes 1994)

> Max a beaucoup vendu de livres 'Max sold many books'
> Max a beaucoup bu de lait 'Max drank a lot of milk.'

The category of *beaucoup* is disputed. In the first example, which involves a count noun, quantification is not over books, but over events of bookselling. Since the scope of the quantifier reflects its syntactic position, the syntactic discontinuity is not neutralized when the structure is semantically interpreted.

As already noted, the phenomenon of determiner spreading is plausibly traced back to a paratactic determiner phrase consisting of two determiner phrases in apposition, one with the noun and one with a null head modifier, as illustrated in Figure 6.6. The noun can be thought of as binding the null head. In an appositional structure, one determiner phrase is predicated of the other; it is natural to assume that the one containing the adjective is predicated of the one containing the noun rather than vice versa. Y2 hyperbaton with definites is simply a discontinuous version of this structure

(59)   τὰ πλοῖα παραπέμψαι τὰ σιτηγὰ Dem 50.20
        ὑπὸ τῶν ἐχθρῶν πεισθεὶς τῶν ἐμῶν Lys 7.39 (v.l.)
        οἱ μὲν τὰ ὑποδήματα ἐργαζόμενοι τὰ παλαιὰ Pl *Meno* 91d
        τοῖς νόμοις χρῆσθαι τοῖς ὑμετέροις Dem 24.210;

and similarly for Y2 genitives

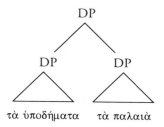

Figure 6.6
Null head modifier analysis of definite Y2 adjective
τὰ ὑποδήματα τὰ παλαιὰ

(59) To provide a convoy for the grain ships (Dem 50.20). Having been persuaded by my enemies (Lys 7.39). Those who mend old shoes (Pl *Meno* 91d). To adopt your laws (Dem 24.210).

(60) τὰς ἐπιστολὰς τὰς τοῦ Φιλίππου Dem 19.51 (continuous)

τὰς δ᾽ ἐπιστολὰς ὑμῖν ἀναγνώσομαι τὰς τοῦ Φιλίππου Dem 19.187.

From a historical point of view, the two determiner phrases have not been split; rather they failed to coalesce into a contiguous structure; the null head modifier is adjoined to the nuclear verb phrase, so that the predication applies at a distance across the superordinate head. This is clear from the Homeric antecedents of Y2 hyperbaton, which we cite again at this point.

(61) μακάρεσσι θεοῖς ἀντικρὺ μάχεσθαι | τοῖς ἄλλοις *Il* 5.819

θεοὺς δ᾽ ὀνόμηνεν ἅπαντας | τοὺς ὑποταρταρίους *Il* 14.279.

The null head modifier theory inserts a null head after the adjective also in Y1 hyperbaton

τας ἰδίας Ø κατεσκευάκασιν οἰκίας.

This immediately creates a problem that does not arise with the discontinuous theory. If Y1 hyperbaton is interpreted as involving discontinuity of the noun phrase, then it would be reasonable to assume that definiteness continues to be projected throughout the YXY structure across the intervening superordinate head X. For instance, in

(62) τοῖς τοὺς γυμνικοὺς νικῶσιν ἀγῶνας Dem 20.141

ἀγῶνας is taken to be definite because definiteness is projected from the determiner τοὺς. However, for null head modifier theories, the null head would presumably be a barrier to the projection of definiteness. This means that, while a simple appositional theory with two definite noun phrases would in principle be available for the null head modifier analysis of Y2 hyperbaton, it will not work for Y1 hyperbaton. ἀγῶνας is not definite since it has no article and definiteness is not projected from the determiner. The difference between ordinary phrasal apposition and Y1 hyperbaton is clearly illustrated by the following example of a regular apposition

(63) τὸν μιαρὸν καὶ ἀναιδῆ φυλάξομεν ἀμφότεροι τὸν Φιλοκράτην
Dem 19.13;

note that the determiner is repeated and the Y1 adjectives are descriptive (and not restrictive as they would be in Y1 hyperbaton). This seems to be a modernized version of the old Homeric appositional structure already discussed (τὴν ὀλοὴν ὑπεκπροφύγοιμι Χάρυβδιν). A closer analogue to Y1 hyperbaton might

(60) Philip's letters (Dem 19.51). I will read you Philip's letters (Dem 19.187).

(61) To fight opposite the other blessed gods (*Il* 5.819). He named all the gods under Tartarus (*Il* 14.279).

(62) To those who win in the athletic games (Dem 20.141).

(63) That we should both keep tabs on that unprincipled bastard, Philocrates (Dem 19.13).

be the integrated type of apposition found with proper names, particularly geographic ones

(64)   τὸν Ζαπάταν ποταμόν Xen *An* 2.5.1
        τὸν Κέρβερον κύνα Xen *An* 6.2.2.

But this type is very resistant to discontinuity in the classical language, although the constraint is not unequivocally syntactic; in order to be discontinuous in prose, the apposition would presumably require a pragmatic context in which a second river or dog is excluded by strong focus.

Our provisional conclusion is that, for the hull head modifier theory, Y_1 hyperbaton is a syntactic apposition but not an ordinary one: there must be some special factor that licenses the bare noun for the Y_2 element. To get a better idea what that factor might be, we shall need to look more closely at the range of interpretations available for noun phrases. This rather difficult subject has been investigated from three different, and only partially integrated, perspectives: structural-syntactic (Abney 1987; Stowell 1989, 1991; Longobardi 1994); functional-typological (Timberlake 1975; Givon 1981; Hopper & Thompson 1980, 1984); and typetheoretic-semantic (Partee 1987; Diesing 1992; de Hoop 1996; Ramchand 1997; McNally 1997; van Geenhoven 1998). The last approach distinguishes broadly speaking three basic readings for noun phrases. Dispensing with the formalism of category to type mapping, we shall simply call them generalized quantifier, referential and predicate

> Every student came early
> That student came early
> He is a student.

Problems arise both because it is not always clear to which class particular uses are to be attributed and because there is not necessarily a one-to-one mapping between the various readings and the morphosyntactic categories found in noun phrases.

Nonreferential noun phrases

By themselves, verbs and nouns are rather "conceptual" entities. They are disconnected from the discourse and from actual world situations that are the subject matter of the discourse. Just as it is a function of tense auxiliaries to relate the verb to the time of the discourse, so it is a basic function of determiners to relate common nouns to the referents of the discourse either by identifying them or by quantifying over them. A determiner can be seen as a sort of operator that takes as its input a simple common noun (which is just a predicate) and combines with it to output an argument noun phrase. Various terminology is used to capture this distinction. The common count noun is said to be a type or a kindlike expression, while the corresponding noun phrase is said

(64)   The river Zapatas (Xen *An* 2.5.1). The dog Cerberus (Xen *An* 6.2.2).

to be an object or token or the instantiation of a kind, and to be individuated in the discourse. There is often a strong tendency to generalize the use of determiners as a syntactic rule, which distorts the correlations. Nevertheless, in many languages there are situations in which determiners are optionally or obligatorily absent, and these sometimes correspond to nonreferential uses of nouns. The most familiar example is that of predicate descriptions involving jobs or professions in languages like German and Italian

> Hans ist Zahnarzt
> Hans ist ein Zahnarzt
> 'Hans is a dentist'
>
> Giovanni è dentista
> Giovanni è un dentista
> 'Giovanni is a dentist.'

This use of the unarticulated noun is not referential. Perhaps the bare noun is used for the type and the articulated noun for a member, token or instantiation of the type. Significantly from our perspective when an evaluative modifier is added, the article becomes obligatory

> Hans ist ein guter Zahnarzt
> Giovanni è un bravo dentista
> 'Hans/Giovanni is a good dentist.'

But we are still dealing with a property, not a referent

> A. A good dentist came in.   B. Who/*What did you say came in?
> A. Hans is a good dentist.   B. What/*Who did you say Hans is?

The following examples are plausibly analyzed as bare primary and secondary predicate nouns in Greek

> (65) νὺξ ἡ ἡμέρη ἐγένετο Her 1.103
>   ὁ Ζεὺς ταμίας ἐστὶν Isoc *Bus* 13
>   ἑαυτὸν δεσπότην πεποίηκεν Xen *Cyr* 1.3.18
>   ἡρέθη κατάσκοπος Thuc 4.27.3
>   τὸν Γωβρύαν σύνδειπνον παρέλαβεν Xen *Cyr* 5.2.14.

Even when nouns are not used as predicates but function as syntactic arguments, they can have nonreferential readings. Sometimes nonreferential uses are not distinguished morphosyntactically from referential uses. When they are, it is usually the case that the nonreferential use lacks some of the coding normally found with regular determiner phrases; in particular, either the article or some inflection or both may be missing. In English, object bare plurals are consistently associated with narrow scope and a nonreferential reading: *write*

(65) The day became night (Her 1.103). Zeus is the dispenser (Isoc *Bus* 13). He has made himself master (Xen *Cyr* 1.3.18). He was chosen inspector (Thuc 4.27.3). He invited Gobryas along as his dinner companion (Xen *Cyr* 5.2.14).

articles, teach students, buy houses in town. We also find bare unarticulated nouns in prepositional phrases indicating location of institutions or instruments, particularly means of transportation

to/at university	to/at lunch
to/in gaol	to/in hospital
by train	by boat.

There is usually a connotation of characteristic function: if you are *in hospital*, you are a patient rather than someone who has been hired to paint the walls. These prepositional phrases do not involve individuated discourse referents, either definite or indefinite. Similar prepositional phrases are found in Greek, although given the absence of an indefinite article the bare noun does not unequivocally encode a nonspecific reading

(66)   ἐπὶ δεῖπνον Xen *Mem* 1.3.6
       ἀπὸ ἵππου Xen *An* 1.2.7
       ἐπὶ μάχην Xen *An* 1.4.12.

The nonreferentiality in examples of this type is particularly evident in coordination with ellipsis

Jack is at church, and so is Angus
Jack jumped ship, and so did Angus.

Jack and Angus can be at different churches and jump different ships. But if we introduce a definite (or specific indefinite) article (*at the church, off the ship*), then only a single church and a single ship can be involved.

Nonreferential readings also occur with articulated noun phrases. English noun phrases with the indefinite article are particularly difficult to evaluate. Consider the following examples

Jack wants to buy a house
Jack wants to buy a house next to the refinery.

The verb *wants* encourages an intensional, nonspecific reading, in which *a house* has narrow scope relative to *wants*. This reading is favoured in the first example, one possible paraphrase for which is as follows: 'for every world *w* such that *w* is compatible with what Jack wants (Jack's wants are satisfied in *w*), Jack buys a house in *w*' (Heim 1982). In the second example, in most real world situations, the descriptive richness of the noun phrase would induce an extensional, specific reading in which *a house* has broad scope relative to *wants* and is in some sense a referring expression: 'There is a particular house that is next to the refinery and Jack wants to buy it.' The concept of specificity is notoriously difficult to define, both in general and as it relates to individual constructions in different languages (Enç 1991). What the speaker intends

(66) To dinner (Xen *Mem* 1.3.6). On horseback (Xen *An* 1.2.7). To battle (Xen *An* 1.2.7). To battle (Xen *An* 1.4.12).

may not be the same as what the listener understands him to mean, unless specific and nonspecific uses are differently encoded, for instance by the use of different cases. Consider this Spanish example (Hopper et al. cit.)

> Busco (a) un empleado que habla inglés
> 'I am looking for an employee who speaks English.'

If the speaker is looking for a specific employee, *a* is required; if he is looking for any old employee, *a* is omitted. If *a* is used, the discourse can continue with a sentence like 'His name is Pablo.' If *a* is not used, it can continue with a sentence like 'Where can I find one?'. But not vice versa. Note also that the intensional reading can answer the question 'What are you looking for?', while the extensional reading answers the question 'Who are you looking for?'.

Nonspecific readings are not limited to the intensional contexts illustrated in the preceding paragraph. Particularly in the case of routinized activities like *buy a beer, write an article*, the indefinite is unlikely to be treated by the speaker as an individuated entity playing a participant role in the situation. This is even the case with the socalled weak reading of certain definite noun phrases

> He washed the dishes
> He watched the telly
> He turned on the light.

Despite the presence of the definite article, the noun phrases are low on referentiality. The sentences are not designed to answer the implicit questions 'What did he wash/watch/turn on?' nor the implicit questions 'What did he do to the dishes/telly/light?'. Rather, they are one type of answer to the question 'What did he do?'. The interpretations with narrow scope weak focus on the verb or on the object are infelicitous because the object is not a separate discourse referent. The whole verb phrase again amounts to a single recognizable activity. The difference between *wash dishes* and *wash the dishes* lies more in the latter being situation specific than in it having a discourse referential object. What is syntactically a transitive verb plus object is semantically comparable to a simple intransitive verb. The syntactic object is interpreted as a sort of predicate modifier which serves to narrow the range of the activity in question (here narrowing *washing* to something closer to *dishwashing*) and not to specify the discourse referent that bears the patient or theme role. So washing the dishes is something you do, washing the teapots is, under normal circumstances, something you do to the teapots.

Certain contexts have the potential to complicate or interfere with these weak readings. One is coordination with an individuated argument

> He washed the dishes and the crystal vase.

Another is anaphora. The status of the following English examples is not quite clear but seems to involve a contextual inference

The next thing he did was lodge a complaint. It was long and
   querulous.
Prof. Jones wrote glyconics. His wife typed them.
He washed the dishes. They were piled up in the sink.

Bare noun prepositional phrases present a similar problem

The bride's mother drove to church and decorated it with flowers.

In languages like Mohawk, Southern Tiwa and West Greenlandic (Sadock
1991; Baker 1996; van Geenhoven 1998) an incorporated noun can serve as
an antecedent for anaphora. On the other hand, in Persian, the marker *ye* is
used with specific indefinites and omitted with nonspecific ones; anaphora is
not possible when *ye* is omitted (Hopper et al. cit.). Another factor that interferes with nonreferential readings is modification. If we add a restrictive modifier (always a matter of interest to us), the weak reading again becomes more
difficult in English, because the richer description is more specific

He washed the blue dishes
He hired a tall lawyer.

In Hindi, some nonreferential nouns can join with verbs to form a type of
complex predicate which has its own particular syntactic properties, but this
does not happen when the noun is modified (Mohanan 1997). The adjective
implies a contrast between those entities at which the verbal activity is directed
and those at which it is not. When the adjective is rather vacuous or prototypical, it ceases to be fully restrictive, and the weak reading seems to reappear
in English with both definites and indefinites

wash the dirty dishes
hire a good lawyer.

Projection of definiteness

With this sketch of noun phrase readings in hand, we are in a position to look
at the projection of definiteness in modified noun phrases. This concept is
familiar from the behaviour of possessives. Consider complex noun phrases
like

the daughter of a wellknown tenor
a daughter of the wellknown tenor.

In the first example, the daughter is definite relative to the tenor and so has the
definite article, and the tenor is indefinite relative to the context and so has the
indefinite article. The whole noun phrase is indefinite relative to the context
because the tenor is not unambiguously identified; there is a different daughter
for every different person to whom the indefinite expression is assigned. In the
second example, the tenor is uniquely identifiable in the discourse context but
the daughter is not definite relative to the tenor: he has more than one daugh-

ter. In these complex noun phrases, each simple noun phrase contributes its own definiteness component. Now something interesting happens when we use the Saxon genitive and put the possessive phrase in the determiner position

> a wellknown tenor's daughter
> the wellknown tenor's daughter.

We keep the definiteness distinction for the tenor but we seem to lose it for the daughter (Woisetschlaeger 1983): only definite readings are fully felicitous. Definiteness is projected from the possessive determiner phrase through the whole noun phrase. There is something awkward about

> The/A wellknown tenor's daughter stole her sister's credit card.

In a slightly different system, definiteness or indefiniteness is projected from the article of the possessor to the whole phrase. This principle is discernible in the tightly knit Semitic construct state construction when there is an additional modifier (Fassi Fehri 1989; Ritter 1991). The construct state construction can be used for 'the house of the man' or 'a house of a man,' but not for 'a house of the man' nor for 'the house of a man.' When the possessed is modified by an adjective ('large house'), the adjective has the definite or indefinite article depending on the definiteness of the possessor.

What we want to suggest is that under certain conditions in Greek we have the converse of what happens to the tenor's daughter. When the complex noun phrase *the/a daughter of the tenor* is recast as the simple noun phrase *the tenor's daughter*, the possessive ends up in a specifier position from which definiteness is projected throughout the phrase. When a Greek modifier is a null head modifier, it becomes a separate noun phrase from the noun, and definiteness is no longer projected from one to the other. Let us review the data.

In classical Greek, there is normally a single value for definiteness in adjectivally modified noun phrases: for Y2 adjectives, the determiner is doubled and for Y1 adjectives definiteness is projected from the determiner through the whole phrase

> (67)   τὸν δὲ πατέρα τὸν ἐμὸν Andoc 1.41
>   τὸν ἐμὸν πατέρα Antiph 1.15
>   οἱ ἄγριοι οἶες καὶ οἱ ὄνοι οἱ ἄγριοι Xen *Cyr* 1.4.7 (v.l.).

However, certain conditions license the use of an unarticulated noun with an articulated adjective. This type represents a survival of the earlier structure of this type

> (68)   τοίχου τοῦ ἑτέροιο *Il* 9.219.

---

(67) My father (Andoc 1.41). My father (Antiph 1.15). Wild sheep and wild donkeys (Xen *Cyr* 1.4.7).
(68) The other wall (*Il* 9.219).

Its frequency varies in different authors depending on the degree of evolution of their language (Brunel 1964:71). The conditions on the noun are pairing or government by a preposition, or any other factor that would encourage omission of the article, such as unique reference (θάλασσα, ἀγορά, βασιλεύς). The conditions on the adjective are that it is mostly a first or second person possessive pronoun or a superlative. In many cases, both the noun and the adjective conform to these conditions

(69) ἐκ πέτρης τῆς αὐτῆς Her 4.90
     κατὰ γνώμας τὰς ἡμετέρας Her 4.53, 9.71
     ἀπὸ παρασκευῆς τῆς ἐμῆς Lys 21.10
     εἰς κινδύνους τοὺς ἐσχάτους Dem 59.1

     ἔργῳ τῷ αἰσχίστῳ οὔνομα τὸ κάλλιστον ἔθευ Her 3.155
     χώραν τὴν αὐτὴν... καὶ γυναιξὶ ταῖς αὐταῖς Xen Cyr 4.4.10
     τί γὰρ διαφέρει... ἄνθρωπος ἀκρατὴς θηρίου τοῦ ἀμαθεστάτου
       Xen Mem 4.5.11.

The conditions on the noun have already been discussed in their application to unmodified nouns. The conditions on the adjective involve strong uniqueness. The two persons involved in the utterance situation, the interlocutors, are maximally identifiable and unambiguous, and the possessive personal pronoun restricts possible referents to just that one possessed by the interlocutor in question. Superlatives in -est, along with ordinals and ὁ αὐτός 'the same' (Xenophon Cyr 4, Herodotus 4 cit.), uniquely restrict reference by picking out a single member of a set; definiteness is associated with the unique individual selected and not with the set in general. In short, the NDA structure that concerns us here involves a nonreferential noun plus adjective, a more integrated version of 'at university, the best one,' 'he was eating apples, the biggest ones.' The indefinite noun can even have a cardinality attribute

(70) εἰς δώδεκα ναῦς τὰς ἄριστα πλεούσας Xen Hell 5.1.27

'on board ships twelve in number that were the fastest sailing ones.' Definiteness is not spread consistently throughout the phrase, but applies only to the modifier. This association of definiteness with the adjective in restrictively modified noun phrases has a morphological manifestation in the definite adjective declension of languages like Lithuanian (Senn 1966)

     gēras vaĩkas 'a good child'
     geràsis vaĩkas 'the good child'

(69) Out of the same rock (Her 4.90). In our opinion (Her 4.53). By my arrangement (Lys 21.10). Into extreme danger (Dem 59.1). You have given the noblest name to the most disgraceful deed (Her 3.155). The same land... and the same wives (Xen Cyr 4.4.10). What difference is there between a man with no selfcontrol and the humblest animal? (Xen Mem 4.5.11).
(70) On his twelve best-sailing ships (Xen Hell 5.1.27).

the definite form is used in null head modifier structures like

> visì geríeji 'all good people.'

It is also worth noting that the scope of the determiner in relative clauses was the subject of debate in early generative times: [Det N] RC, Det [N RC] and [Det RC] N were the options. It was pointed out (Partee 1973) that the first required the relative clause to be descriptive and the last (which has the structure we are interested in for adjectives) seemed to leave the noun hanging in limbo.

The NDA structure that we discussed in the preceding section sometimes appears in Y2 hyperbaton (NVDA)

(71)   εἰς μνήμην εἶναι τὴν ἐμὴν Aesch 2.180
       ἐπ᾽ εὐνοίᾳ φασὶ τῇ ὑμετέρᾳ Lys 22.13
       εὐνοίᾳ γὰρ ἐρῶ τῇ σῇ Pl *Gorg* 486a
       εἵματά τε ἐφόρεον τὰ κάλλιστα Her 3.27
       σκεύεσι χρῆσθαι τοῖς ἐμοῖς Dem 27.5
       φύσιν ἔχοντες τὴν ἄλλην ὁμοίην τοῖσι ἄλλοισι ἀνθρώποισι
       Her 3.116.

The prepositional examples are of the usual nonreferential type. The verbal objects are open to a weak reading, leaving the articulated adjective as the real argument. This interpretation is pretty much required for the two Herodotus examples: 'they wore as clothes their best ones.' A strong narrow topic reading would give 'As for clothes, they wore their best ones,' which is inappropriate in the context. An individuated argument reading (with weak focus plus amplificatory adjective) would give 'They wore clothes (rather than something else), and their best ones at that,' which is even less appropriate. Even some Y2 hyperbata in which both Y elements are articulated

(72)   τοῖς νόμοις χρῆσθαι τοῖς ὑμετέροις Dem 24.210

are open to the same pragmatic interpretation.

Let us briefly recapitulate. The paratactic null head modifier structure [[DP] [DP]] is derived from an earlier structure in which only the modifier was articulated [[NP] [DP]]. This structure reflects the fact that the information producing definiteness is contributed by the restriction. It survives under certain conditions in classical Greek in both continuous and discontinuous form. In these structures, definiteness is not projected through the whole structure, and the unarticulated noun tends to have a nonreferential interpretation.

(71) To the best of my recollection (Aesch 2.180). They say that it was out of consideration for you that... (Lys 22.13). I shall speak with goodwill towards you (Pl *Gorg* 486a). They put on their best clothes (Her 3.27). To use my furniture (Dem 27.5). Having the rest of their nature like other men (Her 3.116).
(72) To adopt your laws (Dem 24.210).

In chapter 2, we noted that, particularly in spontaneous conversation, nouns modified by a restrictive adjective tend to represent information already established in the discourse, while the adjective attracts focus (whether weak or strong). Chapter 2 was devoted to pragmatic structure, and our aim there was to establish the pragmatic status of Y_2 nouns and to clarify its relationship to that of Y_2 nouns in continuous modified YPs. However, the effects of modification are not limited to pragmatics; we are now in a position to complete the picture by pointing out that the potential effects of modification on the status of the noun extend to the semantics: the adjective also attracts definiteness, in fact probably referentiality in general, leaving the noun open to a weak, nonreferential reading. As we shall see, both the typical pragmatic and the typical semantic properties of the Y elements become stronger and more consistent in Y_1 hyperbaton.

Y_1 hyperbaton

As already noted, the articulated modifier phrase can appear to the left of the noun too in Homer

(73)   τὸν ἐμὸν χόλον *Il* 4.42
        τὰ μακρότατ' ἔγχε' ἑλόντες *Il* 14.373.

Although both this Y_1 modifier type and the Y_2 modifier type analyzed in the previous section can coalesce into a single complex noun phrase, this result is not optimal from the point of view of the complexity constraint. One might rather expect [τὰ μακρότατ'] [ἔγχε' ἑλόντες] 'taking spears, those which are the longest.' This analysis is supported by the fact that the phrase is parallel to the preceding ἀσπίδες ὅσσαι ἄρισται (*Il* 14.371), which is a quantifying relative clause. There is direct evidence that the latter phrasing occurred even in historical Greek. In the *Lex Opuntiorum*, the use of punctuation with articulated modifiers is variable, but the following punctuations clearly indicate that the noun can be phrased with the verb in both Y_2 and Y_1 structures, even when they are continuous

    : διομοσαι hορϙον : τον νομιον : *Locr* 45
    τοις Ναυπακτιοις : νομιοις χρεσται : *Locr* 19 (cp. perhaps 25).

Both hορϙον and νομιοις can be interpreted as nonreferential: 'to swear as an oath the prescribed one,' and 'to use as laws the NAUPACTIAN ones.' In the Y_1 example, τοις Ναυπακτιοις has strong contrastive focus. It is quite easy to produce canonical Y_1 hyperbaton from both examples by changing the pragmatics and applying simple movements. Making τον νομιον a strong focus and fronting it gives

    : τον νομιον : διομοσαι hορϙον :

(73) My anger (*Il* 4.42). Taking the longest spears (*Il* 14.373).

and making νομιοις a clear tail and inverting the order inside the V′ gives

: τοις Ναυπακτιοις : χρεσται νομιοις :.

In order to get the first example in a derivational framework, one starts with the attested structure (: διομοσαι hορϙον : τον νομιον :) and then moves τον νομιον so that, instead of stopping to the left of the noun hορϙον, it lands to the left of the verb. This is illustrated for two real Y₁ hyperbata in Figure 6.7, which maintains the integrity of the X′ provisionally posited in earlier chapters. But with a null head Y₁ the tree can be reanalyzed into a more Y₂-like structure with the noun attached outside the core X′ as phrase level tail material.

We have already given some examples illustrating the Homeric appositional antecedents of Y₁ hyperbaton with definites. Here are a few more; as before, they all have a clear contrastive Y₁ focus

(74)   δείδω μὴ τὸ χθιζὸν ἀποστήσωνται Ἀχαιοὶ | χρεῖος *Il* 13.745 (v.l.)
       τοὺς ἄλλους κελόμην ἐρίηρας ἑταίρους *Od* 9.100
       ὁ δ᾽ ἕβδομος ἑστήκει μείς *Il* 19.117
       αἱ Φηρητιάδαο ποδώκεες ἔκφερον ἵπποι *Il* 23.376 (v.l.) (genitive Y₁).

In a pronominal argument framework, both the Y₁ null head modifier and the Y₂ noun are coindexed with a pronominal argument inside the nuclear verb phrase: 'the others, I ordered them, trusty comrades.' The problem we encoun-

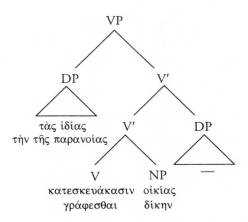

Figure 6.7
Derivational analysis of Y₁ hyperbaton with null head modifier
τὰς ἰδίας κατεσκευάκασιν οἰκίας Dem 23.208
τὴν τῆς παρανοίας γράφεσθαι δίκην Pl *Laws* 929d

(74) I am afraid that the Achaeans will pay back in full the debt of yesterday (*Il* 13.745). I ordered my other faithful comrades (*Od* 9.100). The seventh month had come (*Il* 19.117). The swift-footed mares of Eumelus shot ahead (*Il* 23.376).

ter at a later period of deciding between "movement" to the left (fronting) and "movement" to the right (extraposition) does not arise at this stage, since by definition a YXY order entails both left and right adjuncts. When the pronominal argument is lost, the Y elements are presumably reanalyzed as some form of appositional structure in which the noun specifies the null head. From a diachronic perspective, the question of fronting versus extraposition amounts to deciding whether the nuclear clause is expanded to the left or to the right. Classical prose Y1 hyperbaton seems to maintain an appositional structure in the overt syntax; but semantically the bare noun is interpreted as a predicate modifier. According to some theories, this would be represented by moving the noun so that it forms a complex predicate with the verb at logical form: $[[\kappa\alpha\tau\epsilon\sigma\kappa\epsilon\upsilon\dot\alpha\kappa\alpha\sigma\iota\nu]_V [\text{οἰκίας}]_N]_{V^0}$.

For the complex predicate theory, definiteness is not projected from the determiner; in fact, the Y2 noun is not even referential. For it to be definite, one needs to use genitive hyperbaton, not regular Y1 hyperbaton, irrespective of whether Y1 is itself definite or not. Compare the following sets of examples

(75)   τὴν πλείστην εἰλήφασιν νομοθεσίαν Pl *Laws* 768d
       πρὶν τὰς πλείστας οἰκισθῆναι τῶν Ἑλληνίδων πόλεων Isoc *Paneg* 37
       τὰ πλεῖστα φαίνεται τῶν προειρημένων διαπραξάμενος Isoc *Evag* 37

       πλείστους δὲ τιθέμενοι νόμους Isoc *Pax* 50
       πλείστους διαφθεῖραι τῶν πολιτῶν ibid.

In the *Pax* 50 passage, νόμους is part of a complex predicate ('lawmaking'), while τῶν πολιτῶν is an independent partitive genitive phrase ('of the citizens').

This type of semantic predicate modifier is not quite the same as a regular nominal secondary predicate, although they are both bare nouns. The two types can be compared in clauses with the verb χρῆσθαι. In the regular type

(76)   ταῖς τέχναις ταύταις παραπετάσμασιν ἐχρήσαντο Pl *Prot* 316e

the meaning is to use an entity x for the function normally associated with a different entity y. The Y1 hyperbaton construction involves a slightly different meaning: roughly to use as y a subset of y. When the secondary predicate is preverbal, the two types are syntactically distinct, since nouns in Y1 hyperbaton are postverbal. But if the intervening verb is a matrix verb, the resulting serial order can be the same for both types

(77)   ἄλλοις δ᾽ αὖ πειρῶνται δούλοις χρῆσθαι Xen *Oec* 1.22

---

(75)   Have already received the largest part of their legislation (Pl *Laws* 768d). Before the majority of the Greek cities had been founded (Isoc *Paneg* 37). He clearly accomplished the majority of the abovementioned achievements (Isoc *Evag* 37). Passing very many laws (Isoc *Pax* 50). To corrupt the largest number of our citizens (ibid.).

(76)   They used these arts as a front (Pl *Prot* 316e).

(77)   They try to use others as slaves (Xen *Oec* 1.22).

(78) οὐ γὰρ ἄλλοις τισὶν ὑμᾶς δεῖ περὶ τῶν ἀξίων ὄντων βουλεύειν
      τεκμηρίοις χρῆσθαι ἢ ὑμῖν αὐτοῖς Lys 31.34.

Whereas Y2 is a bare nonreferential noun and semantically part of the predicate, in the syntax the construction remains an apposition. Our assumption
that the Y2 noun in hyperbaton is not part of a complex predicate already in
the syntax is based on fairly strong evidence. It retains a considerable degree of
syntactic autonomy. It can be modified (i.e. in addition to the Y1 modification)

(79) ἄλλα ἀποδεξάμενος μεγάλα ἔργα Her 1.59
      τοιούτους τινὰς εἶπε βραχεῖς καὶ μετρίους λόγους Dem 19.14

and coordinated

(80) μεγίστους ὑμῖν ὑπάρχειν συμμάχους καὶ βοηθούς Dem 11.2,

and although it frequently appears immediately adjacent to the superordinate
head X, it is not restricted to that position: even a subject can intervene if the
following quantifier/demonstrative examples count as evidence

(81) πολλὴν γὰρ πάνυ κατέλιπεν ὁ πατὴρ αὐτῷ οὐσίαν Aesch 1.42
      ταῦτα ἐς τοὺς πάντας Ἕλληνας ἀπέρριψε ὁ Κῦρος τὰ ἔπεα
      Her 1.153.

Finally, note that in one way or another the Y2 noun is construed with both
verbs in the following disjunctive example

(82) τοὺς Σόλωνος ἀνεγνωκέναι νόμους ἢ συνιέναι Dem 20.103.

Light verb complex predicates can be discontinuous in English too

> The Democrats made the Republicans an offer
> Penelope gave the soup a stir,

and they can be modified

> give the soup a good stir,

as can nonreferential indefinites and bare plurals

> buy a new car, buy new tires.

The general idea of a mismatch between a particular type of apposition with a
bare noun in the syntax and a complex predicate reading in the semantics

---

(78) You do not have to use anyone other than yourselves as a standard for membership
of the Council (Lys 31.34).

(79) Having performed other great deeds (Her 1.59). He made a short and moderate
speech along these lines (Dem 19.14).

(80) That they are your greatest allies and assistants (Dem 11.2).

(81) His father left him a great deal of property (Aesch 1.42). These words Cyrus
directed at the whole Greek people (Her 1,153).

(82) That he has read or understands the laws of Solon (Dem 20.103).

should not be a source of concern. The apparently parallel syntax of the complex predicate *give* construction and the simple ditransitive hides significant semantic differences: *gave Sue a cuddle, gave Sue a kettle, cuddled Sue, *kettled Sue, (*)gave a cuddle to Sue, gave a kettle to Sue*.

The complex predicate theory extrapolates fairly easily across categories

> your own for-the-sake-of-ease
> the worst ones responsible-for-disasters
> unrelated ones the insertion-of-topics.

However, Y₁ hyperbaton in which prepositional phrases are split by an intervening verb are less transparent, since the Y₂ noun does not relate to the verb in the usual way. This applies both to adjectival and to genitive hyperbaton

> (83)   ἐν τοῖς φονικοῖς γέγραπται νόμοις Dem 9.44
> ἐν τοῖς δημοσίοις ἀναγέγραπται γράμμασι Aesch 2.58
> ὑπὸ ταύτης ἀγόμενοι τῆς ἐλπίδος Pl *Phaedo* 68a
> τὰ κατ᾽ ἐκεῖνον ἐπελθόντα τὸν χρόνον εἰς τοῦτον ἀποθέσθαι
> τὸν καιρόν Isoc *Panath* 127
> κατὰ τοὺς τοῦ πατρὸς ἐπιτάττοντι νόμους Pl *Criti* 120b
> εἰς τὴν τῶν ἐλευθέρων ἐμπεσόντες ἐπιστήμην Pl *Soph* 253c
> εἰς ἀρετῆς ἕπεσθαι κτῆσιν Pl *Laws* 812c.

ἐπιτάττοντι νόμους 'imposing laws' means something quite different from ἐπιτάττοντι κατα νόμους 'issuing orders according to laws.' The semantics uses the preposition to interpret both Y elements in the hyperbaton construction

> κατὰ τοὺς τοῦ πατρὸς ἐπιτάττοντι <κατὰ> νόμους.

Semantic relations expressed by case marking only are overtly encoded on both Y elements, while those that are expressed independently by a preposition may be encoded just once. Nonrepetition of a preposition is well attested in other constructions

> (84)   ὡς πρὸς παῖδας ἡμᾶς παιζούσας Pl *Rep* 545e
> ἀπὸ τῆς αὐτῆς ἀγνοίας ἧσπερ πολλὰ προΐεσθε τῶν κοινῶν
> Dem 18.134.

Even compounds can be formed with adjuncts, so one might compare 'pan-fried in teflon ones,' 'farmraised in unionized ones,' 'fleabitten by humongous ones.'

---

(83) It is written in the homicide laws (Dem 9.44). They are registered in the public archives (Aesch 2.58). Inspired by the hope ... (Pl *Phaedo* 68a). To postpone what occurred to me at that time till this occasion (Isoc *Panath* 127). Issuing orders according to their father's laws (Pl *Criti* 120b). Coming upon the science of free men (Pl *Soph* 253c). To follow towards the acquisition of virtue (Pl *Laws* 812c).

(84) Making fun of us like children (Pl *Rep* 545e). From the same ignorance that caused you to sacrifice many of your common interests (Dem 18.134).

The Y₂ noun

The question that remains is why Y1 hyperbaton accesses just the otherwise relatively rare structure in which the noun is unarticulated and the adjective articulated. While there are semantic factors that support such an analysis for many types of Y1 hyperbaton (just as there are semantic factors controlling the N(V)DA structure), there are also pragmatic factors peculiar to Y1 hyperbaton that are the principal feature licensing this particular structure. Let us start with the semantic factors, considering indefinites as well as definites. Some of this material has already been discussed more briefly in chapter 2. The point is that in many instances of Y1 hyperbaton, the noun is nonreferential and low on individuation. Consequently it is a suitable candidate for interpretation as a bare nonargument noun. Verbs with internal or cognate accusative objects are formally transitive but semantically comparable to intransitive verbs in that the noun is just a lexical expression of the verbal event: *die a gruesome death* or *sigh a weary sigh* are tantamount to *die gruesomely* and *sigh wearily* (Jones 1988). In fact, a number of Australian languages have intransitive subject case marking in certain cognate object combinations (Austin 1982). This type, which as already noted occurs with null head modifiers

(85) ἱππάδα στολὴν ἐνεσταλμένους Her 1.80 (YP)
τὴν αὐτὴν ἐσκευασμένοι Her 7.84
τὴν αὐτὴν ταύτην ἐσταλμένοι Her 7.62,

is well represented in Y1 hyperbaton

(86) πλείστας μὲν στρατηγήσαντες στρατηγίας Andoc 1.147
ταύτην ἐγὼ ὑπολαμβάνω μαρτυρίαν μεμαρτυρῆσθαι Aesch 1.85
πλείους τραπόμενος τροπὰς τοῦ Εὐρίπου Aesch 3.90
ὀλίγας ἄρξας ἀρχὰς Lys 20.5
τοιαῦτα ἁμαρτάνει ἁμαρτήματα Lys 31.23
ὅτε τὴν προτέραν ἐπρεσβεύομεν πρεσβείαν Aesch 2.81.

Light nouns serve to fill the syntactically projected argument position but contribute little of semantic substance beyond the natural gender of the referent of the Y1 null head modifier

(87) πᾶσιν ἔδειξεν ἀνθρώποις Dem 18.93
τοῖς λοιποῖς ἐπιχειροίη πράγμασιν Dem 18.27

(85) Dressed in cavalry uniform (Her 1.80). Equipped in the same way (Her 7.84). Equipped in this same way (Her 7.62).

(86) Having held very many military commands (Andoc 1.147). I understand that this testimony was given (Aesch 1.85). Turning more turns than the Euripus (Aesch 3.90). Having held few offices (Lys 20.5). Offends with such offences (Lys 31.23). When we were serving on the first embassy (Aesch 2.81).

(87) It demonstrated to all men (Dem 18.93). He could proceed with his remaining business (Dem 18.27).

(88)   τί γὰρ ἄν τις τοιούτῳ πιστεύσειεν ἀνθρώπῳ Aesch 2.130
       ἑτέρων παρεμβολῇ πραγμάτων Aesch 3.205
       ὁ πάντων σχετλιώτατος ἀνθρώπων Andoc 1.124
       πασῶν ἦν ἀνοητοτάτη γυναικῶν Dem 21.149.

In the case of light verbs (Kearns 1989), the verb is formally the predicate but the semantic content of the predicate is actually located in the nonreferential internal argument of the verb, for instance *have a drink, take a walk*. They easily develop into fixed phrases, and are often open to analysis as complex predicates in various languages (Mohanan 1997). There is an obvious intuitive difference between *take a walk* and *take an apple*, and early formulations of complex predicate theory involved light verb plus deverbal noun structures (Jackendoff 1974; Cattell 1984). Here are some Y1 hyperbaton examples

(89)   τὴν αὐτὴν ἔχετε γνώμην Lys 24.14
       ἀληθεῖς κατ᾽ ἀλλήλων ἔχοντες δόξας Aesch 3.213
       πλείστην δὲ εἰκότως ἐποιήσατο διατριβὴν πρὸς τοὺς ἐμοὺς λόγους
          Aesch 2.38
       πολὺν ποιήσονται λόγον Aesch 3.28
       τοιούτους ποιεῖσθαι λόγους Lys 22.13
       τὴν ὑπόλοιπον ποιήσασθε ἀκρόασιν Aesch 3.59
       πλεῖστον ἁπάντων ἀνθρώπων εἶχε νοῦν Dem 21.149.

If this type of complex predicate takes a complement, it is the noun rather than the verb that controls subcategorization, as in Aeschines 2.38 just cited (ποιῶ διατριβὴν πρὸς = διατρίβω πρὸς). Abstract nouns, often occurring with light or lightish verbs, are low on the transitivity scale (they tend to be unaffected by the verbal action), and so open to a weak reading

(90)   ἅπασαν ἐρῶ τὴν ἀλήθειαν Dem 23.187
       τὰς ἐσχάτας οἱ νόμοι διδόασι τιμωρίας Dem 18.12
       τὴν μεγίστην αὐτοῖς ὀφείλειν χάριν Lys Frag 8.1.3 Albini.

It is interesting that in Hungarian complex predicate formation with bare nouns is lexically restricted to high frequency combinations (Kiss 1994)

---

(88) Why would anyone trust such a man (Aesch 2.130). By the introduction of extraneous matters (Aesch 3.205). The most wicked of all men (Andoc 1.124). She was the silliest of all women (Dem 21.149).

(89) You hold the same opinion (Lys 24.14). Holding true opinions of each other (Aesch 3.213). Naturally he devoted most time to what I had to say (Aesch 2.38). They will argue at length (Aesch 3.28). To make this sort of statement (Lys 22.13). Listen to the remainder of my argument (Aesch 3.59). She was the most sensible person in the world (Dem 21.149).

(90) I will tell the whole truth (Dem 23.187). The laws prescribe the ultimate penalties (Dem 18.12). That I owed them the greatest thanks (Lys Frag 8.1.3).

read book(s)
write book(s)
*tear book(s)
*read certificates.

The semantic factors illustrated point towards a complex predicate analysis for this type of example, irrespective of whether the incidence of this sort of semantically light complement is higher in Y₁ hyperbaton than overall or not. However, they do not account for all instances. Y₁ hyperbaton is perfectly acceptable with ordinary referential objects, both inanimate and animate

(91)   ἑτέρους ἐμισθωσάμην ναύτας Dem 50.12
        πολλὰς προσθέντες κλίμακας Thuc 3.23.1.

Where these nouns differ from regular arguments is in their pragmatic status. As already noted, the adjective attracts both focus and referentiality in any case. This effect is particularly strong in Y₁ hyperbaton because the adjective has strong narrow focus and the noun is tail material, established or predictable information. Whereas weak readings of complement noun phrases typically arise even out of the blue, particularly when the whole verb phrase represents a recognizable repeated activity like *rent a car* or *wash the dishes*, weak readings of the noun in this type of Y₁ hyperbaton arise because the noun loses its independent argument status for pragmatic reasons. The noun by itself meets the condition of being recognized and repeated material because it has already been established, or is implicit, or at least backgrounded, in the discourse. Sometimes, it just functions like a long range anaphor. Just as we do not have to keep repeating a noun in its lexical form (a pronoun will do), so in some languages we do not have to keep repeating information about the reference and quantification of the noun, particularly when the assertion is about a subset of the nominal class. When discourse referents are first introduced, they are foreground entities with strong readings. Further into the discourse, they can recede into the background "scenery," displaced by the greater salience of more recently introduced referents, in the case of hyperbaton the Y₁ subset with its strong narrow focus. In the example just cited from Demosthenes 50.12, ναύτας picks up a preceding ναυτῶν

(92)   ἀντὶ τῶν ἀπολιπόντων… ναυτῶν ἑτέρους ἐμισθωσάμην ναύτας,

and in the Thucydides 3.23 example the whole XY₂ complex is repeated material

(93)   κλίμακας προσθέντες… πολλὰς προσθέντες κλίμακας.

(91) I hired other sailors (Dem 50.12). Placing many ladders (Thuc 3.23.1).
(92) In place of those who had deserted I hired other sailors (Dem 50.12).
(93) Placing ladders… placing many ladders (Thuc 3.23.1).

So not only is the focus mapped to a c-commanding Y1 position, but according to the complex predicate theory the noun in the cofocus does not have the status of a semantic argument; it plays the subsidiary role of predicate modifier, which leaves the Y1 null head modifier as the complete referential argument, as in the following rough and ready tripartite representation

FOC $[x = \text{ἑτέρους}]$ $[\text{ἐ-ναύτο-μισθωσάμην } (x)]$.

Semantic and context-dependent predictability seem to be very generally copresent and interactive in the interpretation of discourse. Consider the case of implicit arguments. Whereas Y2 nouns are predictable and overt, implicit arguments are predictable and covert. When a verb such as *eat* or *read* is used intransitively, it is interpreted relative to a prototypical, vague or nonspecific default complement. If you are eating, then obviously there exists something that you are eating; the question is what that something is taken to be. In a sentence like

Jack eats faster than Bill

the implicit argument is the default argument *food*, not some specific food like *oysters* or *mortadella*. However, in the context of a conversation about oyster-eating competitions, the implicit argument is the context-dependent *oysters* (which could have truthconditional consequences, if Jack was a slow eater of food in general but a fast shucker of oysters). So it is not unreasonable to assume that if predictability licenses complex predicate formation and context dependency is an inextricable component of predictability, then weak readings of Y2 nouns will be licensed by both semantic and context-dependent predictability. This conclusion receives empirical support from some of the typological evidence cited in the next section. It follows that restrictive modification, referentiality and predictability are not simply three autonomous linguistic properties, as one might at first sight think, but, up to a certain point, interdependent. What is restrictively modified tends to be predictable or at least background information relative to the subclass associated with the modifier. And what is predictable or background tends to lose referentiality. So 'He bought the red shirt' easily becomes 'He shirtbought the red one.' This way of structuring information is particularly favoured when the focus on the adjective is strong (and the noun is predictable), and Y1 hyperbaton is direct syntactic evidence for it.

The null head modifier theory and the complex predicate theory taken in combination motivate the syntactic discontinuity of Y1 hyperbaton by constructing a categorially shifted representation on the basis of the pragmatic status of the Y elements. When either Y1 or Y2 is deleted from a prose Y1 hyperbaton, the result is still a grammatical structure. When Y2 is deleted

τὰς ἰδίας κατεσκευάκασι,

the identity of the null head is inferred by contextual anaphora: 'they have built their own ones.' When Y1 is deleted

κατεσκευάκασιν οἰκίας,

the result is eligible for a complex predicate reading, like an English verb phrase with a bare plural: 'they have built houses, they have housebuilt.' Under the particular pragmatic conditions of Y₁ hyperbaton, the two structures combine. More or less implicit in the theories as presented is that in prose they generalize to indefinite YPs with restrictive adjectives having strong focus, but not to restrictive adjectives without strong focus nor to descriptive adjectives. (We are not considering quantifiers here.) Suppose this is indeed the case. Then the structural distinction between internal and external Y₁ positions established in chapter 4 corresponds to a categorial one. Null head modifiers appear in the external position, ordinary premodifying adjectives in the internal position. In other words, strong focus licenses adjectives to appear in the external position by changing them into null head modifiers in that position. While verse continues to admit ordinary adjectives in the internal position and null head modifiers in the external position, prose disallows the former category. In prose, null head Y₁ modifiers can be discontinuous but regular premodifying adjectives have to be continuous.

TYPOLOGICAL SUPPORT

Although the null head modifier and complex predicate theories are less transparent than the discontinuous YP theory and involve more machinery, there is an intriguing range of crosslinguistic evidence that points in their direction.

Evidence from Romance

In colloquial Italian besides the continuous noun phrase in sentences like

> Se n'è comprata una rossa di camicia
> he CL-has bought himself a red of shirt
> 'He has bought himself a RED shirt,'

there is a discontinuous variant with fronted null head modifier

> Una rossa se n'è comprata di camicia.

The construction is related to the German *was für* split (p. 275) and to the predicative *N of a N* type (*fior di camicia* 'gem of a shirt'). The pragmatics of this null head modifier construction are practically the same as those of Y₁ hyperbaton. The discontinuous type arises when Y₁ is focus fronted, stranding Y₂; Y₂ is not extraposed. Some relevant details of the discontinuous version of the construction in the Sardinian dialect emerge from a recent study (Jones 1993), although it is not clear that all the properties of the continuous type are replicated in the discontinuous variant. The construction cannot be used unless the Y₁ element is independently licensed as a null head modifier. Y₁ can be an adjective or a possessive. The Y₂ noun can itself be modified. Y₂ need not be placed directly after the verb but can be separated from the verb by another constituent. The somewhat problematic split preposition phrase YP also occurs

> Kin sa mea keljo iscriere de pinna
> with the mine I want to write of pen
> 'I want to write with MY pen.'

All these properties are also found in Y₁ hyperbaton in Greek, a fact which tends to support the null head modifier theory of hyperbaton.

Another intriguing item of evidence involves body part nouns. These tend to have low categoriality and are liable to appear uninflected or to get incorporated in a range of different languages (Hopper & Thompson 1984; Evans 1996); the owner of an (undetached) body part gets promoted to argument status. They also occur in a French construction, dative external possession, which can be interpreted as covert complex predicate formation (Vergnaud & Zubizarreta 1992)

> La fille leur a lavé la main sale
> 'The girl washed their dirty hand.'

Furthermore, this French construction is not available when the body part is modified by a descriptive adjective

> *La fille leur a lavé le visage sale
> 'The girl washed their dirty face.'

The descriptive adjective cannot modify the noun by being included inside the complex predicate, since modification blocks the stricter forms of complex predicate formation. But modification from outside the complex predicate would be a type of stranding incompatible with the strictly adnominal character of descriptive modifiers; it would force a restrictive reading. This would apply a fortiori to restrictive modifiers having strong focus, since these are semantically and syntactically even more independent of the noun. Recall that descriptive adjectives are rare or nonoccurring in Y₁ hyperbaton. In chapter 2 we pointed out that they are incompatible with the semantics of focus: there can be no set of alternates for the Y₁ focus to range over if the denotation of the noun is a subset of the denotation of the modifier (rather than the denotation of the modified noun phrase being a proper subset of the denotation of the noun). We can now add that descriptive adjectives in Y₁ position are incompatible with a complex predicate structure too. Furthermore, there is also a strong association of null head modifiers (or their counterparts with pronominal heads) with a restrictive reading: *the tall one* is naturally restrictive, although it could have a secondary descriptive use as a nickname for a person of greater than average height. So one can conclude that the absence of descriptive adjectives in Y₁ hyperbaton position in prose fits well with the null head modifier and complex predicate framework, quite apart from the contribution of strong focus.

Incorporation

In English, the demotion of tail nouns is most noticeable in the prosody

> We eat MEAT on Sundays, but we don't eat meat on Fridays.

When *meat* is new information, it has a pitch accent (small caps in the example), but when it is old information it does not. Some languages can use noun incorporation to encode the tail status of an argument, usually the direct object or unaccusative subject. In Mayali, incorporated nouns have the same semantic properties as nouns in Yı hyperbaton: they tend to be generic, nonreferential, less specific than external nominals. They also have the same sort of pragmatic properties as nouns in Yı hyperbaton: "new, stressed, contrasted or conjoined nominals are external, while given or unstressed nominals are incorporated... Incorporated generics... typically carry given information and... progress from external to incorporated status through the discourse" (Evans 1996). Here is an example from a Mayali discourse about dingo pelts (Evans 1995b)

> *In the old days I used to put down baits and collect their pelts. I*
> *wanted to take the pelts to the police station. I would pelts-give to*
> *him and he would give me money.*

The following is one of a number of similar examples in Nahuatl (Merlan 1976)

A. *You never eat meat*
B. *I always meat-eat.*

In Nahuatl, incorporation is regularly used for weak readings of nouns as in *wash the dishes.* One says

> *He door-opened*
> *He door-closed.*

Use of the unincorporated noun in such Nahuatl phrases is pragmatically marked. Body part nouns are most likely to be incorporated; when they are not incorporated, they tend to have focus. Pragmatically triggered noun incorporation is also reported for Caddo and Tuscarora (Mithun 1984, 1995).

In complex predicate formation, the noun with a weak reading remains a separate morphological word, whereas in noun incorporation it actually joins together with the verb into a single word. Evidently, incorporation is an overt morphosyntactic manifestation of what is assumed to occur interpretively in complex predicate formation. Now certain incorporating languages also allow hyperbaton. The following examples are from Southern Tiwa (Allen et al. 1984; Baker 1996)

> Yede seuan-ide a-mū-ban (YP X)
> that man-SUF 2SG.3SG-see-PAST
> 'You saw that man'

Yede ti-mū-ban seuan-ide (Y₁XY₂)
that   1SG.3SG-see-PAST man-SUF
'I saw that man.'

Yoadeu a-mū-ban   seuan-ide
which 2SG.3SG-see-PAST man-SUF
'Which man did you see?'

What is interesting is that Southern Tiwa also has a hyperbaton-like structure in which the noun is not independent but incorporated, so that the Y₁ modifier is left stranded

Yede a-seuan-mū-ban (Y₁ Y₂-X)
that   2SG.3SG-man-see-PAST
'You saw that man.'

Yoadeu a-seuan-mū-we
which 2SG.3SG-man-see-PRES
'Which man do you see?'

In principle, a three-point strength hierarchy would not be impossible, for instance: focus > independent (mostly referential) > incorporated (mostly non-referential). Compare further examples like

(94) ἀλόντας μιᾷ ψήφῳ μόνον Andoc 4.9 (XYP μόνον)
μιᾷ μόνον ἀλῶναι ψήφῳ Dem 21.75 (Y₁ μόνον XY₂)

with the following Southern Tiwa pair

Wim'a musade-tin ti-tuwi-ban (YP only X)
one   cat-only   1SG.3SG-buy-PAST

Wim'a-tin ti-musa-tuwi-ban (Y₁ only Y₂-X)
one-only   1SG.3SG-cat-buy-PAST
'I bought only one cat.'

It is also suggestive in light of Greek conjunct hyperbaton that alongside co-ordinate noun phrases with plural object agreement there is a variant in which one conjunct is incorporated and the verb has singular object agreement

Kanide-'an bakade-'an bi-tuwi-ban
horse-with cow-with   1SG.3PL-buy-PAST

Ti-kan-tuwi-ban   ba   bakade-'an
1SG.3SG-horse-buy-PAST and cow-with
'I bought a horse and a cow.'

Disjunct stranding as well as modifier stranding is reported for West Greenlandic (Sadock 1991; Bittner 1998).

_____

(94) Convicted on a single vote only (Andoc 4.9). That he was convicted by only a single vote (Dem 21.75).

Therefore, in Southern Tiwa and some other languages, incorporation can strand Y₁ modifiers and second conjuncts just like hyperbaton. Incorporation can be triggered inter alia by the same sort of semantic and pragmatic factors as Y₁ hyperbaton in Greek. Incorporation is overt complex predicate formation. It follows that Y₁ hyperbaton in Greek can be understood as covert complex predicate formation, which was just the hypothesis advanced in the preceding section. More generally, a number of recent studies have made the connection between incorporation and indefinites having a weak reading (Ackema 1994; Platzack 1994; van Geenhoven 1998).

We have remarked that the complex predicate theory applies more straight-forwardly if Y₁ is interpreted as a null head modifier than if it is interpreted as an adjective somehow modifying at a distance. The parallel of incorporation lends some support to this claim, since in some languages verbs having incorporated nouns can additionally have ordinary lexical direct objects (which are external adjuncts in pure pronominal argument languages). Although the situation can be complicated by questions of agreement and transitivity, it provides some support for the idea that Y₁ elements stranded by incorporation could be null head modifier direct object phrases. As already noted, for the most part if a modifier can be stranded by incorporation, it can also be a null head modifier. Whereas in Mayali, an incorporated noun can be modified by an external adjective, demonstrative, or numeral, in Southern Tiwa (Rosen 1989) only numerals and demonstratives may be stranded by incorporation. (Both languages additionally allow relative clauses modifying incorporated nouns.) In Southern Tiwa, only numerals and demonstratives are allowed to occur as ordinary null head modifiers ('I like that one' etc.): unfortunately, it is not reported whether this language has other adjectival modifiers.

Hyperbaton in a typological perspective

Typological evidence cited in the preceding paragraph indicated that modifier stranding occurs with or without incorporation. So discontinuity can arise both from the complexity constraint and from complex predicate formation. These are not unrelated factors but ultimately both manifestations of non-configurationality. In complex predicate formation, the head-complement relation is simplified and replaced by head plus modifier; this is morphologically actuated by noun incorporation in a number of nonconfigurational languages. Discontinuity is automatic with incorporation, since incorporation strands modifiers. Discontinuity can also occur without noun incorporation. So the complexity constraint does not reduce to incorporation, which at least suggests that it does not reduce to complex predicate formation either. On the adjective side, it is reasonable to think that strong focus adjectives are more likely to be discontinuous than others, but again discontinuity is not limited to strong focus adjectives. As already argued, modification and predictability by themselves can induce nonreferentiality in the noun, thereby setting the stage for one type of discontinuity. So both for nouns and for adjectives, there is a hierarchy of conditions triggering discontinuity. In prose, with its more progressive syntactic typology, hyperbaton requires an optimal combination of the strongest adjective condition (strong narrow focus) with the strongest noun condition (tail status and complex predicate formation). Verse with its less configurational typology allows Y_1 hyperbaton under a broader range of conditions.

In light of this analysis of discontinuity, it becomes clear that it is rather superficial and nonexplanatory to account for hyperbaton simply in terms of a mechanical disturbance of serial word order. This approach amounts to little more than a formalization of the initial reaction of a speaker of English to a piece of nonconfigurational syntax. A Warlpiri discourse or a chorus from Greek tragedy strikes us at first sight as a random unstructured shambles. Noone would talk that way; or, if they did, they certainly would not write that way. Such a reaction to nonconfigurationality has already been criticized in chapter 5. Now consider the converse scenario: what would be the equally glossocentric initial reaction of an early bronze age warrior to a piece of English configurational syntax? Perhaps he would say that the monotonously hierarchical phrase structure snuffs out the more variable and textured style of syntax that is free to surface in his own language. English syntax takes comparatively little notice of the pragmatic status of noun phrases, treating them fairly uniformly (once grammatical relations are established) irrespective of whether they are topics, foci or tails. It is also largely insensitive to the semantic distinction between nouns that are referential and nouns that are predicate modifiers. As for adjectives, instead of surfacing in a variety of syntactic contexts potentially reflecting subtle nuances of meaning—attributive modifiers, different types of adjunct predicates (Hale 1983), null head modifiers—they are rather uniformly assigned attributive premodifier status. All this is illustrated by the translations at the foot of the page in this book, which regularly neutralize the effects of hyperbaton. Some of the missing work may be done by the prosody in English, but from a syntactic point of view one could argue that, in this regard, the configurational languages are impoverished relative to the nonconfigurational ones, and not vice versa.

ARGUMENT RANKING

Even the most cursory inspection of the examples on any page of this book will show that the various arguments and adjuncts of the verb are not equally represented in prose Y_1 hyperbaton. This means that a student writing a Greek prose composition cannot use hyperbaton ad lib.; some sort of rules will be required to block difficult or illicit hyperbata. These rules will reflect the following observations about the status of YP in Y_1 hyperbaton:

(1) YP cannot be the subject of a transitive verb, except under a few conditions to be specified later

(2) YP can be the subject of a passive verb

(3) YP can be the subject of an unaccusative intransitive verb

(4) YP can be the subject of an unergative intransitive verb, perhaps under certain conditions only

(5) YP can be the direct object (DO) of a transitive verb

(6) YP can be an indirect object (IO) or an oblique complement or an adjunct phrase provided no unequivocally lower ranked noun phrase occurs in the clause, where ranking in gross terms is as follows: DO < IO/oblique complement < adjunct < transitive subject

(7) Pronouns and adverbs are invisible to this calculus.

Before we proceed to set out examples of each constraint, we need to point out that the mere existence of these distributional inequalities in texts does not necessarily entail their syntactic significance. Since subjects tend to be topics, particularly in transitive clauses, subject adjectives are easily superfluous; there is no need to repeat the restriction of an already established referent. Consequently, subject adjectives are rare in spontaneous conversation (Thompson 1988). Although it is not difficult to construct examples of strong narrow subject adjective focus alongside its object counterpart

> The TALL centurion killed the Gaul
> The centurion killed the TALL Gaul,

one has to take seriously the proposition that the absence of the former in prose Yı hyperbaton is simply a reflex of its overall low textual incidence. The argument ranking constraints would then have everything to do with the pragmatic structure of discourse and nothing to do with the syntax of hyperbaton. The rule would simply be that if a modifier has strong narrow focus, pragmatic factors ensure that it will almost always modify the lowest ranked argument in the clause, irrespective of whether it appears in hyperbaton or not. The irrelevance of unfocused pronouns also follows automatically. Our Greek prose composition rules would then have the same status as an English prose composition rule forbidding more than the occasional use of words beginning with the letter z.

Interestingly enough, the same sort of dilemma arises for discontinuous ergative YPs in some Australian languages (Pensalfini 1992). However, Yidin informants expressed some dissatisfaction when actually presented with split ergative YPs (Dixon 1977), which suggests that the problem may not be purely a matter of the pragmatic structure of the examples. One might argue that the occurrence of argument ranking violations in postclassical Greek also suggests that the constraints are syntactic

(95)   τούτοις τὸν νεανίαν... ἐχειρώσατο τοῖς λόγοις Philostratus 150 Kayser
τοὺς τοῦ Χριστοῦ στρατιώτας ἡ ἱερὰ τοῦ ξύλου προσκαλεῖται ἠχὴ
    Theodorus of Petra 86 Usener
ἄρτου ἐπὶ τριάκοντα μὴ γευσάμενος ἔτη ibid. 20.

The idea would be that postclassical Greek authors were no longer aware of the classical rules. However, in this style of Greek any Y₁ adjective can appear in hyperbaton (not only those with strong focus) and argument positions are in general more likely to be filled by complex, not to say overburdened, phrases. So no useful comparison is possible with classical Greek. Furthermore, there seem to be some argument ranking effects in modern Greek hyperbaton.

The main reason why we believe that the hyperbaton argument ranking rules are not entirely the reflex of pragmatic factors is that there is a substantial body of typological evidence linking various types of discontinuity with argument ranking constraints. This typological evidence is derived from living languages, where informants have explicitly rejected examples with argument ranking violations as degraded or ungrammatical. In the following sections, we will present the various constraints in terms of specific asymmetries, giving some Greek examples along with the relevant typological support. Principal sources of evidence are the discontinuous version of quantifier float in Japanese and the *was für* split interrogative in German. Examples for the former are from Kumahira Comrie (1987); Miyagawa (1989); Tsujimura (1989); Fukushima (1991); Yoshida (1993); Yatabe (1993); Kawashima & Kitahara (1993). Examples for the latter are from den Besten (1985); Diesing (1988, 1992); Grewendorf (1989); Shannon (1992); Lee & Santorini (1994).

Subject-complement asymmetry

The sole complement of a transitive verb can appear in Y₁ hyperbaton but the subject cannot

(96)   μίαν ἔχειν ἀμφότερα τὰ γένη δόξαν Pl *Polit* 310e
    (*)ἀμφότερα ἔχειν μίαν δόξαν τὰ γένη

    μόναις ταύταις ἀπαγορεύουσιν οἱ νόμοι ταῖς γυναιξὶ Dem 59.86
    (*)μόνοι οὗτοι ἀπαγορεύουσι ταῖς γυναιξὶν οἱ νόμοι.

The asterisked examples are rare or nonoccurring in prose. The same subject-complement asymmetry appears with Japanese quantifiers: an object phrase can be split but an ordinary transitive subject phrase cannot

(95) He so cowed the young man with these words (Philostratus 150). The holy sound of the cross summons the soldiers of Christ (Theodorus 68). Not having tasted bread for thirty years (ibid. 20).

(96) That both classes hold the same opinion (Pl *Polit* 310e). The laws forbid these women alone (Dem 59.86). *Only these laws forbid women.

Go-hon gakusei-ga   sake-o   nonda
Five-CL student-NOM sake-ACC   drank
'The students drank five bottles of sake'

*San-nin   sake-o   gakusei-ga   nonda
Three-CL sake-ACC student-NOM drank
'Three students drank sake.'

In another type of Japanese construction, a sort of Y2 hyperbaton known as right dislocation, the quantifier appears discontinuously after the verb, for instance '*Students are reading books, 3-persons*'; there is no subject-object asymmetry for short distance dislocation but there is for long distance dislocation in the judgement of many speakers. In Halkomelem (British Columbia: Gerdts 1984)

> *All baked the children the bread*

means 'The children baked all the bread' and not 'All the children baked the bread.'

There is a construction in German (and some other Germanic languages) known as the *was für* split, in which the interrogative is extracted out of its phrase; the detailed conditions for the use of this construction are not entirely clear (Diesing 1992; Shannon 1992; Haider 1993). It is a sort of interrogative counterpart of the Italian null head modifier construction already discussed. Here is an example with a *was für* direct object phrase:

> Was hast du deinem Mann für einen Roman geschenkt?
> 'What kind of novel did you give your husband?'.

This construction is judged (by our informants) far less acceptable or unacceptable with the subject of a transitive verb, even when it is adjacent to the verb:

> (*)Was haben deine Mutter für Ameisen gebissen?
> 'What kind of ants bit your mother?'

although the unsplit version with a subject phrase is acceptable:

> Was für Ameisen haben deine Mutter gebissen?

In Dutch child language subextraction (p. 35), there were no examples of split subject phrases, although it is not clear if this observation is statistically significant relative to the incidence of the unsplit type

> Welke wil jij liedje zingen?
> 'Which want you songs to sing?'

> (*)Welk leest kind een boekje?
> 'Which reads child a book?'.

Active-passive subject asymmetry

Passive subject phrases are well attested in hyperbaton

(97) μηδεμίαν καταλείπεσθαι πρόφασιν Dem 25.17
      ἄπαντα γὰρ αὐτοῦ κατελέλειπτο τὰ ἐπιτήδεια Lys 32.8.

Note that with the active form of the verb only the object can appear in hyperbaton; the subject is illicit even with the appropriate pragmatics

(98) τὸν εὐκλεᾶ θάνατον ἀθάνατον περὶ τῶν ἀγαθῶν καταλείπειν λόγον
      Lys 2.23 (v.l.)
      (*) τὸν εὐκλεᾶ καταλείπειν θάνατον ἀθάνατον λογόν.

It is not clear whether there is any ranking of arguments and adjuncts in passive clauses

(99) πολλοὶ μὲν δὴ συγκατακαίονται τοῖσι μάντισι βόες Her 4.69
      οἱ μὲν χρόνοι τῆς αἱρέσεως καὶ τὰ τῶν πρεσβευσάντων ὀνόματα ἐν
      τοῖς δημοσίοις ἀναγέγραπται γράμμασι Aesch 2.58 (heavy
      subject phrase).

In Japanese, split quantifier subject phrases are disallowed in regular transitive clauses, as just noted, but permitted in passive clauses:

      Yuube 2-dai doroboo-ni kuruma-ga nusumareta
      Last night 2-CL thief-by car-NOM   were stolen
      'Last night two cars were stolen by a thief.'

The German *was für* split, which is difficult with active subjects in transitive clauses, as just noted, is fine with passive subjects:

      Was ist deinem Mann für ein Roman geschenkt worden?
      'What kind of novel was given to your husband?'.

Unergative-unaccusative asymmetry

There is clear evidence from a variety of languages that intransitive verbs fall into two classes, often termed unergative and unaccusative. Unergative verbs include "verbs of manner of motion, communication, bodily processes, gestures and signs, and involuntary emission of stimuli"; unaccusative verbs include "verbs of inherently directed motion, change of location, change of state, and appearance and existence" (Rappaport et al. 1993). The distinction is ultimately a semantic distinction between more agentive and more patientive

(97) So that no reason remains (Dem 25.17). All their provisions had been left there (Lys 32.8).

(98) That a glorious death leaves behind an immortal reputation (Lys 2.23).

(99) Many oxen are burned to death along with the diviners (Her 4.69). The dates of the appointments and the names of the ambassadors are registered in the public archives (Aesch 2.58).

and thematic, as well as correlating with the aspectual property of telicity. It shows up with various grammatical manifestations in different languages and with some indeterminacy in classification of verbs between languages (Italian *è bastato*, German *hat genügt*), particularly with verbs (like *blush* and *bloom*) that can be interpreted either as an activity or as a change of state. The best known instantiation of the distinction involves the choice of the perfect auxiliary for intransitive verbs in various languages including Italian, which, unlike English with its systematic *have* auxiliary, use *have* for some verbs and *be* for others. In Italian, unaccusatives take *essere* (*sono arrivato*), unergatives take *avere* (*ho lottato*) like transitives. The classification is usually lexically determined, but there are cases of fluid usage

> Sono corso in casa 'I ran into my home' (change of location;
>   theme subject)
> Ho corso in casa 'I ran at home' (manner of motion; agent subject).

The relevance of this distinction for Y1 hyperbaton in Greek prose is difficult to assess. Semantically unaccusative subject phrases are well attested

(100)   πολλοὶ παρ' ὑμῖν... γεγόνασι ῥήτορες Dem 18.219
        τοῦ γὰρ Φωκικοῦ συστάντος πολέμου Dem 18.18
        οὐκ ἂν ἡ ἡμετέρα κατέστη μήτηρ Isae 3.5
        εἴ τις ἄλλη πώποτε τοιαύτη ἐγένετο προθεσμία Aesch 1.39 (v.l.),

as well as predicate copula phrases

(101)   πλείστη ἐστὶν Ἀθήνησιν ἀκολασία Xen *Ath Pol* 1.10
        μακρὸς ἂν εἴη λόγος Andoc 3.9.

But likely unergative subject phrases also occur in hyperbaton

(102)   ἅπαντες γὰρ ἀπαγορεύουσιν οἱ νόμοι Aesch 3.50
        ὁ παλαιός κελεύει νόμος Dem 20.99,

where a transitive use of the same verb would be illicit

(103)   (*)ὁ παλαιὸς κελεύει νόμος τοὺς πολίτας.

However, these instances of split unergative subjects are stative, with inanimate referents: what is not clear from the examples is whether unergative intransitive verbs, detransitivized verbs or object prodropped transitive verbs can be used in prose with split agentive subject phrases in a regular predicational structure

----

(100) You have had many orators (Dem 18.219). When the Phocian war began (Dem 18.18). Our mother would not have become ⟨heiress⟩ (Isae 3.5). Any other amnesty of this type that has ever occurred (Aesch 1.39).

(101) There is extreme licence at Athens (Xen *Ath Pol* 1.10). It would be a long story (Andoc 3.9).

(102) All the laws forbid (Aesch 3.50). The old law requires (Dem 20.99).

(103) *The old law requires the citizens.

(104) (*)οἱ ἄλλοι (κατ)ἐγέλασαν στρατιῶται.

In Japanese, split subject quantifier phrases in intransitive clauses are in principle permitted with unaccusative verbs but not with unergative verbs

> 2-ri ryokan-ni kyaku-ga tuita
> 2-CL to the inn guests-nom arrived
> 'Two guests arrived at the inn'

> *3-nin geragerato kodomo-ga waratta
> 3-CL   loudly   children-nom laughed
> 'Three children laughed loudly.'

Addition of a goal of motion phrase can again change an unergative into an unaccusative

> *Gakusei-ga kodomo-to sannin hasitta
> student-NOM children-with 3-CL ran
> 'Three students ran with the children.'

> Gakusei-ga kooen-made san-nin hasitta
> student-NOM park-as-far-as 3-CL   ran
> 'Three students ran to the park.'

Similar data are cited for Hindi numerals (Terada 1991):

> *Books on the desk two were put* (passive)
> *Girls with difficulty four arrived* (unaccusative)
> *Girls with loud voice four laughed* (unergative),

and Bengali quantifiers (Dasgupta 1988)

> *Today I letters wrote some* (object)
> *Here flowers have blossomed some* (unaccusative subject)
> *Today boys ran some* (unergative subject).

The Sardinian discontinuous null head modifier construction already discussed is licensed with unaccusative but not with unergative subjects (Jones 1993)

> Su tuo no' est ghiratu de cane
> 'YOUR dog hasn't returned'

> *Su meu at appeddatu de cane
> 'MY dog has barked.'

The German *was für* split has been reported as allowed in intransitive clauses with unaccusative verbs but not with unergative verbs

> Was sind für Leute angekommen?
> 'What sort of people have arrived?'

(104)   *The other soldiers laughed.

*Was haben für Leute gearbeitet?
'What sort of people worked?'

Unergative verbs become more acceptable in this German construction with a richer spatiotemporal context (Shannon 1992). This behaviour of unergative verbs is replicated in other languages. Italian *ne*-cliticization, a classical unaccusative diagnostic, can occur with unergatives too, provided the discourse overtly or implicitly furnishes a topic such as a locative or a conditional; the evidence of agreement, intonation and adverb placement in the northeastern dialect of Conegliano indicates that in such cases the unergative subject is verb phrase internal (Saccon 1993). Note that this creates a conflict between (mostly) lexically assigned auxiliary selection and discourse conditioned verb phrase structure as evidenced by *ne*-cliticization. Similar data have been cited from Spanish (Torrego 1989) and from Japanese for split quantifiers even in transitive clauses (Kawashima & Kitahara 1993). These data probably all ultimately relate to the distinction between socalled thetic and categorical sentences (Sasse 1987). Categorical sentences are propositional: there is a subject of which something is predicated. Thetic sentences are either nonpropositional descriptions of happenings or they are predicated of a semantic subject that is an implicit discourse topic, a reason, for instance, or a spatiotemporal location (*tum et ibi accidit ut*). The distinction seems to be one of the factors contributing to the likelihood of destressing in English, as in the following examples (caps = stress)

DOGS BARK (generic)
The DOG barked (eventive)

PETER CALLED (Italian *Pietro ha telefonato*) (outgoing call)
PETER called (Italian *Ha telefonato Pietro*) (incoming call)

Prof. Jones' ARTICLES are LOUSY
I don't want to hire Prof. Jones: ⟨the reason is because⟩ his ARTICLES
   are lousy.

So it is worth considering whether it could be the stativity that licenses the prose Y1 hyperbaton examples with prima facie unergative verbs: 'the state of affairs is such that it is legally forbidden' rather than 'the law is such that it actively forbids.'

Direct-indirect object asymmetry

Y1 hyperbaton of an indirect object phrase in clauses having a lexical direct object is rare or nonoccurring, and this may represent a real constraint

(105)   τὴν δὲ ἄλλην ἀνάγουσι ὁρτὴν τῷ Διονύσῳ Her 2.48
   (*) τοῖς δὲ ἄλλοις ἀνάγουσι θεοῖς τὴν ὁρτὴν

(105) They celebrate the rest of the festival to Dionysus (Her 2.48). *They celebrate the festival to the other gods.

(106)   πολλὴν γὰρ πάνυ κατέλιπεν ὁ πατὴρ αὐτῷ οὐσίαν Aesch 1.42

(*)πολλοῖς γὰρ πάνυ κατέλιπεν ὁ πατὴρ υἱέσι τὴν οὐσίαν.

The second example shows rather clearly that it is the rank of the split argument and not the surface distance between Y₁ and Y₂ that is critical. Single indirect object or dative oblique complements are well attested

(107)   πᾶσιν ἤρεσκε ταῦτα τοῖς ἄλλοις πρέσβεσιν Dem 19.157

πᾶσι βεβοηθήκατε τοῖς ἐν τοῖς ἔργοις ἐργαζομένοις Dem 42.31.

In a transitive sentence in Japanese, an indirect object quantifier phrase (which is probably a postpositional phrase in this context) cannot be split (unlike the direct object)

> *San-nin John-ga   gakusei-ni hon-o   ageta
> 3-CL   John-NOM student-to book-ACC gave
> 'John gave books to three students.'

Details aside, in Tzotzil (Aissen 1984) and Pima (Munro 1984) a Y₁ discontinuous quantifier is interpreted as modifying the direct rather than the indirect object. The German *was für* split is fine with direct objects but disallowed with indirect objects in transitive clauses. In intransitive clauses it is less objectionable, but speaker reaction varies; it is fine with unsplit indirect object phrases:

> (*)Was hast du für Leuten geholfen?
> Was für Leuten hast du geholfen?
> 'What sort of people did you help?'.

Complement-adjunct asymmetry

Adjunct phrases (optional phrases typically expressing information like time, instrument, manner, and location other than goal of motion) should not stand in Y₁ hyperbaton if the clause has a complement of any sort

(108)   ἄλλα τρόπῳ τῷ αὐτῷ ποιεῦνται πλοῖα Her 1.194

(*)τῷ αὐτῷ ποιεῦνται ἄλλα πλοῖα τρόπῳ

ὅστις γὰρ περὶ τοὺς ἑαυτοῦ ἀναγκαίους τοιαῦτα ἁμαρτάνει
    ἁμαρτήματα Lys 31.23

(*)ὅστις γὰρ περὶ τοὺς ἑαυτοῦ ἁμαρτάνει ἀναγκαίους τοιαῦτα
    ἁμαρτήματα.

In intransitive clauses (clauses not having any complement), adjuncts can occur in Y₁ hyperbaton without difficulty

---

(106) His father left him a great deal of property (Aesch 1.42). *The father left his property to many sons.

(107) This pleased all the other ambassadors (Dem 19.157). You have helped all those engaged in mining. (Dem 42.31).

(108) They make other boats in the same way (Her 1.194). Anyone who commits such offences towards his own relations (Lys 31.23).

(109)   μιᾷ μόνον ἁλῶναι ψήφῳ Dem 21.75
        ταῖς μεγίσταις κολάζουσα ἀτιμίαις Pl *Polit* 309a
        κατὰ τοὺς τοῦ πατρὸς ἐπιτάττοντι νόμους Pl *Criti* 120b.

In Japanese, complement postpositional phrases can be discontinuous but adjunct postpositional phrases in transitive clauses should not be discontinuous

    *Go-ken   John-ga   mise-kara torakku-o karita
    Five-CL   John-NOM   shop-from   truck-ACC rented
    'John rented the trucks from five shops.'

Pronouns and adverbs

Nonlexical arguments (pronouns, demonstratives) are invisible to the argument ranking calculus

(110)   ἐν ἑτέρῳ γράψας αὐτὰ γραμματείῳ Isae 1.25
        ⁽*⁾ἐν ἑτέρῳ γράψας γραμματείῳ τὰς διαθήκας

        ἀπὸ τῶν ὑμετέρων ὑμῖν πολεμεῖ συμμάχων Dem 4.34
        ⁽*⁾ἀπὸ τῶν ὑμετέρων τοῖς Ἀθηναίοις πολεμεῖ συμμάχων

        ἐν τοῖς ἐφεξῆς ὑμᾶς πειράσομαι λόγοις διδάσκειν Aesch 1.137
        ⁽*⁾ἐν τοῖς ἐφεξῆς τοὺς Ἀθηναίους πειράσομαι λόγοις διδάσκειν

        πάντων μαρτυρούντων καὶ ἐπαινούντων με τῶν συμπρέσβεων
            Aesch 2.122
        ⁽*⁾πάντων μαρτυρούντων καὶ ἐπαινούντων τὸν πρεσβευτὴν
            τῶν συμπρέσβεων.

Hyperbaton is also unaffected by adverbs

(111)   ἐν ἁπάσαις ἀεὶ βοᾷ ταῖς ἐκκλησίαις Dem 25.64
        οὐδεμίαν πώποτε φανήσεται πρεσβείαν... καλέσας Aesch 3.76
        δαιμονίᾳ τινὶ καὶ θείᾳ παντάπασιν ἔοικεν εὐεργεσίᾳ Dem 2.1.

In Polish hyperbaton, pronouns, clitics and adverbials can intervene between the verb and the Y₂ constituent, but a (lower ranked?) argument cannot

(109) That he was convicted by a single vote (Dem 21.75). Punishing them with the greatest types of disfranchisement (Pl *Polit* 309a). Issuing orders according to their father's laws (Pl *Criti* 120b).
(110) Writing them in a separate will (Isae 1.25). *Writing his will in a separate document. He is making war on you at the expense of your allies (Dem 4.34). *He is making war on the Athenians at the expense of your allies. I will try to show you in my subsequent remarks (Aesch 1.137). *I will try to show the Athenians in my subsequent remarks. When all my fellow-ambassadors testified and praised me (Aesch 2.122). *When all his fellow-ambassadors testified and praised the ambassador.
(111) He always loudly announces in all the assemblies (Dem 25.64). He will be found not to have ever invited a single embassy to the seat of honour (Aesch 3.76). This seems to be an entirely divine and heaven-sent blessing (Dem 2.1).

(Siewierska 1984). In Japanese, a split quantifier subject phrase is not allowed in regular (nonthetic) transitive clauses if the intervener is a direct or indirect object, or a verb phrase internal adjunct like an instrumental or comitative:

> *Gakusei-ga   hon-o 4-satu katta
> Students-NOM book-ACC 4-CL bought
> 'Four students bought books'

> *2-ri naifu-de kodomo-ga roopu-o kitta
> 2-CL knife-by children-NOM rope-ACC cut
> 'Two children cut the rope with a knife.'

Time and place adverbs and postpositional phrases are more acceptable splitting subject quantifier phrases preceding an object; not only do they not themselves obstruct discontinuity, they also sometimes seem to license subject phrase discontinuity by acting as the subject of predication, so that the clause has an eventive or thetic reading with a verb phrase internal subject

> Gakusei-ga kinoo/tosyokan-de go-nin hon-o yonda
> Student-NOM yesterday/library-in five-CL book-ACC read
> 'Five students read books yesterday/in the library.'

Analysis

The typological evidence adduced suggests that argument ranking in Y_1 hyperbaton does not just automatically fall out of discourse structure, but is also grammatically motivated. It would be a great coincidence if all these other languages had grammatical constraints on hyperbaton, while Greek had an almost identical distribution of hyperbaton for purely pragmatic reasons. So the question that confronts us next is the following: why are the rules for Y_1 hyperbaton just the way they are (rather than, for instance, their mirror image), and, in fact, why should there be any rules at all? The answers that can be given to such questions depend to a great degree on the sort of syntactic theory one is disposed to adopt. For instance, structural-derivational theories have attempted to express the constraints in terms of the government of traces, while relational grammar casts them in terms of different strata of grammatical relations. Our particular concern is with their relevance for the theory of Y_1 hyperbaton that we have been developing. So we will try to bypass foundational issues of syntactic theory and present a very brief discussion of the constraints with particular reference to their ultimate semantic determinants.

Agents are often topical and discourse old entities. Agents are the highest ranked arguments not so much because they are intrinsically salient as because they are in a sense independent from the nuclear event described by the predicate (Kratzer 1996). They tend to exist outside and potentially prior to the nuclear events in which they are involved and which they initiate (Keenan 1984; Croft 1991). For instance, the event might be one in which an archduke gets assassinated, and the throwing of a bomb or the firing of a pistol would be conceived of as a separate causative phase. Having these properties, agents make very suitable subjects of predication. Complete events are grammaticalized as propositions in which the nuclear event is predicated of its initiator. If the Y2 noun is to be a predicate modifier, then it will have to be an element of the predicate; it cannot be outside the predicate. In other words, the predicate can only be modified by an entity that is part of the nuclear event it describes, which, in this perspective on events, does not include its initiator (unless it surfaces as a *by*-phrase adjunct in the passive).

Not all subjects are agents. Some nonagent semantic roles, experiencers for instance (those who see, hear, love, hate, etc.), are sufficiently like agents that they can be aligned with agents and encoded as subject; they mostly behave like subjects for the purposes of hyperbaton too. However, there is some fuzziness at the edges. In the following transitive Japanese sentence, in which the subject is a theme and the object a locative path, discontinuity of the subject phrase is licensed

> Tekihei-ga   hashi-o   san-nin watatta
> Enemy-soldiers-NOM bridge-ACC three-CL crossed
> 'Three enemy soldiers crossed the bridge.'

Unlike transitive subjects, passive and unaccusative subjects, while grammatically subjects of predication, are semantically nuclear event internal. When the archduke is assassinated (passive) and dies (unaccusative), he is internal to the event, which is not initiated by his active participation (but by that of the assassin). This might be reflected in their being assigned to a verb phrase internal position even in the surface syntax. In any case, their internal status makes them perfectly acceptable as predicate modifiers. The status of unergative subjects in Greek is not entirely clear, as already noted. The typological evidence indicates that they should in principle be treated like transitive subjects; the attested exceptions give unergatives the appearance of a category intermediate between transitives and unaccusatives, but they might be explained away as lacking full agentivity. However, there are also instances (cited in the next section) of subject Y1 hyperbaton with prima facie transitive verbs having a pronominal object and of transitive verbs having heavy object phrases external to the nuclear verb phrase. The theoretical significance of this indeterminacy is that if all these cases are admitted as true subject Y1 hyperbaton, then, despite the typological evidence, the Greek rule is simply that Y1 hyperbaton is licensed with the lowest ranking overt nominal argument or adjunct, irrespective of its predicational status. We will stick with the (typologically) more conservative approach. In particular, the evidence already cited from a number of different languages relating to eventive readings with time-place adverbial topics points to the critical relevance of predicational structure for discontinuous subject phrases.

So far we have accounted for the constraints with the simple and natural rule that only predicate internal entities can be predicate modifiers. The next constraints we have to consider, namely the direct-indirect object constraint and the complement-adjunct constraint, involve a hierarchy within the predicate. The hierarchy differs from the familiar argument hierarchies found with relativization, verb agreement and case marking both in its direction of application and in the relative ranking of objects and obliques. The hyperbaton constraints are not absolute: the Y_2 predicate modifier can be any of the verb phrase internal arguments or adjuncts so long as it is the lowest ranked on the hierarchy. The hierarchy is sometimes called a salience hierarchy. The least salient argument is then eligible to become a predicate modifier. But this is not really explanatory. Why not the most salient? and why should salience be relevant at all? What exactly is the connection between salience and discontinuity? If we find a rule like "Only nouns denoting round, blue entities can be used with verbs in the imperfect subjunctive," it won't help very much to say that round, blue entities are salient. The concept of argument ranking can be made a bit more substantive if it is interpreted in the framework of compositional semantics. The formulations of predicate logic suggest a single, flat or structure-free relationship between a verb and its arguments: in symbols $V(x,y,z)$, for instance an introduction relationship pertaining between Mary, Bill and Sue. In this scheme, the semantic roles are read off the serial order: Mary (x) introduced Bill (y) to Sue (z). The more compositional approach found in categorial grammar and Montague semantics is related to the unstructured approach via a logical operation known as currying. In this latter system, the arguments are combined with the verb one at a time by recursive functional application, and intermediate structures are consequently generated just as in a binarily branching tree structure: in symbols, reducing some of the parentheses, $(((Vy)z)x)$. Here (Vy) is 'introduced Bill'; $((Vy)z)$ is 'introduced Bill to Sue' and $((Vy)z)x$ is 'Mary introduced Bill to Sue.' In this perspective, salience reflects the (inverse of the) order in which arguments are combined with the predicate for semantic interpretation (Dowty 1982; Bierwisch 1990; Strigin 1994; Kiparsky 1997). It is a further reasonable assumption that adjuncts compose later than arguments. The result is that there is a semantic constituent corresponding to each V' projection, with the proviso that the order of semantic composition is that of the argument ranking, which is not necessarily the same as that of the surface order in the syntax. It follows quite naturally that the predicate has to combine with its modifier before the resulting complex predicate is composed with regular referential and quantified arguments and with adjuncts. The process of building the predicate has to be completed before composition begins. Once the verb has composed with a regular argument, it is no longer accessible to modification by Y_2. Hence Y_2 must always be the lowest ranked nominal. Noun incorporation, which is an overt process of morphological coalescence, is subject to much the same sort of argument ranking constraints (Mithun 1984), no doubt for the same reason. For instance, Mohawk basically allows incorporation of direct objects and unaccusative subjects, but not of transitive subjects, unergative subjects or indirect objects (Baker 1996). Mayali incorporates direct objects and intransitive subjects (including perhaps unergatives) but not subjects in transitive clauses or indirect objects in ditransitive clauses (Evans 1996). This is a further parallel between Y1 hyperbaton and incorporation and, consequently, further evidence in favour of the complex predicate theory.

Apparently, pronouns (overt as well as prodropped) are invisible. The process of complex predicate formation can jump over pronouns to the next higher ranked internal argument. Perhaps this is not too surprising. Syntactically clitic pronouns, at least, can wander off to a parking lot in sentential second position, and there is much psycholinguistic and neurolinguistic evidence pointing to the separate processing of nonlexical words in general. Some double object constructions are easier if one of the objects is a pronoun both in Latin (Bradley's Arnold §231) and in English.

The invisibility of adverbs is to be expected. Adverbs can modify the predicate directly, or they can also modify larger constituents (Travis 1988). In the former case, they could perfectly well modify a complex [VY2] predicate, in the latter they would be external to a larger constituent including the complex predicate. By contrast, adverbial adjunct phrases containing nominals are not "transportable" in this way; they often add participants to the event and are composed with the verb after the arguments.

Verse

The situation in verse is somewhat different, since verse practice partly reflects the more varied syntactic typology of discontinuity posited for nonconfigurational languages. In a pronominal argument setting, if both Y elements are adjuncts, there is no complex predicate formation and discontinuity is licensed even for transitive subjects. It is also possible for one of the Y elements to be internal to the nuclear clause and the other an external adjunct or apposition (preadjunct plus internal noun or internal null head modifier plus appositional noun). Furthermore, if a lower ranked argument is externalized as a fronted topic or focus, this leaves a higher ranked argument available for hyperbaton within the nuclear clause. Consequently one sometimes finds in verse a sort of surface hemistich hyperbaton which is not subject to argument ranking constraints

(112) τὸν δ' ἐς Ἀχαιῶν νῆας ἐΰσκαρθμοι φέρον ἵπποι *Il* 13.31
       λαΐνους πύργους πέριξ | ὀρθοῖσιν ἔθεμεν κανόσιν *Troad* 5.

(112) His prancing horses carried him to the ships of the Achaeans (*Il* 13.31). We put towers of stone all around with straight plumblines (*Troad* 5).

The rather rare double hyperbaton discussed in chapter 3, which in prose survives mainly with the figura etymologica, also seems to go back to this earlier typology.

Exceptions

Finally, we need to cite the relatively rare prose examples that violate the argument ranking constraints. Judgements about discontinuity in living languages tend to be rather fuzzy and indeterminate. Informants vary from one to another, and from one generation to another, and reactions can be quite sensitive to subtle syntactic and semantic differences between examples. So it is hardly surprising that our Greek prose texts should offer a (comparatively small) number of examples of Y₁ hyperbaton that violate the argument ranking constraints. It is also reassuring that these violations are apparently not random. In fact, their structure may throw some additional light on how argument ranking works.

We will start with a simple violation of argument ranking, a Y₁ adjunct (or possible source complement) hyperbaton in a transitive clause with a lexical direct object

> (113)   ἐκ τούτου τὴν μορίαν ἀφανίζειν ἐπεχείρησα τοῦ χωρίου, ἐν ᾧ...
>   Lys 7.28.

This exception seems to be licensed by the fact that the whole speech is about the established criminal offences of sacred-olive-removal (τὴν μορίαν ἀφανίζοντα ibid. 22, μορίαν ἀφανίζειν ibid. 29) and sacred-stump-removal (σηκόν ἀφανίζειν ibid. 2). We probably have a contextually promoted version of our old friend *wash the dishes*. If τὴν μορίαν ἀφανίζειν is itself a single predicate, then the adjunct phrase is free to occur in Y₁ hyperbaton.

The other exceptions involve movements of some type, which result in syntactically and/or prosodically separate constituents. The lower ranked constituent is outside the domain of the hyperbaton argument calculus. If it leaves a trace, the trace behaves like an overt pronoun, that is it does not affect the calculus. One example involves a fronted branching interrogative object phrase

> (114)   τίν' οὖν ῥαστώνην τοῖς πολλοῖς ὁ σός, ὦ Λεπτίνη, ποιεῖ νόμος...;
>   Dem 20.28.

The resulting subject hyperbaton is another legal prescription to add to the unergative instances already cited. In the remaining exceptions, the lower ranked argument appears adjoined to the left or right margin of the hyperbaton domain. The former involves topicalization, and the latter is reminiscent of heavy noun phrase shift. Many instances of both types involve heavy coordinated constituents. If the topics are the semantic subjects of predication, that

---

(113) I tried to remove the sacred olive from this plot of land in which... (Lys 7.28).

(114) What relief does your law, Leptines, give the populace (Dem 20.28).

would help to license the subject hyperbata, especially as part or all of the subject phrase could be seen as verb phrase internal even in the surface syntax. Here are some examples

(115)   τὰ δὲ περὶ τὰς τριήρεις καὶ τοὺς τριηράρχους ἁρπάγματα τίς ἂν
        ἀποκρύψαι χρόνος δύναιτ᾽ ἄν; Aesch 3.222
        κυνέας δὲ καὶ οἱ ἄλλοι ἅπαντες ἐφόρεόν τε βασιλέες καὶ ἐτύγχανον
        τότε ἔχοντες Her 2.151
        πατρίδος δὲ τοιαύτης ἐπ᾽ αἰσχίσταις στερηθεὶς αἰτίαις Lys 7.41.

In the next example, the object phrase is a fronted contrastive focus

(116)   οὐδ᾽... ἀποδιδόντας... ὑμῖν τὰ ὑμέτερα, ἀλλ᾽ ὁμολογουμένως τὰς
        πατρῴας οὐσίας εἰς τὴν πρὸς ὑμᾶς ἀνηλωκότας φιλοτιμίαν
        Aesch 3.19.

The following are cases of the right margin type

(117)   πᾶσιν ἔδειξεν ἀνθρώποις τήν τε τῆς πόλεως καλοκαγαθίαν
        καὶ τὴν Φιλίππου κακίαν Dem 18.93
        ταῖς μεγάλαις ἐπικληρῶσαι συμμορίαις μέρος ἓν χρήστων ἑκάστῃ
        Dem 14.21
        ἥδε ἔτεκεν ἡ γῆ τοὺς τῶνδέ τε καὶ ἡμετέρους προγόνους
        Pl *Menex* 237e.

Without movement, the two Demosthenes examples would violate the direct-indirect object constraint. The Plato example would give a straight transitive subject hyperbaton, but perhaps the language is poetic, as one commentator suggests; compare

(118)   ὧν ἥδε κεύθει σῶματ᾽ Ἰδαία κόνις *Hec* 325
        ὅδ᾽ οὐ θυραίων πημάτων ἄρχει λόγος *Alc* 814.

According to the null hypothesis, argument ranking in prose Y1 hyperbaton is an automatic consequence of discourse structure; it is a purely pragmatic epiphenomenon. As we saw, the null hypothesis is suspect on typological grounds. At first sight, the fact that there are exceptions to argument ranking

(115) What passage of time could hide your rapacious conduct relative to the triremes and the trierarchs (Aesch 3.222). All the other kings both used to wear helmets and did have them on right then (Her 2.151). Deprived of so dear a native land on the most disgraceful charges (Lys 7.41).

(116) Nor repaying you what belongs to you, but, as generally acknowledged, having spent their family fortunes for the sake of public honour (Aesch 3.19).

(117) It demonstrated to all men the nobility of the city and the disgraceful character of Philip (Dem 18.93). That one part of the debtors should be assigned by lot to each of the large boards (Dem 14.21). This land of ours has given birth to the ancestors of both these men and ourselves (Pl *Menex* 237e).

(118) Whose bodies this soil of Ida covers (*Hec* 325). This speech announces a sorrow that is not someone else's concern (*Alc* 814).

might be though to support the pragmatic theory, since what is pragmatically rare is predicted to occur on rare occasions. However, the structure of the exceptions just analyzed indicates rather clearly that argument ranking is a real constraint. Coordination occurs in the exceptions at a far higher rate than it does in nonexceptions (or in simple clauses without hyperbaton). On the face of it, this is a counterintuitive result, since violations ought to be easier with lighter internal arguments (as with the pronoun rule). In any case, there is no pragmatic reason why coordination in a lower ranked argument should be particularly associated with strong narrow focus on a higher ranked argument. Strong object topicalization increases the likelihood of weak or strong focus on the other argument phrase, but so do tail objects, and they do not easily license argument ranking violations

$^{(*)}$ἐπ᾽ αἰσχίσταις στερηθεὶς πατρίδος τοιαύτης αἰτίαις.

Heavy shifted object phrases have weak focus (as in English) and so do not encourage another focus in the clause; and uncoordinated, unshifted weak focus objects do not easily license argument ranking violations

$^{(*)}$πᾶσιν τὴν Φιλίππου κακίαν ἔδειξεν ἀνθρώποις.

So one has to conclude that the exceptions are syntactically licensed by coordination or some property like heaviness correlated with coordination.

Theoretical implications

It follows from the analysis of exceptions that arguments are composed with verbs according to the inverse of their rank within the domain of the verb phrase. If a lower ranked argument is moved out of this domain and placed at the left or right periphery of the verb phrase or higher in the clause, then it is excluded from the calculus and so a higher ranked nominal takes its place as the one available for Y_1 hyperbaton. This in turn implies that argument ranking itself is a properly grammatical effect, not a pragmatic one. So the internal Greek evidence points in the same direction as the typological evidence: argument ranking is a grammatical constraint. Such a conclusion, in its turn, has far-reaching theoretical implications for our understanding of Y_1 hyperbaton and of Greek syntax in general.

As far as Y_1 hyperbaton is concerned, the syntactic theory of argument ranking entails the complex predicate theory of Y_1 hyperbaton, or something very like it. If the Y_2 noun were an ordinary nominal argument, why should it be subject to argument ranking constraints at all? There must be something special about the Y_2 noun. If that something special is predicate modifier status, then the details of the argument ranking hierarchy and its direction of application follow quite naturally, as already pointed out.

More generally, the grammatical theory of argument ranking forces us to look at the familiar concepts of free word order and nonconfigurationality in a different light. If Greek word order is free, it is free in the sense that the order of argument and adjunct phrases is not consistently grammatically determined in the surface syntax. But the phenomenon of argument ranking indicates that however syntactically free Greek word order may be, it is semantically fixed in grammatically determined configurations. In this regard—to put it in the most mischievous and provocative way possible—the Greeks spoke in Greek but they thought in English.

So as not to end on quite such an anglocentric note, we hasten to point out that if Greek semantics is configurational in the sense just suggested, it does not follow that Greek syntax is (grammatically) configurational too. For the most radical illustration of this, consider again the implications of overt focus "movement" in light of the predicational theory of focus discussed in chapter 2 and of the compositional ideal of isomorphic prosodic, syntactic and informational (pragmatic) constituency. A predicational interpretation of focus movement gives the syntax a cleft-like flavour (just as, conversely, clefts have various monoclausal properties). On this approach, the fronted focus is one syntactic constituent and the presupposition is the other (even if it contains the grammatical subject). There is a predicational relationship between the presupposition (the complex property described by the lambda abstract) and the focus. A syntactic incarnation with bound variables was suggested over twenty years ago (in Cresswell's lambda categorial language). More recently, verb phrase internal subjects have become commonplace, but fluid binarily branching constituency and traceless extraction are still principally (though not exclusively) associated with categorial grammar. The cost of admitting this sort of flexible and unorthodox constituency is not so great in a language like Greek, where the syntax can be liberated from the requirement to replicate the work done by the morphology. In return, we would get a deeper and more explanatory account of the intuition that pragmatics drives free word order.

GLOSSARY

accommodate   Suppose you are discussing Prof. Jones' Greek literature seminar with Jack. You don't know which authors the students chose to write papers on. Jack says *The students that wrote papers on Aeschylus all got good grades.* When interpreting this sentence, you first have to enter into your knowledge store the information that some students chose Aeschylus, which was not directly asserted by Jack; this step is called accommodation. Then you add the information that those students all got good grades.

adjoin   If a phrase YP is adjoined to a phrase XP, they combine to form a larger phrase of category XP: $_{XP}[YP[XP]]$, $_{XP}[[XP]YP]$.

adjunct   An element, for instance a modifier, that is added to the lexical projection of a head as opposed to being one of its arguments. In the sentence *Brutus stabbed Caesar in the senate*, *Caesar* is the complement of the verb *stabbed* while *in the senate* is an adjunct. The term is also used in a purely structural sense for any element that has been adjoined to a node, consequently including moved arguments in a derivational theory.

adjunct clause   The argument-adjunct distinction also applies to clauses. Purpose clauses, for instance are adjunct clauses, whereas indirect statements are complement clauses.

adnominal quantification   Quantification the restriction of which is limited to a nominal and which often forms a syntactic constituent with the nominal. Opposed to adverbial and other types of quantification. *Many hoplites were killed* has adnominal quantification; contrast *The hoplites were killed in large numbers*, which relates more to event(s) of hoplites getting killed.

allophonic duration   The duration of a vowel or consonant is the time taken to pronounce it. Each vowel and consonant has its own intrinsic duration, reflecting in part the nature of the articulatory gestures it involves. One and the same vowel or consonant also has different durations in different contexts, reflecting in part the extent to which articulators have to move in getting from one sound to the next: this is called allophonic duration.

alternates   Prof. Jones' Latin class has six students, of whom two passed the midterm (+) and four failed (−), giving the following matrix: Sue (+), Jack (−), Bill (−), Pete (+), Nigel (−), Pat (−). Then we can say *SUE and PETE passed the midterm*. In the terminology used in this book, the students are the set of alternates, Sue and Pete are the foci, and the rest of the students are the alternatives to the focus.

AP   Adjective phrase, phrase headed by an adjective: *keen, fond of children.*

argument   Syntactically, any phrase that is required to be present with a head; semantically, an element that is required to occur with a predicate. Syntactically, the verb *stab* has two arguments, the subject and the object. Semantically, *stab* expresses a relationship between the stabber and the one who gets stabbed. In the sentence *Brutus stabbed Caesar in the senate*, Brutus and Caesar are arguments, but *in the senate* is an adjunct. Although events necessarily take place in some location, the location does not have to be specified to make a complete sentence.

argument composition   The process of combining arguments with their head to produce an interpretation.

argument ranking   A hierarchical ordering of arguments in terms of their semantic roles required for the formulation of certain syntactic regularities, for instance assigning grammatical relations (subject, object). The nature of the hierarchy and the details of the ranking have been disputed. A typically assumed ranking is as follows: agent < beneficiary < goal < instrument < patient/theme < locative.

asymmetric c-command   If a relation between A and B also holds between B and A, it is a symmetric relation. If it does not, it is asymmetric. If a node A c-commands B but B does not c-command A, then A asymmetrically c-commands B.

branching   A branch is a line connecting two nodes in a tree structure. If a phrase XP does not branch, it consists of the head only; for instance, the intransitive verb *runs* in the sentence *Jack runs* is a nonbranching verb phrase. If in addition to the head XP contains a complement, as in *Jack killed the cat*, then XP branches. Specifiers and adjoined modifiers also produce branching structures.

broad scope focus   The scope of an element such as a modifier or an operator is the range or domain to which it applies. It is very important in the study of informational structure to be specific about the scope of focus. For instance *A BLACK cat came in* has narrow scope focus on the adjective; *A BLACK CAT came in* has broad scope focus on the noun phrase; *A black cat KILLED THE QUAIL* has broad scope focus on the verb phrase; and so on.

c-command   Abbreviation for constituent command. According to the most prevalent definition, A c-commands B if neither A nor B dominates the other and the first branching node dominating A also dominates B. If an operator has semantic scope over a domain, it is often located in the syntax so that it c-commands that domain.

cataphora   Inverse anaphora; reference is fixed by what follows rather than by what has preceded, as in *His$_i$ mother loves John$_i$.*

categoriality   Nouns with high categoriality appear in regular, fully fledged autonomous syntactic phrases. Nouns with low categoriality can easily get merged into compounds, incorporated, or deprived of their inflections; they tend to be non-referential or not treated by the discourse as independent participants in an event.

category-type mapping   The mapping of syntactic categories onto semantic types. Type theory is a system for classifying expressions semantically in terms of how they combine with other expressions. Typically, there are very few basic types and most expressions are complex. For instance, the semantic correspondent of an intransitive verb like *runs* is defined as a function from an individual (e) to a formula (t): $\langle e,t \rangle$. An adverb modifying *runs*, for instance *quickly*, would be a function $\langle\langle e,t \rangle,\langle e,t \rangle\rangle$ from $\langle e,t \rangle$ (intransitive verb) to $\langle e,t \rangle$ (intransitive verb); and so on.

closed class   Major categories like nouns and verbs contain a vast number of different members and can be added to by neologism; so they can be called open class words. Minor categories like determiners, pronouns, conjunctions, and particles contain relatively few members and can hardly be added to by neologism; so they can be called closed class words.

cofocus   The part of a sentence that remains when the focus is removed in a simple binary analysis of focus structure.

cohead   On a single head analysis, *red shirt* is a noun phrase and *red* is an adjective phrase modifying *shirt*. On a cohead analysis, *red shirt* is still a noun phrase, but it is also an adjective phrase in the sense that *red* is seen as a head taking *shirt* as its complement.

coindexed   Elements are coindexed with the same subscript letter to indicate that they have the same referent: *Jack$_i$ loves his$_i$ wife.* Also used in derivational theories to associate moved elements with their traces: *Which hole$_i$ did that mouse crawl out of —$_i$?*

common ground   The sum of information that is known to or believed by the parties to a conversation.

complement (grammatical)   Argument(s) of a head other than the subject. In *Jack put the book on the table*, both the direct object (*the book*) and the locative (on the table) are complements.

complement (logical)   If A is all the items for sale in a shop and B is the set of shirts, the complement of B relative to A is all the items for sale that are not shirts.

complement clause   See **adjunct clause**.

compositionality   The idea that the meaning of an expression is determined by the meanings of its parts and how they are combined. This definition may be understood as raising various problems for discontinuous structures like the hyperbaton YP. First, is YP an expression? Second, what are the syntactic and semantic categorial types of its parts, Y_1 and Y_2? Third, how can they be combined (not being adjacent they are not simply concatenated)?

configurational   See nonconfigurational.

constituent   Structural units of various sizes that combine to make a sentence. The constituents are represented by nodes in a tree diagram. This means that for discontinuous structures to be represented in trees, either the tree has to be three-dimensional or the lines have to cross.

continuous   A constituent is continuous if its subconstituents are adjacent. In $Y_1 Y_2 X$, YP is continuous; in $Y_1 X Y_2$, YP is discontinuous.

contrastive focus   A type of strong focus used to contrast members of the set of alternates.

coordinate structure constraint   A conjunct cannot be moved out of a coordinate structure, and no element contained inside a conjunct can be moved out of it. Across the board movements, which affect each conjunct in a parallel way, are permitted. *Jack likes papyrology and epigraphy but not literary theory* can become *Papy-*

rology and epigraphy Jack likes but not literary theory with both conjuncts fronted, but **Papyrology Jack likes and epigraphy but not literary theory* is not permitted unless the second conjunct is an afterthought. Conjunct hyperbaton violates the coordinate structure constraint if Y₁ καὶ Y₂ is treated as a coordinated phrasal structure (just as Y₁ hyperbaton violates the left branch condition if Y₁ is treated as a left branch of YP).

copy theory of movement   According to the traditional conception of movement, an element moves from its site of origin to its landing site, typically leaving a trace in the former now empty position. According to the copy theory, a copy of the "moved" element is placed in the landing site, leaving the original in situ.

counterassertive focus   Used to correct an existing erroneous assumption of the addressee.

covert movement   Movement not in the overt syntax but at some preinterpretive stage such as logical form. For instance, covert movement of focus to a position adjacent to *only* in *Jack only likes STATIUS* gives a logical form *Jack only STATIUS$_i$ likes — $_i$.*

CP   Complementizer phrase; traditionally used as a shorthand for 'clause' whether there is an overt complementizer like *that* or not.

crosscategorial   Applying across categories, irrespective of syntactic category. X-bar syntax is a crosscategorial theory of phrase structure.

de dicto/de re   There is an ambiguity in a sentence like the following: *Jack believes that a student who passed the Latin test will apply to Oxford.* On the de re reading, the speaker says that there is a student who passed the Latin test and that Jack believes he will apply to Oxford. On the de dicto reading the speaker simply reports Jack's belief; the speaker may not know whether any student actually did pass the test. One way of formalizing this distinction is in terms of broad and narrow scope relative to the matrix verb.

defeasible   Unlike logical entailments, pragmatic implicatures are typically defeasible; they can be cancelled by additional information. *Jack has broken his arm* entails *Jack's arm is broken*: one cannot say **Jack has broken his arm but it is not broken.* It may also implicate *He can't play soccer next Saturday*, but this implicature can be suspended or cancelled: *Jack has broken his arm, and I don't know whether he can play soccer next Saturday/but he is going to play soccer next Saturday anyway.*

denotation   On a settheoretical, extensional approach to meaning, the denotation of the noun *cat* is the set of entities that are cats, and the denotation of the verb phrase *purr* is the set of entities that purr.

dependent marking   Languages in which morphological marking of syntactic relations is heavily concentrated on arguments and modifiers (rather than on heads), as in the nominal case marking systems of Latin and Greek.

derivational   Theories of syntax which allow a structure to pass through successive stages of derivation. Derivational frameworks are convenient for situations in which discontinuous structures are optional variants of their continuous counterparts, since the former can often be thought of as derived from the latter by movement.

descriptive adjective   An adjective that does not restrict reference. *White wine* typically means 'wine that is not red or rose,' but *white snow* typically means 'snow, which (it is important in this context to bear in mind) is white.'

determiner   A class of nonlexical words like articles, demonstratives and quantifiers that serve to express the reference of or to quantify over noun phrases. English determiners include *the, that, my, which, some, most, each*. Syntactically determiners appear in the specifier position of noun phrases, sealing them off to the left. The class of syntactic determiners varies from language to language, and some languages may not have determiners at all. Possessive pronouns, for instance, are determiners in English but in Greek they seem to be more like regular adjectives (as also in Italian).

directionality   The direction (left or right) in which arguments or complements appear relative to their head.

discontinuous   A constituent is discontinuous if its subconstituents are not adjacent: in $Y_1 Y_2 X$, YP is continuous; in $Y_1 X Y_2$, YP is discontinuous.

discourse configurational   Configurational languages have grammatically determined hierarchical phrase structure. Nonconfigurational languages have a much flatter phrase structure in which arguments and modifiers often do not form hierarchically structured phrases with their heads. Discourse configurational languages have hierarchical phrase structure that is sensitive to pragmatic rather than to grammatical properties.

dislocation   Location of a constituent in a left or right peripheral position, often intonationally demarcated from the clausal nucleus which may contain a resumptive pronoun.

ditransitive   Taking two direct objects or a direct and an indirect object, as *teach Jack Latin, give Jack a book*.

donkey anaphora   A theoretically important type of anaphora in which the antecedent is an indefinite overtly or, arguably, covertly in the scope of another quantifier. Here is a classic example, from which the term is derived: *Every farmer who owns a donkey beats it.*

DP   Determiner phrase, phrase assumed to be headed or coheaded by a determiner. See **determiner**.

E-type pronoun   Pronouns interpreted like definite descriptions constructed from material in preceding clauses: in *A man was shot in the park. He was wearing a green shirt*, the pronoun *he* is interpreted as 'the man who was shot in the park' if the anaphora is resolved by an E-type strategy.

echo question   A question in which the speaker repeats or paraphrases the words of another interlocutor, querying one or more constituents in order to ascertain that the message has been accurately received, often to suggest that the message is so preposterous that it must have been misheard. *Wh*-words remain in situ in echo questions.

ergative   In accusative languages like Latin and Greek, the single argument of intransitive verbs has the same case marking as the agent of an active transitive verb (and aligned roles). In ergative languages, it has the same case marking as the patient of an active transitive verb (and aligned roles). The ergative case is the one used for transitive verb agents.

experiencer   A semantic role associated with the person affected by experiences, perceptions or feelings, for instance someone who *loves, enjoys, sees, hears, feels*.

extension   Roughly speaking, the extension of the predicate *red* is the set of entities that are red, whereas the intension of *red* can be thought of as the property of being red.

extraction   Movement of one constituent out of another, for instance an interrogative object out of a verb phrase as in *Who did he stab?* or out of a subordinate clause as in *Who did she say that he stabbed?*

extraposition   Movement of a constituent out of a superordinate constituent and adjunction to the right, as in *I saw a review yesterday of Prof. Jones' new book.* Some analyses of hyperbaton assume extraposition of Y$_2$ out of YP.

floating quantifier   A quantifier that does not appear in the more usual prenominal position, for instance *He gave the children all a balloon; The children all found an egg.*

functional application   In the arithmetical expression 2³, ³ denotes the cubing function and 2 is the argument it is applied to. Similarly a lexical head, for instance *destroy* or *fond* can be thought of as a function applying to its arguments; then phrases like *destroy Carthage* or *fond of oysters* arise by functional application.

gapping   The absence of a verb, by itself or with additional material, from coordinated structures: *Jack read Aeschylus and Sue Plato.* Whether omission is from the first or the second conjunct in any language relates to its canonical word order.

gender resolution   Rules for assigning gender to plural adjectives agreeing with conjuncts of different genders: *Pater et mater mortui/*mortuae sunt.*

generalized quantifier   Interpretation of a noun phrase as a set of sets or equivalently, and more simply, in terms of a quantificational relationship with another set. For instance, *Some students came to the lecture* is taken to mean that the intersection between the set of students and the set of lecture attenders is not null; *No student came to the lecture* that it is null; and *Every student came to the lecture* that the set of students is a subset of the set of lecture attenders.

group formation   *The team* is a noun phrase denoting a group. *The eleven players* is a noun phrase which denotes a group when it gets a collective, as opposed to a distributive, reading. A collective reading is indicated for *The eleven players won the match*, and a distributive reading for *The eleven players laced up their boots.*

hanging topic   Left dislocated topic that is not integrated into the nuclear clause, as evidenced in modern Greek by intonational demarcation, failure of case agreement, tonic resumptive pronoun, insensitivity to island constraints.

head   That element in a phrase from which the whole phrase is projected, the verb in a verb phrase, the adjective in an adjective phrase, and so on. For instance, the head of the adjective phrase *very fond of soccer* is the adjective *fond*; the head of the prepositional phrase *straight to the edge of the cliff* is the preposition *to*.

head marking   Languages in which marking of syntactic relations is mainly achieved by agreement affixes or pronouns associated with heads (rather than with dependents), giving structures like *The conspirators killed-they-him the emperor*. Head marking can favour a syntax of adjunction as opposed to a syntax of complementation.

heavy noun phrase shift   Postponement typically of a focused direct object that is in some way syntactically and/or phonologically complex: *Jack studied at Oxford Livy, Lucretius and Plato* is allowed, but not **Jack studied at Oxford Livy*.

illocutionary   Relating to the type of speech act associated with a sentence, for instance assertive (declaring, denying, predicting), directive (ordering, requesting, advising), commissive (promising, threatening), and so on.

implicature   An inference that can be made from an utterance but is not entailed by the content of the utterance. Implicatures, unlike entailments, are defeasible (q.v. for examples).

incorporation   Formation of a single compound-like word out of a head and its internal complement. For instance, in Nahuatl instead of *He closed the door* it is usual to say *He doorclosed*, unless the door is individuated for pragmatic reasons. According to the syntactic theory noun incorporation arises by head movement (e.g. adjunction of N to V); according to the lexicalist theory it is simply a type of compounding.

individual level   Individual level predicates are more or less permanent stative properties of individuals like *being smart* or *knowing the third declension*. Stage level predicates are episodic properties of individuals, more temporary, associated with events or with transitory states, like *being hungry* or *learning the third declension*. The terminology reflects the idea that stages are "temporal slices" of individuals. The two types of predicate are awkward in coordination without a special supporting context: *Jack is hungry and tall*.

informational   Informational focus is simple weak focus, so called because it fills a gap in the addressee's knowledge without the exhaustive, contrastive or counterassertive connotations of strong focus. More generally, informational structure is the analysis of an utterance in terms of informational categories like topic, focus and tail. The term pragmatic is commonly used in place of informational, although strictly speaking informational structure is one aspect of pragmatics.

intensional   This term is used in a variety of different ways. While the extension of a predicate is just the set of its members, the intension of a predicate can be thought of as the property characteristic of that set, a conceptual description of it. A construction is intensional if its denotation does not depend only on the extensions of its components. Classical examples are intensional verbs like *resemble, look for, need* and intensional adjectives like *former, ostensible*.

intersective adjective   Simple, extensional predicates like *four-legged, married* permitting a directly intersective interpretation with little or no reference to a comparison set or to the meaning of the noun.

intrinsic duration   See **allophonic duration**.

inverse scope   *Two professors taught every class* can mean that it is true of a certain pair of professors that they taught all the classes or that it is true of every class that it was cotaught (not necessarily by the same pair of professors). In the first reading the semantic scope preserves the syntactic c-command relationship, in the second it inverts it. Sometimes, an inverse scope reading is unavailable: *Two professors* *taught few classes* cannot mean that only a few classes were cotaught; it can only mean that two professors were less than optimally productive.

IP   Inflectional phrase; traditionally used as shorthand for 'clause' excluding the complementizer position. This terminology derives from an abstract analysis of the clause as headed by the verbal inflection.

island   A structure from which extraction is difficult or illicit: *the archduke who the murder of started the war; the pork chop which I don't like the supermarket that sold; Aeschylus Jack chose or Sophocles.*

kind   Natural or well-established class of entities; expressed by either count or mass nouns: *cat, tree, coal.* The extension of a kind is the set of entities in the world that instantiate it: *cats, trees, quantities of coal.* Some predicates, notably *become extinct,* require a kind subject: *A cat became extinct* can only mean that a feline subspecies died out, not that Whiskers passed away.

lambda abstraction   A formal device for expressing complex properties. *Red* is a simple property that characterizes the set of entities that are red. To express a complex property like *red shirt that Jack gave to Peter,* we need a device to change the proposition *Jack gave Peter a red shirt* into the property characterizing the set of entities meeting that description. For instance, the modified noun could be represented as $\lambda x\,[\mathrm{shirt}\,(x) \wedge \mathrm{red}\,(x)]$, and the relative clause informally as $\lambda y\,[\mathrm{Jack\ gave\ }y\mathrm{\ to\ Peter}]$. Then these could be combined to give $\lambda x\,[\mathrm{shirt}\,(x) \wedge \mathrm{red}\,(x) \wedge \lambda y\,[\mathrm{Jack\ gave\ }y\mathrm{\ to\ Peter}]\,(x)\,]$.

left branch condition   A specifier, modifier or complement that precedes its head is on a left branch. In *Jack's older sister, Jack's* and *older* are on left branches. According to the (generalized) Left Branch Condition, such elements cannot be moved to a position outside their phrase: **Jack's I met older sister, *Jack's older I met sister, *That give me apple, *How is Jack's sister old?, *A much I found less expensive car.*

lexical   The lexical categories are noun, verb, adjective and (in syntax) preposition. Nonlexical categories include determiners, auxiliaries and conjunctions. Lexical categories typically express denotational meaning, while nonlexical categories tend to have a more grammatical function. Prepositions range from the primarily grammatical like *of* to semantically substantive words like *beyond;* phonologically, prepositions can surface reduced or cliticized, just like nonlexicals.

light   Contributing little semantic or phonological substance. Semantically light nouns like *person, thing* contribute little to the description of the entity beyond a value for animacy. In light verb constructions, the verb is formally the predicate, but the semantic content of the predicate is actually located in the complement: *have a drink, take a walk;* contrast *have a dictionary.* Phonologically light structures have less weight, length, complexity or sonority than their regular counterparts.

logical form   A simple and straightforward semantic interpretation of inverse scope and focus in situ, for instance, seems to require a preliminary covert movement of quantifiers and focused constituents comparable to the overt movement found in languages like Hungarian. This supports the idea that there is a level of representation intermediate between overt syntax and its semantic interpretation, called Logical Form or LF for short, at which the overt syntax is massaged by rules that are still essentially syntactic in character and thereby prepared for direct semantic interpretation.

metalinguistic Pertaining to the use of language to say something about language rather than to say something about the world. Contrastive and counterassertive focus have a metalinguistic flavour when they can be understood as concerned with the correct choice of some linguistic element: *I said HAT not CAT; not RE-generation but DE-generation.*

minimality In informal and theory neutral terms, a requirement for complements to associate with their heads locally rather than across another nongoverning head.

narrow focus Short for narrow scope focus. The scope of an element such as a modifier or an operator is the range or domain to which it applies. It is very important in the study of informational structure to be specific about the scope of focus. For instance *A BLACK CAT came in* has broad scope focus on the noun phrase, while *A BLACK cat came in* has narrow scope focus on the adjective.

nonconfigurational Configurational and nonconfigurational languages differ in a number of features and along various parameters. The basic difference is that configurational languages have grammatically determined hierarchical phrase structure, while nonconfigurational languages have a much flatter phrase structure in which arguments and modifiers often do not form a hierarchically structured phrase with their heads.

nonderivational In a derivational theory of syntax arguments start out realised within the phrasal projection of their heads and in a canonical order reflecting their semantic roles. They are subsequently liable to movement in the derivation, resulting in a surface order that does not directly reflect the underlying phrasal projection. For instance, a derivational approach to hyperbaton might derive *Magnas Caesar delevit urbes* from *Caesar delevit magnas urbes*. In a nonderivational (monostratal) framework, *magnas* has to be directly placed in the Y_1 position and linked with *urbes* across the intervening material. The derivational framework is still a convenient metaphor for those who do not subscribe to it.

nonlexical See **lexical**.

nonreferential A referent is that entity in the world (person, object, event, etc.) denoted by an expression. This leaves room for a range of uses, and the details are difficult to pin down. For our purposes, a determiner phrase is referential if the speaker is referring to a particular object in the world; other determiner phrases are nonreferential, for instance pure quantifiers (*more than three students, no student*), objects of intensional verbs (*needs a secretary*), predicates (*He is a student*) and predicate modifiers (*rent a car*). Note that according to this characterization *a car* is nonreferential even though, if you rent a car, there exists in the world some car that gets rented and probably even though that car can be referred to by intersentential anaphora (*It was red*).

NP Noun phrase; phrase headed by a noun. Narrowly as the noun phrase not including the determiner (*love, love of chocolate*), or more broadly in its traditional sense including the determiner (*her love of chocolate*).

nuclear scope The tripartite operator structure consists of an operator, a restriction and a nuclear scope. To illustrate with a quantifier, *Most first year students took verse composition* is analyzed as *Most [first year students] [took verse composition]*; the determiner (*most*) is the operator, the rest of the noun phrase (*first year students*) is the restriction and the verb phrase (*took verse composition*) is the nuclear scope.

null head modifier   Modified noun phrase with a silent head: *the wise, the fourth, the best*. English usually requires pronominal support: *a nice one, the red one*.

operator   There are two types of keys on a keyboard: the alphanumeric keys have a straightforward "denotational" function, while other keys, such as caps, delete, change font, etc. serve to perform operations on alphanumeric characters. The same sort of division of labour is found in semantics and syntax. The major lexical categories are basically denotational, but quantifiers, negatives, conjunctions, tense markers, interrogatives and focus have a more logical function, and so they are often called operators.

optimality   A system for selecting among a range of competing structures. Structures are evaluated on the basis of how well they satisfy a set of constraints which are said to be universal but arranged in a language specific hierarchy. The structure selected as optimal is the one which incurs the least serious violations along the constraint hierarchy.

patient   In a prototypical transitive relationship like *stab, kiss, break*, the agent is the one who initiates the action and the patient is the one who undergoes it. The agent is the stabber, kisser, breaker and the patient is the stabbee, kissee, object that gets broken.

piedpiping   When a constituent moves and, instead of moving by itself, takes along with it other material with which it forms a larger constituent, it is said to piedpipe that material. In English, a left branch cannot move without piedpiping the rest of the constituent: one says *Which ministers responsible for the fiasco did you fire?*, not **Which did you fire ministers responsible for the fiasco?* nor **Which ministers did you fire responsible for the fiasco?*

polysynthetic   Polysynthetic languages make extensive use of affixation and incorporation, with the result that they might express in a single word what is expressed by one or more clauses in English. For instance, the Mohawk word *sahʌtsyahserunháhna* means 'he went back to prepare the fish.'

PP   Prepositional phrase; phrase headed by a preposition: *over the edge, on the table*.

predicate modifier   A nominal that is interpreted as a nonreferential restriction on a syntactically transitive verb rather than as an independent individuated (referential or quantified) complement. For instance, it could be claimed that in *He was shucking oysters* the object *oysters* is a predicate modifier restricting the range of the shucking activity by excluding clams, peanuts and other shuckables; this claim would not be possible for *He shucked the largest oyster* nor for *He shucked every oyster*.

premodifier   Modifier located to the left of its modifiee.

prodrop   Whereas Latin and Greek allow null subject and, under certain conditions, even null object pronouns (*Habent* 'They have them'), English does not allow pronouns to be dropped in this way.

projection   An expansion of a head. For instance, when the prepositional head *on* takes the complement *the table*, it projects the prepositional phrase *on the table*; when the verbal head *slaughter* takes the complement *the hostages*, it projects the verb phrase *slaughter the hostages*.

propositional attitude verbs These are matrix verbs expressing someone's attitude (assertion, belief, desire) towards the proposition in the subordinate clause. Accusative and infinitive clauses in Latin mostly depend on propositional attitude verbs: *Sperat Caesarem Gallos superaturum esse* is taken to mean that he stands in the hoping relation to the proposition that Caesar will overcome the Gauls.

prosodic phrasing The segmentation of an utterance into normally hierarchical prosodic units ranging from word through clitic group, minor phrase, major phrase all the way up to the sentence and the paragraph.

prosody The prosodic (suprasegmental) properties of speech are duration (how long something lasts), intensity (how loud it is) and tone (its pitch or fundamental frequency).

quantifier In a broad sense, any word that expresses quantity. In a narrow sense, a determiner forming a generalized quantifier phrase. These two usages can conflict. In the phrase *the numerous soldiers*, the former might treat *the* as a definite article and *numerous* as a quantifier, whereas in the latter *the* might be considered a quantifier and *numerous* an attribute.

quantifier float See **floating quantifier**.

raising In a broad sense, the movement of any element to a higher position, for instance quantifier raising or clitic raising. In a narrower sense, the raising of one element out of a subordinate clause into the matrix clause. In its narrowest sense, specifically subject raising with verbs like *seem* or subject raising from an underlying verb phrase internal position.

reconstruction Movement at logical form of an extracted element back into its position of origin for the purposes of semantic interpretation. Metaphorically, access to a position other than the overt syntactic position for some interpretive purpose. For instance, in an analysis of Y_1 hyperbaton in terms of a discontinuous YP, Y_1 is interpreted in its overt position for pragmatic purposes but adjacent to Y_2 in its semantic function as a premodifier.

referent See **nonreferential**.

relational grammar A theory of syntax centered on a hierarchy of grammatical relations (subject, object, etc.). These can be reassigned as the derivation proceeds through various strata. For instance, a passive sentence starts out as an active sentence, so that *Caesar was stabbed by Brutus* starts out as *stabbed, Brutus (1), Caesar (2)*. At a later stratum the object is promoted to subject $(2 \rightarrow 1)$ and the subject is demoted to adjunct (called 'chomeur': $1 \rightarrow$ Cho), giving *Stabbed, Brutus (Cho), Caesar (1)*.

restrictive adjective An adjective that serves to restrict reference. If, in *the red shirt*, the adjective identifies the shirt the speaker is referring to via its colour, the adjective is restrictive; if the shirt in question has already been identified and introduced into the discourse, the adjective is descriptive (q.v.).

restrictor/restriction The description restricting a variable in the scope of an operator in the tripartite structure. *Most students like Ovid* is given a tripartite structure of the following type: Most_x [student (x)] [likes-Ovid (x)]. *Student* restricts the domain over which *x likes Ovid* is evaluated.

right node raising Postponement of a phrase on a right branch until after a final conjunct or disjunct: *Jack praised but Sue criticized Prof. Jones' lecture.*

scalar adjective Adjectives like *big, slow, bad* that are not all or nothing but involve grades usually evaluated relative to a contextually derived comparison class: *slow jet, slow snail.*

scope The extent of material to which a modifier or an operator applies. In *the old men and women*, if *old* scopes over both conjuncts, the meaning is 'the old men and the old women'; if it scopes only over the first conjunct, the meaning is 'the old men and the women.' For examples of scopal ambiguity with quantifiers see **inverse scope**.

scrambling Grammatically, but usually not pragmatically, free order of arguments and adjuncts: *Brutus Caesarem in senatu interfecit; Caesarem Brutus in senatu interfecit; In senatu Brutus Caesarem interfecit*, etc.

semantic roles A classification of arguments and adjuncts according to the role they play in the situation associated with a predicate: *Mary* (agent) *kissed Jack* (patient) *in the garden* (location); *Sprocket* (agent) *kicked the ball* (theme) *across the field* (path).

shell The VP shell is an abstract structure having two heads, one of which is empty, proposed for the analysis of certain complex verb phrases like causatives and ditransitives.

sister Two nodes having the same mother (i.e. that are immediately dominated by the same node) are sister nodes in a tree structure.

slash Device used in monostratal theories of syntax to indicate an extraction site by incrementally marking each superordinate node with a "slash." For instance, in *Caesar Brutus stabbed*, the empty object noun phrase is marked with a slash feature, as is the superordinate verb phrase *stabbed* indicating that it is short one argument.

specifier Structurally, a sister of X', where X' is the head X plus a complement YP if the head is transitive. Notionally, specifiers tend to limit the head by relating it to the discourse context via reference or quantification (like determiners) or by indicating degree or extent (*very smart, right across the field*).

split coordination Conjunct hyperbaton.

stage level See **individual level**.

strand When a subconstituent is moved, as in subextraction, that part of the constituent which remains in situ is said to be stranded. In *Quod in eum excogitabitur supplicium?*, if *quod* is subextracted out of a constituent *quod supplicium*, then *supplicium* is stranded.

string vacuous Movement posited for theoretical consistency which is not empirically discernible in terms of the linear sequence of words. For instance, in subject questions (*Who killed the cat?*), if the interrogative is extracted like object interrogatives (*Who did Jack kill?*), as some theories posit, then the supposed movement is string vacuous.

stripping A type of elliptical construction in which material identical to that in an antecedent clause is omitted (stripped from) a conjoined clause: *The students read Aeschylus in Prof. Jones' class, and Sóphocles too.*

strong focus   Focus that does not merely fill a gap in the addressee's knowledge but additionally evokes and excludes alternatives. The term covers exhaustive listing (strong focus in the narrow sense), contrastive focus and counterassertive focus.

subextraction   In a broad sense, extraction of a subconstituent. More narrowly, extraction of a left branch. Most specifically, the German *was für*/Dutch *wat voor* construction.

subjacency   General conditions regulating extraction relative to depth of embedding expressed for instance in terms of clauses and noun phrases.

subject control verbs   When the subject of an infinitive is the same as the subject of the matrix verb, the latter is said to control the former: *Jack wanted/promised/managed to take Prof. Jones' Ennius course.*

subject raising verb   When the subject of a subordinate clause raises to become the subject of what would otherwise be an impersonal matrix verb, the latter is called a subject raising verb: *Jack seemed/appeared/happened to be rather drunk.*

subsective adjective   Adjectives that modify not an entity extensionally but some contextually relevant property of an entity: *great chess player, lousy husband.*

superiority effect   Some but not all languages have a rule regulating the order of interrogatives in multiple questions: *Who bought what?; *What did who buy?* Contrast *Which car did which customer buy?*, which is licensed by the fact that *which* is a type of partitive that ranges over a fixed set (here of customers) rather than being open ended like *who.*

superordinate   If X is the head of XP and Y is the head of YP and YP is a constituent of XP, then X is the superordinate head of YP.

synchronic   Pertaining to a single moment in time.

tail   A component of informational structure, namely material in a sentence that is neither topic nor focus.

terminal node   The lowest nodes in a tree that do not dominate any other node but are normally associated with a lexical item.

ternary branching   In binary branching, a node is connected to two lower nodes, in ternary branching it is connected to three. If a hyperbaton structure YXY has ternary branching, it is a flat structure $_{XP}[YXY]$. If it has binary branching, it is a hierarchical structure, either $_{XP}[Y[XY]]$ or $_{XP}[[YX]Y]$.

theme   A distinction is often made between a patient (an entity affected by the verbal action) and a theme (an entity in some state or location or changing state or location): if you smash a ball, the ball is a patient; if you throw a ball, the ball is a theme.

thetic   Whereas categorical sentences are propositional, thetic sentences either lack predicational structure or are predicated of an implicit spatiotemporal or causal subject. They include weather sentences (*It's raining*) and simple eventive sentences (*The postman rang*).

token   Instance of a type. The two cats next door are tokens of the type cat.

topicalize   Typically adjunction of topical material in a left peripheral position: *Latin verse composition we only teach to our graduate students.*

trace   An empty element thought to be left behind at the site out of which a constituent has been moved: *Who$_i$ did you see —$_i$?*

tripartite structure   Logical representation for binary operators (operators taking two arguments): [Operator] [Restrictor] [Nuclear Scope]. For an adnominal subject phrase quantifier, the restrictor is typically the noun and the nuclear scope is the predicate (see **restrictor** for an example). For a posited focus operator, the restrictor is the presupposition and the nuclear scope is the focus.

unaccusative   Unaccusative verbs include "verbs of inherently directed motion, change of location, change of state, and appearance and existence." The distinction between unaccusative and unergative is ultimately a semantic distinction between more agentive and more patientive and thematic, as well as correlating with the aspectual property of telicity.

unergative   Unergative verbs include "verbs of manner of motion, communication, bodily processes, gestures and signs, and involuntary emission of stimuli." See **unaccusative**.

universal quantification   Quantification such that a property is true of *all* or *every* entity, or with an obligatorily distributive sense, of *each* entity in a discourse domain.

valence   The number and type of arguments projected by a head.

variable   Unspecified entity in a logical representation. Variables can be thought of as similar to unassigned pronouns, as in *He is running* when the reference of *he* is not fixed and the property of running is predicated of an unspecified person. The sentence can only be interpreted when the pronoun gets associated with a referent. Variables are particularly useful for the representation of quantification, since they permit one to range over entities and quantify them without listing them individually: *Someone is running* = $\exists x\,[\mathrm{run}\,(x)]$; *Everyone is running* = $\forall x\,[\mathrm{run}\,(x)]$.

VP   Verb phrase; phrase headed by a verb: *read, read the document*.

weak focus   See **informational**.

wrapping   The wrapping of a discontinuous head X around its complement YP giving $X_1 YP X_2$. More generally, to cover also the infixation of a head X inside its complement YP giving $Y_1 X Y_2$.

X-bar   Theory of phrase structure based on the premise that phrase structure is uniform across categories. Typically, a head X combines with a sister complement to form X′, which in turn combines with a sister specifier to form the maximal projection XP, irrespective of category: hence $_{PP}[\mathrm{Spec}\ _{P'}\ [P\ YP]]$, $_{AP}[\mathrm{Spec}\ _{A'}\ [A\ YP]]$, and so on.

TRANSLITERATED EXAMPLES
WITH WORD-FOR-WORD TRANSLATIONS

One example is given from each numbered batch of comparable examples. Transliteration is according to a slightly modified version of the system in *Journal of Hellenic Studies* 67 (1947) xix. This is a letter-for-letter system, which suppresses most suprasegmental information (accent and vowel length). In the interests of legibility, morphological information is not normally provided in the word-for-word translations; coindexation is marked where it would be difficult to retrieve from the footnote translations in the main text.

Chapter 1

(1) tina dunamin echei 'what power it-has' (Pl *Laws* 643a); tina echei dunamin 'what it-has power' (Pl *Rep* 358b).

(2) tin' echei loipen doreian, Leptine? oudemian depou (*scil.* echei loipen doreian) 'what has-he left reward, Leptines? None evidently (*scil.* he-has left reward) (Dem 20.123).

(3) poson gar edemegorei chronon Timarchus? polun (*scil.* edemegorei chronon) 'how-much PRT was-speaking-in-public time Timarchus? Much (*scil.* was-speaking-in-public time) (Dem 19.286).

(4) poias polites patridos Hellenos 'of-which citizen state Greek' (*IT* 495); Pheraias tesde kometai chthonos 'of-Pheraean this inhabitants land' (*Alc* 476).

(5) tinos... epistemon technes 'of which knowledgeable art' (Pl *Gorg* 448e); rhetorikes... epistemon technes 'of rhetorical knowledgeable art' (Pl *Gorg* 449c).

(6) tinos heneka kairou 'of which for-the-sake-of advantage' (Dem 23.182); telikouton heneka... tekmerion 'so-great for-the-sake-of evidence' (Dem 57.64).

(7) tina echei dunamin 'what does-it-have power' (Pl *Rep* 358b); oudemian echei dunamin 'no it-has power' (Pl *Euthyd* 296c).

(8) en hoiois keimeth' athlioi kakois 'in-what do-we-find-ourselves wretched evils' (*Phoen* 1639); en toioisde keimene kakois 'in such finding-myself evils' (*Hec* 969).

(9) aph' hes omosath' hemeras 'from which you-swore day' (Dem 18.26).

(10) ti malist' en hapasi diespoudastai tois nomois? 'what most in all has-been-guarded-against the laws?' (Dem 20.157).

(11) en hois oi peri tes eirenes egignonto logoi 'in which the about the peace took-place debate' (Aesch 2.74).

(12) houtoi de ti poiousin hoi nomoi? 'these PRT what accomplish the laws?' (Dem 21.30).

(13) ei polla katelipe chremata 'if much he-left property' (Andoc 1.119).

(14) heteron parembolei pragmaton 'of-other by-introduction matters' (Aesch 3.205).

(15) heteron choran presbeon 'of-other the-function ambassadors' (Aesch 2.105).

(16) ten ton pollon doxan anthropon 'the of-the many opinion men' (Pl *Prot* 353a).

(17) ho toutou eros tou anthropou 'the of-this love the man' (Pl *Symp* 213c).

(18) mestei pollon agathon 'full of-many goods' (Xen *An* 3.5.1); pollon meston aga-thon 'of-many full good-things' (Pl *Laws* 906a).

(19) ton ison aitios... kakon 'for-the equal responsible disasters' (Dem 19.29).

(20) touton... enioi ton andron 'of-these some the men' (Dem 20.64).

(21) peri ton allon technon 'about the other skills' (Pl *Clit* 410c); ton allon peri nomeon 'the other about herdsmen' (Pl *Polit* 268b).

(22) tes idias rhathumias heneka 'the own ease for-the-sake-of' (Dem 10.25); tes idias heneka rhathumias 'the own for-the-sake-of ease' (Dem 8.49).

(23) pasan eblapte ten polin 'all he-harmed the city' (Dem 3.13).

(24) toutois epartheis tois psephismasi 'by-these having-been-encouraged the de-crees' (Dem 18.168).

(25) pleiston ek tes politeias eilephos argurion 'very-much from the politics having-taken money' (Aesch 3.173).

(26) hapanton metaschon ton ponon tei polei 'all sharing the toils with-the city' (Aesch 3.191).

(27) megiston aition hemin agathon 'for-greatest responsible to-us benefits' (Pl *Phaedr* 266b).

(28) pros humas hapasan ero ten aletheian 'to you all I-will-tell the truth' (Dem 23.187).

(29) eirekamen d' humin pasan ten aletheian 'we-have-told PRT to-you all the truth' (Thuc 6.87.1).

(30) me mikropsuchou poiein ergon anthropou 'not of-a-meanspirited to-do work man' (Dem 18.269).

(31) Euxenou d' aphikomen pontou pros aktas 'of-the-Euxine PRT I-arrived sea to the-shores' (*Rhes* 428).

(32) polles meston onta hormes 'of-much full being desire' (Pl *Ep* 325e).

(33) chlorais hup' elatais 'green beneath pines' (*Bacch* 38).

(34) en tois phonikois gegraptai nomois 'in the homicide it-has-been-written laws' (Dem 9.44).

(35) apo ton humeteron humin polemei summachon 'from the your against-you he-makes-war allies' (Dem 4.34).

(36) kai peri toutou Demosthenes men kai Ktesiphon polun poiesontai logon 'and about this Demosthenes PRT and Ctesiphon much will-make speech' (Aesch 3.28).

(37) ponera phusis... demosias apergazetai sumphoras 'an-evil nature public pro-duces disasters' (Aesch 3.147).

(38) peri hon... megalas... hoi nomoi didoasi timorias 'about which great the laws prescribe punishments' (Dem 18.12).

(39) megalas epethekan timorias 'great they-imposed punishments' (Dem 47.2).

(40) pollen gar panu katelipen ho pater autoi ousian 'much PRT very left the father to-him property' (Aesch 1.42).

(41) ouch ho pater autoi ten pollen ousian katelipen 'not the father to-him the much property left' (Isae 5.37).

(42) pasin ereske tauta tois allois presbesin 'to-all pleased these-things the other ambassadors' (Dem 19.157).

(43) tauta es tous pantas Hellenas aperripse ho Kuros ta epea 'these to the all Greeks directed the Cyrus the words' (Her 1.153).

(44) ou polun... [see text]... chronon endiatripsei 'not much... time will-spend' (Ar *Frogs* 708).

(45) hippoi agrioi 'horses wild' (Her 4.52).

(46) apodexamenoi erga megala 'having-performed deeds great' (Her 7.139); alla te megala erga apedexanto 'other and great deeds they-performed' (Her 8.17); alla apodexamenos megala erga 'other having-performed great deeds' (Her 1.59).

(47) allos bomos megas 'another altar large' (Her 1.183).

(48) ton kedesten ton emon 'the father-in-law the my' (Dem 50.24).

(49) ton helikioton ton emon 'the contemporaries the my' (Isoc *Are* 66).

(50) epi tes emes neos 'on the my ship' (Lys 21.7).

(51) tes emes hippikes 'the my riding' (Lys 24.10).

(52) ten palaian paroimian 'the old proverb' (Pl *Rep* 329a).

(53) ta eleina tauta dramata 'the pitiable these dramas' (Pl *Apol* 35b).

(54) tauta ta kala onomata 'these the noble words' (Pl *Crat* 411a).

(55) endedukasi de kithonas lineous 'they-wear PRT tunics of-linen' (Her 2.81); metebalon on es ton lineon kithona 'they-changed-it PRT to the linen tunic' (Her 5.87).

(56) tois Naupaktiois : nomiois chrestai 'the Naupactian : laws to-be-subject-to' (*Locr* 19).

(57) marturas pseudeis parechomenon 'witnesses false producing' (Dem 29.5); pseudeis marturias paraschomenos 'false evidence having-produced' (Dem 47.17); pseudeis anagnonta marturias 'false having-read depositions' (Dem 45.48).

(58) en tois phonikois gegraptai nomois 'in the homicide it-has-been-written laws' (Dem 9.44).

Chapter 2

(1) pollas eiche elpidas 'many he-had hopes' (Her 5.36).

(2) oudemian humas pothein akousai prophasin 'no you to-desire to-hear excuse' (Lys 14.1).

(3) tous tautei chromenous tei ergasiai 'the this using the profession' (Aesch 1.119).

(4) ex alles elthonta komes 'from another coming village' (Her 1.196).

(5) tois demosiois agosin 'the public lawsuits' (Aesch 1.2).

(6) pseude suntaxas kath' hemon kategorian 'a-false having-put-together against us charge' (Aesch 2.183).

(7) idious d' heuriskein polemous 'personal PRT to-find wars' (Dem 2.28).

(8) ep' ekeinon trepsetai ton logon 'to that he-will-have-recourse argument' (Isae 5.3).

(9) *tois epartheis psephismasin 'by-the encouraged decrees.'

(10) tes gar pephuka metros 'of-that PRT I-was-born mother' (*OT* 1082).

(11) ten gar auten toutoi poiesamenos ton gegrammenon taxin 'the PRT same as-this-man adopting of-the accusations order' (Dem 18.56).

(12) brachus moi leipetai logos 'Short to-me remains speech' (Aesch 3.175).

(13) pollon erxe trieron 'many he-commanded triremes' (Lys 14.36).

(14) medemian paraleipein hemeran 'not-one to-leave day' (Aesch 3.220).

(15) miai monon halonai psephoi 'by-one only to-be-condemned vote' (Dem 21.75).

(16) proten d' exelthon strateian 'on-first PRT going-out expedition' (Aesch 2.168).

(17) pollas au heurekamen aretas mian zetountes 'many again we-have-found virtues one seeking' (Pl *Meno* 74a).

(18) tei neogamoi gunaiki 'the newly-wed wife' (Her 1.37).

(19) tou kataratou Kurebionos 'of-the accursed Cyrebio' (Dem 19.287).

(20) ten kalen tauten niken nenikekos 'the glorious this victory having-won' (Aesch 1.64).

(21) tou koinou toutou biou 'of-the combined this life' (Pl *Phil* 22d).

(22) kalen g'... apeilephasin... charin 'a-fine PRT they-have-received reward' (Dem 9.65).

(23) ton iatron Eruximachon 'the doctor Erixymachus' (Pl *Symp* 185d).

(24) diasoizontes ten palaian paroimian 'maintaining the old proverb' (Pl *Rep* 329a).

(25) ho palaios keleuei nomos 'the old prescribes law' (Dem 20.99).

(26) pollas archas erxen... oligas arxas archas 'many magistracies he-held... few having-held magistracies' (Lys 20.5).

(27) klimakas prosthentes... pollas prosthentes klimakas 'ladders placing... many placing ladders' (Thuc 3.23.1).

(28) toiauta hamartanei hamartemata '(with-)such offends offences' (Lys 31.23).

(29) tois loipois epicheiroie pragmasin 'at-the remaining he-could-work business' (Dem 18.27).

(30) to pornikon telos... tous tautei chromenous tei ergasiai 'the prostitution tax... those this using the profession' (Aesch 1.119).

(31) eis ten eschaten empesoien athumian 'into the worst they-should-fall despondency' (Aesch 3.65).

(32) chlanidion leukon periballomenos 'mantle white putting-on' (Her 1.195).

(33) choris tes alles aischunes kai adoxias... kai megaloi kindunoi periestasin ek touton ten polin 'apart-from the other shame and disgrace... also great dangers threaten from this the city' (Dem 19.83).

(34) somata de agatha kai kala poteron ek Boioton oiei pleio an eklechthenai e ex Athenaion? 'bodies PRT good and beautiful PRT from Boeotians do-you-think more PRT to-be-selected or from Athenians?' (Xen *Mem* 3.5.2).

(35) hos oun kainotomountos sou peri ta theia gegraptai tauten ten graphen 'as PRT being-a-radical; against-you; about the religious-matters he-has-lodged this the accusation' (Pl *Euthyph* 3b).

(36) kouphon hamartematon aition 'for-minor offences responsible' (Pl *Laws* 863c); megalas epethekan timorias 'heavy they-imposed penalties' (Dem 47.2).

(37) toi kallistoi onomati chromenos deinotaton ergon didaskalos katastas 'the most-excellent phraseology using of-the-most-terrible deeds teacher having-become' (Lys 12.78).

(38) tauten men oun eis ton mellonta chronon anegrapsan ten politeian 'this PRT PRT into the future time they-wrote the constitution' (Arist *Ath Pol* 31.1).

(39) pollous men echon philous Iphikrates, polla de chremata kektemenos 'many PRT having friends Iphicrates, much PRT money having-acquired' (Dem 21.62).

(40) anthropoi.. apethanon... polloi, kai chremata polla healo 'men died many and property much was-captured' (Thuc 7.24.2).

(41) ton men dexion hupodeitai poda, ton de aristeron epilethetai 'the PRT right he-puts-a-shoe-on foot, the PRT left he-forgets' (Pherecydes).

(42) polloi men de sunkatakaiontai toisi mantisi boes, polloi de perikekaumenoi apopheugousi 'many PRT PRT are-burned-up with-the diviners oxen, many PRT scorched escape' (Her 4.69).

(43) panta tauta ta kala legousi poiemata 'all these the beautiful they-compose poems' (Pl *Ion* 533e).

(44) pollous kai megalous oikous 'many and great houses' (Isoc *De Pace* 4).

(45) pollous hadrous choirous 'many fine pigs' (Xen *Oec* 17.10).

(46) paralabon Sikelias pollas kai megalas poleis 'taking-over of-Sicily many and great cities' (Pl *Ep* 7.331e).

(47) ta polla kai megala agatha 'the many and great benefits' (Dem 19.35).

(48) chruseon kai argureon metallon 'gold and silver mines' (Her 3.57).

(49) pollas echonti sarkas allotrias 'much having flesh superfluous' (Pl *Rep* 556d).

(50) polla men chrusea poteria... polla de argurea 'many PRT gold cups.. many PRT silver-ones' (Her 7.190).

(51) pollous kai agathous 'many and good-men' (Lys 13.28).

(52) pollous kai thraseis... epairomenos logous 'many and insolent uttering words' (Dem 18.222).

(53) panton epikratein ton anthropinon logismon 'all to-prevail-over the human reasoning' (Aesch 1.84).

(54) touton archein pason ton technon 'of-these to-be-master all the arts' (Pl *Gorg* 517e).

(55) panton... megiston aitios kakon 'for-all greatest responsible evils' (Dem 18.143).

(56) treis de monai psephoi 'three PRT alone votes' (Dem 23.167).

(57) toisi patrioisi mounon chrasthai theoisi 'the ancestral only to worship gods' (Her 1.172).

(58) ten Hellada pasan, ouchi tas idias adikousi monon patridas 'the Greece all, not the own they-are-injuring only countries' (Dem 19.11).

(59) monos houtos eremei ho logos 'alone this remained-safe the argument' (Pl *Gorg* 527b).

(60) monen d' an moi dokoumen tauten tois enthade keimenois apodounai charin 'alone PRT PRT to-me we-seem this to-those here lying to-give thanks' (Lys 2.75).

(61) hapantas men oun chre nomizein megalous einai tous demosious agonas... malista de touton 'all PRT PRT it-is-right to-think great to-be the public trials, most-of-all PRT this-one' (Lyc 7).

(62) ei de kai tautes kurios tes chores genesetai 'if PRT also of-this master the land he-will-become' (Dem 3.16).

(63) ouk an heteron edei soi marturon 'not PRT of-other there-would-be-need to-you witnesses' (Lys 7.22).

(64) metaschonta theleias phuseos 'sharing-in female nature' (cp. Pl *Laws* 872e).

(65) pollen gar panu katelipen ho pater autoi ousian 'much PRT very left the father to-him property' (Aesch 1.42).

(66) [ton d' iphthimos balen Aias] [teichei hupo Troon] [Helenes posin eukomoio] [dexiteron kata mazon] '[him PRT strong struck Ajax] [the-wall under of-the-Trojans] [of-Helen the-husband having-lovely-hair] [the-right on breast].'

(67) martures d' ei men polloi paregenonto 'witnesses PRT if PRT many there-had-been-present' (Antiph 2.9).

(68) marturas, hos apheka auton ton enklematon, paresketo pseudeis 'witnesses, that I-had-released him from-the-charges, he-produced false' (Dem 45.5).

(69) *tauten tote eisballousin eis to ploion to grammateidion hina echoien emoi ten aitian epipherein 'this; then they-throw into the boat the note so-that they-may-have against-me the charge; to-bring' (cp. Antiph 5.55).

(70) *en autoi ouden isasi prin g' ede osi toi kakoi 'in actual; nothing they-know until PRT already they-are the evil;' (cp. Antiph 1.29).

(71) chopos men ek tond' ouket' oid' apollutai 'and-how PRT after this not I-know she-perished' (OT 1251).

(72) boulomai de tauten hos estin alethes epideixai saphos pasin humin 'I-wish PRT this-ACC that it-is true to-show clearly to-all of-you' (Dem 29.10).

(73) toutous de tous desmous elegon hoti chalepon ouden sundein 'these PRT the bonds I-said that difficult-is not to-tie' (Pl *Polit* 310e).

(74) horais ton eutrapezon hos hedus bios 'you-see the luxurious-ACC how sweet-is life-NOM' (Eur Frag 1052.3).

(75) toiouton mentoi kai ego oida hoti pathos pathoimi an 'such PRT too I know that fate I-would-suffer' (Pl *Gorg* 522b).

Chapter 3

(1) ep' aroteras... strateuometha andras 'against farmers we-are-making-war men' (Her 7.50); ep' andras strateuometha agathous 'against men we-are-making-war valiant' (Her 7.53).

(2) parechomenoi neas ogdokonta 'supplying ships eighty' (Her 8.44); neas parechomenoi ogdokonta 'ships supplying eighty' (Her 6.8).

(3) odmen de barean parechetai 'a-smell PRT strong it-gives-off' (Her 2.94); odmen parechomenon barean 'a-smell giving-off strong' (Her 6.119).

(4) chronou bracheos dielthontos 'time short having-elapsed' (Dem 5.5); epeidan de chronos dielthei brachus 'when PRT time elapsed short' (Dem 20.86).

(5) pantes hoi polemoi gegonasi hoi Hellenikoi 'all the wars have-occurred the Greek' (Dem 9.22).

(6) oikian oikodomeken Eleusini tosauten 'a-house he-has-built at-Eleusis so-great' (Dem 21.158).

(7) ges periodos pases 'of-the-earth a-map whole' (Ar *Clouds* 206); aischunes peri kakes 'dishonour about disgraceful' (Pl *Laws* 647b).

(8) hippomachia tis egeneto braxeia 'cavalry-battle some occurred short' (Thuc 2.22.2).

(9) ho palaios keleuei nomos 'the old prescribes law' (Dem 20.99); nomos d' eie patrios 'a-law PRT there-is old' (Andoc 1.110).

(10) andron ero presbuteron.. onomata kai meirakion 'of-men I-shall-say older names and of-youths' (Aesch 1.155).

(11) theous nemesizeto aien eontas 'the-gods he-was-in-awe-of always being' (*Od* 1.263).

(12) epesti kolossos lithinos 'there-is-on-top a-colossus of-stone' (Her 2.149); krepis d' hupen lithine 'a-foundation PRT there-was-below of-stone' (Xen *An* 3.4.7).

(13) Ares enarize miaiphonos 'Ares was-stripping murderous' (*Il* 5.844).

(14) Hippotherides anetheken Acharneus 'Hippotherides dedicated-this the-Acharnian' *DAA* 246.

(15) Solonos eipontos Athenaiou ten gnomen 'Solon speaking the-Athenian the opinion' (Aesch 3.108).

(16) Prodikos hode 'Prodicus this' (Pl *Prot* 340c).

(17) Hupo toutoui tou Marsuou 'by this the Marsyas' (Pl *Symp* 215e).

(18) ho nomos hode 'the law this' (Andoc 1.99).

(19) houtosi ho nomos 'this the law' (Andoc 1.87).

(20) out' en tautei tei machei out' en tais allais 'neither in this the battle nor in the others' (Thuc 6.69.1).

(21) polesi gar tautais monais 'cities PRT these alone' (Thuc 7.55.2).

(22) tauten ten machen... krino ischurotaten genesthai 'this the battle I-consider the-hardest to-have-been' (Her 1.214).

(23) ek tautes tes polios 'from this the city' (Her 2.41); peri tes chores tautes 'about the country this' (Her 2.13); tas en tei poli tautei gunaikas 'the in the city this women' (Her 2.60).

(24) ho chronos dieleluthen houtos 'the time has-passed this' (Dem 2.25).

(25) ou monon... dia ten praxin orgizesthai tauten alla kai dia ton logon touton 'not only because-of the behaviour to-be-angry this but also because-of the speech this' (Lyc 58).

(26) tauta de legontos tou patros tou emou 'these-things PRT saying the father the my' (Andoc 1.22).

(27) ten metera gemantos ten emen 'the mother having-married the my' (Dem 45.3).

(28) hoi chrestoi presbeis houtoi 'the excellent ambassadors these' (Dem 18.30).

(29) treis men bioi... tou koinou toutou biou 'three PRT lives... of-the combined this life' (Pl *Phil* 22d).

(30) hot' en pais hede moi 'when there-was child this to-me' (Eur *Suppl* 1098).

(31) : ai de tir ta graphea : tai kadaleoito : 'if PRT anyone the writings : these damages' (*LSAG* 42.6).

(32) hos g' heliou tod' eisoran emoi phaos monos dedokas 'who PRT of-the-sun this to-see to-me light alone have-given' (*Philoct* 663).

(33) hin' eideth' helika pragmath' he miare kephale taraxas' haute diken ouk edoke 'so-that you-may-know how-much trouble the hateful person*ᵢ* having-stirred-up this*ᵢ* punishment not incurred' (Dem 18.153).

(34) theous de sebontai mounous tousde 'gods PRT they-worship alone these' (Her 5.7).

(35) paida anoeton chaironta ede eides?... andra de oupo eides anoeton chaironta? 'a-child foolish rejoicing already did-you-see? a-man PRT ever didn't-you-see foolish rejoicing?' (Pl *Gorg* 497e).

(36) grammat' ektitheis pseude 'letters publishing false' (Dem 25.50).

(37) hote hippeuen... hippous ektesato lamprous 'when he-served-in-the-cavalry horses he-procured fine' (Lys 19.63).

(38) estheti de chreomenous Medikei 'clothes PRT using Median' (Her 5.9).

(39) toutois ousian ho pater katelipe pollen 'to-these property the father left much' (Isae 7.5).

(40) tas d' emas tuchas tis ar' Achaion... echei? 'the PRT my fortunes who PRT of-the-Achaeans controls?' (*Troad* 292).

(41) soi te gar paidon ti dei? 'to-you and PRT of-children what there-is-need?' (*Med* 565).

(42) soi de pos phainetai? 'to you PRT how does-it-appear?' (Pl *Crat* 403b).

(43) eisphoras logizei posas? 'taxes you-calculate how-great?' (Isae Frag 2).

(44) paidas de de ti tousd' apokteinai theleis? 'boys PRT PRT why these to-kill you-wish?' (*HF* 206).

(45) onkon gar allos onomatos ti dei trephein metroon? 'the-pride PRT in-vain of-the-name why should cherish of-a-mother?' (*Trach* 817).

(46) chronon d' emeinat' allon en Troiai poson? 'time PRT did-you-stay other in Troy how-much?' (*Hel* 113).

(47) poson chronon gar diapeporthetai polis 'how-much time PRT has-been-destroyed the-city?' (*Hel* 111).

(48) ego d' epeide chronon emein' hoson me chren 'I PRT when time I-remained as-much-as for-me it-was-required' (*Hel* 612).

(49) chronon men ouk an emen en Thrakei polun 'time PRT not PRT we-would-have-been in Thrace much' (Ar *Ach* 136).

(50) ho gar aner kai dunamin echei megalen kai onomastos estin 'the PRT man both power has great and famous is' (Xen *Hell* 6.1.4).

(51) tas naus ton Athenaion 'the ships of-the Athenians' (Thuc 7.74.2); ton Athenaion toi peri tas naus erumati 'of-the Athenians the around the ships fortification' (Thuc 8.55.3); tas ton Athenaion naus 'the of-the Athenians ships' (Thuc 7.23.3); holon to strateuma to ton Athenaion 'whole the army the of-the Athenians' (Thuc 8.50.5).

(52) to stratopedon ton Athenaion 'the army of-the Athenians' (Thuc 4.94.2); to ton Athenaion stratopedon 'the of-the Athenians army' (Thuc 2.25.2).

(53) hoi men hoplitai ton Chalkideon... nikontai hupo ton Athenaion... hoi de hippes ton Chalkideon... nikosi tous ton Athenaion hippeas 'the PRT hoplites of-the Chalcidians are-conquered by the Athenians, the PRT cavalry of-the Chalcidians conquer the of-the Athenians cavalry' (Thuc 2.79.3).

(54) ta teiche ton Athenaion 'the walls of-the Athenians' (Thuc 7.3.4).

(55) paroikodomesantes kai parelthontes ten ton Athenaion oikodomian 'building-across and passing the of-the Athenians construction' (Thuc 7.6.4).

(56) meta de ten ton andron es ten neson diakomiden 'after PRT the of-the men to the island transfer' (Thuc 3.76.1).

(57) ton Surion tous klerous 'of-the Syrians the farms' (Her 1.76).

(58) deisantes ton Athenaion to tolmeron kai ten neoteropoiian 'fearing of-the Athenians the daring and the revolutionary-spirit' (Thuc 1.102.3).

(59) ton hopliton to stiphos 'of-the hoplites the mass' (Thuc 8.92.5).

(60) ten choran autou 'the country his' (Dem 17.6); tas heautou choras 'the of-himself lands' (Dem 7.82).

(61) ten gunaik' autou 'the wife his' (Dem 18.204); ten heautou gunaik' 'the of-himself wife' (Dem 59.110).

(62) proseballon auton toi teichei 'they-were-attacking of-them the wall' (Thuc 3.52.2).

(63) tes oikias tautes hesteke ta oikopeda 'of-the house that stand the foundations' (Aesch 1.182); he stratia hexei ton Athenaion 'the army will-come of-the Athenians' (Thuc 4.42.3).

(64) ten tes poleos horon rhomen 'the of-the city seeing strength' (Pl *Alc* 1.135e).

(65) tas d' epistolas humin anagnosomai tas tou Philippou 'the PRT letters to-you I-will-read the of-the Philip' (Dem 19.187).

(66) son men echthairon lechos kaines de numphes himeroi peplegmenos 'your PRT hating bed, of-a-new PRT bride by-love struck' (*Med* 555); e son echthairon lechos 'or your hating bed' (*Med* 697).

(67) son demas theromenos 'your person looking-for' (*Phoen* 699); kai son eksosai demas 'and your to-save person' (*Hel* 1092).

(68) anax tesde chthonos 'king of-this land' (*HF* 8); tesde koiranos chthonos 'of-this ruler land' (*Med* 71).

(69) hos kakon tond' aitios 'who for-evils these is-responsible' (*IA* 895); tond' hos aitios kakon 'for-these who is-responsible evils' (*Med* 332).

(70) en teid' hemerai 'on this day' (*Hipp* 22); teid' en hemerai 'this on day' (*Hipp* 726).

(71) lipousa tousde... domous 'leaving this house' (*Hel* 1526); tousd' an eklipoi domous 'this PRT he-would-leave house' (*Hipp* 796).

(72) hupo tautes agomenoi tes elpidos 'by this induced the hope' (Pl *Phaedo* 68a).

(73) tousde ge sterxeis nomous 'these PRT you-will-like laws' (*Hipp* 461).

(74) toisd' episteneis teknois 'over-these you-lament children' (*Med* 929).

(75) touth' humin anagnosetai to epigramma 'this to-you he-will-read the inscription' (Dem 20.112).

(76) ou tauten houtos agei ten hesuchian 'not this he practises the tranquility' (Dem 18.308).

(77) ou gar s' egoge teid' emei thapso cheri 'not PRT you I with-this my shall-bury hand' (*Alc* 665).

(78) out' elthes es tond' ex emou kletheis taphon 'nor you-came to this by me invited funeral' (*Alc* 629).

(79) tonde dialusis kakon 'of-these the-termination evils' (Phoen 435).

(80) tende diasoisai polin 'this to-save city' (*Phoen* 783).

(81) ton son Hellas apoteisei phonon 'for-the your Greece will-atone murder' (*IT* 338).

(82) Skamandrious gar tasde diaperon rhoas 'of-the-Scamander PRT these crossing streams' (Troad 1151).

(83) hoi dierotontes humas houtoi pephenasi rhetores 'the questioning you these have-shown-up orators' (Dem 3.22).

(84) chloran d' an' hulen 'green PRT in the-forest' (*Hipp* 17).

(85) es telouron hekomen pedon 'to a-distant we-have-come land' (*PV* 1).

(86) sen molont' eph' hestian 'your coming to hearth' (*Hec* 1216).

(87) eunas eluthon pros Hektoros 'bed I-came to Hector's' (*Rhes* 660).

(88) epi skenen iontes ten Xenophontos 'to the-tent coming the of-Xenophon' (Xen An 6.4.19).

(89) leukon edidosan gala 'white they-gave milk' (*Bacch* 700).

(90) stikton t' enduta nebridon 'of-dappled and garments fawnskin' (*Bacch* 111).

(91) apeirona ponton 'the-endless sea.'

(92) pikron oiston 'the-bitter arrow' (*Il* 4.118).

(93) heileto d' oxun akonta 'he-took PRT a-sharp javelin' (*Od* 14.531).

(94) xanthen apekeirato chaiten 'golden he-cut-off hair' (*Il* 23.141).

(95) pleiston hapsamenos logon 'very-many having-touched-on topics' (*Alc* 964).

(96) megiston aitios kakon 'for-the-greatest responsible evils' (*Med* 1080).

(97) megiston aitios kakon 'for-the-greatest responsible evils' (Dem 18.143).

(98) chruseen epetheke koronen 'a-golden he-put-on tip' (*Il* 4.111).

(99) tous te Skuthas katestrepsato kai tous Threikas 'the both Scythians he subdued and the Thracians' (Her 2.103).

(100) su te gar Hellen ei kai hemeis 'you-SG both PRT Greek are and we' (Xen An 2.1.16).

(101) Gorgous ommat' echon ede brotoloigou Areos 'of-the Gorgon the-eyes having and of-men-destroying Ares' (*Il* 8.349).

(102) ei me Nux dmeteira theon esaose kai andron 'if not Night tamer of-gods had-saved-me and of-men' (*Il* 14.259).

(103) apo kteneon zoousi kai ichthuon 'from livestock they-live and fish' (Her 1.216).

(104) neon apo kai klisiaon 'the-ships from and the-huts' (*Il* 16.45).

(105) enoreei pisunoi kai kartei cheiron 'in-valour trustful and in-the-strength of-their-hands' (*Il* 11.9).

(106) pollous logous kai tapeinous 'many words and humble' (Dem 21.186).

(107) megalois lithois kai olistherois 'with-big stones and slippery' (Xen An 4.3.6).

(108) polla kai pathontes kaka kai poiesantes 'many both having suffered losses and having-inflicted' (Aesch 2.172).

(109) daimonie tis ginetai horme 'heaven-sent some occurs impulse' (Her 7.18).

(110) ei tina tes Attikes leistai topon katalaboien 'if some of-the Attica pirates place were-to-seize' (Dem 7.4).

(111) ei tina pros allon deoi 'if anyone to other it-was-necessary' (Thuc 5.37.2).

(112) ei tis bouloito ton Lakedaimonion 'if anyone wanted of-the-Lacdaemonians' (Her 7.34).

(113) gunaika de gameten ean aner di' orgen kteine tina tis 'wife$_i$ PRT wedded$_i$ if husband$_k$ through anger kills any$_i$ any$_k$' (Pl *Laws* 868d).

(114) es ton tina komeon 'to of-the any villages' (Her 1.185).

(115) ton tis dokimon allos Medon 'of-the$_i$ some$_k$ notable$_i$ other$_k$ Medians$_i$' (Her 1.124).

(116) ei gar tis polis ploutei xulois... ti d' ei tis sideroi.. ploutei polis? 'if PRT some city is-rich in-timber, what PRT if some in-iron is-rich city?' (Xen *Ath Pol* 2.11).

(117) polu gar ton hippon etrechon thatton 'much PRT than-the horses they ran faster' (Xen An 1.5.2).

(118) edoke Gorgiai argurion toi Leontinoi 'he-gave to-Gorgias money the one-from-Leontini' (Xen An 2.6.16).

(119) kai min bale meron oistoi dexion 'and him struck on-the-thigh with-an-arrow right' (*Il* 11.583).

(120) apoluo kai humas tes aitias kai Agasian 'I-absolve both you of-the accusation and Agasias' (Xen *An* 6.6.15).

(121) spondas epoiesanto hekaton Athenaioi ete kai Argeioi 'treaty made for-a-hundred the-Athenians years and the-Argives' (Thuc 5.47.1).

(122) tous de doulous hoi Skuthai pantas tuphlousi 'the PRT slaves$_i$ the Scythians all$_i$ blind' (Her 4.2).

(123) toiauten dia telous gnomen echo 'such through-to the-end opinion I-have' (Lys 25.17).

(124) echei gunaikas hekastos pollas 'has wives each many' (Her 5.5).

(125) tini chromenos tekmerioi? 'what using evidence?' (Dem 20.115); toi autoi... chresometha tekmerioi 'the same we-will-use evidence' (Pl *Symp* 195e).

(126) horo de thiasous treis gunaikeion choron, hon erch' henos men Autonoe, tou deuterou meter Agaue se, tritou d' Ino chorou 'I-see PRT bands three of-female dancers, of-which one PRT Autonoe led, the second mother Agave your, the-third PRT Ino band' (*Bacch* 680).

(127) apangellein tis tina auton timai ton enthade. Terpsichorai... tous en tois chorois.. tei d' eratoi tous en tois erotikois... tei de... Kalliopei... tous en philosophiai diagontas 'to-announce which which of-them honours of-those here. To-Terpsichore those in the dances, to-the PRT Erato those in the love, to-the PRT Calliope those in philosophy passing-life' (Pl *Phaedr* 259c).

(128) toi men diokonti elatto epoiesan ta epitimia... toi de pheugonti megalas epethekan timorias 'for-the PRT prosecution less they-made the penalty, for-the PRT defendant great they-imposed punishments' (Dem 47.2).

(129) : ton Loqron topiwoiqoi : kai ton epiwoiqon toi Loqroi : 'of-the Locrians for-the-colonist and of-the colonists for-the Locrian' (*Locr* 34).

(130) ho d' adikos logos... pharmakon deitai sophon 'the PRT unjust argument remedies needs sophisticated' (*Phoen* 471).

(131) tauten men oun es ton mellonta chronon anegrapsan ten politeian, en de toi paronti kairoi tende 'this PRT for the future time they-wrote the constitution, in PRT the present crisis this' (Arist *Ath Pol* 31.1).

(132) duoin ge pantes anthropoi logoin ton kreisson' ismen 'of-two PRT all men arguments the stronger we-know' (Eur *Suppl* 486).

(133) lepta ep' ommaton phare balousa ton son 'fine$_i$ on eyes$_k$ veil$_i$ putting the your$_k$' (Eur *Suppl* 286).

(134) pedia de panta... okeia margois phlox edainuto gnathois 'plain PRT whole the-swift$_i$ with-fierce$_k$ flame$_i$ devoured jaws$_k$' (Phrynichus 5.3).

(135) hen ouden houto dunamin echei paideion mathema megalen 'one$_i$ none$_i$ so power$_k$ has instructional$_i$ discipline$_i$ big$_k$' (Pl *Laws* 747b).

(136) hos mega pasin herkos Achaioisin peletai polemoio kakoio 'who a-great for-all protection the-Achaeans is of-war evil' (*Il* 1.283).

(137) epiballomenan chaitaisin euode rhodeon plokon antheon 'putting on-her-hair a-fragrant$_i$ of-rose$_k$ wreath$_i$ blossoms$_k$' (*Med* 842).

(138) touton hapasas ton tropon eilephenai tas boulas 'in-this$_i$ all$_k$ the way$_i$ to-have-received-it the councils$_k$' (Dem 22.6).

(139) meden... hetton heteran heteras psuchen psuches einai 'no less one than-another; soul soul; to-be' (Pl *Phaedo* 93d).

(140) hetera d' aph' heteron kaka kakon kurei 'one; PRT from another_k evil; evil_k occurs' (*Hec* 690).

(141) tous diaphaneas lithous toi puri 'the red-hot stones with-the fire' (Her 4.75).

(142) ta ton parodon ton eis Pulas choria kuria 'the of-the approaches the to Ther-mopylae places controlling' (Aesch 2.132).

(143) ten metaxu polin Heraias kai Makistou 'the between city Heraea and Macis-tus' (Xen *Hell* 3.2.30).

(144) tei de proteraiai hemerai xunebe tes maches tautes 'on-the PRT previous day it-happened to-the battle this' (Thuc 5.75.4).

(145) epi tous paratetagmenous hippeas 'against the drawn-up-opposite cavalry' (Xen *Hell* 3.4.23).

(146) en tais polesi tais stasiazousais 'in the cities the politically-unstable' (Xen *Ath Pol* 3.10).

(147) kata tas pulas tas eis ten akran pherousas 'towards the gates the to the citadel leading' (Xen *An* 5.2.23).

(148) tous hupo ton leiston haliskomenous barbarous 'the by the patrols captured barbarians' (Xen *Hell* 3.4.19).

(149) tas polemousas pros allelas poleis 'the fighting against each-other cities' (Xen *Vect* 5.8).

(150) ten ex hapantos tou aionos sunethroismenen tei polei doxan 'the from all the time accumulated to-the city glory' (Lyc 110).

(151) ton rheonta potamon dia tes poleos 'the flowing river through the city' (Xen *Hell* 5.2.4).

(152) tas meta tou Demosthenous naus epelthousas 'the with the Demosthenes ships coming-after' (Thuc 7.55.1).

(153) ton tetagmenon chronon en tois nomois 'of-the prescribed times in the laws' (Dem 24.26).

(154) hoi d' ek ton Surakouson tote meta ten tou Plemmuriou halosin presbeis oichomenoi es tas poleis 'the PRT from the Syracuse then after the of-the Plemmyrium capture ambassadors going to the cities' (Thuc 7.32.1).

(155) tei mellousei tou ontos hikanos te kai teleos psuchei metalepsesthai 'the going-to of-the reality sufficiently both and completely spirit partake' (Pl *Rep* 486e).

(156) aitian legontes pseude 'reason saying a-false' (Dem 20.133).

(157) oudemian ekeinou peri touton poiesamenou diatheken 'no him about these-things having-made will' (Isae 8.40).

(158) ego te gar lexasa kouphisthesomai psuchen kakos se 'I and PRT having-spoken shall-be-relieved in-heart badly about-you' (*Med* 472).

(159) tautes tes presbeias ou kategoreis mou didontos tas euthunas 'of-this the em-bassy not you-accuse me giving the account' (Aesch 2.96).

(160) ten stolen ekdus edoke ten Mediken 'the robe having-taken-off he-gave the Median' (Xen *Cyr* 5.1.2).

(161) deka naus apesteilet' echonta kenas Charidemon 'ten ships you-sent having empty Charidemus' (Dem 3.5).

(162) hekei pseude suntaxas kath' hemon kategorian 'he-comes a-false having-concocted against us charge' (Aesch 2.183).

(163) ex heteras oicheto presbeuon poleos 'from another he-went being-ambassador city' (Dem 19.147).

(164) megisten hegoumai peri emautou tei demokratiai pistin dedokenai 'the-greatest I-believe about myself to-the democracy assurance to-have-given' (Lys 25.17).

(165) oudemian popote phanesetai presbeian... kalesas 'no ever he-will-appear embassy having-invited' (Aesch 3.76).

(166) ten heterou zeton epitimian aphelesthai phainetai 'the of-another trying civil-rights to-take-away he-seems' (Dem 18.15).

(167) tis an apokrupsai chronos dunait' an 'what PRT to-hide time would-be-able PRT' (Aesch 3.222).

(168) pleista emellon pragmata hexein 'most I-was-going-to trouble have' (Lys 3.32).

(169) posa emelles pragmata hexein 'how-much were-you-going-to trouble have?'

(170) hoposa an hekastos dunaito porisai moi chremata 'how-much PRT each could provide to-me money' (Xen Cyr 8.2.16).

(171) gunaikas de nomizontes pollas echein hekastos 'wives PRT having-the-custom many to-have each' (Her 4.172).

(172) hegoumenos ten megisten autois opheilein charin 'believing the greatest to-them to-owe thanks' (Lys Frag 8.1.3); en pollei an echesthai humas aporiai doko 'in great PRT to-be-held you difficulty I-think' (Antiph 5.65); ean humin eipein hapanta dunetho ta pepragmena 'if to-you to-say all I-am-able the deeds' (Lys 1.5); megala touton oimai semeia deixein humin 'great of-these-things I-think proof to-be-about-to-show to-you' (Aesch 3.177); ou prosekontas emautoi doxo proeiresthai logous 'not befitting myself I-will-seem to-have-chosen topics' (Dem 18.129); ek toutou ten morian aphanizein epecheiresa tou choriou 'from this the sacred-olive to-remove I-tried the plot-of-land' (Lys 7.28).

(173) hopos oun esesthe andres axioi tes eleutherias hes kektesthe 'so-that PRT you-will-be men worthy of-the freedom which you-possess' (Xen An 1.7.3).

(174) pollen ephe pronoian huper eusebeias echein 'much he-said consideration for piety to-have.'

(175) hegeomai, oimai, dokeo, phainomai, nomizo, hupolambano, aisthanomai, peiraomai, mello, zeteo, boulomai, dei, dunamai, exesti, epicheireo, prosekei, sumpherei. For translation, see footnote in text.

(176) pollen prosekei pronoian huper eusebeias echein 'much it-befits-him consideration for piety to-have' (Aesch 2.114).

(177) me de pantas emous epielpeo muthous eidesein 'not PRT all my hope words to-know' (Il 1.545).

(178) polees te min eresanto hippees phoreein 'many and it prayed horsemen to-wear' (Il 4.143).

Chapter 4

(1) he min egeire Nausikaan eupeplon 'and-she her awakened Nausicaa beautifully-dressed' (Od 6.48).

(2) he de diapro eluthen encheie 'it PRT right-through went the spear' (Il 7.260).

(3) tei rha paradrameten pheugon, ho d' opisthe diokon 'there PRT they-ran-by fleeing-SG, he-PRT from-behind pursuing-SG' (Il 22.157).

(4) hoi de duo skopeloi, ho men ouranon eurun hikanei 'those PRT two cliffs, the-one PRT heaven wide reaches' (*Od* 12.73).

(5) tes d'... anagnousei 'her-GEN PRT... recognizing-DAT' (*Od* 23.205).

(6) Zeu pater... Eelios th' 'Zeus-VOC father-VOC... Sun-NOM and' (*Il* 3.276).

(7) amphi de chaitai omois aissontai 'around PRT mane on-the-shoulders streams' (*Il* 6.509).

(8) elth' ho geron Dolios, sun d' huieis toio gerontos 'came that old-man Dolios, together PRT sons of-that old-man' (*Od* 24.387).

(9) Tudeiden d' ouk an gnoies poteroisi meteie 'the-son-of-Tydeus-ACC PRT not PRT you-could-know to-which-side he-belonged' (*Il* 5.85).

(10) hina min pauseie ponoio dion Achillea 'so-that him he-might-restrain from-labour, noble Achilles' (*Il* 21.249).

(11) he d' en gounasi pipte Diones, di' Aphrodite 'she PRT at the-knees fell of-Dione, beautiful Aphrodite' (*Il* 5.370).

(12) autar ho boun hiereusen anax andron Agamemnon piona 'but he an-ox*ᵢ* sacri-ficed king of-men Agamemnon fat*ᵢ*' (*Il* 2.402).

(13) piona meria kaie boos 'fat thighs he-was-burning of-an-ox' (*Il* 11.773).

(14) polin aipen olesa 'city lofty I-destroyed.'

(15) polin Kilikon olesa 'city of-the-Cilicians I-destroyed.'

(16) polin kai astu olesa 'inhabitants and city I-destroyed.'

(17) eprathon kai olesa polin 'I-sacked and destroyed city.'

(18) epi d' alphita leuka palune 'on-it PRT barley white she-sprinkled' (*Il* 11.640); epi d' epia pharmaka passe 'on-it PRT soothing medications sprinkle' (*Il* 11.830); epi de rhizan bale pikren 'on-it PRT herb he-put bitter' (*Il* 11.846); epi d' aigeion kne turon 'on-it PRT goat he-grated cheese' (*Il* 11.639).

(19) he de Ladike apedoke ten euchen tei theoi 'the PRT Ladice fulfilled the vow to-the goddess' (Her 2.181).

(20) xenia edokan tei stratiai 'gifts they-gave to-the army' (Xen *An* 5.5.14).

(21) toutois de choran kai oikous edoke 'to-these PRT land and houses he-gave' (Xen *Cyr* 8.4.28).

(22) ton chrematon kratein : ton epiwoiqon 'of-the property take-possession : the colonist' (*Locr* 31).

(23) en Naupaktoi : karuxai en tagorai : 'in Naupactus : announce in the-market-place :' (*Locr* 20).

(24) ton au Pheidippos te kai Antiphos hegesasthen 'these PRT Phidippus both and Antiphus led-DUAL' (*Il* 2.678).

(25) pro gar heke pater alloi te gerontes 'out PRT sent-SG his-father the-other and old-men' (*Od* 21.21).

(26) doio d' Atreida meneten kai dios Odysseus 'the-two PRT sons-of-Atreus remained-DUAL and noble Odysseus' (*Il* 19.310).

(27) tacheos d' Admatos hiken kai Melampos, eumeneontes anepsion 'quickly PRT Admetus came-SG and Melampus, wishing-well-to-PL their-cousin' (Pi *Pyth* 4.126).

(28) e men de tharsos moi Ares t' edosan kai Athene 'PRT PRT PRT courage to-me Ares both gave-PL and Athena' (*Od* 14.216).

(29) See footnote in text.

(30) ei de k' Ares archosi maches e Phoibos Apollon 'if PRT PRT Ares start-PL battle or Phoebus Apollo' (*Il* 20.138).

(31) oureas men proton epoicheto kai kunas argous 'the-mules PRT first he-attacked and the-dogs swift' (*Il* 1.50).

(32) Dios angeloi ede kai andron 'of-Zeus messengers and also of-men' (*Il* 7.274).

(33) polin hairesomen euruaguian 'the-city we-will-capture with-broad-streets' (*Il* 2.329); ek de polin persen Kilikon 'out PRT the-city he-wiped of-the-Cilicians' (*Il* 6.415).

(34) enth' alochon te philen elipon kai nepion huion 'where wife both dear I-left and infant son' (*Il* 5.480).

(35) mela phulassemenai patroia kai helikas bous 'the-sheep to-guard paternal and the-curved oxen' (*Od* 12.136).

(36) ton rh' Eous ekteine phaeines aglaos huios 'whom PRT of-Dawn killed bright the-glorious son' (*Od* 4.188).

(37) chlainan kalen balen ede chitona 'cloak beautiful she-put-on and tunic' 10.365); chlainan bale phoinikoessan 'cloak he-threw-off purple' (*Od* 14.500).

(38) kai min bale meron oistoi dexion 'and him he-hit on-the-thigh*ᵢ* with-an-arrow right*ᵢ*' (*Il* 11.583).

(39) : diomosai horqon : ton nomion : 'to-swear an-oath : the prescribed' (*Locr* 45).

(40) en tepiaroi k' enechoito : toi 'ntaut' egramenoi 'to the-penalty PRT he-should-be-liable : the here written' (*LSAG* 42.6).

(41) ha de bola potelato : hantituchonsa 'the PRT council shall-enforce-it : the-one-in-office' (IG 4.554).

(42) qoi basileus edoq' hoiguptios 'and-the king gave the-Egyptian' (Masson et al. 1988).

(43) phrazon halosin Iliou t' anastasin 'indicating the-capture, of-Troy and the-destruction' (*Ag* 589).

(44) labon chlanida kai peribalomenos purren 'taking a cloak*ᵢ* and putting-on red*ᵢ*' (Her 3.139).

(45) hai sumphorai ton anthropon archousi kai ouki honthropoi ton sumphoreon 'the circumstances the men govern and not the-men the circumstances' (Her 7.49).

(46) epea pteroenta proseuda 'words winged he-addressed.'

(47) thuoen nephos 'fragrant cloud' (*Il* 15.153).

(48) rhodoenti de chrien elaioi 'with-rose-scented PRT she-anointed-him oil' (*Il* 23.186).

(49) aner chalkeus 'man smith' (*Od* 9.391); ten chalkees kamon andres 'which smiths made men' (*Il* 4.187).

(50) pentekonta d' helon diphrous 'fifty PRT I-seized chariots' (*Il* 11.748).

(51) euru gar amph' omoisin echei sakos 'broad PRT around his-shoulders he-has shield' (*Il* 11.527).

(52) hos ar' ephan apiontes, emon d' egelasse philon ker hos onom' exapatesen emon 'so PRT they-spoke leaving, my PRT smiled dear heart how name deceived my' (*Od* 9.413).

(53) leukous d' eperesen odontas 'his-white PRT it-pierced teeth' (*Il* 5.291).

(54) chruseia pater etitaine talanta 'the-golden the-Father held-up scales' (*Il* 8.69).

(55) adakruto echen osse 'tearless he-held his-eyes' (*Od* 4.186).

(56) tachees d' ekpipton oistoi 'the-swift PRT fell-out arrows' (*Il* 21.492).

(57) tarpheiai niphades Dios ekpoteontai psuchrai 'thick the-snowflakes from-heaven fly-down cold' (*Il* 19.357).

(58) aure d' ek potamou psuchre pneei 'a-breeze PRT from the-river cold blows' (*Od* 5.469).

(59) neoutatou ⟨eouses⟩ erree cheiros 'from-newly-wounded ⟨being⟩ it-ran-down arm' (*Il* 13.539).

(60) epempsan... estephanomenous duo kerukas 'they sent garlanded two heralds' (Xen *Hell* 4.7.3).

(61) melan d' anekekien haima 'dark PRT gushed blood' (*Il* 7.262).

(62) eeri d' enchos ekeklito kai tache' hippo 'on-a-cloud PRT his-spear was-leaning and his-swift horses' (*Il* 5.356); chrusampukas eiteen hippous 'the-having-golden-front-lets she-asked-for horses' (ib. 358); doke chrusampukas hippous 'he-gave-her the-having-golden-frontlets horses' (ib. 363).

(63) Troon rhegnunto phalangas 'of-the-Trojans they-broke the-ranks' (*Il* 13.718).

(64) e tis sphoe poren theos antibolesas 'or some you gave god having-met' (*Il* 10.546).

(65) teon d' ex euchetai einai andron? 'from-what PRT he-claims to-be men?'

(66) poluphorbou peirata gaies 'of-the-bountiful the-ends earth' (*Il* 14.200).

(67) hieres para puthmen' elaies 'of-the-sacred by the-trunk olive' (*Od* 13.372).

(68) kakon epilethon hapanton 'of-misfortunes causing-oblivion all' (*Od* 4.221).

(69) melainaon apo neon 'the-black from ships' (*Il* 24.780).

(70) hon korunetes geinat' Areithoos kai Phulomedousa boopis 'whom the-mace-bearer begat Areithous and Phylomedusa ox-eyed' (*Il* 7.10).

(71) Peneleos de Lukon te sunedramon 'Peneleus PRT Lycon and ran-together' (*Il* 16.335).

(72) hechi rhoas Simoeis sumballeton ede Skamandros 'where their-streams Simois join-DUAL and Scamander' (*Il* 5.774).

(73) oinon emisgon eni kretersi kai hudor 'wine they-were-mixing in bowls and water' (*Od* 1.110).

(74) to engus monon horon kai to parachrema 'the near only seeing and the imme-diate' (Pl *Crat* 395d).

(75) harmoniai monon kai mekei 'in-tone only and in-duration' (Pl *Crat* 416b).

(76) sunebouleue... gunaika me agesthai teknopoion es ta oikia 'he-advised woman not to-bring child-bearing into the-home' (Her 1.59).

(77) ep' andras strateuometha agathous 'against men we-are-waging-war valiant' (Her 7.53); es gen epleuse Troiad' 'to the-land he-sailed Trojan' (Eur *El* 3).

(78) kai toi nedumos hupnos epi blepharoisin epipte negretos, hedistos, thanatoi anchista eoikos 'and to-him pleasant sleep on his-eyelids fell sound, very-sweet, to-death most-closely resembling' (*Od* 13.79).

(79) pedas chruseias ebale 'fetters gold he-put-on'; Abanta kai Polueidon metoicheto 'Abas and Polyidus he-went-after.'

(80) opa chalkeon 'voice brazen' (*Il* 18.222).

(81) theleia d' hippos kale ou kalon...? 'female PRT horse beautiful-FEM not beauti-ful-NEUT-is?' (Pl *Hipp Mai* 288b).

(82) lithoi te kai plinthoi kai xula kai keramos ataktos men errimena ouden chresima estin 'stones and and bricks and timber and tiles without-order PRT thrown-together not useful-NEUT is' (Xen *Mem* 3.1.7).

(83) epeita de chili' hupeste aigas homou kai ois 'then PRT a-thousand-NEUT he-promised goats together and sheep' (*Il* 11.244).

(84) amphi de min rhakos... balen ede chitona rhogalea rhupoonta 'around PRT him a-cloak she-put and a-tunic torn-NEUT and filthy-NEUT' (*Od* 13.435).

(85) estheta de phoreousi hoi hirees lineen mounen 'clothing PRT wear the priests linen only' (Her 2.37).

(86) heimata te ephoreon ta kallista 'clothes and they-wore the best' (Her 3.27).

(87) cheir' hele dexiteren 'her-hand he-took right' (*Od* 1.121); thuras epetheke phaeinas 'the-doors she-closed shining' (*Il* 14.169).

(88) peri kouleon een argureon 'around-it a-scabbard there-was silver' (*Il* 11.30); kretera pherein Megapenthe' anogen argureon 'bowl to-bring Megapenthes he-told silver' (*Od* 15.103); ho d' ara kretera phaeinon thek' autou proparoithe pheron krateros Megapenthes argureon 'he PRT PRT bowl shining placed him before bringing mighty Megapenthes silver' (*Od* 15.121).

(89) entha hoi aule hupsele dedmeto periskeptoi eni choroi kale te megale te, peridromos 'where to-him high was-built visible-around in place beautiful and great and, with-open-space-around' (*Od* 14.5).

(90) See footnote in text.

(91) Troes d' epi dourat' echeuan oxea pamphanoonta 'the-Trojans PRT on-him spears poured sharp gleaming' (*Il* 5.618).

(92) koruthi d' epeneue phaeinei tetraphaloi 'with-his-helmet PRT he-nodded bright four-bossed' (*Il* 22.314).

(93) plokamous eplexe phaeinous kalous ambrosious 'her-hair she-plaited glossy beautiful divine' (*Il* 14.176).

(94) thamnos ephu tanuphullos elaies herkeos entos akmenos thalethon 'a-bush grew longleaved of-olive the-courtyard inside fullgrown flourishing' (*Od* 23.190).

(95) lithon heileto cheiri pacheiei keimenon en pedioi melana trechun te megan te 'a-stone she-seized in-her-hand stout lying on the-ground black rough and great and' (*Il* 21.403).

(96) epi de Troes keladesan nepioi; ek gar spheon phrenas heileto Pallas Athene 'thereat PRT the-Trojans applauded foolish; from PRT them sense took Pallas Athene' (*Il* 18.310).

(97) pardaleei men prota metaphrenon euru kalupse poikilei 'with-a-leopard-skin PRT first his-back broad he-covered spotted' (*Il* 10.29).

(98) he hoi hapasas | esch' odunas 'which to-him all | stopped pain' (*Il* 11.847).

(99) par de hoi alloi | naion Boiotoi 'beside PRT him other | live Boeotians' (*Il* 5.710).

(100) megiston | tekmor 'the-greatest | guarantee' (*Il* 1.525).

(101) hos ken emes ge | choinikos haptetai 'whoever PRT my PRT | food shares' (*Od* 19.27).

(102) e mala lugres | peuseai angelies 'PRT very miserable | you-will-learn news' (*Il* 18.18).

(103) houneka kalon | eidos ep' 'because handsome | appearance there-belongs-to-him' (*Il* 3.44).

(104) chruseoisin / aorteressin 'with-golden / rings' (*Il* 11.31).

(105) hieroio domoio | 'of-the-holy house |' (*Il* 6.89).

(106) kope | arguree 'a-hilt | silver' (*Od* 8.403).

(107) hedus hupnos 'sweet sleep.'

(108) hupnon | hedun 'sleep | sweet' (*Od* 1.364); ex hupnou m' anegeireis | hedeos 'from sleep me you-are-waking | sweet' (*Od* 23.16).

(109) heure de phokas | zatrepheas 'he-found PRT the-seals | fat' (*Od* 4.450).

(110) homophrosunen opaseian | esthlen 'harmony may-they-grant-you | good' (*Od* 6.181).

(111) hai men leptas othonas echon, hoi de chitonas | heiat' eunnetous 'these PRT fine dresses had, those PRT tunics | wore well-woven' (*Il* 18.595).

(112) panta [peresamen eurea ponton] 'all [we-crossed the-wide sea]' (*Od* 24.118); [eurea peresamen ponton] '[the-wide we-crossed sea]'; panta [peresamen ponton] 'all [we-crossed the-sea].'

(113) mega gar min Olumpios etrephe pema 'as-a-great PRT him the-Olympian reared woe' (*Il* 6.282).

(114) eutrichas hoplisath' hippous 'having-beautiful-manes he-prepared horses' (*Il* 23.351).

(115) tout' echoi geras 'this could-have privilege' (*LGS* 370.14).

(116) touto geras apeneime 'this privilege he-attributed' (Pl *Prot* 341e).

Chapter 5

(1) touton authis ho makarios periptuxamenos Markianos epi to tou sitou apegage katagogion, "Eulogeson" legon "pater, hoste tas tes apothekes aneoixai thuras hemas kai ek ton ageorgeton drepsasthai karpon 'him PRT the blessed having-embraced Marcianus to the-of-the grain lead store, "Bless" saying "father, so-that the-of-the granary may-open doors we and from the uncultivated pluck harvest' (Theodorus 75).

(2) pollen moi aporian parechei 'much to-me difficulty it-affords' (Lys 19.1).

(3) megala ektesato chremata... megala hoi chremata anatheinai 'great she-obtained wealth... great to-her wealth to-ascribe' (Her 2.135).

(4) oud'...dolies epeletheto technes 'nor his-deceitful did-he-forget ways' (*Od* 4.455).

(5) kakon epilethon hapanton 'of-misfortunes inducing-forgetfulness all' (*Od* 4.221).

(6) doru t' esche kai aspida 'his-spear both he-held and his-shield' (*Il* 5.300).

(7) cheiressi pepoithotes ede biephi 'in-their-hands trusting and in-their-strength' (*Il* 12.135).

(8) dolon at' ede ponoio 'of-guile insatiable and of battle-toil' (*Il* 11.430).

(9) arnon knises aigon te teleion 'of-sheep the-sacrificial-aroma of-goats and un-blemished' (*Il* 1.66).

(10) megale gar rhope 'great PRT weight' (Dem 2.22).

(11) chlorais hup' elatais anorophois hentai petrais 'green under pines on-roofless they-sit rocks' (*Bacch* 38).

(12) krounon ek megalon koiles entosthe charadres 'springs from great hollow inside gorge' (*Il* 4.454).

(13) neon apo kai klisiaon 'the-ships from and the-huts' (*Il* 13.273); epeon kecholomenos ede kai ergon 'at-words enraged and and at-deeds' (*Il* 11.703).

(14) mestei pollon agathon 'full of-many good-things' (Xen *An* 3.5.1); pollon agathon mestai 'of-many good-things full' (Xen *Cyr* 4.1.9); pollon meston agathon 'of-many full good-things' (Pl *Laws* 906a).

(15) met' allon murion 'with others countless' (*Andr* 697).

(16) cheiros asiderou meta 'hand unarmed with' (*Bacch* 736); pollon met' allon 'many with others' (*Andr* 1152).

(17) allotrias ges peri 'a-foreign land for' (Thuc 3.13.5).

(18) ton d' allon peri blapseon 'the PRT other about injuries' (Pl *Laws* 932e).

(19) chronon epi makron 'time for long' (Her 1.81).

(20) *ton tolmerotaton meta lochagon 'the boldest with commanders.'

(21) polemion para 'enemies from' (*Orest* 875).

(22) polu pro ton allon 'much ahead-of the others' (Thuc 2.91.2).

(23) polu sun phronemati meizoni 'much with confidence greater' (Xen *An* 3.1.22).

(24) chthona | eis tend' 'land | into this' (Eur *Suppl* 1191).

(25) hupselon d' epi | naon 'high PRT on | temples' (Eur *El* 6).

(26) melainaon apo neon 'the-black from ships' (*Il* 16.304); melaineon herm' odunaon 'of-black carrier pains' (*Il* 4.117).

(27) basilikon domon huper 'the-royal palace for' (*Phoen* 1326).

(28) ouranion hupsipetes es melathron 'the-heavenly lofty to hall' (*Hec* 1100).

(29) poluanori d' en xenoenti thronoi 'crowded PRT at the-full-of-foreigners throne' (*IT* 1282).

(30) etea men es eikosi kai hekaton tous pollous auton apikneesthai 'years PRT up-to twenty and a-hundred the majority of-them reach' (Her 3.23).

(31) tinos g' hup' allou? 'who PRT by else?' (*Hec* 774).

(32) hagnois en hierois 'the-holy in shrine' (*Andr* 1065).

(33) tina boais logon? 'what are-you-shouting words?' (*Hipp* 571).

(34) tin' hupageis m' es elpida? 'what are-you-leading me to hope?' (*Hel* 826).

(35) tou theou para 'the god from' (*OT* 95); paidos toud' emanthanon para 'boy this I learned from' (*Ant* 1012).

(36) apo krenes melanudrou 'from a-spring dark-watered' (*Il* 16.160); melainaon apo neon 'the-black from ships' (*Il* 16.304); *melainaon neon apo 'the-black ships from.'

(37) kranaen Ithaken kata koiraneousi 'rocky Ithaca over they-rule' (*Od* 1.247).

(38) koilei para nei melainei 'the-hollow by ship black' (*Od* 3.365); *koilei nei para melainei 'the-hollow ship by black.'

(39) astu periplomenon deion hupo thumoraisteon 'a-town surrounding enemies by life-destroying' (*Il* 18.220).

(40) porphureois peploisi kalupsantes malakoisin 'with-purple robes covering-them soft' (*Il* 24.796).

(41) auton peri 'them about' (*Soph* 226b).

(42) peri auton 'about them' (*Euthyph* 6b).

(43) touton peri 'these-things about' (*Meno* 92c).

(44) tou peri? 'what in-respect-of?' (*Soph* 222d).

(45) tinon de peri? 'what PRT about?' (*Laws* 809d).

(46) hedones peri monon 'pleasure about only' (*Laws* 658a).

(47) tautes de peri... tes metaboles 'this PRT about the change' (*Laws* 676c).

(48) ta men oun de ton archaion peri... ta de ton neon 'those PRT PRT PRT of-the ancients about... those PRT of-the moderns' (*Laws* 886d).

(49) ta men thanasima... ton d' allon peri blapseon 'the PRT fatal-ones... the PRT other about injuries' (*Laws* 932e).

(50) ton te oun allon eulabeisthai peri plemmelein eis diken, diapherontos de... 'the and PRT other-things to-beware about of-offending against justice, particularly PRT' (*Laws* 943e).

(51) hon an erein peri mellei 'which PRT to-speak about he-intends' (*Phaedr* 259e).

(52) e peri phonous e peri hieron klopas 'either about murder or about of-sacred-things theft' (*Euthyph* 5d).

(53) tou hosiou te peri kai tou anosiou 'the pious both about and the impious' (*Euthyph* 4e).

(54) ton allon peri nomeon 'the other about herdsmen' (*Polit* 268b).

(55) ton megiston peri kindunon 'the greatest about dangers' (Thuc 1.75.5).

(56) iatron de peri panton 'doctors PRT about all' (*Laws* 865b).

Chapter 6

(1) See footnote in text.

(2) ten allen diexelthon presbeian 'the other I-went-through embassy' (Aesch 2.48).

(3) tous geuomenous kunas ton probaton 'the tasting dogs the sheep' (Dem 25.40).

(4) polu allous emou deinoterous 'much others than-me more-skilled' (Xen *Oec* 2.16).

(5) he stratia hexei ton Athenaion 'the army will-come of-the Athenians' (Thuc 4.42.3).

(6) tous daknontas kunas 'the biting dogs' (Xen *Hell* 2.4.41).

(7) agathoi 'in-a-good-man' (Pl *Tim* 29e).

(8) he husteraia 'the following'; he eutheia 'the straight.'

(9) naumachesantas mian 'having-naval-battle-fought one-FEM' (Ar *Frogs* 693).

(10) ek de hoi tautes tes gunaikos oud' ex alles paides eginonto 'from PRT to-him this wife nor from another children were-born' (Her 5.92).

(11) prophaseis anti ton alethon pseudeis metathenta 'reasons in-place-of the true false substituting' (Dem 18.225).

(12) pater epetelleto Peleus 'your-father ordered Peleus' (*Il* 9.252).

(13) aipoloi andres 'goatherd men' (*Il* 2.474).

(14) alkimon huion 'valiant son' (*Il* 6.437).

(15) pater hoi doken emos 'father to-him gave-it my' (*Od* 1.264).

(16) en tois demosiois anagegraptai ⟨grammasi⟩ 'in the public they-have-been-registered ⟨archives⟩' (Aesch 2.58); tas t' idias dikas kai tas demosias 'the both private cases and the public-ones' (Dem 18.210).

(17) hupo tes metruias tes emes exapatomene 'by the stepmother the my deceived' (Antiph 1.19); hupo ton echthron peistheis ton emon 'by the enemies persuaded the my' (Lys 7.39); homologoumenon de ton semeion kai para tes toutou gunaikos kai para tes emes 'being-acknowledged PRT the seals both by the of-this-man wife and by the mine' (Dem 41.21).

(18) he polis en kakois tois megistois egigneto 'the city in evils the greatest was getting' (Andoc 1.58); ten de polin en kakois ousan tois megistois 'the PRT city in evils being the greatest' (Andoc 1.51); ton men tois echthrois huparchouson dunameon tas megistas aphelein 'of-the PRT to-the enemy accruing strengths the biggest to remove' (Dem 18.302).

(19) tous idious polemous epanorthosai 'the private wars to-fix' (Dem 14.5); tas idias kateskeuakasin oikias 'the private they-have-built houses' (Dem 23.208); tas holes ge tes patridos spondas... ou monon tas idias 'the to-whole PRT the country obligations... not only the personal-ones' (Dem 19.191).

(20) lege kai ten epistolen ten tou Berisadou 'read also the letter the of-the Berisades' (Dem 23.174); tes epistoles ekouete tes Proxenou 'the letter you-heard the of-Proxenus' (Aesch 2.134); kata to Kleonumou psephisma.. kata de to Peisandrou 'according-to the of-Cleonymus decree... according-to PRT the of-Pisander' (Andoc 1.27).

(21) iasomenoi to Demosthenous dorodokema 'to-remedy the of-Demosthenes bribery' (Aesch 3.69); to Demosthenous epigraphein onoma 'the of-Demosthenes to-write name' (Aesch 3.159); eis tas leitourgias apochoresetai. tas pot' e pou gegonuias? tas tou patros? 'to the public-services he-will-have-recourse. The when or where occurring? The of-the father?' (Dem 25.78).

(22) to teichos to makron to notion 'the wall the long the south' (Andoc 3.7); en tei archaiai tei hemeterai phonei 'in the archaic the our language' (Pl *Crat* 398b).

(23) ho men de nautikos ho ton barbaron stratos 'the PRT PRT naval the of-the barbarians force' (Her 7.196); trieres he strategis ede exormei he Lamachou 'trireme the commanding already was-at-sea the of Lamachus' (Andoc 1.11); ten lithon tauten heorakas ten kalen ten diaphane 'the stone that have-you-seen the beautiful the transparent' (Ar *Clouds* 766).

(24) hedion gar an komoidias tes phaulotates... akousaien 'sooner PRT PRT comedy the most-low-brow they-would-hear' (Isoc 2.44).

(25) ta teuchea kala 'that armour beautiful' (*Il* 21.317).

(26) toichou tou heteroio 'wall that other' (*Il* 9.219).

(27) emati toi proteroi 'day that previous' (*Il* 21.5).

(28) ton opithen 'those behind' (*Od* 11.66); toisin Odusseos 'with-those of-Odysseus' (*Od* 22.221).

(29) theous d' onomenen hapantas tous hupotartarious 'the-gods PRT he-named all those under-Tartarus' (*Il* 14.279).

(30) ton ariston Achaion 'the best of-the-Achaeans' (*Il* 5.414).

(31) ton emon cholon 'the my anger' (*Il* 4.42).

(32) tous de kata prumnas te kai amph' hala elsai Achaious 'those PRT among the-ships both and next-to the-sea to-hem-in Achaeans' (*Il* 1.409).

(33) tous men lipen autou 'those PRT he-left there' (*Il* 4.364).

(34) tous men heous erukake monuchas hippous 'the PRT his-own he-restrained single-hooved horses' (*Il* 5.321).

(35) tous sous elenxo, meter, ei sapheis logoi 'the yours I-shall-test, mother, if are-true words' (Eur *Phaeth* 62).

(36) ten tes paranoias graphesthai diken 'the of-the insanity to-bring accusation' (Pl *Laws* 929d).

(37) gnoi men ton Heras hoios est' autoi cholos 'he-may-learn PRT the of-Hera of-what-sort is for-him anger' (*HF* 840).

(38) pragma gar... mega kai lampron... aneileto 'prize PRT great and glorious he-has-carried-off' (Dem 10.47); pragma heurekenai mega kai pollou axion 'a-matter to-have-discovered great and of-much worth' (Lys 12.68); pos hemin he polis hoia t' estai polemein... allos te kan pros megalen te kai plousian anankasthei polemein 'how for-us the

city able PRT will-be to-fight-a-war... particularly PRT if against great both and rich it-is-compelled to-fight' (Pl *Rep* 422a).

(39) polla kai megala pragmata 'many and great things' (Pl *Meno* 99d); tous men polla kai megala poiesantas humas agatha 'those PRT many and great having-done you good-things' (Dem 26.7); me smikron morion hen pros megala kai polla aphairomen 'not small part one with large and many let-us-contrast' (Pl *Polit* 262a).

(40) ho kalon aleison anairesesthai emelle chruseon amphoton 'he a-beautiful cup to-raise was-about-to gold two-handled' (*Od* 22.9).

(41) limenas elthes es euenemous 'a-harbour you-came to sheltered' (*Andr* 749).

(42) ek pontou bas ioeideos 'from the-sea coming purple' (*Od* 5.56); en pontoi pathet' algea ichthuoenti 'in-the-sea you-suffered hardships fish-teeming' (*Od* 10.457).

(43) oinon echous' en cheiri meliphrona dexiterephi 'wine having in hand delicious right' (*Il* 24.284).

(44) hina pantes Achaioi ophthalmoisin idosi 'so-that all the-Achaeans with-their-eyes may-see' (*Il* 19.173).

(45) ou... pantes basileusomen enthad' Achaioi 'not... all we-will-reign here Achaeans' (*Il* 2.203).

(46) hoi d' ara pantes aken egenonto siopei 'they PRT PRT all quiet became in-silence' (*Il* 7.398).

(47) hoi d' ara pantes epiachon huies Achaion 'they PRT PRT all applauded sons of-the-Achaeans' (*Il* 7.403).

(48) ton pantes anastenachousin Achaioi 'whom all mourn the-Achaeans' (*Il* 23.211).

(49) tauta pantes isasin hoi hippeis 'these-things all know the knights' (Dem 21.174).

(50) tois allois hapasin anthropois 'to-the other all men' (Din 1.106).

(51) pantas apektonesan autous 'all they-have-killed them' (Xen *Hell* 7.2.4).

(52) nekuos de de amphimachontai gumnou 'the-corpse PRT PRT they-are-fighting-around stripped' (*Il* 18.20); gastera tupse mesen 'in-the-belly he-struck-him mid' (*Il* 4.531).

(53) meteorous exekomisan tas hamaxas 'on-high they-lifted the wagons' (Xen *An* 1.5.8).

(54) to ton summachon akuron pepoiekos dogma 'the of-the allies void having-made decree' (Aesch 2.62).

(55) polloi apethanon 'many died' (Xen *Hell* 4.8.29); polloi auton apethanon 'many of-them died' (Xen *Hell* 5.2.42); polloi apethanon auton 'many died of-them' (Thuc 3.108.3); polloi epeisthesan ton marturon 'many are-typically-persuaded of-the witnesses' (Lyc 20).

(56) pollous echon ton epitedeion 'many having of-the friends' (Lys 3.38).

(57) polla men esose ton chrematon toisi Perseisi, polla de kai autos periebaleto 'many PRT he-saved of-the precious-objects for-the Persians, many PRT also himself appropriated' (Her 8.8).

(58) tas idias kateskeuakasin oikias 'the private they-have-built homes' Dem 23.208).

(59) hoi men ta hupodemata ergazomenoi ta palaia 'those PRT the shoes mending the old' (Pl *Meno* 91d).

(60) tas epistolas tas tou Philippou 'the letters the of-the Philip' (Dem 19.51); tas d' epistolas humin anagnosomai tas tou Philippou 'the PRT letters to-you I-shall-read the of-the Philip' (Dem 19.187).

(61) makaressi theois antikru machesthai tois allois 'the-blessed gods opposite to-fight those others' (*Il* 5.819).

(62) tois tous gumnikous nikosin agonas 'to-those the athletic winning contests' (Dem 20.141).

(63) ton miaron kai anaide phulaxomen amphoteroi ton Philokraten 'the disgusting and shameless we-will-beware-of both the Philocrates' (Dem 19.13).

(64) ton Kerberon kuna 'the Cerberus dog' (Xen *An* 6.2.2).

(65) nux he hemere egeneto 'night the day became' (Her 1.103).

(66) epi deipnon 'to dinner' (Xen *Mem* 1.3.6).

(67) ton de patera ton emon 'the PRT father the my' (Andoc 1.41); ton emon patera 'the my father' (Antiph 1.15).

(68) toichou tou heteroio 'wall that other' (*Il* 9.219).

(69) ek petres tes autes 'out-of rock the same' (Her 4.90); ergoi toi aischistoi ounoma to kalliston etheu 'to-deed the most-disgraceful name the noblest you-gave' (Her 3.155).

(70) eis dodeka naus tas arista pleousas 'onto ships twelve the best sailing' (Xen *Hell* 5.1.27).

(71) phusin echontes ten allen homoien toisi alloisi anthropoisi 'nature having the rest similar to-the other men' (Her 3.116).

(72) tois nomois chresthai tois humeterois 'the laws to-use the your' (Dem 24.210).

(73) ta makrotat' enche' helontes 'those longest spears taking' (*Il* 14.373).

(74) tous allous kelomen erieras hetairous 'those others I-ordered faithful comrades' (*Od* 9.100).

(75) pleistous de tithemenoi nomous 'very-many PRT passing laws' (Isoc *Pax* 50); pleistous diaphtheirai ton politon 'very-many to-corrupt of-the citizens' (ibid.).

(76) tais technais tautais parapetasmasin echresanto 'the arts these as-a-front they-used' (Pl *Prot* 316e).

(77) allois d' au peirontai doulois chresthai 'others PRT PRT they-try as-slaves to-use' (Xen *Oec* 1.22).

(78) ou gar allois tisin humas dei peri ton axion onton bouleuein tekmeriois chresthai e humin autois 'not PRT other any you ought about the worthy being to-be-a-council-member evidence to-use than you yourselves' (Lys 31.34).

(79) alla apodexamenos megala erga 'other having-performed great deeds' (Her 1.59).

(80) megistous humin huparchein summachous kai boethous 'the-greatest for-you to-be allies and assistants' (Dem 11.2).

(81) pollen gar panu katelipen ho pater autoi ousian 'much PRT very left the father to-him property' (Aesch 1.42).

(82) tous Solonos anegnokenai nomous e sunienai 'the of-Solon to-have-read laws or to-understand' (Dem 20.103).

(83) en tois demosiois anagegraptai grammasi 'in the public it-has-been-registered archives' (Aesch 2.58); kata tous tou patros epitattonti nomous 'according-to the of-the father instructing laws' (Pl *Criti* 120b).

(84) hos pros paidas hemas paizousas 'as of children us making-fun' (Pl *Rep* 545e).

(85) hippada stolen enestalmenous 'in-cavalry uniform dressed' (Her 1.80); ten auten eskeuasmenoi 'in-the same equipped' (Her 7.84).

(86) pleious trapomenos tropas tou Euripou 'more having-turned turns than-the Euripus' (Aesch 3.90).

(87) tois loipois epicheiroie pragmasin 'to-the remaining he-could-turn-his-hands matters' (Dem 18.27).

(88) ho panton schetliotatos anthropon 'the of-all most-wicked men' (Andoc 1.124).

(89) polun poiesontai logon 'much they-will-make speech' (Aesch 3.28).

(90) hapasan ero ten aletheian 'all I-will-tell the truth' (Dem 23.187).

(91) heterous emisthosamen nautas 'other I-hired sailors' (Dem 50.12); pollas pros-thentes klimakas 'many placing ladders' (Thuc 3.23.1).

(92) anti ton apoliponton... nautōn heterous emisthosamen nautas 'in-place-of the having-deserted sailors other I-hired sailors.'

(93) klimakas prosthentes... pollas prosthentes klimakas 'ladders placing... many plac-ing ladders.'

(94) halontas miai psephoi monon 'convicted on-one vote only' (Andoc 4.9); miai monon halonai psephoi 'by-one only to-be-convicted vote' (Dem 21.75).

(95) tous tou Christou stratiotas he hiera tou xulou proskaleitai eche 'the of-the Christ soldiers the holy of-the cross calls sound' (Theodorus 86).

(96) monais tautais apagoreuousin hoi nomoi tais gunaixin 'to-alone these forbid the laws the women' (Dem 59.86); *monoi houtoi apagoreuousi tais gunaixin hoi nomoi 'alone$_i$ these$_i$ forbid to-the women the laws$_i$.'

(97) medemian kataleipesthai prophasin 'no to-be-left reason' (Dem 25.17).

(98) ton euklea thanaton athanaton peri ton agathon kataleipein logon 'the glorious death an-immortal about the good-things to-leave reputation' (Lys 2.23); *ton euklea kataleipein thanaton athanaton logon 'the glorious to-leave death an-immortal reputa-tion.'

(99) polloi men de sunkatakaiontai toisi mantisi boes 'many PRT PRT are-burned-up-together with-the diviners oxen' (Her 4.69).

(100) tou gar Phokikou sustantos polemou 'the PRT Phocian having-begun war' (Dem 18.18).

(101) makros an eie logos 'long PRT would-be speech' (Andoc 3.9).

(102) ho palaios keleuei nomos 'the old commands law' (Dem 20.99).

(103) *ho palaios keleuei nomos tous politas 'the old commands law the citizens.'

(104) *hoi alloi (kat)egelasan stratiotai 'the other laughed soldiers.'

(105) ten de allen anagousi horten toi Dionusoi 'the PRT remaining they-celebrate festival to-the Dionysus' (Her 2.48); *tois de allois anagousi theois ten horten 'to-the PRT other they-celebrate gods the festival.'

(106) pollen gar panu katelipen ho pater autoi ousian 'much PRT very left the father to-him property' (Aesch 1.42); *to-many PRT very left the father sons the property.'

(107) pasi beboethekate tois en tois ergois ergazomenois 'all you-have-helped those in the mining working' (Dem 42.31).

(108) alla tropoi toi autoi poieuntai ploia 'other in-manner the same they-make boats' (Her 1.194); *toi autoi poieuntai alla ploia tropoi 'in-the same they-make other boats manner.'

(109) tais megistais kolazousa atimiais 'with-the greatest punishing-them dishonours' (Pl *Polit* 309a).

(110) en heteroi grapsas auta grammateioi 'in another writing them document' (Isae 1.25); *en heteroi grapsas grammateioi tas diathekas 'in another writing document the will.'

(111) en hapasais aei boai tais ekklesiais 'in all always he-shouts the assemblies' (Dem 25.64).

(112) lainous purgous perix orthoisin ethemen kanosin 'stone towers around with-straight we-put plumblines' (*Troad* 5).

(113) ek toutou ten morian aphanizein epecheiresa tou choriou, en hoi... 'from this the sacred-olive to-remove I-tried the plot-of-land, in which...' (Lys 7.28).

(114) tin' oun rhaistonen tois pollois ho sos, o Leptine, poiei nomos...? 'what PRT relief to-the many the your, O Leptines, gives law?' (Dem 20.28).

(115) patridos de toiautes ep' aischistais steretheis aitais 'of-country PRT such on most-disgraceful deprived charges' (Lys 7.41).

(116) oud'... apodidontas... humin ta humetera, all' homologoumenos tas patroias ousias eis ten pros humas anelokotas philotimian 'nor repaying to-you the your-things, but as-acknowledged the inherited property to the with you having-spent honour' (Aesch 3.19).

(117) pasin edeixen anthropois ten te tes poleos kalokagathian kai ten Philippou kakian 'to-all it-showed men the both of-the city nobility and the of-Philip evil-character' (Dem 18.93).

(118) hon hede keuthei somat' Idaia konis 'whose this covers bodies of-Ida soil' (*Hec* 325).

BIBLIOGRAPHY

Abney, S. 1987. *The Noun Phrase in its Sentential Aspect*. Ph.D. diss., MIT.

Ackema, P. 1994. Theta-theory and the locality of noun incorporation. *OTS Yearbook* 1994:1.

Anagnostopoulou. E. 1997. Clitic left dislocation and contrastive left dislocation. *Materials on Left Dislocation*, ed. E. Anagnostopoulou et al.: 151. Amsterdam.

Aissen, J.L. 1984. Themes and absolutives. *Syntax and Semantics* 16:169.

Aissen, J.L. 1989. Agreement controllers and Tzotzil comitatives. *Language* 65:518.

Aissen, J.L. 1992. Topic and focus in Mayan. *Language* 68:43.

Alexiadou, A. and C. Wilder. 1998. *Possessors, Predicates and Movement in the Determiner Phrase*. Amsterdam.

Allen, B., D. Gardiner and D. Frantz. 1984. Noun incorporation in Southern Tiwa. *International Journal of American Linguistics* 50:292.

Andrews, A. 1985. The major functions of the noun phrase. *Language Typology and Syntactic Description*, ed. T. Shopen 1: 62. Cambridge.

Androutsopoulou, A. 1994. The distribution of the definite determiner and the syntax of Greek DPs. *Chicago Linguistic Society* 30:16.

Androutsopoulou, A. 1996. The licensing of adjectival modification. *WCCFL* 14:17.

Androutsopoulou, A. 1998. Split DPs, focus, and scrambling in Modern Greek. *WCCFL* 16:1.

Aoun, J. and E. Benmamoun. 1999. Gapping, PG merger, and patterns of partial agreement. *Fragments*, ed. S. Lappin and E. Benmamoun: 175. New York.

Atlas, J.D. and S.C. Levinson. 1981. *It*-clefts, informativeness, and logical form. *Radical Pragmatics*, ed. P. Cole: 1. New York.

Austin, P. 1982. Transitivity and cognate objects in Australian languages. *Syntax and Semantics* 15:37.

Bach, E. 1981. Discontinuous constituents in Generalized Categorial Grammars. *North Eastern Linguistics Society* 11:1.

Baker, M. 1992. Unmatched chains and the representation of plural pronouns. *Natural Language Semantics* 1:33.

Baker, M. 1996. *The Polysynthesis Parameter*. New York.

Bakker, E.J. 1990. Homeric discourse and enjambement. *Transactions of the American Philological Association* 120:1.

Baltin, M.R. 1982. A landing site theory of movement rules. *Linguistic Inquiry* 13:1.

Baltin, M.R. 1991. Head movement in logical form. *Linguistic Inquiry* 22:225.

Bartsch, R. 1975. Subcategorization of adnominal and adverbial modifiers. *Formal Semantics of Natural Language*, ed. E.L. Keenan: 175. Cambridge.

Bergson, L. 1960. *Zur Stellung des Adjektivs in der älteren griechischen Prosa.* Stockholm.

Bernstein, J.B. 1993. *Topics in the Syntax of Nominal Structure across Romance.* Ph.D. diss., CUNY.

Bierwisch, M. 1967. Some semantic universals of German adjectivals. *Foundations of Language* 3:1.

Bierwisch, M. 1989. The semantics of gradation. *Dimensional Adjectives,* ed. M. Bierwisch and E. Lang: 71. Heidelberg. ·

Bierwisch, M. 1990. Verb cluster formation as a morphological process. *Yearbook of Morphology* 3:173.

Bittner, M. 1998. Crosslinguistic semantics for questions. *Linguistics and Philosophy* 21:1.

Bittner, M. and K. Hale. 1995. Remarks on definiteness in Warlpiri. *Quantification in Natural Languages,* ed. E. Bach et al.: 81. Dordrecht.

Blake, B.J. 1983. Structure and word order in Kalkatungu. *Australian Journal of Linguistics* 3:143.

Blevins, J.P. 1990. *Syntactic Complexity. Evidence for Discontinuity and Multidomination.* Ph.D. diss., University of Massachusetts.

Boeder, W. 1989. Verbal person marking, noun phrase and word order in Georgian. *Configurationality: The Typology of Asymmmetries,* ed. L. Marácz and P. Muysken: 159. Dordrecht.

Bolinger, D.L. 1952. Linear Modification. *Publications of the Modern Language Association of America* 67:1117.

Bolinger, D.L. 1967. Adjectives in English. Attribution and predication. *Lingua* 18:1.

Brunel, J. 1964. *La construction de l'adjectif dans les groupes nominaux du grec.* Paris.

Bunt, H., and A. van Horck. 1997. *Discontinuous Constituency.* Berlin.

Butt, M. 1997. Complex predicates in Urdu. *Complex Predicates,* ed. A. Alsina et al.: 107. Stanford.

Calcagno, M. 1996. Presupposition, congruence and adverbs of quantification. *OSU Working Papers in Linguistics* 49:1

Carden, G. 1968. English quantifiers. *Mathematical Linguistics and Automatic Translation,* Report no. NSF-20. Computation Laboratory, Harvard University.

Carstens, V. 1985. Proper government in Yoruba. *West Coast Conference on Formal Linguistics* 4:58.

Cattell, R. 1984. *Composite Predicates in English.* Syntax and Semantics 17. Sydney.

Chafe, W.L. 1985. Linguistic differences produced by differences between speaking and writing. *Literacy, Language and Learning,* ed. D.R. Olson et al.: 105. Cambridge.

Chantraine, P. 1953. *Grammaire homérique II. Syntaxe.* Paris.

Chao, W. 1988. *On Ellipsis.* New York.

Choi, H.-W. 1996. *Optimizing Structure in Context.* Ph.D. diss., Stanford.

Chomsky, N. 1957. *Syntactic Structures.* The Hague.

Chomsky, N. 1976. Conditions on rules of grammar. *Linguistic Analysis* 2:303.

Chung, C. 1998. Argument composition and long distance scrambling in Korean. *Syntax and Semantics* 30:159.

Cinque, G. 1994. On the evidence for partial N-movement in the the Romance DP. *Paths towards Universal Grammar,* ed. G. Cinque et al.: 85. Washington, D.C.

Clark, M. 1997. *Out of Line.* Lanham.

Coleman, R. 1975. Greek influence on Latin syntax. *Transactions of the Philological Society* 1975:101.

Comorovsky, I. 1996. *Interrogative Phrases and the Syntax-Semantics Interface*. Dordrecht.

Comrie, B. 1993. The phonology of heads in Haruai. *Heads in Grammatical Theory*, ed. G. Corbett et al.: 36. Cambridge.

Corbett, G. 1983. Resolution rules. *Order, Concord and Constituency*, ed. G. Gazdar et al.: 175. Dordrecht.

Corver, N. 1990. *The Syntax of Left-Branch Extractions*. Ph.D. diss., Brabant.

Corver, N. and H. van Riemsdijk. 1994. *Studies on Scrambling*. Berlin.

Crain, S. and H. Hamburger. 1992. Semantics, knowledge, and NP modification. *Formal Grammar*, ed. R. Levine: 372. New York.

Croft, W. 1991. *Syntactic Categories and Grammatical Relations*. Chicago.

Croft, W. 1993. A noun is a noun—or is it? *Berkeley Linguistics Society* 19:369.

Culicover, P. 1993. Focus and grammar. *Workshop on the Semantic and Syntactic Analysis of Focus*. OTS-WP-TL-93-012. Utrecht.

Dahlstrom, A. 1987. Discontinuous constituents in Fox. *Native American Languages and Grammatical Typology*, ed. P.D. Kroeber and R.E. Moore: 53. Bloomington.

Dahlstrom, A. 1995. *Topic, Focus and other Word Order Problems in Algonquian*. Belcourt Lecture, Winnipeg.

Dalrymple, M., S. Shieber and F. Pereira. 1991. Ellipsis and higher-order unification. *Linguistics and Philosophy* 14:399.

Dasgupta, P. 1988. Bangla quantifier extraction, unaccusative in situ, and the ECP. *Linguistic Inquiry* 19:691.

de Hoop, H. 1996. *Case Configuration and Noun Phrase Interpretation*. New York.

de Hoop, H. and J. Solà. 1996. Determiners, context sets and focus. *West Coast Conference on Formal Linguistics* 14:155.

de Swart, H. 1992. Intervention effects, monotonicity and scope. *SALT II*: 387.

de Vries, J. 1938. *Untersuchungen über die Sperrung von Substantiv und Attribut in der Sprache der attischen Redner*. Göttingen.

Delsing, L.-O. 1993. On attributive adjectives in Scandinavian and other languages. *Studia Linguistica* 47:105.

den Besten, H. 1985. The ergative hypothesis and free word order in Dutch and German. *Studies in German Grammar*, ed. J. Toman: 23. Dordrecht.

Denniston, J.D. 1952. *Greek Prose Style*. Oxford.

Déprez, V.M. 1989. *On the Typology of Syntactic Positions and the Nature of Chains*. Ph.D. diss., MIT.

Derbyshire, D.C. 1985. *Hixkaryana and Linguistic Typology*. Arlington.

Devine, A.M. and L.D. Stephens. 1994. *The Prosody of Greek Speech*. New York.

Diesing, M. 1988. Bare plural subjects and the stage/individual contrast. *Genericity in Natural Language*, ed. M. Krifka: 107. Tübingen.

Diesing, M. 1992. *Indefinites*. Cambridge, Mass.

Dik, H. 1995. *Word Order in Ancient Greek*. Amsterdam.

Dik, H. 1997. Interpreting adjective position in Herodotus. *Grammar as Interpretation*, ed. E.J. Bakker: 55. Leiden.

Dixon, R.M.W. 1972. *The Dyirbal Language of North Queensland*. Cambridge.

Dixon, R.M.W. 1977. *A Grammar of Yidin*. Cambridge.

Doetjes, J. 1994. Quantification at a distance and event relatedness. *Linguistics in the Netherlands* 1994:13.

Dover, K.J. 1968. *Lysias and the* Corpus Lysiacum. Berkeley, Ca.

Dowty, D. 1982. Grammatical relations and Montague grammar. *The Nature of Syntactic Representation*, ed. P. Jacobson and G.K. Pullum: 79. Dordrecht.

Dowty, D. 1988. Type raising, functional composition, and non-constituent coordination. *Categorial Grammars and Natural Language Structures*, ed. R.T. Oehrle et al.: 153. Dordrecht.

Drubig, H.B. 1994. *Island Constraints and the Syntactic Nature of Focus and Association with Focus*. Arbeitspapiere des Sonderforschungsbereichs 340, Tübingen.

Duhoux, Y. 1968. La syntaxe mycénienne à propos de la notion de "faute." *Atti e memorie del 1° Convegno Internazionale di Micenologia*: 781. Rome.

Duhoux, Y. 1973. L'ordre des mots en mycénien. *Minos* 14:123.

Dunkel, G.E. 1990. Jacob Wackernagel und die idg. Partikeln *só, *ke, *kem und *an. *Sprachwissenschaft und Philologie*, ed. H. Eichner and H. Rix: 100. Wiesbaden.

Dwivedi, V. 1994. *Syntactic Dependencies and Relative Phrases in Hindi*. Ph.D. diss., University of Massachusetts.

Edwards, M.W. 1966. Some featrues of Homeric craftsmanship. *Transactions of the American Philological Association* 97:115.

Enç, M. 1991. The semantics of specificity. *Linguistic Inquiry* 22:1.

Evans, N. 1995. *A grammar of Kayardild*. Berlin.

Evans, N. 1995b. A-quantifiers and scope in Mayali. *Quantification in Natural Languages*, ed. E. Bach et al.: 207. Dordrecht.

Evans, N. 1996. The syntax and semantics of body part incorporation in Mayali. *The Grammar of Inalienability*, ed. H. Chapell and W. McGregor: 65. Berlin.

Faltz, L.M. 1995. Towards a typology of natural logic. *Quantification in Natural Languages*, ed. E. Bach et al.: 271. Dordrecht.

Fanselow, G. 1988. Aufspaltung von NPn und das Problem der 'freien Wortstellung.' *Linguistische Berichte* 114:91.

Fassi Fehri, A. 1989. Generalized IP structure, case and VS word order. *MIT Working Papers in Linguistics* 10:75.

Fiengo, R., J. Huang, H. Lasnik and T. Reinhart. 1988. The syntax of *wh*-in situ. *West Coast Conference on Formal Linguistics* 7:81.

Fleiss, J.L. 1973. *Statistical Methods for Rates and Proportions*. New York.

Foley, W. 1991. *The Yimas Language of New Guinea*. Stanford.

Fraser, J. 1910. The σχῆμα ἀλκμανικόν. *Classical Quarterly* 4:25.

Friedrich, P. 1977. *Proto-Indoeuropean Syntax*. Butte.

Fukushima, K. 1991. Phrase structure grammar, Montague semantics and floating quantifiers in Japanese. *Linguistics and Philosophy* 14:581.

Gazdar, G. 1979. *Pragmatics*. New York.

Gerdts, D.B. 1984. A relational analysis of Halkomelen causals. *Syntax and Semantics* 16:169.

Giejgo, J.A. 1981. *Movement Rules in Polish Syntax*. Ph.D. diss., University College, London.

Gigante, M. 1951. A Ps. Senofonte ʾAθ. Πολ. 3.11. *Parola del Passato* 21:448.

Gil, D. 1982. *Distributive Numerals*. Ph.D. diss., University of California, Los Angeles.

Gil, D. 1983. Stacked adjectives and configurationality. *Linguistic Analysis* 12:141.

Gil, D. 1991. Aristotle goes to Arizona, and finds a language without *and*. *Semantic Universals and Universal Semantics*, ed. D. Zaefferer: 96. Berlin.

Ginzburg, J. 1992. *Questions, Queries and Facts*. Ph.D. diss., Stanford.

Giorgi, A. and G. Longobardi. 1991. *The Syntax of Noun Phrases*. Cambridge.

Giseke, B. 1864. *Homerische Forschungen*. Leipzig.

Givón, T. 1979. *On Understanding Grammar*. New York.

Givón, T. 1981. Logic vs. pragmatics, with natural language as the referee. *Journal of Pragmatics* 6:81.

Givón, T. 1995. *Functionalism and Grammar*. Amsterdam.

Golston, C. 1988. *Phrasal Morphology in Homeric Greek*. M.A. diss., University of California, Los Angeles.

Goody, J. 1986. *The Logic of Writing and the Organization of Society*. Cambridge.

Goody, J. 1987. *The Interface between the Oral and the Written*. Cambridge.

Grewendorf, G. 1989. *Ergativity in German*. Dordrecht.

Grewendorf, G. and J. Sabel. 1994. Long scrambling and incorporation. *Linguistic Inquiry* 25:263.

Gross, D. , U. Fischer and G.A. Miller. 1989. The organization of adjectival meanings. *Journal of Memory and Language* 28:92.

Gumperz, J.J. and S.C. Levinson. 1996. *Rethinking Linguistic Relativity*. Cambridge.

Haider, H. 1993. *Deutsche Syntax – Generativ*. Tübingen.

Hainsworth, J.B. 1968. *The Flexibility of the Homeric Formula*. Oxford.

Hale, K. 1976. The adjoined relative clause in Australia. *Grammatical Categories in Australian Languages*, ed. R.M.W. Dixon: 78. Canberra.

Hale, K. 1981. *On the Position of Walbiri in a Typology of the Base*. Indiana University Linguistics Club.

Hale, K. 1983. Warlpiri and the grammar of nonconfigurational languages. *Natural Language and Linguistic Theory* 1:5.

Hale, K. 1994. Core structures and adjunctions in Warlpiri syntax. *Studies in Scrambling*, ed. N. Corver and H. van Riemsdijk:185. Berlin.

Halliday, M.A.K. 1989. *Spoken and Written Language*. Oxford.

Halpern, A. 1995. *On the Placement and Morphology of Clitics*. Stanford.

Hamblin, C. 1973. Questions in Montague grammar. *Foundations of Language* 10:41.

Hausser, R. and D. Zaefferer. 1979. Questions and answers in a content dependent Montague grammar. *Formal Semantics and Pragmatics for Natural Languages*, ed. F. Guenthner and S.J. Schmidt: 339. Dordrecht.

Heath, J. 1984. *Functional Grammar of Nunggubuyu*. Canberra.

Heath, J. 1986. Syntactic and lexical aspects of nonconfigurationality in Nunggubuyu. *Natural Language and Linguistic Theory* 4:375.

Heim, I.R. 1982. *The Semantics of Definite and Indefinite Noun Phrases*. Ph.D. diss., University of Massachusetts.

Herburger, E. 1997. Focus and weak noun phrases. *Natural Language Semantics* 5:53.

Higbie, C.. 1990. *Measure and Music*. Oxford.

Higginbotham, J. 1985. On semantics. *Linguistic Inquiry* 16:547.

Higginbotham, J. and R. May. 1981. Questions, quantifiers and crossing. *The Linguistic Review* 1:41.

Hirschberg, J. 1985. *A Theory of Scalar Implicature*. Ph.D. diss., University of Pennsylvania.

Hoekstra, T. and P. Jordens. 1994. From adjunct to head. *Language Acquisition Studies in Generative Grammar*, ed. T. Hoekstra and B.D. Schwartz: 119. Amsterdam.

Hoepelman, J. 1983. Adjectives and nouns. *Meaning, Use, and Interpretation of Language*, ed. R. Bäuerle et al.: 190. Berlin.

Hopper, P.J. and S.A. Thompson. 1980. Transitivity in grammar and discourse. *Language* 56:251.

Hopper, P.J. and S.A. Thompson. 1984. The discourse basis of lexical categories in universal grammar. *Language* 60:703.

Horn, L. 1981. Exhaustiveness and the semantics of clefts. *North Eastern Linguistics Society* 11:125.

Horrocks, G.C. 1980. *Space and Time in Homer*. Salem, N.H.

Huck, G.J. and A.E. Ojeda. 1987. *Discontinuous Constituency*. Syntax and Semantics 20.

Hyman, L.M. 1975. On the change from SOV to SVO. *Word Order and Word Order Change*, ed. C.N. Li: 115. Austin.

Iatridou, S. 1991. *Topics in Conditionals*. Ph.D. diss., MIT.

Jackendoff, R.S. 1972. *Semantic Interpretation in Generative Grammar*. Cambridge, Mass.

Jackendoff, R.S. 1974. A deep structure projection rule. *Linguistic Inquiry* 5:481.

Jackendoff, R.S. 1977. *X-Bar Syntax*. Cambridge, Mass.

Jacobs, J. 1991. Focus ambiguities. *Journal of Semantics* 8:1.

Jeffery, L.H. 1990. *The Local Scripts of Greece*, rev. A.W. Johnston. Oxford.

Jelinek, E. 1984. Empty categories, case, and configurationality. *Natural Language and Linguistic Theory* 2:39.

Jelinek, E. 1996. Definiteness and second position clitics in Straits Salish. *Approaching Second*, ed. A.L. Halpern and A.M. Zwicky: 271. Stanford.

Johannessen, J.B. 1998. *Coordination*. New York.

Jones, M.A. 1988. Cognate objects and the case filter. *Journal of Linguistics* 24:89.

Jones, M.A. 1993. *Sardinian Syntax*. London.

Kamp, H. and B. Partee. 1995. Prototype theory and compositionality. *Cognition* 57:129.

Karttunen, L. 1989. Radical lexicalism. *Alternative Conceptions of Phrase Structure*, ed. M.R. Baltin and A.S. Kroch: 43. Chicago.

Kawashima, R. and H. Kitahara. 1993. On the distribution and interpretation of subjects and their numeral classifiers. *SALT III*: 97. Cornell.

Kayne, R.S. 1994. *The Antisymmetry of Syntax*. Cambridge, Mass.

Kearns, K. 1989. Predicate nominals in complex predicates. *MIT Working Papers in Linguistics* 10:123.

Keenan, E.L. 1984. Semantic correlates of the ergative/absolutive distinction. *Linguistics* 22:197.

Keenan, E.L. and L.M. Faltz. 1985. *Boolean Semantics for Natural Language*. Dordrecht.

Kenesei, I. 1994. Subordinate clauses. *Syntax and Semantics* 27:275.

Kester, E.-P. 1996. Adjectival inflection and the licensing of empty categories in DP. *Journal of Linguistics* 32:57.

King, T. 1993. *Configuring Topic and Focus in Russian*. Ph.D. diss., Stanford.

Kiparsky, P. 1997. Remarks on denominal verbs. *Complex Predicates*, ed. A. Alsina et al.: 473. Stanford.

Kiss, K.E. 1994. Sentence structure and word order. *Syntax and Semantics* 27:1.

Kiss, K.E. 1995. Introduction. *Discourse Configurational Languages*, ed. K.E. Kiss: 3. New York.

Kitahara, H. 1997. *Elementary Operations and Optimal Derivations*. Cambridge, Mass.

Koenig, J.-P. 1991. Scalar predicates and negation. *Chicago Linguistic Society* 27.2:190.

Koizumi, M. 1994. Layered specifiers. *North Eastern Linguistics Society* 24:255.

Komlósy, A. 1994. Complements and adjuncts. *Syntax and Semantics* 27:91.

Kratzer, A. 1996. Severing the external argument from its verb. *Phrase Structure and the Lexicon*, ed. J. Rooryck and L. Zaring: 109. Dordrecht.

Krause, W. 1924. Die Entwickelung einer alten elliptischen Konstruktion in den indogermanischen Sprachen. *Kuhns Zeitschrift* 52:223.

Krifka, M. 1996. Frameworks for the representation of focus. *5th CSLI Workshop on Logic, Language and Information*. Stanford.

Kumahira Comrie, A. 1987. *On So-Called Quantifier Floating in Japanese*. Ph.D. diss., USC.

La Roche, J. 1867. Die Stellung des attributiven and appositiven Adjectivs bei Homer. *Wiener Studien* 19:161.

Langacker, R.W. 1987. Nouns and verbs. *Language* 63:53.

Langdon, M. 1970. *A Grammar of Diegueño*. Berkeley.

Larson, R. 1983. *Restrictive Modification*. Ph. D. diss., University of Wisconsin, Madison.

Lasersohn, P. 1995. *Plurality, Conjunction and Events*. Dordrecht.

Laughren, M. 1989. The configurationality parameter and Warlpiri. *Configurationality. The Typology of Asymmetries*, ed. L. Marácz and P. Muysken: 319. Dordrecht.

Lee, Y.S. and B. Santorini. 1994. Towards resolving Webelhuth's paradox. *Studies on Scrambling*, ed. N. Corver and H. van Riemsdijk: 459. Berlin.

Leino, P. 1986. *Language and Metre*. Helsinki.

Levinson, S.C. 1983. *Pragmatics*. Cambridge.

Lewis, D. 1976. General Semantics. *Montague Grammar*, ed. B.H. Partee: 1. New York.

Liberman, A. 1990. "Afterthought" as a feature of Old Icelandic syntax. *Syntax gesprochener Sprachen*, ed. B.K. Halford and H. Pilch: 45. Tübingen.

Lindhamer, L. 1908. *Zur Wortstellung im Griechischen*. Ph.D. diss., Munich.

Lobeck, A. 1995. *Ellipsis*. New York.

Löbner, S. 1985. Definites. *Journal of Semantics* 4:279.

Löbner, S. 1990. *Wahr neben Falsch*. Tübingen.

Longobardi, G. 1994. Reference and proper names. *Linguistic Inquiry* 25:609.

Mahajan, A. 1990. *The A/A-Bar Distinction and Movement Theory*. Ph.D. diss, MIT.

Marácz, L.K. 1989. *Asymmetries in Hungarian*. Ph.D. diss., Groningen.

Masson, O and J. Yoyotte. 1988. Une inscription ionienne mentionannant Psammétique Ier. *Epigraphica Anatolica* 11:171.

Matsumoto, Y. 1992. *On the Wordhood of Complex Predicates in Japanese*. Ph.D. diss., Stanford.

Matthei, E. 1982. The acquisition of prenominal modifier sequences. *Cognition* 11:301.

McCloskey, J. 1986. Inflection and conjunction in Modern Irish. *Natural Language and Linguistic Theory* 4:245.

McGregor, W.B. 1990. *A Functional Grammar of Gooniyandi*. Amsterdam.

McNally, L. 1993. Comitative coordination. *Natural Language and Linguistic Theory* 11:347.

McNally, L. 1997. *A Semantics for the English Existential Construction.* New York.

Merlan, F. 1976. Noun incorporation and discourse reference in Modern Nahuatl. *International Journal of American Linguistics* 42:177.

Michelini, G. 1987. ὁ, ἡ, τό nell' uso non relativo ed il suo funzionamento come articolo. *Studi Italiani di Linguistica Teorica ed Applicata* 16:93.

Mithun, M. 1984. The evolution of noun incorporation. *Language* 60:847.

Mithun, M. 1988. The grammaticization of coordination. *Clause Combining in Grammar and Discourse*, ed. J. Haiman and S.A. Thompson: 331. Amsterdam.

Mithun, M. 1995. Morphological and prosodic forces shaping word order. *Word Order in Discourse*, ed. D. Dowty and M. Noonan: 387. Amsterdam.

Miyagawa, S. 1989. *Structure and Case Marking in Japanese.* San Diego.

Mohanan, T. 1997. Multimensionality of representation. *Complex Predicates*, ed. A. Alsina et al.: 431. Stanford.

Moltmann, F. 1997. Intensional verbs and quantifiers. *Natural Language and Linguistic Theory* 5:1.

Moltmann, F. 1997b. *Parts and Wholes in Semantics.* New York.

Mommsen, T. 1895. *Beiträge zu der Lehre von den griechischen Präpositionen.* Berlin.

Monachesi, P. 1998. Italian restructuring verbs. *Syntax and Semantics* 30:313.

Morpurgo-Davies, A. 1968. Article and demonstrative. *Glotta* 46:77.

Morrill, G. 1995. Discontinuity in categorial grammar. *Linguistics and Philosophy* 18:175.

Müller, G. and W. Sternefeld. 1993. Improper movement and unambiguous binding. *Linguistic Inquiry* 24:461.

Munn, A.B. 1993. *Topics in the Syntax and Semantics of Coordinate Structures.* Ph.D. diss., University of Maryland.

Munro, P. 1984. Floating quantifiers in Pima. *Syntax and Semantics* 16:269.

Newman, P. 1970. *A Grammar of Tera.* Berkeley.

Nishigauchi, T. 1990. *Quantification in the Theory of Grammar.* Dordrecht.

Norden, E. 1958 (1898). *Die antike Kunstprosa.* Darmstadt.

Nordlinger, R. 1997. *Constructive Case.* Ph.D. diss., Stanford.

O'Grady, W. 1997. *Syntactic Development.* Chicago.

O'Shaughnessy, D. and J. Allen. 1983. Linguistic modality effects on fundamental frequency in speech. *Journal of the Acoustical Society of America* 74:1155.

Olsen, S. 1987. On non-overt and pronominal head nouns in the English noun phrase. *Linguistische Berichte* 112:470.

Ong, W.J. 1982. *Orality and Literacy.* London.

Palm, J. 1960. *Zur Funktion und Stellung des attributiven Demonstrativums im Griechischen.* Lund.

Parry, M. 1971. *The Making of Homeric Verse.* Oxford.

Parsons, T. 1980. Modifiers and quantifiers in natural language. *Canadian Journal of Philosophy* 6:29.

Parsons, T. 1990. *Events in the Semantics of English.* Cambridge, Mass.

Partee, B. 1973. Some transformational extensions of Montague grammar. *Journal of Philosophical Logic* 2:509.

Partee, B. 1987. Noun phrase interpretation and type shifting principles. *Studies in Discourse RepresentationTheory and the Theory of Generalized Quantifiers*, ed. J. Groenendijk et al.: 119. Dordrecht.

Partee, B. 1988. Many quantifiers. *ESCOL '88*:383.

Partee, B. 1995. Quantificational structures and compositionality. *Quantification in Natural Languages*, ed. E. Bach et al.: 541. Dordrecht.

Payne, D.L. 1986. Basic constituent order in Yagua clauses. *Handbook of Amazonian Languages*, ed. D. Derbyshire and G.K. Pullum 1:440. Berlin.

Payne, D.L. 1993. Meaning and pragmatics of order in selected South American Indian languages. *The Role of Theory in Language Description*, ed. W.A. Foley: 281. Berlin.

Payne, D.L. and T.E. Payne. 1990. Yagua. *Handbook of Amazonian Languages*, ed. D. Derbyshire and G.K. Pullum 2:249. Berlin.

Pensalfini, R. 1992. *Degrees of Freedom. Word Order in Pama-Nyungan Languages*. Honours Thesis, University of Westerrn Australia.

Pensalfini, R. 1996. Nonconfigurationality as restrictions on encyclopedic information. ConSOLE 5. MIT.

Platzack, C. 1994. The relation between lexicon and syntax. *Paths towards Universal Grammar*, ed. G. Cinque et al.: 277. Washington, D.C.

Progovac, L. 1996. Clitics in Serbian/Croatian. *Approaching Second*, ed. A.L. Halpern and A.M. Zwicky: 411. Stanford.

Pullum, G.K. 1982. Free word order and phrase structure rules. *North Eastern Linguistics Society* 12:209.

Pulman, S.G. 1997. Higher order unification and the interpretation of focus. *Linguistics and Philosophy* 20:73.

Pustejovsky, J. 1993. Type coercion and lexical selection. *Semantics and the Lexicon*, ed. J. Pustejovsky: 73. Dordrecht.

Pustejovsky, J. 1995. *The Generative Lexicon*. Cambridge, Mass.

Radford, A. 1993. Head-hunting. *Heads in Grammatical Theory*, ed. G.G. Corbett et al.: 73. Cambridge.

Radford, A. 1997. *Syntactic Theory and the Structure of English*. Cambridge.

Raible, W. 1981. Von der Allgegenwart des Gegensinns. *Zeitschrift für romanische Philologie* 97:1.

Ramchand, G.C. 1997. *Aspect and Predication*. Oxford.

Rapoport, T.R. 1992. Adjunct predicate licensing and D-structure. *Syntax and Semantics* 25:159.

Rapoport, T.R. 1995. Specificity, objects, and nominal small clauses. *Syntax and Semantics* 28:153.

Rappaport, M., M. Laughren and B. Levin. 1993. Levels of lexical representation. *Semantics and the Lexicon*, ed. J. Pustejovsky: 37. Dordrecht.

Raubitschek, A.E. and L.H. Jeffery. 1949. *Dedications from the Athenian Akropolis*. Cambridge, Mass.

Reinhart, T. 1991. Elliptic conjunctions. *The Chomskyan Turn*, ed. A. Kasher: 360. Oxford.

Risch, E. 1974. *Wortbildung der homerischen Sprache*. Berlin.

Risselada, R. 1984. Coordination and juxtaposition of adjectives in the Latin NP. *Glotta* 62:202.

Ritter, E. 1991. Two functional categories in noun phrases. *Syntax and Semantics* 25:37.

Roberts, C. 1995. Domain restriction in dynamic semantics. *Quantification in Natural Languages*, ed. E. Bach et al.: 661. Dordrecht.

Roberts, C. 1996. Information structure in discourse. *OSU Working Papers in Linguistics* 49:91.

Rooth, M. 1985. *Association with Focus*. Ph.D. diss., University of Massachusetts.

Rooth, M. 1992. A theory of focus interpretation. *Natural Language Semantics* 1:75.

Rooth, M. 1996. Focus. *The Handbook of Contemporary Semantic Theory*, ed. S. Lappin: 271. Oxford.

Rosén, H.B. 1967. *Strukturalgrammatische Beiträge zum Verständnis Homers*. Amsterdam.

Rosen, S.T. 1989. Two types of noun incorporation. *Language* 65:294.

Rosen, S.T. 1990. *Argument Structure and Complex Predicates*. New York.

Rudin, C. 1986. *Aspects of Bulgarian Syntax*. Columbus, Oh.

Russell, K. and C. Reinholz. 1996. Hierarchical structure in a nonconfigurational language. *West Coast Conference on Formal Linguistics* 14:431.

Russell, K. and C. Reinholz. 1997. Nonconfigurationality and the syntax-phonology interface. *West Coast Conference on Formal Linguistics* 15:441.

Saccon, G. 1993. *Postverbal Subjects*. Ph.D. diss., Harvard University.

Sadler, L. and D. Arnold. 1994. Prenominal adjectives. *Journal of Linguistics* 30:187.

Sadock, J.M. 1974. *Towards a Linguistic Theory of Speech Acts*. New York.

Sadock, J.M. 1991. *Autolexical Syntax*. Chicago.

Saeed, J.I. 1984. *The Syntax of Focus and Topic in Somali*. Hamburg.

Saito, M. 1992. Long distance scrambling in Japanese. *Journal of East Asian Linguistics* 1:69.

Sasse, H.-J. 1987. The thetic-categorical distinction revisited. *Linguistics* 25:511.

Sasse, H.-J. 1992. Predication and sentence constitution in universal perspective. *Semantic Universals and Universal Semantics*, ed. D. Zaefferer: 75. Berlin.

Schachter, P. 1973. Focus and relativization. *Language* 49:19.

Schein, B. 1995. Small clauses and predication. *Syntax and Semantics* 28:49.

Schmitt, R. 1967. *Dichtung und Dichtersprache in indogermanischen Zeit*. Wiesbaden.

Schwartz, L. 1985. Plural pronouns, coordination and inclusion. *Papers from the Tenth Minnesota Regional Conference on Language and Linguistics*: 152.

Senn, A. 1966. *Handbuch der litauischen Sprache*. Heidelberg.

Shannon, T.F. 1992. Split intransitivity in German and Dutch. *Recent Developments in Germanic Linguistics*, ed. R. Lippi-Green: 97. Amsterdam.

Shipp, G. P. 1972. *Studies in the Language of Homer*. Cambridge.

Siegel, M. 1976. *Capturing the Adjective*. Ph.D. diss., University of Massachusetts.

Siewierska, A. 1984. Phrasal discontinuity in Polish. *Australian Journal of Linguistics* 4:57.

Simpson, J. 1991. *Warlpiri Morpho-Syntax*. Dordrecht.

Sławomirski, J. 1988. Une construction syntaxique négligée dans la langue homérique. *Revue des Etudes Anciennes* 90: 325.

Speas, M. 1991. Generalized transformations and the D-structure position of adjuncts. *Syntax and Semantics* 25:241.

Sproat, R. and C. Shih. 1991. The crosslinguistic distribution of adjective ordering restrictions. *Interdisciplinary Approaches to Language*, ed. C. Georgopoulos and R. Ishihara: 565. Dordrecht.

Stavrou, M. 1996. Adjectives in Modern Greek. *Journal of Linguistics* 32:79.

Steedman, M. 1996. *Surface Structure and Interpretation.* Cambridge, Mass.

Steele, S. 1989. *Agreement and Anti-agreement.* Dordrecht.

Stowell, T. 1989. Subjects, specifiers, and X-bar theory. *Alternative Conceptions of Phrase Structure*, ed. R. Baltin and A. Kroch: 232. Chicago.

Stowell, T. 1991. Determiners in NP and DP. *Views on Phrase Structure*, ed. K. Leffel and D. Bouchard: 37. Dordrecht.

Strigin, A. 1994. Topicalization, scrambling and argument scope in German. *Journal of Semantics* 11:311.

Szabolcsi, A. 1983. Focussing properties, or the trap of first order. *Theoretical Linguistics* 10:125.

Szabolcsi, A. 1986. Comparative superlatives. *MIT Working Papers in Linguistics* 8:245.

Szabolcsi, A. 1997. *Ways of Scope Taking.* Dordrecht.

Szabolcsi, A. and F. Zwarts. 1993. Weak islands and an algebraic semantics for scope taking. *Natural Language Semantics* 1:235.

Takizala, A. 1973. Focus and relativization. *Syntax and Semantics* 2:123.

Tannen, D. 1982. *Spoken and Written Language.* Norwood..

Tannen, D. 1984. *Coherence in Spoken and Written Discourse.* Norwood.

Tenenbaum, S. 1977. Left- and right-dislocation. *Haya Grammatical Structure.* Southern California Occasional Papers in Linguistics 6:161.

Terada, H. 1991. Types of floating quantifiers and the landing site of scrambling. *Nagoya Working Papers in Linguistics* 7:47.

Thomas, R. 1992. *Literacy and Orality in Ancient Greece.* Cambridge.

Thompson, S.A. 1988. Adjectives in discourse. *Explaining Linguistic Universals*, ed. J. Hawkins: 167. Oxford.

Thomson, G. 1939. The postponement of interrogatives in Attic drama. *Classical Quarterly* 33:147.

Timberlake, A. 1975. Hierarchies in the genitive of negation. *Slavic and East European Journal* 19:123.

Torrego, E. 1989. Unergative-unaccusative alternations in Spanish. *MIT Working Papers in Linguistics* 10:253.

Travis, L. 1988. The syntax of adverbs. *McGill Working Papers in Linguistics* May 1988: 282.

Tredinnick, V. 1992. Movement in the Modern Greek noun phrase. *Penn Review of Linguistics* 16:194.

Tsujimura, N. 1989. Unaccusative mismatches in Japanese. *ESCOL '89*:264.

Tuller, L. 1992. The syntax of postverbal focus constructions in Chadic. *Natural Language and Linguistic theory* 10:303.

Untermann, J. 1984. Beobachtungen zum attributiven Adjektiv bei Homer. *Athlon: Satura Grammatica in Honorem F.R. Adrados*, ed. A. Bernabé et al.: 1.471. Madrid.

van Geenhoven, V. 1998. *Semantic Incorporation and Indefinite Descriptions.* Stanford.

van Kampen, J. 1997. *First Steps in Wh-Movement.* Ph.D. diss., Utrecht.

van Leusen, N. and L. Kálmán. 1993. *The Interpretation of Free Focus.* ILLC Prepublication Series for Computational Linguistics CL-93-01. Amsterdam.

van Oirsouw, R.R. 1987. *The Syntax of Coordinatioon.* London.

van Riemsdijk, H. 1982. Locality principles in syntax and phonology. *Linguistics in the Morning Calm*: 693. Seoul.

van Riemsdijk, H. 1989. Movement and regeneration. *Dialect Variation and the Theory of Grammar*, ed. P. Benincà: 105. Dordrecht.

Vergnaud, J.-R. and M.L. Zubizarreta. 1992. The definite determiner and the inalienable constructions in French and English. *Linguistic Inquiry* 23:595.

Vieira, M.D. 1995. The expression of quantificational notions in Asurini. *Quantification in Natural Languages*, ed. E. Bach et al.: 701. Dordrecht.

von Fintel, K. 1994. *Restrictions on Quantifier Domains*. Ph.D. diss., University of Massachusetts.

Wackernagel, J. 1875. Zum homerischen dual. *Kuhns Zeitschrift* 23:302.

Waugh, L. 1976. The semantics and paradigmatics of word order. *Language* 52:82.

Webelhuth, G. 1990. Diagnostics for structure. *Scrambling and Barriers*, ed. G. Grewendorf and W. Sternefeld: 41. Amsterdam.

Webelhuth, G. 1992. *Principles and Parameters of Syntactic Saturation*. New York.

Woisetschlaeger, E. 1983. On the question of definiteness in "An old man's book." *Linguistic Inquiry* 14:137.

Yatabe, S. 1993. *Scrambling and Japanese Phrase Structure*. Ph.D. diss., Stanford.

Yoshida, T. 1993. Verb movement and proper head-government in Japanese. *Formal Linguistics Society of Midamerica* 3:373.

Zwicky, A. 1986. Concatenation and liberation. *Chicago Linguistics Society* 22:65.

INDEX NOMINUM

INDEX RERUM